FORGING GENIUS

Baseball Biography and History from Potomac Books

Bob Feller: Ace of the Greatest Generation
John Sickels

Mickey Mantle: America's Prodigal Son
Tony Castro

Paths to Glory: How Great Baseball Teams Got That Way
Mark L. Armour and Daniel R. Levitt

The Baseball Rookies Encyclopedia
David Nemec and Dave Zeman

Wrigley Field: The Unauthorized Biography
Stuart Shea

*Chasing Steinbrenner: Pursuing the Pennant
in Boston and Toronto*
Rob Bradford

Deadball Stars of the National League
SABR

Getting in the Game: Inside Baseball's Winter Meetings
Josh Lewin

Throwbacks: Old-School Players in Today's Game
George Castle

Weaver on Strategy
Earl Weaver and Terry Pluto

Baseball: The Writer's Game
Mike Shannon

The World Series' Most Wanted
John Snyder

Baseball's Most Wanted
Floyd Conner

Baseball's Most Wanted II
Floyd Conner

FORGING GENIUS

THE MAKING OF CASEY STENGEL

STEVEN GOLDMAN

Potomac Books, Inc.
Washington, D.C.

Library of Congress Cataloging-in-Publication Data

Goldman, Steven, 1970–
　　Forging genius : the making of Casey Stengel / by Steven Goldman.—1st ed.
　　　　p.　cm.
　　Includes bibliographical references and index.
　　ISBN 1-57488-873-0 (hardcover : alk. paper)
　　1. Stengel, Casey.　2. Baseball managers—United States—Biography.　I.
Title.
　GV865.S8G65　2005
　796.357′092—dc22　　　　　　　　　　　　　　　　　　　　2004028056

Hardcover 1-57488-873-0 (alk. paper)

Printed in Canada on acid-free paper that meets the American National
Standards Institute Z39-48.

Potomac Books, Inc.
22841 Quicksilver Drive
Dulles, Virginia 20166

First Edition

10　9　8　7　6　5　4　3　2　1

For my parents, Reuven and Eliane Goldman,
who instilled in me an unquenchable curiosity about everything

and

In memory of Charlot Amici,
another wily old man.
‘‘I reserve the right to think.’’

CONTENTS

ACKNOWLEDGMENTS

Recently I chanced upon a copy of Eddie Epstein's football book, *Dominance*, published by the same house that has brought forth this current volume. Mr. Epstein's acknowledgements begin, "I want to thank Chris Kahrl . . . for believing in this project and Keith Law for being the catalyst." Funny you should mention that, Eddie . . . but let's begin at the beginning.

This book had an unusually long genesis, and its author is indebted to many for its publication. To all whose names are inscribed below I owe many thanks. First and foremost, much gratitude is due my big-hearted friend Andrew Baharlias, whose continual support, belief, encouragement, and introduction to the chaotic world of the New York Yankees front office made most of what followed possible. In a tempestuous, uncertain world, Mr. Baharlias is a rock of reliability. I cannot praise him too highly nor thank him too much. Later, he critiqued many versions of the chapters and even helped me assemble the final version of the manuscript, deepening a debt which I can never fully repay.

Due to Mr. Baharlias's efforts, the mysterious, mercurial Tim Wood, then Yankees director of publications, read an early version of the book and thought I would be a worthy contributor to team publications and later, in the early days of baseball on the Internet, fulfilled a life's dream by making me a columnist (I recently heard Phillip Lopate say that no one grows up wanting to be a columnist, but from the day I read my first Robert Benchley, I did) for the huge network of web sites for which he was responsible, including the original incarnation of Yankees.com.

For the survival and continuance of that column, which has been my entry to the hearts and minds of so many Yankees fans and is therefore directly responsible for the existence of this book, I am also grateful to Joe Violone, Jim Banks of MLB.com, and Bryon Evje, then of American Cities Studios. Mr. Evje has been a reliable supporter, a friendly source of honest criticism, and helped me continue the Pinstriped Bible by giving me access to his endless circle of professional friends, first at MLB Advanced Media and then at the Yankees Entertainment and Sports Network, and also encouraged this Casey Stengel project.

My sister, the industrious Ilana Goldman, frequently offered her sui generis brand of militant motivational techniques, reminding me to either finish the book or do *something*. I generally chose to work on the book. The opportunity to draft energy from the self-empowered is a boon to those of us in the chronically indolent set.

The trio of wise men at YES—Fred Harner, Will Weiss, and Chris Corbellini—have been lavish in their praise and support and have let me have my head with so many things, from columns of serious baseball analysis that swerved into history, politics, music, and comparing the Yankees to famous cheeses and the poetry of Rudyard Kipling. I am one of those rare human beings who looks forward to going to work, and it is because of these fine gentlemen. The rebirth of the column led directly to the rebirth of the book; Casey Stengel believed that you make your own luck, that nothing happens by chance. The slow chain reaction that led to *Forging Genius* proves him right.

Darren Viola of baseballprimer.com introduced his audience to the Pinstriped Bible, bringing me a wider following than I ever had before. Darren's generosity led directly to Keith Law of the Toronto Blue Jays seeking me out for a memorable luncheon that concluded with his saying, "So why haven't you shown your book to Chris Kahrl?" I have already told Mr. Law that I'm buying lunch from now on; though he has modestly declined any special credit, let the appearance of these words in print serve as my bond: Mr. Law, it's on me. I must also thank the readers of the Pinstriped Bible itself, who have been kinder to me than any Internet columnist has a right to expect.

Additional thanks are due to Jonah Keri, Will Carroll, and Ryan Wilkins of the *Baseball Prospectus*, who offered their encouragement at critical moments. Jay Jaffe offered indispensable assistance in choosing photographs at Cooperstown. Clifford Corcoran, fastest of fast friends, has offered sympathy, professional-level insight, and license to eat rich desserts whenever I needed it.

My editor, Chris Kahrl, has been as accessible and understanding as Buddha, without the inscrutability. I had always eagerly read Chris's columns and now she's my editor, which is a bit like writing your first song and then having it arranged by Nelson Riddle. Chris's inexhaustible patience when personal illness and a seemingly endless stream of household disasters caused deadline after deadline to sail by like so many Flying Dutchmen will always be greatly appreciated.

Home stretch now: My oldest friend, the spectacularly perspicacious and versatile Dr. Richard Mohring, read every version of this manuscript and was reliably and disconcertingly able to pick out errors I missed in each one. Rick has been there for me with everything I've written since I was seven years old, and yet he's still my friend.

My fascination with baseball dates to my cousin Jonathan Blum opening up the 1979 Statis-Pro baseball board game (1978 statistics) and offering to play me. Jon always did like an easy target; I knew so little about baseball that I thought a pinch-runner stood at home plate and ran as soon as the batter hit the ball. I was challenged to do better. The first book I bought in my effort to learn more was the 1985 *Bill James Baseball Abstract*. A new world was opened up to me, and the rest is history. Thank you, Jonathan, even if you never did let me manage the Yankees, made me bench Willie Stargell, and required me to pitch Glenn Abbott against the Red Sox. And Bill James, thank you, too.

I can't figure out how to list all of my wife Stefanie's contributions to this project without diminishing them. Suffice it to say she was and is my sun, moon, and stars, and if not for her this project would have neither begun nor finished.

Finally, in completing this book there was the ceaseless pleasure of looking up from my work to see my beautiful little girl, Sarah, who always asked, "Daddy, can I help you?" You did, Sarah Baby, you did.

It's a good thing that this is a book and not the Academy Awards ceremony; Henry Mancini and the boys would have played me off a long time ago.

Steven Goldman
New Jersey, December 30, 2003

CHAPTER 1

WHO WAS CASEY STENGEL?

It has now been over half a century since the New York Yankees took what was perceived to be a great risk and hired Charles Dillon Stengel as manager. Engaging this obscure, comical figure worked out better than even the Yankees imagined, but more importantly the hiring launched an enduring and ubiquitous personality whose mark can be found everywhere from *Bartlett's Familiar Quotations* to the Smithsonian Institution.

Six years after Stengel's death, the great sportswriter Red Smith observed that, "It seems to me that those of us who covered Casey in his time owe it to history to reintroduce him to readers . . . at least once a decade." He then reproduced at length a monologue from the 1950s, rendered in Stengel's uniquely rambling "Stengelese." Both mask and prop, Stengelese was a language, Smith said, "only superficially resembling Sanskrit," but full of, "rich, crunchy goodness."

Stengel's speech rambled through a survey of recent Yankees history and careened and lurched to its triumphal summation. "It's that carry-on spirit that the Yankees have and everybody in this country wants somebody to be a Yankee or live like a Yankee which don't mean just baseball but to be somebody for the United States."

Casey Stengel was somebody for the United States. Like his Missouri contemporary, Harry Truman, he labored for years in obscurity until at last he emerged in the foremost position in his profession. He shared with fellow Missourian Samuel Clemens a talent for both the humorous anecdote and the biting rejoinder. Thus he embodied the iconic qualities of the quintessential American: the scrappy wit of the frontiersman, a relentless optimism, and the resiliency of the rags-to-riches myth. "I have been up and down the ladder," Stengel said. "I've learned a lot and

1

picked up a few ideas of my own." He had the kind of life that is imagined to be typically American, going up that ladder one more time than he went down. Of course, outside the realm of fantasy such stories are the exception rather than the rule; as Gore Vidal once wrote, "Americans . . . change class almost as fast—downward, at least—as they shift from city to city or job to job." Casey Stengel's rise to the top of his profession represents a rare occasion when the American dream came true. Stengel unwittingly referred to himself when he said, "Our ball club has been successful because . . . we have the spirit of 1776."

Today, over forty years after the era of his greatest triumphs ended, Casey Stengel is remembered as the manager of the New York Yankees dynasty of 1949 to 1960, the greatest sustained success in baseball history. Stengel's Yankees won ten pennants in his twelve seasons as manager, an unprecedented run which will probably never be equaled (though the record of Bobby Cox's Atlanta Braves from 1991 to 2003 is, in a lower-case way, as impressive). Given his many ostensible failures as a manager prior to his fifty-ninth year, Stengel's achievements afterwards seemed to many observers unexpected and even unearned. Yet it is those moments of failure and rejection that hold the key to understanding the man and his achievements. Stengel was forged by the journey, not the arrival. The seeds of the Yankees championships were planted during the years that Stengel was believed to have wasted.

Stengel's greatest asset was his resiliency. In his 1964 book, *The Quality of Courage*, Mickey Mantle, Stengel's protégé and intended monument, wrote (or perhaps dictated to his ghost, Robert Creamer), in a chapter titled "Casey Never Quit,":

> He had a terrible managerial record [before joining the Yankees]. . . . But people forget that after Casey hit .223 at Maysville one year he led his league in batting the next. They forgot that after he was traded from a seventh-place club to an eighth-place club, he was traded to a pennant-winner and starred in two World Series. They forgot that after looking all washed up, he batted .368 and .339 in successive seasons. They forgot that Casey knew how to come back.

Mantle didn't know the half of it. Stengel was out of baseball nearly half a dozen times over the course of his career. On the eve of the Great War, before the government had insisted that ballplayers work or fight, he risked being blacklisted in the major leagues by walking away from his contract with the Pittsburgh Pirates and joining the Navy. Traded to the Philadelphia Phillies, he refused to report and was placed on the restricted list. Later, when he was looking for his first major league coaching assignment, it was rumored that the commissioner, Judge Kennesaw

Mountain Landis, had forbidden his return to the majors. After his tour as manager of the Brooklyn Dodgers came to a premature end after the 1936 season, he spent a full year away from the game pursuing oil investments in Texas.

When Stengel ended a five-year term at the helm of the Boston Braves, easily the most derided club in baseball at that time, probably even he was tempted to believe that his career was beyond resurrection—but only tempted, not convinced. "I have been discharged fifteen times and rehired," he said later. "As far as I'm concerned, from drawing a salary and from my ups and downs and being discharged, I always found that that there was somebody ready to employ you, if you were on the ball."

Stengel not only returned from his setbacks but advanced himself each time, winning world championships and eventually transcending the narrow definition of success versus failure that is games won and lost. Fred Lieb, who covered the manager in every decade of his long career, wrote that with the exception of Babe Ruth, Stengel was the most widely known and best-loved man in baseball. Whitey Herzog said that he was the best ambassador baseball ever had. Baseball, he wrote, is like physics. "The field is ruled by properties you can't see, but those properties make everything happen that you *can* see. Only the best teachers know the laws and have the sense to make them clear to the young and the brainless. In Casey, I had an Einstein."

Joe Torre, who (at this writing) has managed the Yankees to four championships, said, "Around here, you are measured against Casey and what he did with the Yankees. People made fun of him, but Casey was a deep thinker. He had a great grip on the game. Casey was the best." Sparky Anderson wrote, "Casey Stengel is the most dominant figure ever to bless baseball. To me, Casey Stengel is more dominant than Babe Ruth! . . . Nobody was sharper than The Old Man. He was scientist and artist combined. Baseball only happened to be his vehicle. Casey was the master entertainer. He was also a guru on life . . . Casey Stengel was every person's person. Casey Stengel was America."

On October 9, 1970, Stengel, retired from managing for over five years, wrote a column for the op-ed page of the *New York Times*. In the box at the bottom of the column where the contributor's credentials are listed, it said, "Casey Stengel is the philosopher of baseball." No additional résumé was needed. The man who had once been referred to derisively as "The Ol' Perfesser" had become Professor Emeritus.

Stengel earned that title, in part, by outlasting his critics. Herbert Hoover, who for many years was the most vilified of ex-presidents, said towards the end of his long life, "If you live long enough, the wheel turns, the pendulum swings." More succinctly: "I outlived the bastards." Unlike Hoover, who was buoyed up as he made the inexorable transition from partisan politician to nonpartisan elder statesman, Stengel not only outlived but outfought. He remained in the fray until a few days before his seventy-fifth birthday. "A lot of people my age are dead at the present time," he was given to saying in his later years. A lot of enemies were too, but it didn't matter; he minted new loyalists and detractors with each new generation and kept going regardless of which group had the upper hand.

Stengel's career covered almost every era of baseball history, from the dead ball to the lively ball. It witnessed presidential administrations from William Howard Taft to Lyndon Johnson. It covered multiple ages of vice, from speakeasies to drug dens. He crossed paths with most of the greatest figures in baseball history and interacted with literally every one of the game's figures of importance over a sixty-year span. It's hard to fathom, but Stengel batted against Christy Mathewson and managed Tug McGraw. He chased the balls that Babe Ruth hit in the first World Series game at Yankee Stadium and a half-century later was George Steinbrenner's guest at the same ballpark. The first important influence on his managerial career, Wilbert Robinson, was born during the Civil War. His last players were Baby Boomers. Play "Six Degrees of Separation" with Casey Stengel and you can travel from Abraham Lincoln to Alex Rodriguez in just a few steps. As Red Smith wrote, "Certainly Casey was one of the greatest managers . . . but it isn't the record that is significant . . . you could no more write the history of baseball without mentioning him than you could do a military history without Napoleon, a history of England without Wallis Simpson or a history of the movies without Mack Sennett."

Stengel did not achieve such incredible longevity by accident. His early career, replete with so many discouraging episodes, hardened him into someone who, though he never lost his sense of fun, steadfastly refused to go away. This aspect of his character has rarely been acknowledged. Instead, as with all successful managers, Stengel has sometimes been accused of riding the coattails of his players. The winning tradition of the Yankees rubbed off on Stengel, this reasoning went, and not the other way around. It was often taken for granted that the Yankees Stengel inherited were of such quality that the manager was irrelevant to their performance. One of the most vocal proponents of this attitude has been the team's shortstop, Hall of Famer Phil Rizzuto. "You or I could have managed and gone away for the summer and still won those pennants," he has said. "That's how good we were." In his view, Stengel "Fell into it . . . he inherited a great team." Billy Johnson, who played to Rizzuto's right, said, "Stengel might have been a good manager, but anybody could have managed the Yankees at [that] time."

Eddie Joost, who briefly played for Stengel in 1943, asserted that with the Yankees, "Stengel was never a good manager. . . . He never made the decisions. . . . Stengel was in the dugout not having any idea what was going on. When he would make a decision, it was usually wrong."

Bill Werber, a journeyman infielder who played for Stengel at Toledo in 1931, said in his autobiography:

> In nine years of managing in the National League with Brooklyn and Boston, he never reached the first division. . . . The Yankees' success in [Stengel's] years had much to do with general manager George Weiss and his legion of scouts who . . . assembled teams with tremendous talent. A manager of a great team typically has little to do with the success of the team, other than to not screw up a good thing. Consistent pitching and timely hitting turned Stengel into a genius and convinced the sportswriters of the day that his nonsensical utterances were in fact the learned pontifications of a master.

Ah, those lucky managers of great teams, haplessly stumbling into good fortune. As time goes by, athletes have a way of remembering their best moments while forgetting the context that allowed them to happen. "That's why I don't go to old timers' games," Yankees second baseman Jerry Coleman has said, "because they sit there, 'Member when, 'member when, 'member when?' They don't know how lousy they really were. Everything is perfect forty years later."

The idea that anyone could have managed the Yankees because the talent was deep or it doesn't take that much intelligence to know when to flash the bunt sign represents a fundamental misunderstanding of the role of manager. The manager's job is primarily supervisory and logistical (tactics take a distant third). They neither pitch nor hit and in that sense do not contribute to their team's wins and losses in the field, but it is equally true that during the entirety of World War II, Dwight Eisenhower (who shared Stengel's year of birth, Midwestern upbringing, and appreciation for baseball) did not fire a single shot in anger. The similarity between field generalship and military generalship has been vastly overstated but for this: both jobs are primarily about deployment of resources. The manager/general picks his team, prepares it to fight, and gets it to the place of battle in good order. Luck, Branch Rickey said, is the residue of design; if your plan is thorough and intelligently constructed, you can slant the odds in your favor. That's what managers—and generals—do. They try to maximize their advantages and hide their disadvantages by planning that takes place primarily before, not during, the battle.

Certainly, the experienced players and deep resources of the New

York Yankees organization did not handicap Stengel in executing his role (though the team was run frugally in those days, in no way resembling George Steinbrenner's spendthrift operation today), but even the Yankees fielded imperfect teams. Even the Yankees were subject to the forces of entropy, age, and injury that tear down even the best-run ballclubs. When Stengel joined the Yankees in 1949, and for most years thereafter, the team required a wise hand to smooth over its flaws. The years Stengel spent managing untalented ball clubs prepared him to recognize talent, distinguish it from the chaff, and utilize it in ways that enabled his teams to exceed the sum of their parts. At the moment when the tools available to him matched his ability to manipulate them, he was ready.

Nonetheless, to many observers Stengel's Yankees were what they always had been and always would be, baseball's biggest gorilla, even at times when the more appropriate primatical point of reference would have been a pygmy marmoset. Stengel was just along for the ride. It was Joe DiMaggio's ride, and then it was Mickey Mantle's ride, even if Stengel had promoted and trained Mantle himself.

Failure to receive due credit for his successes stung Stengel, especially since he had received (as all managers do) an overproportionate share of the blame for his teams' shortcomings. To the public, Casey Stengel claimed to be simply, "a man that's been around for awhile, a man that's been up and down, a man that's played with the dead ball and the lively ball and lived to tell the difference." Inside, he bore scars. Ed Linn, writing about Stengel in the *Saturday Evening Post*, asked,

> What does it do to a man to know that he can do his job better than anybody else in the world—to know in his heart that he knows how it should be done—and not only be denied the opportunity but to be looked upon as a garrulous fool?

The answer is self-evident: it hurts. It hurts badly. Casey Stengel neither gave in to that pain, nor believed his critics. When wounded, he fought off feelings of bitterness by laughing outwardly. He used his time in the wilderness to better his own understanding of his profession and himself, regroup, and attack again. Stengel's life represents the Horatio Alger myth stretched out over two and a half decades. He could not be a boy who made good, so he became an old man who made good. "Defeat does not awe Casey," a columnist observed in 1958, "and he is on good terms with hope." Or as Stengel himself put it, "Don't give up. Tomorrow is just another day, and that's myself."

CHAPTER 2

THE SUMMER OF SECOND CHANCES

Rooting for the Yankees is like rooting for U. S. Steel." The line is variously attributed. It might have been said by the comedian Joe E. Lewis, whose son was the general manager of the hapless Pittsburgh Pirates; the great sports columnist Red Smith; Spinoza; or Maimonedes. Whatever its provenance, it perfectly encapsulated the preferred image of the New York Yankees. New York City's American League ball club liked to portray itself as a horsehide IBM, an organization run with the clockwork precision that generated almost constant success. While the on-field victories that fueled this image were generated by players no less earthy or hard bitten than any of their contemporaries, the Yankees, seen through the lens of that era's sports pages, appeared to succeed through high character, superior morals, management, and discipline, all held together by the *esprit de corps* of an elite military unit. Though the team had ridden to incredible riches on the back of Babe Ruth's boisterous and often boorish exploits, the organization saw Ruth as an excess to be tolerated. It was hoped that the fans, though they loved the Babe, would prefer to identify with the quiet efficiency of Lou Gehrig, "a self-effacing star who never gave a manager a day's trouble."

The Yankee formula meant victories and businesslike comportment. Deviation from the formula was not long tolerated. Hence the almost palpable sense that something had gone wrong when on October 13, 1948, the New York Yankees announced that Charles Dillon "Casey" Stengel had been hired to manage the team for the next two seasons, replacing the popular incumbent, Bucky Harris. Stengel, a fifty-eight-year-old veteran of nine lackluster managerial campaigns, was widely perceived to be a clown, "A second division manager who was entirely satisfied to have a losing ball club so long as Stengel and his wit were appreciated." The general attitude among the newspapermen who covered the team, which they then transmitted to the public, was disbelief.

There was no reason for their skepticism, and the writers knew it. At midcentury, many of the New York sportswriters had been covering baseball since the days of Cobb and Wagner. Stengel had been associated with New York baseball almost as long, having played, coached, or managed in the city for all or parts of fourteen seasons from 1912 to 1917, 1921 to 1923, and 1932 to 1936. The same writers whose mouths were agape at Stengel's hiring had spoken with him, drunk with him, and ridden the rails with him on the long trips to baseball's distant outposts in St. Louis and Chicago (until 1958, baseball thought the American frontier ended at the Mississippi river and that "The Lewis and Clark Expedition" referred to an evening in 1921 when Duffy Lewis and Clark Griffith stayed out all night trying to find the best speakeasy in the District of Columbia). Their coverage of him had always reflected their apprehension of his intelligence and the bonhomie of their relationship.

Stengel's unexpected association with the Yankees changed everything. The sportswriters of 1948, as with the political journalists of today, had only a sideline in reporting the events of the day. Their primary job was to produce storylines, in the soap opera sense of the word. With over a dozen area daily newspapers, game stories were a commodity product. What sold papers were heroes and goats, complex events and personalities reduced to morality plays, fairy tales without the sophistication.

New York City had three baseball teams in those days, and each had long had an established character, unchanging, like the cardboard leading men in the boys' adventure serials of the time; unflinching square-jawed hero in episode one, unflinching square-jawed hero in chapter twenty-five. The Dodgers were bumbling and yet lovable. The Giants were hard-bitten and driven, as exemplified by a managerial line of descent from John McGraw to Bill Terry to Leo Durocher, the momentary interruption of which by the administration of the milquetoast Mel Ott inspired Durocher to quip, "Nice guys finish last."

With the Yankees, the primary characterization was of a methodical, emotionless precision, more suited to a watch factory than an entertainment operation. There were half-truths in this. The Yankees liked to project this image, particularly in the years of owner Jacob Ruppert, secretary ("general manager" in modern parlance) Edward Grant Barrow, and manager Joe McCarthy. It was inspired by many things: a legitimate need to instill a sense of professionalism on the club after the players got out of control in the wild early 1920s, a sincere belief in *esprit de corps*, and the perception that the team's fan-base consisted of snooty types who might otherwise go to the ballet if the ball club had too many rough characters (or African-Americans, or Hispanics . . .). Babe Ruth was a paradox for the Yankee ownership. He brought people to the ballpark—but perhaps he was bringing in the wrong people. Still, management somehow endured him for as long as he was at the top of his game. As soon as he slipped, he was gone. They never doubted they could keep winning without him, and as for the Babe's cult of personality, they didn't want it.

After Ruth, McCarthy would drill his charges in "the Yankee way": "You're a Yankee," he would say. "Act like one." Then he would go off and get blind drunk. "Riding the white horse," they called it around the ballpark, after the manager's preferred poison. Perhaps he would miss a couple of games, even disappear for a week. The writers, who had their own drinks—as well as room, board, and transportation—picked up by the club, would write that Joe's gall bladder had been troubling him or that he had the flu.

Many of the players bought into the myth that McCarthy was creating. "I hope the pride which a player has in being a Yankee does not die out," star outfielder Tommy Henrich said in early 1949:

> It is something more than a tradition. It is a mental, almost physical lift for a player to put on that Yankee uniform. I like to tell the young players new to the club about this pride in being a Yankee. I like to tell them about the days when the Yankees walked out on the field and threw terror into the ranks of the opposition simply because they were Yankees. . . . DiMaggio, Keller, Crosetti and I sit around in the clubhouse sometimes and talk about that very thing. About the history and prestige of this organization of ours.

The players even shared the organization's beliefs about the nature of the men and women who came through the turnstiles. Eddie Lopat, one of the team's pitching aces in the late forties and early fifties said, "Yankee fans were refined people for the most part. You'd hear the cheering but they were kind of sedate generally . . . the fans were controlled and there was control in the ballpark."

There were also many players who did not subscribe. If the player was of only minor consequence, he was made to go away, like Roy Johnson, a reserve outfielder on the 1937 club. When McCarthy groused after the Yankees lost a close game, Johnson said, "What does that guy expect to do—win every game?" Not only was he gone the next day, but he had been sent to the Boston Braves, at that moment about as far as one could go from a pennant race and still be on the major league circuit. He was replaced by the rookie Henrich, who knew the McCarthy doctrine without being told. Then there was outfielder Ben Chapman. He was bigoted, conceited, rowdy, started fights, and was a southerner, which irritated a peculiar McCarthy prejudice. McCarthy dealt him to the Washington Senators for a lesser player, one even more violent, more bigoted (though in those lilywhite days bigotry was just a character trait, not a career-breaking defect)—and another rookie, Joe DiMaggio was on hand to take up any slack.

When no Henrich or DiMaggio was on hand to take the place of a recalcitrant field hand, the bad seed was simply allowed to persist, subject to harassment by management to mend his ways. Milton Gross of the *New York Post* wrote, "Through the years McCarthy has been pictured as some sort of baseball Buddha before whose sacred altar all his players had to prostrate themselves. Characters, individualists, rowdies and malingerers, so the story goes, could not play for McCarthy. . . . This is sheer nonsense. McCarthy never gave away a problem child who had talent without getting his equal in return."

The fireballing lefty Joe Page, an escaped coal miner whose liberation was an excuse to abuse alcohol, was so resistant to coaching and curfews that in 1946 he finally broke McCarthy's spirit (Page's was the last blow in a campaign begun by another even more notorious alcoholic, the team's managing partner). "He was probably the biggest dissipater in the history of baseball," said a contemporary pitcher. "Drinker, women . . . They'd send detectives out to follow him and he'd up getting the detectives drunk." In 1947 Page was a national baseball hero and McCarthy was home in Buffalo with a case of nervous exhaustion.

Essentially, management shouted "semper fidelis" for only as long as it was in its interests to do so. Ruppert and Barrow were ruthless in making their team Ruth-less. Though the aging slugger backed them into a corner by refusing to back off his demand that he replace McCarthy, they made no effort to reach an accommodation. As for Gehrig, though Barrow looked at him as a son, when the first baseman first manifested signs of the illness that would ultimately take his life the secretary was amazingly quick to suggest that "it was about time for Lou to get himself another job." That was it—no pension, no coaching sinecure—just, thanks for the 2,130 games of dedicated service. Good luck in your future endeavors, however brief they are likely to be. It fell to New York Mayor Fiorello La Guardia to give Gehrig a position on the city Parole Board.

Forced to choose among printing the Page version (every man for himself) or the Henrich version (all for one and one for all), or the truth—that the roster was not homogenous, united in pursuit of a single goal, but a blend of Pages, Henrichs, and guys just doing their job—the press went with the Henrich version. The fans were on board from the start, and over the years even the writers began to believe their own corn, began to believe what they were selling.

In Stengel's case, they were selling the story of the stumblebum comic who inherited the world's greatest baseball team. A familiar but indistinct figure to New York baseball fans, Stengel was best known for two things: letting a bird fly out of his cap during a game that took place in the foggily remembered years before the Great War, and hitting a game-winning home run off of Yankees pitcher "Sad" Sam Jones in the 1923 World Series. This would seem to have been a heroic act rather than a comical one, but Stengel corrupted the moment by thumbing his nose at the American Leaguers as he jogged around the bases.

Not only did he act funny, but he *looked* funny. By the time the Yankees got hold of him, Stengel's face looked like a topographical model, creased and furrowed from too many day games spent staring into the sun, too many cigarettes, and late hours. Even his wide, smiling mouth was creased, with a tributary running down from the lower left-hand corner, a souvenir of the time a drunken teammate tore his lip during a fistfight. (In a 1952 *Life Magazine* article, Clay Felker and Ernest Havemann wrote, "At the left side of his mouth, running almost to his chin, is a line as deep as a canyon. It has been worn there through the years by the restless rumble and roar of words pouring out of the side of his mouth like an eternal waterfall," which is more romantic, but not true.) He had a wide, plunging expanse of nose and lively eyes bracketed by two giant jug-handle ears. Talking with sportswriter Tommy Holmes, Stengel referred to them as, "this here pair of palm-leaf fans." "Whereupon Mr. Stengel raised both of his hands," Holmes wrote, "and his fingertips touched a pair of awesome ears of about the same size, shape, and constituency of rib lamb chops."

All of these elements were wonderfully malleable, and working them in concert Stengel could augment any anecdote, of which he had thousands, with a variety of comically contorted expressions. When telling a story about a horse-faced catcher, it was said that he not only looked more like a horse than the catcher, but "he looked more like a horse than Man-O-War." Joe Williams, columnist for the New York *World Telegram* wrote, "No typewriter has yet been invented that can record the facial gyrations of Casey as he illustrates his yarns. He's no Clark Gable to start with and when he gets through one of his workouts children are scared for miles around." Joe Garagiola later called it "Casey Stengel's change of face."

Even in repose, the face was thought-provoking. People admired it in the same way they would a well-traveled trunk or a piece of distressed furniture. Harold Rosenthal of the *New York Herald-Tribune* felt that, "Casey Stengel actually grew better-looking as he got older. Not that he was any beauty contest winner but . . . his face had assumed a seamy dignity." Yankees broadcaster Mel Allen said that Stengel had the face of a "sea captain or a range rider." Jimmy Cannon wrote, "The old man has the face of an eagle who has flown into sleet storms. The lines in Casey Stengel's face are gullies. The left eye winks in the hook-nosed face as he discusses baseball, like a ferocious old bird sitting on the top branch of the highest tree in the world, watching all the ballgames ever played going on beneath him at the same time."

Only when Stengel spoke was the image completed. "Stengelese" had not yet been identified as such, but Stengel had always possessed his unique blend of mangled grammar, *fin de siècle* Midwestern idioms, and stream of consciousness dialogue. Sportswriter Jim Murray wrote, "Casey Stengel is a white American male with a speech pattern that ranges somewhere between the sounds a porpoise makes underwater and an Abyssinian rug merchant chant." Another, on his first meeting with the manager, exclaimed, "My god, he talks the way James Joyce writes!" A bad player was a "road apple," a scatological reference to the horse and buggy days. Someone who displayed naivety was a "Ned in the third reader." To do well was to have "done splendid." One did not begin, one commenced, and a player was not good, but remarkable. To hit down on the ball was to "butcher boy," and on and on, often in reference to something that happened years before. Stengel was both an autodidactic baseball historian and Zelig-like eyewitness to history, and he liked to illustrate a point with examples from the past. There is an oft-repeated story wherein a reporter goes looking for Stengel to find out who the next day's starting pitcher is. The reporter is gone for several hours. When he finally returns, one of his colleagues asks him, "Did Casey tell you who's going to pitch tomorrow?" "No," the beleaguered reporter replies. "He started to, but he got to talking about McGraw and the time he managed in Toledo and the Pacific Coast League and God knows what else. I think tomorrow's pitcher is Christy Mathewson." Once, when Shirley Povich of the *Washington Post* grew impatient after an hour waiting for a specific answer to his question, Stengel snapped, "Don't rush me."

Stengel also possessed a caustic wit, a superb sense of irony, and above all else was an indefatigable talker. The combination meant that he was always entertaining to listen to, if not always easy to understand. The serious listener was ultimately rewarded for his attention, but many dismissed his words as involuntary dadaist babbling, early senescence, or both. Perfectly clear when he wanted to be—and that was almost always behind the scenes—Stengel used obfuscation as a way of putting a distance between himself and the press. Late in Stengel's life, a young reporter interviewed the manager and was shocked to find him speaking in a perfectly comprehensible manner. "That jargon of yours is just a joke," the reporter exclaimed.

"Son," Stengel said, "this is gonna be our little secret, isn't it?"

Before and after Stengel, certain managers were given a free pass by the press despite decades of losing records and disappointing finishes. After the early 1930s, Connie Mack of the Philadelphia A's clearly wasn't trying—to him, a perfect season was one in which the A's got off to a hot start, stimulating attendance, and then dropped off rapidly so players could not demand raises—but he was a beloved Philadelphia institution, so no one called him on it. Mack protégé Jimmy Dykes managed for twenty-two seasons without exceeding eighty-five wins or finishing higher than third, yet no one ever questioned his fitness for the job. Gene Mauch first gained notoriety for managing the Phillies to an astounding September collapse in 1964. His next good season came after nineteen consecutive years of mediocre finishes. Nevertheless, during that time, Mauch was frequently called a genius. (Of Mauch and Alvin Dark, Stengel said, "They're so slick; they think they invented the game.")

Stengel's puckishness encouraged observers both in and out of baseball to judge his record harshly. In an era in which sporting competition was often all-too-glibly contrasted with war (and this in the interwar years, after the stubborn "battle of Waterloo was won on the playing fields of Eton" mentality had been interred beneath Flanders fields), Stengel's willingness to laugh at the bleakest times was interpreted as complacency. One contemporary, observing Stengel delivering a monologue at a party, said, "It never fails. Casey Stengel is funny to everyone except the guy who pays his salary."

The general attitude towards Stengel on the part of baseball writers, observed Fred Lieb, their dean, was that Stengel was a highly amusing fellow, but he lacked the proper pedigree for the Yankee job. One writer asked Lieb, "Is this serious? Are they really going to put a clown in to run the Yankee operation?" Dan M. Daniel, veteran reporter for *The Sporting News*, told Jerome Holtzman, "When Casey Stengel got the Yankee managing job, we thought he was in there to tell jokes and while away a season or two until the club could get tightened up and reorganized." Arthur Daily of the *New York Times* quoted a colleague as saying, "Ole Case had better win the pennant or else be awfully funny." "Stengel?" said another in disbelief, "Why, he won't even be around on June 15." "Casey may not win the pennant," said the *Washington Post*, "but you can bet he'll leave us laughing when he says good-bye." Red Smith summed up: "When the rumor that Stengel would be hired was going around World Series press headquarters, a good many men expressed astonishment. They just couldn't reconcile their conception of Stengel, the court jester, with the Yankee tradition of austere and business-like efficiency." And silence. During World War II, reporters had asked Mc-Carthy who would play second base if his keystone star George Stirnweiss was drafted. "Let me worry about that," McCarthy said, and then proceeded to do his best impression of a cigar-store Indian. In one close game, McCarthy decided that Lefty Gomez was providing an unseemly amount of dugout chatter and ordered him into the clubhouse. "Lefty," McCarthy said, "you go in and stay in, and if we want you we will call you."

Stengel's most vociferous and vituperative critic from his days in Boston, Dave Egan (the self-styled "Colonel" of the tabloid *Boston Daily Record*), sought to bury the manager before he had even begun:

> Well sirs and ladies, the Yankees now have been mathematically eliminated from the 1949 pennant race. They eliminated themselves when they engaged Perfessor [sic] Casey Stengel to mismanage them for the next two years, and you may be sure that the Perfessor will oblige to the best of his unique ability . . . [the New York writers] will love Stengel. If it's stories and mimicry and home-spun humor they want, they'll get it from Stengel by day and by night, each day and each night. They'll get everything from him, indeed, with the exception of the pennants to which they have become accustomed.

On another occasion Egan speculated that Stengel must have been hired because one of the Yankee owners owed him money.

As if Stengel needed one more thing to damn him in the eyes of the public and the press, it was widely felt that he had acquired the job because Yankees general manager George Weiss had long had a hidden agenda to hire his old friend Stengel, and that Bucky Harris, who in two seasons with the club had won the World Series the first year and finished two games out of first place in the second, had been stabbed in the back as a result of it. This was barely half true. Weiss had long wanted to employ Stengel and there was nothing stealthy about it; he had first suggested Stengel to the Yankees earlier in the decade and had used him in the Yankees farm system in 1945. It was also patently unfair to say that Harris had been stabbed in the back or otherwise, unless one considered it a case of self-impalement. The exact circumstances of his dismissal were well known to the writers, but either out of the same misplaced sense of delicacy (and bribery) that had protected McCarthy or willful obtuseness, they refused to see, nevermind say, that the "austere and business-like efficiency" that Red Smith referred to had long been a thing of the past. Stengel's hiring was, paradoxically, an attempt to revive them.

In 1945, Colonel Ruppert's heirs had sold the Yankees to a trio of investors comprised of Del Webb, a construction magnate instrumental in the creation of the modern Las Vegas; Dan Topping, heir to an aluminum fortune; and Larry MacPhail. The mercurial MacPhail would be the active partner, having already successfully run major league teams in Cincinnati and Brooklyn. In each case he had taken a second-rate franchise and transformed it. If the franchises he had left behind were not necessarily winners, he at least left them in far better shape than he found them. MacPhail did not stay long in either Cincinnati or Brooklyn due to his own erratic behavior. Christened "Lucifer Sulphurious," by Dan Parker of the *New York Mirror*, MacPhail was an alcoholic given to dramatic outbursts of temper and public tantrums. As an executive he was effective only up to the moment of his inevitable self-destruction. Leo Durocher, who managed the Dodgers for MacPhail and estimated that the "Roaring Redhead" had fired him twenty-seven times between 1939 and 1942 (only to treat the termination as water on the bridge when he sobered up) wrote, "They always said this about MacPhail: Cold sober he was brilliant. One drink and he was even more brilliant. Two drinks—that's another story."

As befits a man with a rash temperament (at the close of the first World War he had taken part in an unauthorized attempt to abduct the Kaiser. He failed to get the monarch but did manage to kidnap his ashtray), MacPhail was an innovator. His greatest attribute was that he did not accept boundaries, clichés, old beliefs. At his direction the Cincinnati Reds became the first team to install lights, disproving the old notion that night baseball could not succeed in the majors. He repeated the trick in Brooklyn and New York. He began the regular radio broadcast of Dodger home games, shattering the myth that to do so would mean a disastrous decline in attendance. In the process, he unilaterally shattered the pact under which the three New York teams had agreed to embargo such broadcasts (MacPhail's other contribution to baseball radio came when he inaugurated the Brooklyn career of broadcaster Red Barber). He also began Durocher's managerial career, trusting him though many in baseball felt his was a borderline criminal personality.

MacPhail was also a great promoter, inaugurating Ladies' Days, the stadium club, and a wide variety of pregame entertainments, and was a good judge of baseball flesh who took particular pride in foxing his former patron/perennial antagonist Branch Rickey of the St. Louis Cardinals when making a trade. As George Weiss later said, "Larry could have been the best executive in baseball if he had a little more emotional stability." Durocher wrote, "There is not a question in my mind that Larry was a genius. There is a line between genius and insanity, and in Larry's case it was sometimes so thin that you could see him drifting back and forth."

There was no institution with which MacPhail did not feel free to tamper. When he transferred his flag to the Yankees he immediately began to tamper with a New York institution, Yankees manager Joe McCarthy, and rapidly left the man a twitching, quivering wreck who had to be fortified with alcohol. MacPhail, "the extra-colossal, super-spectacular, ring-tailed quintessence of everything Ed Barrow wasn't," questioned, doubted, second-guessed, harassed, and threatened summary dismissal. McCarthy had never had that kind of interference before; that the manager should be insulated from the dilettantes in the executive suite had been one of Barrow's cardinal rules. MacPhail was no "sportsman" as Ruppert had been. He was, as Bill Veeck might have described him, an operator.

In late May 1946, McCarthy had one final blowup with Joe Page. As the Yankees waited for a team flight to take off, McCarthy cornered Page and began asking questions like, "What the devil's the matter with you?" "When are you going to settle down and start pitching?" and, "How long do you think you can get away with this?" These were not questions designed to promote relaxed conversation, and when Page rose to the bait, McCarthy exploded, vowing that Page would be sent to the Yankees farm club at Newark, this time to stay.

For twenty-four hours, Page's career hung by a thread while McCarthy stewed. In fifteen years with the team, he had never before dressed down a player in public. He apparently had an epiphany: "He shouldn't go. I should." He promptly resigned.

In 1841, the United States had three presidents. In the Bronx, 1946 was the year of three managers. McCarthy's replacement, the veteran Yankees catcher Bill Dickey, refused to finish out the season under MacPhail. The season was completed under interim manager/organization man Johnny Neun. Neun "had let it be known after about a week that he knew now what McCarthy and Dickey had been talking about and, by God, he didn't have to take that from anybody either." The second-division Cincinnati Reds seemed a better option, and off he went.

That September, Stanley Raymond "Bucky" Harris was hired to serve in an undefined executive capacity (MacPhail acted as his own general manager, and Weiss, the club's farm director since 1932, was on hand to take care of anything that might escape his notice. Barrow, ostensibly a consultant to the club, was also available, though MacPhail never called) and asked to evaluate the team. Almost a quarter century earlier, Harris had been the twenty-eight-year-old "boy manager" who had guided the Washington Senators to consecutive pennants in his initial seasons at the helm. After that the going was not nearly so smooth. Harris's initial command of the Senators lasted until 1928, at which time owner Clark Griffith terminated him, in part for not following up on his earlier success, and in part for failing to recognize the talents of second base prospect Buddy Myer.

Harris moved on to Detroit, where in five seasons he failed to produce a first-division finish. Still in demand, in 1934 he became the first manager hired by Tom Yawkey as owner of the Boston Red Sox. The team's 76–76 record was its best since 1918, but Harris clashed with general manager Eddie Collins and was dismissed. He returned to Washington, where sentimental Senators owner Clark Griffith was never loathe to re-employ an old pal. In the following eight seasons, the club finished fourth once and otherwise could be counted on for a sixth or seventh place finish. Harris made way for another Griffith buddy, Ossie Bluege.

Harris then briefly managed the Philadelphia Phillies under owner Bill Cox, whose own term was foreshortened by Commissioner of Baseball Judge Landis after it was revealed that Cox had bet on his own club. Cox fired Harris after ninety-two games, claiming that he had called his players "a bunch of jerks." In fact, the players threatened to strike when informed of Harris's termination. Said Harris, "If there is any jerk connected with this ball club, it's the president of it." That seemed to have been the last encore for the graying, forty-six-year-old, non-boy manager. When MacPhail hired him, Harris had been serving as the general manager of the International League's Buffalo club. This was actually fine with Harris; after two decades on the managerial merry-go-round, he desired to become an executive—preferably with the Detroit Tigers, but if their general manager's job wasn't open, a job with the Yankees would have to do.

It was MacPhail's original intention to keep Harris in the front office and lure Durocher back to the Yankees (Durocher had begun his major league career as New York's shortstop. He had been abruptly dumped after demonstrating that he was even less coachable than Babe Ruth. For the Yankees, one loose cannon was enough, especially when this midnight reveler was no slugger but rather the "All-American Out" and did not hesitate to confront the Victorian Barrow with profanity). Durocher was still in Brooklyn working for Rickey, and having experienced the Mahatma's cerebral, civilized ways, he had no desire to re-experience the volcanic tantrum-a-day executive style.

The thought of stealing Durocher from Rickey, or even making him nervous about the possibility, had to be enormously titillating to MacPhail; Durocher's feelings on the matter did not necessarily enter into his calculations. He had already taken a stab at Red Barber, the Brooklyn broadcaster, by offering to make him the highest paid broadcaster in the game. Barber ultimately turned MacPhail down, in part because Rickey was willing to match MacPhail. "My offer didn't hurt you, did it?" MacPhail chortled to Barber. He had made Rickey spend more money. The next salvo, which brought yet another potential manager to the Bronx, involved stealing both of Durocher's coaches, Chuck Dressen and Red Cor-riden.

Dressen, who had managed the Reds for MacPhail, was considered the tactical brains of the Dodgers. He had been hanging around Brooklyn since 1939, waiting for Durocher to slit his own throat (Durocher cooper-ated on more than one occasion, but Durocher was a survivor). Dressen had a guaranteed contract with one out; he could leave the Dodgers only to take a managerial position. MacPhail doesn't seem to have considered him for the Yankees job, but that may not be what Dressen was told.

To this day, it is not clear whether MacPhail actually wanted to hire Durocher, was merely trying to tweak Rickey's tail, or even floated the rumor to help Durocher in salary negotiations with Rickey. Later, Mac-Phail denied having made an offer. Durocher insisted he did, and that he turned it down.

The story gets stranger; this was just the overture of what would be a watershed year for the Yankees. What follows is merely the sketchiest of outlines. In a ghost-written column, Durocher accused MacPhail of con-sorting with gamblers, something of which Durocher was constantly (and correctly) under suspicion. Rickey jumped in: why was there a double standard for MacPhail when everyone was always sniping at Durocher? Suddenly the case was a matter for baseball's second commissioner, Happy Chandler.

As with most commissioners of baseball, Chandler weighed in with all the grace of a ten-ton gorilla and with twice as much mystery. He sus-pended Dressen for thirty days, either because he broke his contract, bet too much on the ponies, or both. He fined both the Yankees and the Dodgers organizations $2,000 apiece. As the *pièce de résistance*, he suspended Durocher for the entirety of the 1947 baseball season. Fi-nally, he slapped a gag order on everyone involved. They couldn't say anything to defend themselves, and Chandler chose not to explain his actions—though the fact that Chandler owed his job to MacPhail might have had some bearing on his thoughts.

With the Yankees now down four managerial candidates, Bucky Harris became the manager by default. He reluctantly agreed to undertake the job, insisting on a two-year contract, after which he expected to return to the front office.

The 1946 Yankees had suffered from the lack of continuity in the man-ager's office. Although the team had stars Joe Gordon, Phil Rizzuto, Joe DiMaggio, Charlie Keller, Bill Dickey, Tommy Henrich, and Red Ruffing together on the roster for the first time since World War II military service broke up the team, New York still finished a distant third, seventeen games behind the Red Sox. Many of the players seemed to have aged badly while away from the game and would clearly not last much longer, but with the team in such disarray it was hard to sort out the keepers. The pitching staff saw eighteen different pitchers take a turn in the starting rotation. Wartime first baseman Nick Etten bombed against regular competition, Joe Gordon hit only .210, there was no regular third baseman, and so on.

The list of problems was long and deep, and MacPhail threatened to gut the team. "Lindell, Johnson, Stirnweiss, Rizzuto, Bevens, Page and Robinson were in MacPhail's doghouse," said Weiss, who was himself desperately trying to get away from MacPhail. "He wanted to trade them, two or three at a crack, to Washington for Jimmy [Mickey] Vernon and to St. Louis for Jack Kramer and Vernon Stephens."

Fortunately, the Dr. Jekyll version of MacPhail prevailed and he and Harris did a good job of sorting out the problems. In 1947 the Yankees ran away with the pennant. Already leading by 4.5 games at the end of June, the team buried the competition with a nineteen-game winning streak. As the boy wonder of Washington, Harris had made a spectacularly perspicacious move in taking pitcher Fred "Firpo" Marberry and converting him into a bullpen ace. This was a time when pitching complete games was a manhood issue for pitchers and the bullpen was considered the last refuge of wasted arms. Harris's willingness to put a fresh arm in the game at the same time that the opposing pitcher was trying to figure out how to get some zip on his 150th pitch gave the Senators a tremendous competitive advantage. Now Harris repeated the move, taking wild, hard-throwing Joe Page—the same man who had helped to break Joe McCarthy's spirits—and turning him into a reliever. At first, it seemed as if Page would break Harris's spirits too, but by the end of the 1947 season he was "The Gay Reliever," possessor of a 14–8 record with a league leading (retroactively figured—the saves statistic had yet to be invented) seventeen saves. Harris fell in love; after each win, he would begin his postgame press conference with a toast to Joe Page.

The Yankees won the 1947 World Series from the Durocher-less Dodgers—barely—with a curious decision by Harris to intentionally put the winning run on base in game four contributing heavily to the "barely." Nonetheless, Harris's job should have been secure. Instead, he was finished. His patron had self-destructed.

At the Yankees victory party, MacPhail came undone. He congratulated George Weiss as "the man who really built the Yankees," and was happily emotional at the team's triumph. He returned shortly thereafter, presumably drunk and in a rage. He found Weiss again, insulted him, struck him, then fired him. He announced to whoever was listening that he was quitting the team and leaving baseball. He then turned on his partner, Topping, who subdued him and led him from the room.

It is doubtful that MacPhail meant what he said; when he was with the

Dodgers these sort of outbursts happened on a regular basis and never amounted to anything. The next morning the injured party or parties would hope that MacPhail had forgotten the excesses of the previous evening, or MacPhail would apologize. "Got a little drunk last night, didn't we?" he would say to Durocher. This time no one was forgetting. First, this had been MacPhail's most extreme outburst; second, this sort of thing did not happen to the Yankees. The next morning, though he attempted to apologize, Topping and Webb forced MacPhail to keep his promise to leave. Bought out for two million dollars, he never returned to baseball.

Harris now had to coexist with Weiss, a man as cold and sober as Mac-Phail was hot-tempered and inebriated, a humorless man who did not know he was humorless:

> The Yankees have often been accused of being a hardheaded, hard-hearted organization of unsentimental businessmen with a bunch of talented but mechanical ballplayers carrying out their functions in the field. This isn't so at all. We have simply always realized that modern-day baseball is a highly practical enterprise that has to be run systematically, and this includes everything from operating a good restaurant for members of the Stadium Club to two-platooning on the field when the circumstances demand it. But don't you believe that there's no sentiment left on the Yankees!

The Yankees ran another strong race in 1948, but Weiss felt a lack of discipline on the club had played a greater role in determining the final standings than anything the front-running Cleveland Indians had done. Weiss thought of Harris as "the four-hour manager." He came to the park, coached his game, and then went home to his wife and an unlisted phone number that not even the Yankees had. When, in spring training, Weiss felt the players needed more practice and less time at the dog-racing track, he was chagrinned to discover that Harris was frequently at the track with them. "I have no objections to seeing them at the track," Harris said. "At least this way I know where they are."

When hiring managers teams inevitably, as if guided by an unseen hand, go from high-pressure to low-pressure personalities. In 1978, when George Steinbrenner of the Yankees fired Billy Martin and replaced him with Bob Lemon, he took the team away from a manager who pushed his team through anger and intimidation and gave it to a man whose basic attitude was, "Let's all have some fun." Joe McCarthy was always in charge. "McCarthy is the strict commander," said outfielder Tommy Henrich. "He wants to be the absolute boss. Not much latitude for you; he likes you to do things his way, and he takes full responsibility." Harris was more interested in maintaining a cordial relationship with his players. In his view, there were only two things a manager needed to know—"When to change pitchers and how to get along with the players." "I really don't care what a player does off the field," he once said. "If he is able to do his job and give me 100 percent, that's all I ask." The problem with this formulation is that 100 percent is in the eye of the beholder, and when a player comes into the clubhouse with bloodshot eyes, just how close to 100 percent he really might be is open to doubt.

The price for employing this kind of manager is a laxity of discipline. Billy Johnson remembered that Harris was, "very quiet, very lenient." He had what Tommy Henrich called a "leave them alone" style of managing. "He treated you with confidence," he said. "He let me go my own way, and it was a pleasure to put out for him." Once, when Henrich asked Harris if he should lay down a bunt in a situation that seemed to call for one, the manager replied that it was up to him. When he managed the Red Sox, Harris surprised his team by promulgating only one rule: No swimming. "You're likely to get sunburned," said Harris. When his players faced Bob Feller, the bullet-throwing "Rapid Robert" of the Indians, Harris had just one instruction: "Go on up there and hit what you see. If you can't see it, come on back."

"Under Bucky we were a very relaxed ballclub," said Henrich, "too relaxed in my opinion." In later years, the players clung to the myth of the jocks who policed themselves. Whitey Ford later said, "If a guy blew a play or a game because he came to work late after a long night of drinking or bouncing around, that's when somebody like Hank Bauer settled it in a hurry. He'd grab you in the dugout and look you right in the eyes and growl: 'Don't fuck around with my money.' And that's maybe the main thing that kept the guys straight, the idea that you're not only screwing yourself but you're also taking money out of everybody else's pocket if you screw up." Even Stengel believed it: "They thought all you had to do at the Yankees is to be there on time, tend to your own business off the field and when they said play ball be sure you go out and play hard and play clean."

But neither Ford, nor Bauer, nor Stengel were with the club in 1948, and it wasn't true then, if it was ever true. Joe Page was a particular problem. After contending for the American League Most Valuable Player award in 1947, Page slumped to 7–8 with a 4.25 ERA. Hard living, and Harris's indifference to it, were blamed. "Page burned himself out. He was drunk all the time for God's sakes," Jerry Coleman recalled. "He had a great year in '47, and he couldn't stand that. He had a terrible year in '48. In fact, DiMaggio in spring training of '48 said [to the pitchers], 'You guys better finish your games this year,' because he knew what was going on."

In 1947, MacPhail had given Page a contract with a "good behavior" clause. On each of baseball's eleven paydays he was to receive a different amount depending on whether Harris thought he had been behaving himself. Weiss abandoned the practice in 1948 and the team paid the price. "He couldn't have two good years in a row," Allie Reynolds told Dom Forker. "You can't relax. He did." Weiss hired a detective. Legend has it that Page seduced her, or vice-versa. Perhaps that was the whole point of the exercise.

Despite the detective's reports that Weiss bombarded him with, Harris would not confront Page. He did fine Page at least once, but it was a half-hearted attempt at discipline. "I don't kid myself," said Harris. "Page's great relief work put me back in business after I had been forgotten. I'd be an ungrateful so and so to turn on him now. This job isn't that important to me." He also subscribed to the conventional wisdom in baseball that alcoholism in players was something a manager sometimes had to put up with. "They told me a certain pitcher was drinking too much," he said, possibly referring to Page. "He was. I didn't say anything to him. I felt like Lincoln when his cabinet fussed about Grant drinking, and Lincoln said he wished some of his other generals would try Grant's brand of whiskey." Such was Harris's loyalty to the reliever that at the end of the season he took Page aside and said, "Joe, whatever happens in the future, if I get let go, which is probably going to happen, it's not on account of you."

A manager less concerned with sparing Page's feelings might have gone as far as to say, "not *wholly* on account of you." Page was not alone in keeping late nights; there were multiple carousers including outfielder Johnny Lindell and pitcher Frank Shea. When the Yankees finished two and a half games out of first, rather than look at the finish as a noble failure, Weiss saw the glass as half-empty. More accurately, he just saw glasses. Beer glasses. Whiskey glasses. Rows of long-stemmed glasses wet with "Lindell Bombers." These were actually extra-dry martinis, but Lindell had become so familiar with the drink that he had personalized it. "Bucky Harris is too damned easygoing," Weiss cursed. "He's lost control of the team."

Control aside, there was also the issue of the club's composition. "DiMaggio and Henrich are reaching the end of the line," Weiss worried in July 1948, "and there's no one in sight to replace them." The Yankees would soon be experiencing a youth movement. Harris, who preferred to work with veterans, lacked a sure touch with young players, rushing some, unnecessarily holding others back. Throughout 1948, he and Weiss struggled over the disposition of players like pitcher Bob Porterfield and outfielder Hank Bauer. Meanwhile, Harris's handling of Yogi Berra threatened to permanently destroy the young catcher's confidence in the field. Because the Dodgers supposedly embarrassed Berra by stealing at will in the 1947 World Series, Harris would not commit to him as a catcher, shuttling him from the plate to the outfield throughout the season.

All of these actions were consistent with Weiss's view of a lackadaisical manager buffeted by fate. "God gets you up in the morning in good health and guides you safely through traffic to the ballpark," Harris said a few year later. "When your turn comes, He takes you by the hand and leads you up to the plate. Then He taps your shoulder. 'Son,' He says, 'you take it from here'—and drops you flat on your puss." Similarly, the fate of the Yankees was also out of Harris's hands. "It all depends on the Big Fellow," Harris would say, referring to Joe DiMaggio. Since Weiss was already envisioning a future without DiMaggio, this could hardly have been reassuring.

As soon as the Yankees' third-place finish was interred in the history books, Harris was let go. He played the victim, saying, "It was like being socked in the head with a steel pipe." Though he had known exactly what was coming, the idea that an assassination had taken place stuck. After the season, two sportswriters observed Del Webb approach Harris at a party. "What does Webb want with Harris now?" one of them asked. "He came back for the knife," said the other. On the day of Stengel's reintroduction to the New York press, John Drebinger of the *New York Times* hinted at the great injustice of it all.

> The fifty-seven-year-old Stengel succeeds Bucky Harris who, engaged by Larry MacPhail before the 1947 campaign, won a pennant and world championship in his first year with the Yanks and this year kept what generally was regarded a badly outmatched club in the race until next to the last day, only to be dismissed for a reason as yet not explained by anyone.

> In the light of this, most observers, always kindly disposed toward the engaging Stengel, were viewing his forthcoming assignment with some misgivings.

Even Bill Veeck, owner of the champion Indians and ostensibly Stengel's friend, said publicly that Harris would return with another team and make "the Yankees executives that fired him eat their words." All of these references to the martyr Harris were disingenuous at best. It was as true in 1948 as it is today that both executives and journalists are familiar with every player's peccadilloes. Baseball is a small community with few secrets. The executives don't employ that information for competitive advantage because as the Good Book says, let he who is without sin cast the first stone. Every team has its malcontents and miscreants and so no one is free to speak. Besides, it doesn't pay to be puritanical because that alcoholic wife-beater might help you win a pennant some day. As for the journalists, their silence was at first secured by perks and then by the importance of maintaining cordial relations with the teams. The stab in the back was alive in the Bronx, all because the real, more compelling story of a ball club with its head in a bottle could not be told.

Casey Stengel wandered into this carnival and then was accused of *being* the carnival. With the writers predisposed towards finding fault with him, that first press conference, held over a sumptuous lunch at the 21 Club, did not go well. Introduced by Dan Topping, Stengel said, "Thank you, Bob . . . uh, Dan." Bob was Topping's sybaritic brother, his partner in the National Football League's Brooklyn Dodgers team (later the New York Yankees of the AAFL; such was the second-tier status of professional football in those days that an association with baseball was seen as a corrective to the pervasive lack of interest in the sport), but otherwise a man of leisure. The great Joe McCarthy had made the very same error in his first press conference when he thanked Colonel Huston, Jacob Ruppert's unlamented former partner of nearly ten years gone by. Nonetheless, for the writers this was strike one.

He seemed indecisive when predicting the club's future, and even acknowledged his unfamiliarity with the team. He had not seen the team play in several years, he said. "Now I must study the Yankee situation and draw my own conclusions." In elaborating, he displayed a guilelessness that belied his reputation as a champion obfuscator. "This is a big job, fellows," he told the writers, "and I have barely had time to study it. In fact, I scarcely know where I am at. There'll likely be some changes, but it's a good club and I think we'll do alright. We'll go slow because you can tear a club down a lot quicker than you can build it up." Throughout his career, Stengel had always showed an uncharacteristic reticence when it came to making predictions. Strike two.

Stengel was asked to express his feelings about managing Joe DiMaggio, who was there at the press conference. In old age, DiMaggio was known as a man who clung to the title of "Baseball's Greatest Living Baseball Player" as though he had received it by divine decree rather than fan poll, a man who would not attend baseball functions unless he were introduced last (even when sharing the bill with a fellow luminary like Mickey Mantle or Ted Williams on a day dedicated to *them*). This was not the eccentric pride of an old man. He had always been that way; when DiMaggio said that he always played hard because, "There is always some kid who may be seeing me for the first or last time. I owe him my best," he was displaying his hyper-developed sense of professionalism, but not altogether selflessly. His dedication had to be acknowledged, honored, or the man was not happy. Pride of accomplishment, in a job well done, was inextricably entwined with pride of self.

Stengel could have been expected to praise his star center fielder. He did not. "I cannot tell you very much about that, being as since I have not been in the American League so I ain't seen the gentleman play, except once in a very great while." DiMaggio, not a loquacious man, was very good at nonverbal communication. He frowned. Insufficient genuflection resulting in team MVP getting his nose out of joint: strike three. You're out.

Stengel was called upon to defend his relationship with George Weiss, something he would be asked to do frequently between the announcement of his hiring and the beginning of the season. Here he was very direct. "I didn't get this job through friendship. The Yankees represent an investment of maybe two, three million dollars. They don't hire you just because they like your company. I got the job because these people think I can produce for them."

Stengel knew he was floundering. "Somebody asked a question about DiMaggio and I said I didn't know DiMaggio. I could hear the hum in the background. When they asked about a pennant I could hear that hum again and I knew what they were talking about. They were saying, 'This bum managed nine years and never got into the first division.'"

"Because I can make people laugh," he said, "some of them think I'm a damn fool. But as a player, coach, and manager I have been around baseball for some thirty-five years. I've watched such successful managers as John McGraw and Uncle Robbie work. I've learned a lot and picked up a few ideas of my own." He was almost sixty years old, nearing retirement age. He had managed for almost twenty-five years, apparently without merit. "Let them think it's a joke," Stengel said, "and maybe I'll laugh when I fool them."

Only Red Smith of the *Herald-Tribune* saw through the hypocrisy inherent in holding Stengel up to a mythical conception of the Yankees:

> The old Yankee tradition ceased to exist several years ago when a man named MacPhail arrived. The old owner was a wholesaler who ran a brewery. His successor was a retailer who opened a saloon in the park. There is a new Yankee tradition now, which resembles the old as a chromium and red barstool resembles Chippendale.

> There is, therefore, nothing incongruous in the notion of a comedian running the Yankees. But it is erroneous and unjust to conceive of Casey Stengel merely as a clown. He is something else entirely—a competitor who has always had fun competing, a fighter with the gift of laughter.

The next day, bravado restored, Stengel and newly appointed pitching coach "Milkman" Jim Turner toured Yankee Stadium and made a cameo appearance at a press luncheon time for Topping's Yankees football team. This time Stengel was a hit, breaking up the room by saying, "When I heard that old Pepper Martin [the former St. Louis Cardinals star] was playing football in Brooklyn, I figured that Dan Topping must have had something of that sort in mind when he brought me here."

CHAPTER 3

I WILL HANDLE THIS SITUATION IN MY OWN WAY

When spring training began, Stengel confronted a group of skeptical players. They had read the newspapers, taking with them to Florida images of greasepaint and big floppy shoes. "I still recall the headline," said Jerry Coleman, a rookie in camp, "and it said, 'Yanks hire clown.'" Ed Lopat, one of the team's top starting pitchers, remembered, "It was a shock. We thought we had got a clown." The young third baseman Bobby Brown: "The only thing we knew about Casey is what we'd read in the papers. That he was eccentric, that he was kind of a baseball clown . . . no one realized the depth of his baseball knowledge."

Stengel went out of his way to treat the players gently that first spring. He interceded with Weiss to prevent five players who had been labeled as "playboys" from receiving pay cuts—he wanted to minimize the number of disgruntled veterans if he could. In direct contradiction of the reason he was hired, he promised a hands-off approach. "I know little about this league," he said in his first meeting with the full team. "I am just going to watch and learn." He promulgated one rule: visits to the greyhounds would be limited to Thursday nights. Otherwise, other than a midnight curfew the players were on their own. "It's like this," he said. "If you have men who make you set up rules, then you have rules. If they don't need rules, then they don't need rules. Anyone over twenty-one ought to have enough sense to take care of himself. You're all over twenty-one." Taking no chances, he added a second daily practice session to the Yankee spring regimen for the first time since 1922. "The two-a-day training scheme," he said, "is calculated to keep the minds of the players on baseball for a longer period of time each day here."

Further distancing himself, Stengel cast himself as the team's CEO, delegating many training functions to his coaches and even to the players themselves. Bill Dickey, lured back to the organization for the first time since his falling out with MacPhail, would instruct catchers, Jim Turner the pitchers. Johnny Neun, another returning MacPhail exile, coached base running and tutored the first basemen. Frank Crosetti, a Yankee since 1932 and the sole holdover from the previous regime, worked with the infielders. DiMaggio, the recognized standard of excellence in the pastures, was the primary outfield coach as he entered the twilight of his career.

In batting practice, DiMaggio and Crosetti coached the right-handed hitters. Stengel, Henrich, Dickey, and Charlie Keller coached the lefties. Using veterans to coach their teammates was something new. "I think any young athlete should welcome advice from such established stars," Stengel said. I know I would have welcomed it had it been available for me when I came up." In his day, veterans were largely hostile to young players, seeing them as competition. "On the other hand, a young fellow probably will pay more attention to the instruction of a star than he would to a manager."

"He didn't tell us all his ideas all at once. He was really pretty humble," Rizzuto told Roger Kahn. "If he had come in with a big speech, telling us a whole lot of stuff up front, there would have been trouble. Casey did a lot of smart things with the Yankees but the smartest thing he ever did was come on slow."

In return for Stengel's humility, the players mocked him. Behind his back the players called him "Casey Stinkle," and "The broken-legged manager" (Stengel had a mildly deformed leg, the result of being hit by a car five years earlier). When Bucky Harris was kicked downstairs to the dugout in 1947, Joe DiMaggio told his teammates, "Harris is a real nice guy. Let's give him all we've got." Now DiMaggio spoke for the rest of the team when he agreed with Arthur Daley of the *New York Times* when the latter said, "I've never seen such a bewildered guy in my life. He doesn't seem to know what it's all about." He found a receptive audience in Rizzuto. "I don't get this guy," he said to the shortstop. "With this guy managing, we can't possibly win." Each morning when training began, DiMaggio was the last to report.

Ten days after camp opened, DiMaggio was spotted at the track on an unsanctioned night. "Oh well," sighed Stengel, as if bowing to the inevitability of the moment, "news for the papers." Weighing his own future against DiMaggio's famous dignity, Stengel ordered DiMaggio to apologize to the team. "Those kind of players, all you have to do is read the records and see how they played for other managers," Stengel said. "They've never loafed. This is a serious business with them, they're as anxious to be ready as I am to have them ready. I know that, but I can't do anything that looks like favoritism."

In the past, Stengel had tried to treat all the players the same way, and with the same degree of disposability. In the case of the canine curfew caper, his first instinct was to take a hard line. "I will handle this situation in my own way if I have to go out to the track myself," he said. "No sense fining a player. If he disobeys rules, get rid of him." Capital punishment was the historic privilege of managers, and no doubt Stengel would have been free to exercise it with almost any other player. Joe DiMaggio, though, was perhaps the best player in baseball and a civic possession as much as an employee of the ball club to boot. As if quickly realizing his lack of stature compared to that of his recalcitrant superstar, he sighed, "DiMaggio admits he feels bad about it," and tried to move on.

But what DiMaggio really felt was a simmering resentment. Since he had been rumored to have been up for the manager's job (as were Bill Terry, Al Simmons, Tommy Henrich, and others), at Stengel's introductory press conference the outfielder was asked if he had any ill-feelings about Stengel's hiring. "You know me, boys," he said. "I'm just a ball player with only one ambition, and that is to give all I've got to help my ball club win. I've never played any other way." In reality, he was angry at not having been consulted by the organization on the disposition of the manager's job. He was also resentful that the Yankees did not offer him the job before giving it to Stengel. He did not want to manage; he only wanted the opportunity to turn the job down. He felt this was a courtesy owed to him as the Yankees' preeminent player.

That spring the Yankee players were all about entitlement. They were pros, the children of McCarthy, smarter than Weiss, and more dignified than Stengel. Unable to see the forest for the trees, they missed the decline of the team as it fell down around them. The Yankees were still McCarthy's Yankees of Gehrig at first, Gordon at second, Henrich, Keller, and DiMaggio in the outfield, somehow avoiding the unpleasant truths that McCarthy was drinking himself out of a job in Boston, Gehrig was dead, Gordon was gone, and the three outfielders had left their youthful health and vigor in the decade of the 1930s.

The ballplayers were incapable of acknowledging their impending obsolescence, but Stengel, looking over the club that spring, was faced with several unpleasant realities.

FIRST BASE: There was no first baseman. There hadn't been one since May 2, 1939, the day Lou Gehrig sat down. He had been followed by a parade of mediocrities, as if in addition to retiring Gehrig's number the team was also retiring his position. Babe Dahlgren couldn't hit and McCarthy also held an unexplained grudge against him. Johnny Sturm came up in 1941, got hot early, and then settled down into the least useful batting season by a first baseman in the franchise's history. Sturm was taken into the military and never returned to the majors, which after the defeat of fascism was probably the best thing to come out of World War II. Sturm was followed by Buddy Hassett, a gift from Stengel to Weiss when Stengel was managing the Braves. A contact hitter without power or patience, Hassett was at his best with the Yankees, which is to say he was only below average. He too then went to fight the good fight, the third best thing . . .

The beleaguered McCarthy of the war years was given a break in the form of minor league veteran Nick Etten, who was terrific with the bat from 1943 to 1945. He and the glove were strangers to each other, and when he flopped against the returning major leaguers in 1946 it was all too easy to label him a wartime fluke and ship him off to the Pacific Coast League. In 1947, the Yankees reacquired George McQuinn, a former team farmhand who had made good with the St. Louis Browns. McQuinn had one good year left, then hit the wall in 1948 and was released.

The candidates to replace him were an uninspiring lot. The twenty-four-year-old rookie Dick Kryhoski could hit but not field after slipping on a cake of soap and falling on his arm during spring training in 1947. As a left-handed hitter going into Yankee Stadium he had some appeal, but he had not yet learned to pull the ball. Another left-handed rookie, Joe Collins, had been signed as a first baseman but had lately been shifted to the outfield. Stengel didn't think he could make it as a first baseman. Another prospect, the right-handed Jack Phillips, had had brief trials with the Yankees in both 1947 and 1948 which failed to suggest a future more glorious than that of a reserve infielder. At twenty-six and twenty-seven respectively, neither Collins nor Phillips fit the traditional definition of "young player," but even as late as 1949, farm systems were still sorting through players whose careers had been preempted by military service.

The only veteran (in the baseball sense) possibility was thirty-three-year-old Norman Robert "Babe" Young, who had first appeared in the majors as a twenty-year-old Giant in 1936. He was up and down after that, finally earning a full-time job in 1941. He showed moderate, Polo Grounds–inflated power (eleven home runs at home, none on the road in 1942) before being traded to Uncle Sam for a free world to be named later. As with many players, Young displayed only glimpses of his former abilities upon his return to civilian employment.

During Young's tour with the Giants, Billy Jurges was the starting shortstop. One exhibition season, as the team barnstormed their way north from Florida, Young got into an argument with a rural policeman and was incarcerated. The team went on without him. When the Giants reached New York, sportswriter Tom Meany asked a team official to go over the starting lineup. "We're all set except for Young," said the Giant. "He may be in jail when the season opens."

"If that's the case," said Meany, "It's going to be a long throw for Jurges."

The preceding comprises the sole contribution to the history and lore of baseball by Norman "Babe" Young. *Sic erat in fatis*.

Harris had confronted McQuinn's slump by moving Tommy Henrich from right field to first base, and most observers felt Stengel would be obligated to follow suit. The aggregate abilities of the non-Henrich contingent underscored Stengel's point when he sighed to Leonard Koppet, "When you got four first basemen, you got no first basemen."

SECOND BASE: George "Snuffy" Stirnweiss was the incumbent, but he did not inspire confidence. A wartime star, Stirnweiss was a gap to gap hitter who used his speed to leg out triples and steal bases, making him one of the few players of his era to place an emphasis on speed. Once Johnny came marching home and raised the level of competition, the gaps seemed to shrink and the distance between bases became longer. His best asset was no longer his bat but his willingness to take a walk. At thirty years of age his speed had diminished and he no longer hit for good averages. Nonetheless, he stood to retain his job by default. The other infielders in camp included Mickey Witek, a thirty-three-year-old veteran who had spent 1948 playing sporadically for the Giants farm team at Jersey City, and twenty-four-year-old rookie war hero Jerry Coleman, who was looked upon as a shortstop or third baseman.

THIRD BASE: Harris had primarily played the right-handed Billy "Bull" Johnson at third. Johnson fielded well and had good power, but was impatient and grounded into more than his share of double plays (he just missed topping the league in 1947 and 1948). As a right-handed hitter he was largely thwarted by Yankee Stadium's enormous left field.

Johnson sometimes gave way to young Bobby Brown. Brown, signed for $55,000 in 1946, was one of the few players to receive a large bonus from the Yankees since the team's farm system was established in 1932. By contrast, Yogi Berra had cost only $500 and Mickey Mantle would require only $1,100 to don pinstripes.

Like Mantle, Brown was a special project of his father's, of whom it was said that he taught his son how to hit but forgot to teach him how to field. Signed as a shortstop, Brown quickly proved unequal to the position, and remained error-prone wherever he played. His glove thwarted his good left-handed, high-average bat. Stengel would later say of him, "Bobby reminds me of a fella who's been hitting for twelve years and fielding one." Harris had never been able to decide what to do with Brown, playing him at second, third, and shortstop.

Johnson was popular, a gamer. Harris had said, "I ask him if he's ready and he shakes his head. The next time I talk to him again at the end of the year and when he says goodbye he shakes his head again." The possibility that Brown might take Johnson's job provoked considerable consternation in his teammates.

SHORTSTOP: The public had barely had a chance to get used to Phil "The Scooter" Rizzuto when the Navy plucked him up after the 1942 season and swept him off for three straight years of chronic seasickness. He played quite poorly upon his return in 1946, so it was not until 1947 that Rizzuto came to be known as the team's indispensable man. "He pulls a miracle out there each day," said Harris. "I wouldn't trade him for any shortstop in baseball. I don't care if he only hits .250, it's what he does with his glove, the way he saves our pitchers, that makes him great."

Harris had articulated a common fallacy about the relative value of a shortstop's defensive and offensive contributions that befuddles baseball to this day, but it didn't really apply in Rizzuto's case. In most years his bat was at worst competitive with the other shortstops in the American League, while his defense was quite a bit better—a win-win combination, unlike many a modern good-field, no-hit shortstops. (Bill James has compared Rizzuto unfavorably to Lou Boudreau, his rival shortstop on the Cleveland Indians, but the comparison is inapt; Boudreau fell off precipitously after his 1948 MVP season, while Rizzuto was just coming into his own. Though Rizzuto was just six weeks younger than Boudreau, the bulk of his career, 977 of 1661 career games, took place after 1948, whereas Boudreau played 1,345 games through 1948, but just 301 after.) "My best pitch," said Vic Raschi, "is anything the batter grounds, lines, or pops in the direction of Rizzuto."

With so much uncertainty surrounding the rest of the roster, Rizzuto came to be seen as a rock of stability, "the big man of our team." Despite his range afield and visible enthusiasm for the game, Rizzuto was a small man, five-foot-six and 150 pounds, and ill-cast as a poster-boy for durability. In 1948, Rizzuto was shelved by pulled leg muscles, experienced dizziness when going back on pop flies, and was pained by bone chips in the elbow of his throwing arm. Hobbled, Rizzuto turned in his worst year with the bat, hitting an empty .252, and the diminished strength of his arm neutralized his great lateral range.

Rizzuto had been advised by the Yankees' medical consultants at Johns Hopkins to forego surgery on his elbow, and as spring dawned he was still learning to use his great hands, accuracy, and quickness to compensate for the weakness of his throws. It was not certain that he ever would. In the season to come, Rizzuto would range far into the hole to snag a grounder, then flip it to Billy Johnson who threw out the runner, 6-5-3. A heady play, yes, even a spectacular play, but also one that spoke volumes about Rizzuto's lack of confidence in his arm.

CATCHER: Yogi Berra was to be the catcher. Maybe. Harris's maladroit handling of the young backstop was his greatest legacy to the team. The Dodgers' seven stolen bases in the first four games of the 1947 World Series caused Harris first to bench Berra, then relocate him to right field. By Berra's own estimation, as well as those of contemporary observers, he was very raw behind the plate. "As a catcher," wrote Milton Gross of the *New York Post*, Yogi is a hindrance to the pitchers." Berra himself recalled, "My catching was awful. My mechanics were all screwed up. So was my throwing. You couldn't blame anyone for not trusting me behind the plate. It didn't help that my fingers were so short that the pitchers had trouble seeing my signs. Joe Page . . . used to tell me to grow a pair of hands."

Berra could not frame pitches, called for too many fastballs because they were easier for him to catch and throw, and, as with the Dodgers in 1947, baserunners took liberties. Baseball in the 1940s was tactically static, with managers eschewing the stolen base due to the prevalence of the home run. This should have made Berra's throwing difficulties seem like a minor consideration. Instead, they were emphasized.

Publicly, Harris stayed in Berra's corner, saying, "We'll make a catcher out of him yet if it kills us," but rather than recommit to Berra as a backstop in 1948, Harris played him there for half a season, then shifted him back to right field to replace Henrich when the latter moved to first. Gus Niarhos, who possessed a good eye but had less power than the Undersecretary of Unicorns, Rainbows, and Puffy Clouds, took over behind the dish.

Harris could never accommodate himself to the idea of Berra as a catcher, and as early as spring training 1947 had Joe Medwick, the old Cardinals left fielder, working with him. Berra's raw physical skills were only part of the problem. From the day he signed, the Yankees were blinded by Berra's appearance. Berra was short and stocky and was unlikely to win any beauty contests. Still, the Yankees were not a team of male models. Joe DiMaggio had bad teeth and a receding chin, and Charlie Keller's eyebrows made it look as if someone had stapled a polecat to his forehead. Yet for some reason, the Yankees reacted as if Berra did not belong. They would scratch their armpits and grunt at him, or yodel like Tarzan. Even Harris would call him "Nature Boy" and "The Ape," as in, "Did you see The Ape hit that ball today?" The press urged him on. "You're not really thinking about keeping Berra, are you?" Rudd Rennie, the longtime *New York Herald-Tribune* Yankees beat writer asked Harris. "He doesn't even look like a Yankee."

Ownership wasn't much better. In 1946, Mel Ott, then manager of the Giants, approached MacPhail and asked to buy one of his four catchers. "In fact," he said, "the Giants are willing to pay $50,000 for one of them." "Who?" asked MacPhail. "I'd like a guy you probably don't even know you've got. He's a kid named Berra."

MacPhail said no. "If the truth must be told," MacPhail said later, "I'd never even heard of Berra, but I figured that if he was worth fifty grand to Ottie he must be worth fifty grand to me." Not long after, MacPhail finally got to make the acquaintance of the prized prospect. "The instant I saw him my heart sank and I wondered why I had been so foolish as to not sell him. In bustled a stocky little guy in a sailor suit. He had no neck and his muscles were virtually busting the buttons off his uniform. He was one of the most unprepossessing fellows I ever set eyes on in my life." Years later, Berra recalled that day to Keller and Pete Sheehy, the clubhouse man. I'll bet when you saw me in my uniform you didn't think I was a ballplayer, Berra said to Keller. "I didn't even think you were a sailor," said Sheehy.

"Yogi is one of nature's noblemen," wrote Arthur Daley of the *Times*, "the honest heart that beats beneath that rough exterior. No ballplayer is ridden as cruelly or unmercifully as he. But he accepts it all with a homely grin. He hasn't the quick wit to retort in kind. So he laughs it all off." Berra bore up, but he still had no position.

LEFT FIELD: There was no left fielder. Since 1939, the standby had been Charlie "King Kong" Keller, a hitter so brutishly powerful that Yankees pitcher Lefty Gomez quipped that he was the first player brought back by Frank Buck. With the ability to hit for high batting averages, along with great power and patience, Keller presented as sort of a Ted Williams Junior who played better defense. Indeed, he outhit fellow rookie Williams .334 to .327 that year.

Thereafter, McCarthy insisted he become a pull hitter so as to take advantage of Yankee Stadium's short right field line—McCarthy had chosen to sacrifice Keller's ability to hit for average in exchange for more home runs. From 1940 to 1946 (excluding military service) Keller averaged .285, slugged .534, and reached base forty-one percent of the time. During the same period, the average player's statistics were, respectively, .268, .385, and .342. Keller hit more home runs during those seasons than any player except for Rudy York and Bill Nicholson, both of whom played straight through the war years (Keller had 151 home runs in 765 games, Nicholson had 155 in 1,000 games, and York hit 168 in 1,078 games; in consideration of all three accomplishments, it is important to remember that Hank Greenberg played only 387 games during this period, Joe DiMaggio 557, Ted Williams 587, and so on).

In 1947, Keller had hit thirteen home runs by June 5. That day, he suffered a severe back injury while running the bases. Not only did the injury end his home run production for that season, it proved to be chronic. His 1948 was ruined by a broken hand. Stengel had no assurances that Keller would even be able to open the season, let alone find his former potency. None of the possible replacements were guaranteed to succeed. Johnny Lindell had surfaced as a pitcher in 1942, but did not throw hard enough to suit McCarthy. World War II baseball was fluid enough that McCarthy thought he could get away with following up a hunch and moved Lindell, a massive six-foot-five, to the outfield. In 1944, baseball's wartime nadir, Lindell blossomed, hitting .300 with sixteen triples, eighteen home runs and 103 RBI.

This was not Lindell's true level of ability, and like so many wartime stars he would have gradually receded, but injuries kept bringing him back. Taking over for Keller in 1948 he hit .317 with thirteen home runs in only eighty-eight games. His other postwar seasons were mediocre, and at thirty-two the likelihood of an encore was small. He had also never learned to field. "I have been trying to think what John's use of his hands and fingers . . . reminds me of," John Lardner mused. "Generally speaking, he fields the ball like a man unwrapping a new razor blade and putting it into his razor." Stengel liked Lindell so much as an outfielder that he gave serious consideration to making him a pitcher again.

Some predicted "the next Charlie Keller for the Yanks" would be rookie outfielder Hank Bauer. Bauer, twenty-six, had begun his minor league career in 1941, but his rise to the majors was interrupted by four years of combat action with the Marines. Jan Murray said that Bauer had a face like a clenched fist; perhaps this was Bauer's reaction to landing under fire at such places as Guam, Guadalcanal, and Okinawa, at the last of which he was wounded by shrapnel. Out of the service, the two-time Bronze Star winner joined the Yankees organization in 1946 and first appeared in the majors in September 1948, hitting .180 with one home run in fifty-six plate appearances.

Stengel's personal choice to win the left field job might have been Gene Woodling, who had made a forceful impression on him by hitting .493 with five home runs against the Oakland Oaks as a member of the 1948 San Francisco Seals. Overall, Woodling hit .385, the leading batting average in the Pacific Coast League.

Woodling looked promising, but he was already twenty-six and not a major league virgin. In fact, he had failed to stick in trials with the Cleveland Indians and Pittsburgh Pirates. He had even played on the Yankees' top farm team at Newark in 1947, where his .288 average and eight home runs had proved insufficient incentive for George Weiss to make a commitment to him. He was allowed to pass to San Francisco. It was only when Seals manager Lefty O'Doul rebuilt his swing that Woodling again became attractive to major league eyes. Woodling would later laugh that he cost the Yankees far more in 1948 than he would have had they simply held on to him in 1947, but the truth was that in the former year they were bidding on a different player, one whose abilities had finally crystalized.

Both Woodling and Bauer had come to camp with injured ankles.

CENTER FIELD: The center fielder was the greatest player in the game, and everyone knew it, including DiMaggio. "DiMaggio candidly accepts the fact that he is good," *Time* reported in 1948. If he forgot, his teammates would hold up a mirror. Henrich: "He does everything better than anybody else." Billy Johnson: "He puts his heart into every inning more than any other player I have ever seen." Jerry Coleman: "He is grace, strength, power, all of it effortless."

He was one of the few athletes who deserved to be described as having a mystique. "Joe DiMaggio had an imperial presence on the field," said Coleman. "Nobody in any sport had the imperial presence that he had on a ball field or the court or the football diamond [sic]. He was in a class by himself . . . Joe knew exactly who he was and why. He never made a mistake, never dove for a ball, always came in *whssht*! Pulled it right off the ground. I never saw him dive for a ball. The guy always caught the god damned thing."

"There was an aura about him," said Phil Rizzuto. "He walked like no one else walked. He did things so easily. He was immaculate in everything he did. Kings of State wanted to meet him and be with him. He carried himself so well. He could fit in any place in the world." DiMaggio was so impressive that he was the one player whose name the oblivious Babe Ruth made a point of remembering. In the Babe's New York, there were six million people named "Kid" and one guy named Joe. After the 1936 World Series, Giants manager Bill Terry, a man not easily given to praise, said, "I saw today why you fellows all say that kid in center made the Yankees a winner. Now I understand how one player can be the difference between an ordinary team and a great one." "The Pride of the Yankees didn't pass with Gehrig and Ruth," said Boston Red Sox general manager Joe Cronin. "DiMaggio is still keeping it alive."

As Stengel was soon to discover, production plus arrogance equaled mystique; arrogance without production is just arrogance. The DiMaggio that he inherited threatened to be a triumph of form over substance. In November 1948, DiMaggio had had surgery to remove a bone spur on his right heel. There seemed to be little risk to this; prior to the 1948 season the same procedure had been performed on his left heel, yet he had been spectacular that year, hitting .320 with thirty-eight home runs, slugging .598, and driving in 155 runs.

DiMaggio did not believe in exercising away from the baseball field, so he spent what would today be called the rehabilitation period smoking cigarettes and doing a little dancing. When he came to camp he found that the heel was still sensitive. While he could go to the plate and hit, running, starting, and stopping caused him excruciating pain. After one day, DiMaggio left camp for medical consultation. He returned the next day having been cleared to play so long as he didn't do too much running; the heel was in a "hot condition" and needed rest. Baseball without running is actually batting practice, which was roughly what DiMaggio was limited to doing. He seemed to think a quick recovery was unlikely. "I suppose I look on the dark side of things, but I think that is wise," he said. "Maybe the pain will disappear. I hope it does, anyway."

RIGHT FIELD: In the years since he had replaced Roy Johnson on the roster in 1937, Henrich had earned a reputation for professionalism second only to DiMaggio's. "It is doubtful that the fans out there [in right field] ever heaped more idolatrous affection upon Babe Ruth himself," wrote Red Smith, "than they have now for Tommy Henrich, the resplendent pro who has been . . . the blood and bone and breath of the Yankees." He was also a balance to the Lindell-Page group of partiers, a solid citizen in the clubhouse. "Henrich never volunteers advice to another Yankee, but when players come to him for help his blue eyes light up," *Time* reported in 1949. "Says one mate: 'He's the kind of guy, you give him a watch and he'll take it apart and put it back together, and then write the watchmaker telling him what's wrong with it.'"

Stengel soon came to see Henrich as an ideal player. "He's a fine judge of a fly ball. He fields grounders like an infielder. He never makes a wrong throw, and if he comes back to the hotel at three in the morning when we're on the road and says he's been sitting up with a sick friend, he's been sitting up with a sick friend."

What Stengel did not know was that upon entering baseball, Henrich had rolled back his age by three years. Rather than the reported twenty-one, Henrich was a twenty-four-year-old rookie in 1937, making him thirty-six in 1949. He had never been the most durable of ballplayers, and he was now well into the part of a baseball player's career when injuries increase in frequency and become chronic; Henrich's knees had already begun to trouble him.

Even if he was healthy, Henrich couldn't play right field and first base at the same time. In the latter scenario, rookie Cliff Mapes might be called to take his place. Mapes, twenty-seven, had all of the hallmarks of a fringe prospect of the time: left-handed bat, great throwing arm, career progression set back by service in the war, marginal hitting ability, marginal attitude. Milton Gross of the *New York Post* wrote that Mapes was, "Lean and lithe as a greyhound . . . but lacking something which keeps him from realizing on his potentialities."

THE STARTING ROTATION: The front end of the rotation appeared set. The rotation would be topped by thirty-year-old, third-year righty (blame those nutty fascists again for the late start) Vic Raschi, Massachusetts's "Springfield Rifle," who had established himself as a major league ace with a 19–8, 3.84 season in 1948. He had a hard fastball, a sweeping curve, was learning a slider, and had made exactly forty-seven major league starts.

Raschi would be followed by Ed "The Junkman" Lopat, a soft-tossing lefty that Weiss had acquired from the Chicago White Sox in February 1948. Among those going to Chicago was catcher Aaron Robinson, an expression of Weiss's commitment to Berra's future. Lopat, nee Edmund Lopatynski, had spent seven years in the minors, partially because pitchers that throw "wads of tissue paper" (as Stengel saw it) instead of fastballs had (and have) a tough time getting respect from scouts, and partially because of an anxiety disorder that caused him to lose his composure whenever the breaks of the game didn't go his way. In 1940, a doctor gave Lopat a simple mantra: "When you are ready to blow your top, count your blessings, not your troubles." With wisdom like that, who needed Prozac? Lopat settled down and became a great control pitcher, amassing a record of 67–60 (69–58 support-neutral) with a 3.28 ERA through 1948, making it all look so effortless that Stengel said, "Every time he wins a game, people come down out of the stands asking for contracts."

The Oklahoman righthander Allie Reynolds, nicknamed "Superchief" on account of his one-quarter Creek blood (political correctness, like Prozac, having not yet been invented), was the third starter. Reynolds had not taken up baseball until he was a junior in college. He threw hard but hadn't mastered the intricacies of control and location. Already thirty-four years old (though his "baseball age" was somewhat younger), Reynolds lacked the poise of many much younger pitchers. "I'm still not a real pitcher," he said, "all because of that late start."

Unschooled in the art of pacing, what Christy Mathewson called "pitching in a pinch," Reynolds tended to break down in the middle of games. He had gone 86–62 through 1948, but frequently needed to be bailed out by either his offense (support neutral 73–75) or his bullpen. "Rightly or wrongly," wrote Milton Gross, "he had been labeled a tabby cat pitcher who didn't like tight ball games." Critics called him "The Vanishing American."

The era's one-size-fits-all mentality did not allow for the existence of pitchers who could be affected by problems of mechanics, health, or, in Reynolds' case, the sheer number of pitches that wildness forced him to throw. No, it had to be a lack of manhood. "They told me," said Stengel, "'Don't count on this guy when the chips are down.'"

The fourth and fifth starters remained to be identified out of a crew including Bob Porterfield, Tommy Byrne, Fred Sanford, Spec Shea, Cuddles Marshall, and Duane Pillette. Today, Erwin Coolidge "Bob" Porterfield would be held up as an example of how to ruin a great pitching prospect. In 1947, the twenty-two-year-old right-hander was allowed to pitch 239 innings for Norfolk of the Piedmont League. The results, a 17–9 record, 203 strikeouts against only eighty-two walks, and 2.37 ERA, established Porterfield as an outstanding prospect, but at a high cost to his arm. As part of that era's the-only-real-pitchers-are-pitchers-who-finish-what-they-start ethos, Porterfield's workload was increased in 1948. Promoted to Newark of the International League, Porterfield averaged almost eight innings a start. Porterfield was dominating, going 15–6 with a 2.17 ERA. By August he had pitched 178 innings, and a telltale sign presented itself, albeit one that no one would have paid attention to at the time: his rate of strikeouts was declining.

Nonetheless, Harris began agitating for Porterfield's promotion to the majors. Weiss resisted but eventually gave way, and on August 8, Porterfield made his major league debut. "He made you want to pitch your arm off at the shoulder," Porterfield said later. "Nobody else gave you Bucky's shot at winning. With Bucky, you didn't get the idea you were going to get yanked if the next guy got a hit." Funny you should mention that, Bob. Harris worked Porterfield hard over the last weeks of the 1948 season, and even pitched him on the last day of the season as a way of thumbing his nose at Weiss. Porterfield's combined minors/majors total of 256 innings pitched was higher than that of all but three American League hurlers. No one noticed.

(A few years later, Harris, back with the Senators—Harris was one among many former Clark Griffith employees, including Bobo Newsom, Goose Goslin, Joe Kuhel, and Mickey Vernon, who Griffith would dispose of and then, overcome by sentimentality, welcome back to the fold—would acquire Porterfield from the Yankees. Acceding to, or concurring with, Weiss's judgment, Stengel never found a use for the pitcher, but the Senators were able to wring four and a half decent years out of him, including a 22–10 season in 1953. Justifying like crazy, Harris pitched Porterfield's arm off—again, with seventy complete games out of 111 starts. When Harris was fired after the 1954 season, he took Porterfield's effectiveness with him.)

Lefty Tommy Byrne had first surfaced in the majors with Joe McCarthy's 1943 Yankees. Byrne looked so good at the plate and so bad on the mound that McCarthy was convinced that he ought to be switched to first base. Byrne went off to war before the issue could be resolved. Byrne's problem was chronic wildness. He threw hard but was afraid to let the opposition put the ball in play. In this, Byrne was the most extreme among many likeminded contemporaries. The late 1940s were the tail end of a kind of pitcher's depression, begun with the introduction of the first lively ball in 1920, in which pitchers were more likely to walk batters than strike them out. Confronted with the home run, it was as if American League pitchers and pitching coaches (National Leaguers were either more sturdy or their umpires more flimsy) went into a persistent state of shock. Rather than try to match batters, power against power, or try to outwit them, they would simply walk anyone with power, pitch to the shortstops and second basemen, and if that didn't work, well, maybe someone could set fire to the stadium. From 1950 to present, fifty-three pitchers have posted a strikeout/walk ratio of less than 1.00 in a season of 200 or more innings pitched. Forty-two pitchers failed to break even in the years 1946 to 1949.

"Tommy Byrne would rather strike somebody out than let him hit the ball. He was like that, 150 pitches, 180 pitches, he'd be out there pumpin'," recalled reserve catcher Charlie Silvera. "Yogi would be, 'Oh, Christ!' and the infielders, 'Oh, Jesus!' But he was goofy! He'd laugh, 'I'm not wild!' After he walked about nine and struck out ten, made about 180 pitches, "I'm not wild!' That's the way he was. He had a lot of fun." In 1948, Byrne had started eleven games and relieved in twenty others. In 134 innings pitched he had walked 101 batters, or 6.78 per nine innings—an excellent rate by his standards—struck out ninety-three, and held opposing batters to a .172 average. Dan Topping couldn't stomach Byrne's wildness, but Stengel soon found a way to cope: "Look," he once told Ralph Houk, "don't watch him pitch. You'll die too young. Just turn away and listen to the crowd. You know he'll walk in a run or two in some situations, but then you'll hear the cheer when he strikes someone out. Listen to the noise. It's easier on your stomach. If you watch him you won't last long."

Fred Sanford had been purchased from the St. Louis Browns for $100,000 after the 1948 season. A World War II–delayed twenty-eight-year-old, Sanford had just completed an uninspiring 12–21, 4.64 season with poor strikeout and walk rates. The normally parsimonious Weiss felt obligated to overspend: "He had a good fast ball, and the Red Sox, who had given us some tough battles the season before, were also after him, so the asking price was high," he wrote. "The truth of the matter is, Casey and I both thought it was too high, but Dan Topping called us long distance and said if we wanted him we'd better buy quick because the Browns were about to be sold and moved to the West Coast."

Clarence "Cuddles" Marshall, twenty-four, had even less control of his pitches than Byrne, but he had Berra's blessing. The catcher was overheard early in spring training giving Marshall his unique brand of encouragement:

"You know, Marshall," Berra said, "you're going to be a much better pitcher this year."

"Thank you, Yogi, and why do you say that?"

"Because," replied Berra, "you're not as good looking as you used to be."

Frank "Spec" Shea, "The Naugatuck Nugget," was a former Stengel Oakland Oak who as a rookie in 1947 had posted a surprising 14–5 record. He was a sensation, picking up the win in the All-Star Game, and winning two of three World Series starts (the third start resulted in a no decision—in another wild bit of strategy, Harris pinch-hit for him in the fifth inning of a tie game). Yet another member of the 1940s–1950s "White Men Can't Throw Strikes" club, Shea suffered a neck injury in 1947 that sent him across the fine line that separated too many walks from just getting by. A clubhouse prankster, Shea was on Weiss's short list of players whom Harris had on too long a leash. He had put on weight; in his 1948 book on the Yankees, Milton Gross called him "bovine looking," "bloated," "blubbery looking" and a "corpulent pixie" in the space of just four pages. Though he had pitched well at times in 1948, it was unknown if he could be a regular part of the rotation in 1949.

Duane Pillette had caught Stengel's attention by pitching well against his Oaks for the Portland team managed by Jim Turner. The two had urged Weiss to bring him to New York. Pillette had signed with the Yankees as a twenty-two-year-old in 1946 after having done his part for Uncle Sam. He had pitched reasonably well in the Pacific Coast League, but there were no markers that identified him as an outstanding prospect, and he had the usual aversion to throwing strikes. In 1948 he had thrown 189 innings. He struck out only eighty-three and walked 115.

THE RELIEF ACE: Joe Page had been the making of the 1947 Yankees and the unmaking of the 1948 Yankees. In Game Six of the 1947 World Series, Page had entered the game in the fifth inning and been raked by the Dodgers, ultimately taking the loss. When Shea was knocked out in the second inning of Game Seven and Bill Bevens (still with the Yankees in early 1949, but trying to overcome an arm injury) could only get through the fourth in relief, Page was again called on in the fifth. Ralph Houk, the bullpen catcher, told Harris to choose someone else. "I can catch Page with my bare hands. He hasn't got a thing."

Phil Rizzuto met Page at the mound and told him to forget about his curve and go after Brooklyn with nothing but heat. Page did as he was told. Using only fastballs, he allowed only one hit while pitching the final five innings for the win and the Series.

After, Harris said his only edge had been Joe DiMaggio (obligatory obeisance to the gods), and Page. The writers agreed. There was no Cy Young award as yet, but Page placed fourth in the Most Valuable Player voting, higher than any other pitcher. After the seventh game, even Joe McCarthy told Page, "I'm proud of you."

If McCarthy had a comment on Page's 1948 season he kept it to himself. Presumably it would have been something along the lines of, "I told you so." With Harris feeling that he was in Page's debt and Weiss having discontinued Page's good behavior clause, Page indulged himself in the nightlife of the city—all cities. Years later, when Joe DiMaggio was asked how marriage to Marilyn Monroe would suit him, he said, "It's got to be better than rooming with Joe Page." Page was DiMaggio's best friend on the team and longtime roommate on the road, but when Page continued to confuse "bed check" with "daybreak," the Clipper asked for and got a divorce. With that, Page was completely untethered. Milton Gross wrote:

> Page had no buddy among the Yankees, only DiMag, whom he shadowed and whose dress and tastes he aped. . . . If you saw DiMag you knew Page was close by. When Joe went to a movie, Page did too. . . . It was a strange, pathetic relationship on Page's part. . . . When DiMag was busy elsewhere, Page wandered about at loose ends. . . . Brass rail friendships of a taproom and forced conviviality were his only substitutes for DiMag and he took them where he found them.

Page blamed his slump on bad coaching. "They tried to take my slider away from me last year," he said. "It was supposed to be hurting my arm. Well, why didn't it hurt in 1947? Oh, I was winning then, eh? I've never met Casey Stengel, but I hear he's the sort of guy who lets you pitch your way. That'll be okay with me."

Whatever Page's attitude and comportment, it was clear that the Yankees needed a pitcher like Page. They were, perhaps, the first team in history where the need for a reliever and the solution were both obvious, though they were never articulated. Admitting that a team needed an all-purpose "fireman," someone who could be rushed into the game and do a reliably *good* job, conflicted with the main principle of pitching manhood, which said that starters had to finish their own games. One could praise Joe Page and condemn Allie Reynolds without fear of self-contradiction, but admitting that one had a need for Page was tantamount to admitting that the starting pitchers were a bit fey. None of it made any sense, but baseball operated by these rules for roughly eighty years.

Harris's use of Page had represented an evolution in strategic thinking. Although teams had always gone to relievers if a starting pitcher had faltered, the relievers themselves were often starting pitchers working on their off days. In 1930, Lefty Grove lead the American League in both wins *and* saves. It was considered a waste to put a good fastball in the pen, and thus the relief field was dominated by rag-arms who were considered too old or slow to start. These were the last people one would call upon to protect a lead. With the occasional exception such as Marberry, the only way that relievers were thought to save games was when they "saved" the manager from having to use a real pitcher to finish out a one-sided contest

Page was one of the first full-time relievers who could be trusted to overpower the opposition. At a time where pitching strategy was inflexibly focused on the complete game, Harris had another option. Whereas in the seventh inning every other manager might think to himself, "It doesn't seem as if my starter's gonna make it. I think I will observe, rhetorically, that he is losing his stuff so everyone knows that the old man is paying attention. Then I will sit back and watch it happen. It's his game to win or lose," or worse, "I guess I'll have to bite the bullet and bring in a reliever," Harris was able to think, "I don't *care* if my starter can go all the way. I want Page now." Going to the bullpen was transformed from a reactive to proactive move.

It would take most of the managerial profession most of the next three decades to perceive the wisdom of Harris's position. Stengel did not let dogma blind him to the facts. With Reynolds and two inexperienced starters on hand, he planned to depend on Page. "I don't have to have my hair parted with an ax," Stengel once said, "to get an idea from the outside." He did not invent relief pitching, but if it was what his team needed, he had no problem jumping on the bandwagon. "What do I care if a starting pitcher finishes or not?" he said later. "We had Joe Page, didn't we?"

Stengel moved quickly to sort out his roster. Some of the problems succumbed to decisive attack. Yogi Berra would be the everyday catcher. Bill Dickey was given the job of working him over until he had improved both his confidence and his mechanics. Berra took to him. "Bill is learning me all his experiences,'' he said in his inimitable way. Stengel added that Berra would be an improved catcher if he put more spirit into his work, a not-so subtle hint to heed Dickey. Berra did, and Stengel spent the rest of the year (and in fact, the rest of his life) as a convinced supporter. He instructed the veterans to stop mocking the catcher's appearance. ''No more of this stuff about him keeping house in a tree or swinging from limb to limb like those apes,'' he said. ''And stop feeding him peanuts.'' Later that season, Berra came upon Stengel as he was praising Rizzuto to the press.

''Phil is the one man who is sure to land on the All-Star team,'' Stengel said.

''How about me?'' asked Berra.

''Yogi,'' Stengel replied, ''you are superlative.''

First base proved to be an intractable problem. Babe Young was the first of the first base candidates to go, quickly followed by Joe Collins, who was demoted to Newark. Desperate, Stengel attempted to move Billy Johnson across the diamond. ''I figure that Bobby Brown at third and Johnson at first would add a punch. Both want to play every day.'' The real rationale was keeping Henrich in right field. ''With Johnson in action I may get the maximum in power since the plan will permit me to use Henrich in right and Berra as catcher. At any rate, we'll give the new arrangement a trial on the way north and see how it works out.''

Privately, Stengel admitted he didn't think it would work out. Told that Johnson had not yet acquired a first baseman's mitt, Stengel cracked that he'd better hurry because he might not need it for very long. Within a week, Stengel was already hedging. ''Johnson . . . hasn't looked graceful, but few right-handers do at first base. I've got to go along with him there.'' Less than a fortnight later, he surrendered. ''Johnson proved too green, and that is not his fault. I tried something and it did not work and not because Johnson did not try his level best . . . Johnson returns to the third base situation. Whether he will play against right-handers, or merely await his chance to be useful, I do not know.'' Though he professed to dislike platooning—an outright lie—Kryhoski and Phillips would split the job for the time being.

First base was a minor problem compared to the gaping hole that was threatening to open in center field. DiMaggio pinch-hit without notable success during the early spring training games. The Yankees had played seventeen exhibitions before he finally played the field. He couldn't play again for five days. On April 12, a demoralized DiMaggio, having finally admitted that his heel was ''no better or worse than when I started,'' left the team and flew to Johns Hopkins for further treatment. Reporters immediately peppered him with questions about his ''impending retirement.''

"I certainly am not going to retire," he sniffed. "There's a lot of folks that would like to see me retire, these sadistic people, you know." He declined to identify the sadists, but by the time he landed in Baltimore he had apparently decided that the reporters could be counted among their group. "Go fly a kite," he shouted. "Do you think I'd tell you if I was through?" Leaving the hospital the next day, he told the writers to leave him alone. "Don't you think you've gone far enough?" he asked. "You guys are driving me batty." "DiMaggio appears phlegmatic," Arthur Daley had observed in 1948, "but that's merely a surface indicator. Down below he's as high-strung and sensitive as the true artist he is."

The team had not been given any warning of, or reason for, DiMaggio's departure. "In the spring of 1949 we went through Fort Worth and DiMaggio disappeared," Jerry Coleman remembered. "Never showed up. Where's Joe?" Finally, Stengel called the team together. "Fellas," he said. "Joe won't be with us for awhile."

His first reaction was to try Johnny Lindell in center, preferring his experience at the position. "There is no reason he should not do an adequate job there," said Stengel, and there was none, except for his glove and his bat. He immediately showed that he could not be trusted to field the position on a regular basis. "Lindell looks better in center to me than he did when we were in Florida," Stengel said lamely. He had already changed his mind—yet he hadn't made it up, either. "You cannot take Henrich out of any outfield which is minus its ace," he said. "I wish I could be sure about Charlie Keller. He has encouraged me lately but he still is a question mark. I think he will make it. Well, suppose we have Keller and Lindell in left, Hank Bauer and Gene Woodling in center, and Henrich in right. Would that be a weak combination? Certainly not. Maybe Bauer will be able to carry the load without help."

But Bauer, though he had impressed Stengel, was still hobbled by a bad ankle. The job passed to Woodling, and Lindell shifted to left field to take over for Keller, who could not work himself into shape. "Keller hits the ball," Rudd Rennie of the *Herald-Tribune* wrote from Florida, "but it does not go places." When Lindell opened the season in a 4-for-33 slump, Stengel kept him in the lineup just long enough for him to have a good game ("I don't want to take him out when he's in a slump. After he gets a couple of hits I'll bench him."), then replaced him with Woodling, thereby opening centerfield for a platoon of Mapes and Bauer. Mapes opened the season by going hitless in his first fifteen at-bats.

Meanwhile, the starting rotation, which Stengel had identified as Raschi, Lopat, Byrne, Porterfield, and Reynolds, did not quite last until the end of the exhibition season. Porterfield had pitched a no-hitter in his final spring training start, which sounded like good news until it was realized that on the final pitch a tendon in his elbow had given way. He was out indefinitely. Stirnweiss, who had played second and led off nearly all the spring training games, and was one of the few consistent hitters in camp, severely injured his hand making a tag play in the first regular season game. He was replaced by Coleman, who no one had ever looked at as a second baseman. Even the unflappable Berra missed a few games after his attention drifted during infield practice. Phillips, not realizing that Berra's eyes had just wandered up to the stands, loosed a throw that crashed into the catcher's right temple, knocking him cold.

As spring training came to an end, 206 baseball writers were asked to pick the American League pennant winner. One hundred and nineteen named the Boston Red Sox as the team to beat. Another seventy-nine writers named Cleveland. Six picked the Yankees.

"The Yankees are a team in disrepair," wrote Boston journalist Harold Kaese. "Joe DiMaggio is on his last legs. Keller's back has given out on him. Henrich is hurting."

Dan Daniel of *The Sporting News wrote,* "As things stand, there does not appear to be a club capable of chasing Cleveland and Boston." His publisher, J. G. Taylor Spink, picked the Yankees to finish fourth. Rud Rennie wrote that the Yankees had, "good pitching generally and weak hitting generally."

Jimmy Powers of the *New York Daily News* impugned the team's depth chart:

Let's face it chums, and stop feeding ourselves a lot of bologna on the famed Yankee farm system and the perspicacious George Weiss. We have been reading charming essays for years in the trade publications, the slick mag and the workaday press on how Weiss is a cool, collected genius. . . . The sudden sinking of Joe DiMaggio's star certainly highlights the weakness of the vaunted Yankee farm system . . . the Yankees should have a harvest of youngsters developing. We know there is no duplicate DiMaggio around. But, nevertheless, what is the farm system coming up with in the way of any crop, for crying out loud?

Stengel was asked if he wanted to revise his preseason estimate of the Yankees' chances now that DiMaggio was out. He had claimed the team was good enough to win the pennant. "Well, the way things shape up we should finish one two three," he said. In giving the reasons for his continued confidence he gave the answer to Powers's question: "If Lindell can't carry the load until Joe comes back, we have Hank Bauer, Gene Woodling, and Cliff Mapes." These were the prospects Powers had overlooked.

On opening day, Stengel watched Mrs. Babe Ruth lay a wreath on the new Babe Ruth monument in center field – the slugger had passed away the previous summer. Then wreaths were laid for Gehrig, for Huggins, for Colonel Ruppert, and finally, one was laid on Stengel himself by a boy from the "Yankee Juniors." The irony was not lost on Rudd Rennie, who wrote, "Somewhere, there should be a wreath for this 1949 edition of the Yankees."

Prior to opening day, veteran sportswriter Grantland Rice took Stengel aside. "You're the luckiest stiff in the world, do you know it?"

"Yeah?" Stengel asked.

"Yes. With DiMaggio, you're supposed to win. Without him, everybody says, 'That's a great job by old Case, finishing fifth with no Joe.'"

Stengel didn't find it funny. Nor did he agree with the general assessment of the Yankees. He had been on too many losing ball clubs to concede defeat before he had even begun, especially in an organization so rich with opportunities as the Yankees. His years of suffering in the second division had given him a very clear idea of what a down club looked like, and in his mind the Yankees weren't it. "There is less wrong with the Yankees than with any club I've ever had," he said. "Anything is good about a first-division club. I tried years to make it."

Strange, unanticipated things began to happen. With Vic Raschi batting with the bases loaded in the second game of the season, Brown, Berra, and Kryhoski pulled a triple steal with Brown scoring. At Yankee Stadium on April 30, after Page failed to prevent the Red Sox tying the game 2–2 in the seventh inning, Henrich told him, "You hold it and I'll win it." Page didn't—the Red Sox went ahead by one in the eighth, but Henrich won it anyway, smashing a home run off of Tex Hughson with Woodling on base for a 4–3 win.

The first base platoon of Kryhoski and Phillips hit a combined .350 over the next several weeks. The third base platoon of Brown and Johnson hit .311. Woodling and Bauer hit .289. Coleman hit .300 and played great defense. Tommy Henrich got hot and stayed hot, driving in the winning run in game after game. The team had extraordinary success with pinch-hitters; eight of the first twelve got hits. At Washington, trailing 4–1 in the top of the ninth, Stengel sent up three consecutive pinch-hitters, Woodling for Bauer, Berra for Silvera, and Keller for Sanford. All three came through with hits and the Yankees took a 5–4 lead. The statistically improbable became commonplace. Said Henrich, "McCarthy and Harris . . . depended on power. Casey has been more alert for the more subtle forms of attack."

In late April, Rennie of the *Tribune* noted, as if with wonder: "Last night Casey Stengel loaded his line-up with right-handed hitters because of the left-handed pitching. Today, he loaded it with left-handed hitters because of the right-handed pitching. The Yankees have only three men, Rizzuto, Henrich and Coleman, who play regularly."

All of these things were typical of the managerial hand of Casey Stengel. He faced severe obstacles in trying to hold the team together. The injuries kept mounting: Porterfield came back, was ineffective, got hurt again; Keller had to be sent to Newark to get back into shape; Coleman developed a severe sinus infection; Berra broke a hand; Henrich broke everything but his hand; DiMaggio's return kept being put off.

Yet, Stengel had an advantage in that his problems were familiar ones. In his career he had faced similar stumbling blocks, including the same disrespect that had followed him to the Yankees. His struggles in New York represented both the culmination of a long apprenticeship and an opportunity to apply principles that he had been laboring to perfect for the previous twenty-five years. The things that happened to him were not new. Perhaps they were to the Yankees, where resources and resourcefulness had traditionally combined to make the problematic transient, but not to him. All of the troubles of that summer resonated with the echoes of years past.

CHAPTER 4

DUTCH, THE LEFT-HANDED DENTIST

"Could be I was born in Brooklyn in 1913."

—Casey Stengel

Charles Dillon Stengel was born, in the biological sense, in Kansas City, Missouri on July 30, 1890. He was the son of an insurance agent, and as such enjoyed what passed for a middle-class childhood in leisurely turn-of-the-century America. This was the same Kansas City that Walt Disney memorialized at five-eighths scale as "Main Street USA," where the trappings of the nineteenth century, gas lamps and hitching posts, were stubbornly giving way to the electric lamps and horseless carriages of the twentieth century. Appropriate to that transitional age, the Stengel family enjoyed a sideline in a business which became an anachronism even as they practiced in it. The Kansas City Improved Street Sprinkling Company sprayed water on the city's unpaved boulevards from a horse-drawn wagon to prevent the streets from literally blowing away. A short time later the streets of Kansas City would be paved and the only call for sprinkling would be for the lawns of the city's wealthier residents.

Everything was up to date in Kansas City, but these changes did not interest the young Charlie Stengel. Instead, like the majority of male American children in those long days before television, he devoted his free hours to competition in sport—any sport. He wasn't sorry to see the sprinkling business fall by the wayside. "I wasn't cut out for that work," he remembered. "The horses had all the fun. So I went in more for football or baseball." Years later, returning to Kansas City for a game against the Athletics, Stengel was jeered in a way that had to be unique in the history of baseball. "G'wan, Stengel," shouted the voice from the stands, "your old man took free water and sold it to the city."

Stengel was engaged in games year-round, playing baseball, football, and basketball and excelling at all of them despite the supposed handicap of being left-handed, an "affliction" for which, starting at age six, he was "corrected" in school—often via the age-old fallback of American pedagogy, physical abuse (today's educators, largely enjoined by the law from manhandling their charges, now exercise their passions through verbal abuse. Thus does the republic make its half-hearted accommodations with progress). "You remember the tough managers and teachers," Stengel said. "I remember John McGraw and I remember Mrs. Kennedy. I write right handed today because of her."

It was on the various playing fields of his youth that he first lost his given name of Charles and was instead called Dutch, a reference to his German ancestry. This was a perfectly typical, inoffensive name for an athlete of German heritage in that day when America was less sensitive about ethnic humor, racial epithets, and lynching. "From 'Dutch' I jumped to 'Irish,'" Stengel recalled in 1959. "I had blond hair, some of which still hangs around, and I had freckles and maybe a nasty disposition. I got into a lot of neighborhood fights"—which in the early-twentieth century Midwest sufficed as a description of Irishness.

In time, it became obvious that baseball was where Charlie Stengel's best talents lay. He displayed equal facility with pitching and hitting and was the star of his high school team. After barnstorming with semipro teams during the summers of 1908 and 1909, education lost its limited appeal. Offered the choice between finishing school and signing with the minor league Kansas City Blues, he dropped out.

His winters were spent in dental school. Continuing his education had been his father's idea, one that took on added importance after Stengel hit only .223 at Maysville of the Bluegrass League. Even in 1910, an outfielder hitting under .250 in the low minors was not considered to have much of a professional future. There had to be a fallback.

In dental school Stengel suffered under the familiar handicap of being left-handed. None of the equipment was made for a southpaw and dental student Stengel had a difficult time getting anyone outside of his own family to allow him to work on their teeth. "I was a left-handed dentist who made people cry," Stengel said. His large knuckles made it difficult for him to get into a patient's mouth at all. "I was not very good at pulling teeth, but my mother loved my work. Some of the people in the clinic didn't share her views."

His batting average rebounded to .352 in 1911 and a future in baseball again seemed possible. When he finally had to choose between baseball and dentistry, he was only one semester short of graduating. On the verge of being called up to the major league Brooklyn Dodgers, he spent his tuition money on a high-quality suitcase and never looked back. "I want to thank my parents for letting me play baseball," he said years later, "and I'm thankful I had baseball knuckles and couldn't become a dentist."

There was a certain fatefulness to Stengel's involvement in the game of baseball. They were mutually compatible, perfectly suited to each other. The beginnings of professional baseball preceded Stengel's birth by less than twenty years. When Stengel was born baseball was still undergoing the slow evolution from the rough and tumble game of the Civil War camps to big-dollar entertainment. Along the way it picked up Casey Stengel as it did hundreds of thousands of other boys, taking them from the small-town sandlots to factory teams and finally into the professional minor leagues. For many of those boys, most of whom hailed from the poorer corners of the country, the tenements and the dirt farms, baseball (in theory) offered a more comfortable, more cheerful living than they could have earned in the coal mines and canneries of their home towns. Hall of Fame outfielder Edd Roush, a native of Oakland City, Indiana, explained his choice of career in terms of bovine affinity, or the lack thereof: "I didn't expect to make it to the big leagues, but I didn't care. I had to get away from those damned cows."

Yet, by the time Stengel reached the majors in 1912, baseball's transformation had not been completed. Baseball at its best can only mirror the context of its time. Like the rest of the country, some of its rowdier elements had yet to be purged. There was still room—barely—for free spirits like Stengel.

Stengel's early career took place during the Progressive Era. Ironically, the period represented the height of American corruption. In 1920, the "Black Sox" scandal erupted when it was revealed that at the instigation of New York gambler Arnold Rothstein and his agents the Chicago White Sox had thrown the previous autumn's World Series. In the wake of the scandal, eight players, many of them stars, were permanently banned from the game. Fan confidence in baseball's integrity was severely damaged, as described by F. Scott Fitzgerald in *The Great Gatsby*:

> I remembered of course that the World Series had been fixed in 1919. . . .
> It never occurred to me that one man could start to play with the faith of fifty million people—with the single-mindedness of a burglar blowing a safe.

We have to take Fitzgerald's word for it; to paraphrase H. L. Mencken, no one ever went broke underestimating the complacency of the American people. The accepted line is that with the legitimacy of baseball games and pennant races in doubt the major-league game was in danger of suffocating under the weight of its broken integrity. The more immediate danger was to the organization of Major League Baseball itself; in the aftermath of the scandal baseball's management structure had disintegrated. The owners, distrustful of the players and each other, were equally distrusted by the public. *Plus ça change, plus c'est la même chose.* To rectify both problems, the owners hired Judge Kennesaw Mountain Landis to be the first commissioner of baseball.

Landis, a federal court judge, represented the jurist as thespian. He had become well known to the public for his decisions in two high profile cases. In 1907 he had assessed a $29.4 million fine against Standard Oil for antitrust violations, an astronomical figure inconceivable even to Standard's owner, John D. Rockefeller. The fine was unenforceable and overturned on appeal, but in those days of Theodore Roosevelt–inspired trustbusting it earned Judge Landis notoriety generally unknown to a federal district court judge.

For an encore, Landis presided over the 1918 trial of over one hundred members of the International Workers of the World (IWW). The Wobblies, as IWW members were called, were rounded up during the infamous raids of attorney general A. Mitchell Palmer, arrested for violating the subversion laws of the first World War. Landis assessed fines totaling $2.3 million and sentences of up to twenty years. "When the country is at peace it is a legal right of free speech to oppose going to war," he said from the bench, "but when once war is declared this right ceases." With Judge Landis around, Americans need not have pined for the coming of John Ashcroft.

This IWW case was typical jurisprudence on the part of Judge Landis. His rulings were based not on understood interpretations of the law, but on his own passions and sense of justice. Landis's decisions were decisive, striking, and frequently overturned on appeal.

Landis was the judge who had begun baseball on the legal road that would eventually lead to its celebrated (or infamous) antitrust exemption. An enthusiastic fan of the game, and therefore in baseball matters a reactionary, he refused to rule in an antitrust suit brought against organized baseball by the Federal League, then trying to establish itself as a third major league circuit. His uncharacteristic reticence doomed the Federal League, which was struggling and desperately needed legal intervention to remain in business, and preserved major league baseball's existing structure.

For this generous act, the lords of baseball remembered Landis fondly. When the Black Sox scandal seemed to demand that an outsider with a reputation for integrity be imposed on baseball, Landis was the obvious choice. He was known and respected by the public for his judicial flights of fancy and he was obviously sympathetic to the interests of the owners. It was Landis, exceeding his mandate in his first act as commissioner, who permanently banned the eight White Sox players and thereby began the process of impressing on the public baseball's commitment to an honest game.

The installation of Landis helped to ease distrust of the product, but this left the bigger problem of providing an incentive that would encourage the fans to forget their distaste and return to the grandstands. A new focus was needed on the field.

When "Shoeless" Joe Jackson was asked why he participated in the conspiracy, he answered that he was afraid to cross one of the leaders of the cabal, White Sox shortstop Charles "Swede" Risberg. "The Swede," Jackson said, "was a hard guy." After the housecleaning of 1920 baseball would still have its share of tough characters, but they would never fascinate the public as they had before the scandal. Baseball players had been expected to be rough and stoic, but the fix had caused the public to sour on that sort of personality. To bring fans back into the seats, baseball would have to provide heroes with which fans could connect with on a more personal level, men who played with exuberance rather than grim determination.

The needed attraction would soon be found in a mammoth figure who hit home runs in a way that no one had ever thought possible. That he chose the exact moment of the scandal to start hitting them was the most fortunate coincidence in baseball history. Babe Ruth was like a vaccine invented on the precipice of pandemic, an incredible athlete who was also a magnificent entertainer.

Ruth's grandiose exploits, his expansive personality and outsized body and ego (asked how he could justify making more money than President Hoover he replied, "I had a better year than he did"—at least 22.8 million Americans agreed), and his prodigious home run hitting mitigated the effects of the scandal and expanded the game's appeal to previously uninitiated millions. He changed the way baseball was played and the way it was perceived. In 1916, *Harper's Weekly* called baseball "The Dullest Sport in the World." After Ruth there was a new atmosphere of fun at the ballpark that rendered such statements inoperable.

Baseball had always been a contest; Ruth reminded that it was also a game. For too many years, tough characters like New York Giants manager John McGraw and perennial batting champion Ty Cobb had talked up "inside" baseball, the game of the bunt and steal, a game controlled from the bench and dedicated to the proposition that nothing spontaneous ever happened. The managers made it sound like war, which everyone was disgusted with having just lived through the first World War, and it turned out to be less fun than just watching a big man hack away with a forty-ounce club anyway.

There was a second pleasant coincidence in the timing of Ruth's arrival in that he appeared at the precise moment that a national media was coming into existence. Ruth and modern technology matured together. In the years immediately prior to Ruth's emergence as a slugger in 1919, mass media existed only in nascent form. There was no television. AM radio was still in the planning stages. Movies were a comparatively recent phenomenon. Only one-third of the country had telephones. There was no such thing as a national celebrity in the sense that we understand it; even presidents were elected sight unseen. Sporting events—baseball games included—were local affairs followed locally in local newspapers. Baseball attendance peaked in 1909 at 7.2 million. The average for the ten full seasons prior to 1919 was 5.5 million, or 344,000 per team. "Major Leagues" was really a misnomer; the American and National Leagues were major in the sense that they had monopolized most of the biggest cities, not in terms of national attention. The same was true of other sports. The NFL, new as of 1920, was just hanging on; in 1927 it would collapse from 30 teams to 12. The NBA had yet to be born.

Ruth came along at the moment that mass media was not only inventing itself, but was searching for a purpose. Within a couple of years of Ruth's 1920 transfer to the Yankees, radios started appearing in people's homes. The first World Series broadcast—starring the Babe—aired in 1921. Newspaper circulation increased dramatically. Syndicates were created to distribute content nationally, so when *New York World* columnist Heywood Broun wrote "The Ruth is mighty and shall prevail" after the Yankees won the 1923 World Series, the entire country read his words. There were more magazines than ever, and soon even movies learned to talk.

There were now a multitude of brand new eyes and ears in the form of cameras and microphones searching for subjects worthy of their attention. Politics weren't going to sell radios, not with bland characters like Calvin Coolidge and Herbert Hoover in the White House. True excitement could be found at the ballpark, where there was a big, brash, uninhibited man-child smashing home runs at a rate never before seen. Forget the home runs—Ruth was quotable. He did outlandish things. He would mug for the camera, wear costumes, fight with his manager, crash his car, succeed grandly and even fail grandly. Ruth had not only power, but personality. That vital combination captured the cameras and the microphones and the printing presses at the exact moment that a national hero became technologically possible. His reach became global, spread overseas. "Who is this Baby Ruth," asked the British playwright George Bernard Shaw, "and what does she do?"

The year of Ruth's arrival the Yankees doubled their attendance. The boom spread throughout the big leagues as more and more people who were otherwise uninterested in the world of the hit-and-run, bunt, and stolen base came out to see Ruth hit. Aided by a livelier baseball, Ruth's style of hitting spread around the leagues, and even more fans were drawn to the ballparks. In 1930, in the midst of a devastating depression, attendance reached an all-time high of 10 million.

Ruth transformed baseball from the national pastime—something people played in their back yards and sometimes went to see—into big-dollar entertainment. Professional athletes moved from the cultural background to the foreground. More, all of the familiar trappings of celebrity—endorsements, gossip in the tabloids, breathlessly reported salary squabbles, and the high salaries themselves—reached their modern form with the Bambino. There were popular athletes before Ruth, but he was the first star. His home runs turned on the lights. His smile set the film rolling. He brought down the spotlight and trained it not on inside baseball, but outside Ruth—make fun, not war.

Fun was a bandwagon Stengel was happy to jump on. Though not possessed of the same talents as Ruth (he hit only sixty home runs over the course of fourteen big league seasons; Ruth hit sixty homers in the 1927 season alone), he shared with him an extroverted personality. He also had a puckish sense of humor that delighted fans. It was a perfect time for a man like Casey Stengel to succeed in baseball.

It did not take the fixing of the World Series to bring out these traits in him. Stengel had played as a happy individualist from the earliest days of his professional career. When he first broke into the minors it was as a pitcher. His new manager asked for a demonstration of his abilities. "I was pitching batting practice and they told me not to throw hard," said Casey. "I wanted to impress the manager, so I threw as hard as I could. The hitters commenced hitting balls over buildings. Then I threw harder and they hit the ball harder. Then I told the manager I was really an outfielder."

Stengel was a good prospect, one scout concluded, but "only from the neck down." A Dodgers scout reported to his masters that Stengel had, "Good hands, good power, runs exceptionally well, nice glove, left-handed line drive hitter. Good throwing arm. May be too damn aggressive, bad temper."

"Bad temper" was a valid observation. Stengel's readiness to fight was a flaw that he wouldn't successfully subdue until he was nearly 40 years old, if not later—the September 13, 1945, edition of *The Sporting News* reported a brawl between the Kansas City Blues and the Milwaukee Brewers: "When the battle ceased, manager Casey Stengel was discovered under the heap of players." Stengel was fifty-five years old. That aside, the scout that concluded Stengel could only be counted on from the neck down misread the man completely. To be fair, Stengel did present a contradiction in terms: a man who loved to talk, but was an excellent listener and observer of others. Before he signed up with the Blues, Stengel sought the counsel of Charles Augustus "Kid" Nichols, a recently retired 361-game winner who had begun pitching in the National League just a few months before Stengel was born. The future Hall of Famer told Stengel to, "Listen to your manager, or if you have an old player teaching you, listen to him. Never say, 'I won't do that.' Always listen." Stengel's older brother Grant, very much an early role model, chimed in with the same advice. A quarter of a century later, the advice still resonated with him: "When I broke in as a rookie, a veteran advised me always to pay attention to what older and more experienced players had to say. 'In this racket,' he told me, 'you never stop learning.' So look no further than this here pair of palm-leaf fans if you wish to see the reasons for my success, if any."

The young Stengel acted as if he didn't get it, but as time went by he followed this advice more and more, observing a lot, as Yogi Berra later put it, by watching. First he had to find sages worth listening to. Surrounded by some of the lower echelon intellects that populated baseball's more obscure outposts, he struggled to follow Nichols's advice. One of his first coaches told him that an outfielder had to learn to play the fence angles. "Play the angles!" he said. "If you want somebody to play the angles, why don't you hire a pool player?"

Stengel's first stop was Kankakee in the Class C Northern Association. The team's home field adjoined the grounds of a mental institution. Stengel quickly became a favorite of the institution's patients, who would watch games from their wardroom windows.

Stengel decided that his sliding needed work. Accordingly, he would practice his sliding as he ran out to his position in centerfield each inning. From the dugout he would slide into first, slide into second, and finally dive into centerfield. As the mental patients cheered their hero, Stengel's manager would only shake his head, point to the ward and say, "It's only a matter of time, Stengel." Another teammate came to the same conclusion: "Stengel is one guy who won't be playing here next year." Where would Stengel be? The teammate pointed past the fence. "Over there," he said.

Fortunately, the league disbanded before any commitment papers could be signed. Taking his uniform in lieu of payment, Stengel latched on with Maysville of the Bluegrass League. "So I got out of Kankakee, Illinois," Stengel told a Congressional hearing in 1959, "and I just go there for the visit now."

Stengel slid into the majors in 1912. "They brought me up to the Brooklyn Dodgers, which at that time was in Brooklyn.," he said. "I think I cost all of $300, but I don't know whether I ever convinced Squire Ebbets that I was a bargain." Even at that low introductory price, Stengel was given a warning—by the ballpark gateman of all eminences—when he arrived for the first time in Brooklyn: "You'd better be good," the man said balefully.

The majors of 1912 was the rough and tumble league of Ty Cobb and "Shoeless" Joe Jackson, "Smokey" Joe Wood, and Christy Mathewson, Tris Speaker, Honus Wagner, Tinkers, Evers, and Chance. It was baseball's golden age, and Stengel had surfaced amidst giants. He would outlast every one of them in the game.

Stengel once said, "I was not so successful at baseball, as it is a game of skill." This was a characteristic exaggeration. Stengel was not a great player, but he was a useful one, a decent power-hitter for the time with a right fielder's arm, and he brought many skills to the Dodgers, not the least of which was the lighthearted way he played the game. This was especially valuable in Brooklyn, where the team's personality was as important as its won-lost record.

Stengel was an audacious young man, constantly scrapping, trying to get ahead. He reached the majors with a flourish. "I broke in with four hits and the writers promptly decided they had seen the new Ty Cobb. It took me only a few days to correct that impression." The lasting impression that he did leave was that of a fighter. When he came to the Dodgers, the veteran players did not let him take batting practice. The thinking at the time was that a rookie was there to take a job from someone already on the club. Undeterred, Stengel had calling cards printed that said, "Hi. My name is Dutch Stengel and I'd like to take batting practice." Stengel got to bat.

He also lost the name Dutch. When Stengel had his luggage engraved, "Charles Stengel, K. C." for his hometown, his fellow ballplayers inevitably renamed him "K. C. Stengel," and then finally "Casey."

Stengel's manager in 1912 and 1913 was "Bad" Bill Dahlen, a former star shortstop who had broken into the majors, such as they were, under Cap Anson in 1891. Just forty-two years old when Stengel made his debut, Dahlen's own playing career had just recently come to an end. He was still sufficiently spry to give Stengel hands-on advice on sliding, which even after the insane asylum was still problematic. One of the stars of the National League at the dawn of the twentieth century, John Mc-Graw had considered the acquisition of Dahlen on December 12, 1903, the key to his Giants pennant winners of 1904 and 1905. When Dahlen joined the Giants—from the Dodgers, where he had been since 1899—he said, "It has always been my ambition to play in New York City. Brooklyn is all right, but if you're not with the Giants you might as well be in Albany."

Dahlen's conduct as manager of the Dodgers suggested that the unfavorable comparison to Albany was still operative in his mind. Dahlen had earned the sobriquet "Bad" because he was always eager for a scrap with umpires. Many of these arguments had been fueled by alcohol. A star player with a chip on his shoulder is compelling, exciting, dangerous. A manager with the same attitude is a belligerent drunk. Dahlen's Dodgers were good at brawling but failed to finish higher than sixth place. Towards the end of Stengel's rookie year a popular rumor had Dahlen not returning in 1914. A member of the press caught Dahlen leaving the ballpark after a game that September.

"Well, Bill, I hear you're losing your job," the writer said.

"I dunno," Dahlen muttered, "but you ain't gonna get it, you slob."

The next manager of the Dodgers was the former captain of the "old" Baltimore Orioles, Wilbert Robinson. Robinson would be remembered as the bumbling, frequently perplexed manager of that Brooklyn aggregation of ham-fisted sluggers known as the Daffiness Boys, but that came later. When his tour began he had been focused by a desire for revenge on his former best friend and boss, New York Giants manager John J. McGraw. He was the first significant influence on Stengel's managerial career.

Like Stengel's New York Mets teams of the early 1960s, the Daffiness Boys were such a celebrated group that they served to obscure much of what Robinson had accomplished before. Wilbert Robinson was one of baseball's most recognizable, respected personalities for the first thirty years of the Twentieth century. As a coach, he was recognized as one of the motivators behind manager John McGraw's New York Giants, the most successful franchise in baseball at the time. As manager of the National League's Brooklyn club, he became literally synonymous with the franchise. He skippered the Dodgers for eighteen seasons, staying so long that for a time "Dodgers" was dropped in favor of "The Robins." Robinson won two pennants and just missed two others, but these were a small part of his legacy. His main contribution to the team and to baseball was his gruff but fun-loving manner, his rotund belly, and his sense of humor. It was Robinson's good-natured persona that made the Dodgers the beloved neighborhood team that is missed even today. It was Uncle Robbie, as he was universally known, not Duke Snider, nor Pee Wee Reese, nor even Jackie Robinson that cemented the love affair between the borough and the team. The great 1940s and 50s rivalry between the "corporate" Yankees and the "neighborhood" Dodgers—a perception that existed despite the fact that for many years the Dodgers were largely owned by a bank—were made possible by this man, the only uncle in the history of the game, whose Dodgers were only sometimes competitive but always fun.

Wilbert Robinson was born on June 6, 1864 (some sources say June 29, 1863) in Bolton, Massachusetts, the son of a butcher. Like many young men of his era, Robinson went to work almost as soon as he was ambulatory. Education was never a priority, and Robinson would be a stranger to spelling and grammar. Like his contemporary, Connie Mack (born in Massachusetts in 1862), Robinson turned to baseball as an alternative to the exploitative, low-wage jobs that were typically available to young men of the working class. Fred Lieb wrote of Mack that his early experiences with these jobs helped to set his personality. "This early experience with child labor," Lieb wrote, "gave Mack much of his human sympathy, broad understanding, tolerance, and appreciation of the other fellow's problem, especially when that fellow was the underdog." Robinson's youthful experiences had a similar effect on him, for while he was a much rougher character than Mack, he had in common with the Tall Tactician an "easy way" with his players, a human quality absent from most of the managers of the day.

Robinson's destiny was set in 1890, when he became the catcher for, then captain of, the National League's Baltimore Orioles. For many years to follow, the gay nineties Orioles were considered the greatest team of all time, particularly by the old Orioles themselves, all of whom fanned out across baseball as managers, coaches, and high priests of their own legacy.

The main promulgators of the Orioles myth were Robinson and the team's third baseman, the arrogant, calculating John J. McGraw. Instant friends, the two could not have been more different. "Robinson was the sugar," McGraw said, "and I was the vinegar." McGraw had a consuming intensity that Robinson lacked, but the latter was more than happy to go along for the ride. The two would be a team for most of the next two decades. After nine years in Baltimore, Robinson and McGraw moved to the St. Louis Cardinals as a package. When McGraw became manager of the nascent American League's Baltimore franchise in 1901 (the National League's Orioles had been phased out in a restructuring a year earlier), Robinson became his coach, one of the first fulltime coaches in baseball.

In 1902, after a series of disputes with American League president Bancroft Johnson, McGraw became the manager of the New York Giants, jumping the Orioles in midseason and taking most of their quality players with him to Manhattan. Robinson was left behind to manage the husk of a team left in Baltimore. Bereft of his stars, the Orioles won only 24 of 81 games (.296) under Robinson. When the team was transferred to New York (ultimately to become the Yankees), Robinson was let go. The experience with the vestigial Orioles had demoralized him. "Every game was like a wake," wrote Fred Lieb. "Uncle Robbie had a team of humpty dumpties and ugly ducklings." He was furious with McGraw for leaving him in the lurch. Just thirty-eight years old, he quit baseball.

Robinson opened up a meat market and spent the next six years behind a butcher's block. Then McGraw called again. Unable to resist his
old friend, Robinson returned to baseball as the Giants first base and
pitching coach. The two old friends picked up where they left off, even
opening a Manhattan billiards parlor together (it was their second ven-
ture together. In Baltimore they had opened a Dutch-pin bowling alley,
supposedly the first of its kind). With Robbie aboard, the Giants won
three pennants in a row, 1911–1913.

In each of the three World Series the Giants were defeated by their
American League opponents. By 1913, McGraw had become bitter. He
lashed out at Robinson, blaming him for a critical caught-stealing late in
the late Series. Robinson responded that whatever mistakes he had
made, they were not nearly so numerous as McGraw's. Robinson was
fired on the spot. But for a ships-that-pass-in-the-night rapprochement
in the 1930s, the breach would never be repaired.

With Robinson free, the Dodgers hurried to hire him, hoping that some
of the Giants' success might rub off on an organization that had been
trapped in the second division since 1902. In this, Dodgers owner
Charles Ebbets might have misunderstood Robinson; he lacked the intensity that a long-time associate of John McGraw's might have been expected to have. He was corpulent, jolly—a profane baseball Santa Claus.
Where McGraw was a harsh taskmaster, Robinson would be a player's
manager. Momentarily, though, his personality was suppressed by the
desire for revenge against his former friend and his Manhattan-based
ballclub. Brooklyn improved in the standings in each of his first three seasons, rising to sixth in 1913, fifth in 1914, and third, far ahead of Mc-
Graw's Giants, in 1915.

In 1916, with the Giants still rebuilding after an unaccustomed last-
place finish (one of two times that McGraw would be out of the first division in thirty seasons) the pennant was there for the taking. Brooklyn
fought it out all summer with the Braves and the Phillies. Unable to accept losing to his former protégé, McGraw frantically goaded his team, at
one point pushing them to a record twenty-six straight wins. The Giants
climbed from last to fourth, but no further. By a quirk of scheduling,
Brooklyn clinched the pennant against the Giants. McGraw was livid. In
the fifth inning of the game he exploded, loudly accusing his team of quitting on him and rolling over for the Dodgers. McGraw himself then quit,
angrily leaving the field. In spite of these theatrics, Brooklyn won the
game and its first National League pennant.

After the game, McGraw was still furious. "I do not say my players did
not try to win, but they refused to obey my orders. . . . It was too much
for me and I lost my patience. Such baseball disgusted me and I left the
bench." Robbie replied, "That's a lot of [expletive]. That's a joke. The

fact is, we're a better ball club, and McGraw knows it. . . . Tell McGraw
to stop [expletive] on my pennant.''

The moment of glory was short lived. In the World Series, Brooklyn ran
up against the 1916 Boston Red Sox, one of the great teams of all time.
The suspense was over quickly as the Red Sox won the Series four games
to one. Particularly mysterious to the Dodgers was the stuff of a young
left-handed pitcher named Babe Ruth, who beat them with a fourteen-
inning complete game in the second contest of the Series. Years later,
Stengel, who was kept on the bench by virtue of being left-handed, would
mournfully remark, "That game was so famous they never used me."

Stengel still played a key role on the team, both on the field and in the
clubhouse. He went 4-for-11 (.364) in the Series, scored two runs, and
even more than Robbie kept the team in the game. Chief Meyers, the
team's catcher, told Lawrence Ritter, "Old Robbie was the manager. He
didn't have to do much managing, though, because it was a team of veterans. . . . I always maintained that Stengel won one more pennant than
the record books show. That was in 1916 . . . Robbie was just a good old
soul and everything. It was Casey who kept us on our toes. He was the
life of the party and kept us old-timers pepped up all season."

Despite the World Series loss, Robinson had arrived as a baseball star
of the first magnitude. In some ways, the sport began to revolve around
him. Together with Cap Huston, the co-owner of the Yankees, Robinson
purchased Dover Hall, a hunting lodge in Georgia. The lodge became an
off-season magnet for the greats of the game. Babe Ruth came there,
and so did Ty Cobb and numerous other players, owners, and writers.
The Hot Stove League lived at Uncle Robbie's house.

Machinations at Dover Hall would exercise an important influence on
the history of the New York Yankees. In 1917, Huston, who owned fifty
percent of the team, decided that Robinson, just coming off of the National League pennant, would be the ideal manager for the historically
weak Yankees franchise. Jacob Ruppert, owner of the other fifty percent,
favored St. Louis Cardinals manager Miller Huggins. When Huston, a military engineer, went to Europe as the United States entered World War I,
Ruppert took advantage of his absence to hire his own choice of managers. Huston never forgave the betrayal, and after his return Yankees ownership was fractured, with Ruppert supporting Huggins and Huston
giving players tacit approval to disrespect the manager. The situation
was untenable, eventually forcing Ruppert to buy Huston out and become sole owner of the Yankees.

In an era when the fans could easily fraternize with ballplayers, Robbie
was well known to the public. His 300-pound girth became his trademark. Some St. Louis roughs nicknamed him "Falstaff," after a popular
beer of the time (or Shakespeare's character; these could have been

well-read roughs). The Oxford Companion to English Literature describes Falstaff as "a fat, witty, good-humored old knight, loving jests, self-indulgent, and over-addicted to sack; a braggart who, when exposed, has presence of mind and resource enough to find some shift to save his face." No wonder Robinson hated the name—it described him perfectly. On September 18, 1931, Robinson got into a tiff with his catcher, Al Lopez, on game-calling. Finally, Lopez said, "Look, Robbie, if I'm so dumb, why don't you call all the signs? I'll look over at the bench and you give 'em to me."

Robinson agreed to call that day's game with the Cubs. The game was a scoreless tie through three innings. In the fourth, Chicago loaded the bases with no one out. Lopez looked up for his sign. Robbie ignored him. Lopez waited. Robbie seemed to be otherwise occupied. The players on the bench succeeded in attracting the manager's attention, but still he sent no sign. Lopez refused to continue without Robinson's input. Finally, Robinson cupped his hands and shouted, "What's the matter with you—didn't you ever catch before?"

The spectacularly educated sportswriter John Kieran of the *New York Times* also saw the Falstaff analogy, apparently without the prompting of a beer bottle or a box of cigars. "Like Falstaff," he wrote of Robinson, "he was not only witty himself but the cause of wit in others. His conversation was a continuous flow of homely philosophy, baseball lore, and good humor."

As the catcher and captain of the old Baltimore Orioles of the National League, Robinson was supposed to be an exemplar of the gangster baseball of the 1890s. Perhaps he would have been, had he possessed the players, but as baseball became more professionalized, there was a corresponding decrease in the intensity of the players. Robbie's men were unquestionably brawlers, but they weren't going to be lectured on how to be killers. Generational change had washed that away.

Rather than become frustrated, as McGraw became over the years, Robinson gave vent to another side of his personality. As he grew ever larger—Joe Williams wrote, "Taking him circumferentially," he is, "the largest manager in baseball. . . . On very hot Florida days Mr. Robinson is a distinct boon to the community, and mothers bring their young out-of-doors to allow them to play their childish games in the soothing shadows cast by the gentleman's superstructure"—his personality became more expansive as well. He and his wife—all of Brooklyn called her "Ma"—lived in the borough, and neighbors were welcome to approach him and argue his decisions. Simultaneously, he did away with many of the authoritarian trappings of management, leaving the players without a curfew. Said *The Sporting News*, "He has grown in grace, as he has in poundage." Unselfconscious, Robbie simply held his huge girth in his arms and said, "I haven't been feeding on oysters and wild duck all these years in Baltimore for nothing."

At the same time, he could be acerbic and sharp-tongued, but he was also friendly and displayed a sense of bemusement. In this Robinson was much like the later Stengel, though the competitive intensity was dialed down. Even then, he was often able to keep a generally undermanned club in contention due to his adroit handling of the pitching staff. The offense and the defense had to fend for themselves. John Lardner wrote, "Robbie played from day to day. One day he worried; the next day he grinned, and on all days he emitted the best cussing in the pastime." Lardner continued:

> The Dodgers arrived in St. Louis faced with the necessity of changing their signals. . . . Robbie called a signal meeting. His advisers began to wrangle. They argued until it was time to play ball without deciding on a set of signals, so they played the game without any. They won. Without signals, they won their next ten games in a row. At last Robbie's sense of fitness was outraged. On the morning of the eleventh day he called another meeting.

> "This has gone far enough!" he bellowed. "No big-league ball club can play without signals. It ain't right. We gotta fix some, and we gotta fix 'em now!"

> So the boys evolved a new set of highly efficient signals, and that day they lost the game . . . they lost twelve in a row. It was a shock to Robbie's deepest instincts, and it proved that anything could happen on the Brooklyn club.

During the period when the team was eschewing coded communications, a writer asked Robinson to account for their absence. He answered directly. "Most of these fellows," he said, "are too dumb to read signs." He was resigned, not resentful.

The most famous moment in Robinson's managerial career, was, ironically, not for managing but for a stunt. It is also the most famous moment of his association with Stengel, though Stengel had little or nothing to do with it. On March 13, 1915, at Daytona Beach, Florida, Robinson agreed to catch a baseball dropped from an airplane by aviatrix Ruth Law. Catching the ultimate pop-up was something of a fad around baseball at this time, with catchers on both circuits trying to top each other by snatching up balls dropped from ever greater heights. The top of the Washington Monument. Pike's Peak. John McGraw's ego.

Law climbed into the sky while Robbie waited below, mitt at the ready.

When Law reached the apex of her flight—approximately 525 feet—she realized that she had forgotten to bring along a baseball. Instead she dropped lunch. A ripe grapefruit was sent plunging towards terra firma. Robinson circled, lined it up—and missed. The grapefruit bounced off the heel of his glove and exploded against Robbie's chest, knocking him down.

His face and chest covered in sticky liquid, Robinson assumed the worst. "Jesus, I'm killed! I'm dead! My chest's split open! I'm covered with blood!" When the laughter of his assembled players awakened him to his actual situation, the first thing he said was, "Who done this, Stengel?" Stengel always denied involvement in the plot, suggesting various other suspects. "When you are younger you get blamed for crimes you never committed," he said as an old man, perhaps thinking of the incident, "and when you're older you begin to get credit for virtues you never possessed. It evens itself out."

Robinson taught Stengel many things, not least that it was okay for the manager to have trouble with names. In later years, Stengel was famous for warping his players' names or dispensing with them altogether, as in his answer to the question, "Who is going to play third base for the Yankees this year?"

Well the fella I got on there is hitting pretty good and I know he can make that throw, and if he don't make it that other fella I got coming has shown me a lot, and if he can't I have my guy and I know what he can do. On the other hand, the guy's not around now. And well, this guy may be able to do it against left-handers if my guy ain't strong enough. I know one of my guys is gonna do it.

"Everyone was 'Hey you,'" said Hank Bauer. "One day I wasn't playing, and in the top of the eighth inning he was looking for a pinch-hitter. He's sitting way down here and I'm way down there [at the other end of the bench]. I heard him holler, 'Hey, Woodling, get a bat!' He came up in front of me and said, 'God damn it, I said get a bat!' and I said 'God damn it, Woodling's playing left field! My name is Bauer!' He said [apologetically], 'Oh, oh, oh, get a bat, get a bat.'" As manager of the New York Mets, Stengel once called the bullpen and asked Bob Miller to warm up. There were two pitchers named Bob Miller on the team. Which one do you want, Stengel was asked. "Surprise me," he said, and hung up the phone.

Robinson was worse. "Robbie always had trouble with names," wrote Tom Meany. "Thus, Lombardi became 'Lumbago,' Bool became 'Bowlo,' and so on. Because of his love for nicknames, one never was quite sure whether Robbie devised the diminutives because he couldn't remember the proper names or whether he thought the diminutives were the proper names. He once, before witnesses, selected Dick Cox to play right field because he couldn't spell Oscar Roettger, his original choice for that position." In one 1930 game, Robinson decided that pitcher Sloppy Thurston had run out of gas. Approaching Gordon Slade, he said, "Joe, go out there and run for Pete."

Robbie demonstrated daily that there was no pitcher who was so old or injured that he could not be rehabilitated. In 1915 he acquired right-hander Jack Coombs. From 1910 to 1912, Coombs posted a combined record of 80–31 with a 2.64 ERA, including a 31–9, 1.30 season in 1910. In 1913 he contracted typhus and was virtually inactive for the next two years as he battled to stay alive. A debilitated thirty-two-year-old, Coombs had lost his control and his stuff. Nonetheless, in his first two years under Robbie he went 28–18 with a 2.61 ERA.

While with the Giants, Robinson had helped tutor Richard "Rube" Marquard in the art of big league pitching. In his first season with Robinson, the twenty-four-year-old Marquard, a career 9–18, 3.15 ERA (against a league average of 2.71) enigma popularly known as the "$11,000 Lemon," blossomed into a 24–7, 2.50 ace. McGraw rode him until he burned out, then discarded him. Robbie got another five years out of him, using him as a reliever in some games, nursing him through starting assignments in others. In 1916, their first full year together, Marquard went 13–6 with a 1.58 ERA. Later, Robinson picked up Dazzy Vance, previously discarded by the Yankees (among others) at thirty-one and turned him into one of the great strikeout pitchers of all time.

Most of all, Robinson showed Stengel that a manager could win while retaining his sense of fun. "There's nothing to be gained in baseball by being in the dumps," Robbie said. "I don't care what stage the pennant race may be in or how hopeless the ball game may seem. There's nothing to be gained by going into the ninth inning with the score against you and your head between your legs. Anything can happen in baseball."

There were limits; in 1931 the Dodgers had a journeyman pitcher named Pea Ridge Day who gave a hog call after every strikeout. After hearing thirty hog calls in twenty-two Day games, Robinson released him, saying, "No man has a right to be sillier than God intended him to be."

At the outset, Stengel had a hard time connecting with the avuncular side of Uncle Robbie. According to sportswriter Fred Lieb, one midnight during the spring training season of 1915 found Stengel standing at the railing of a Daytona Beach bridge. By pure chance a reporter who covered the Dodgers was driving along the bridge and recognized the man at the rail. Pulling over, the reporter hailed Stengel and asked him what he was doing there. "George, I'm trying to get up the guts to jump off," said Stengel. "I'm not hitting. Besides, Uncle Robbie doesn't like me. And I've got the clap."

The reporter talked Stengel off the bridge and into his car, returned him to Dodger camp, and no more was heard of the matter. Whatever the reason—it has also been suggested that Stengel was suffering from typhus—Stengel had his worst season in 1915, hitting only .237. In general, Stengel was up and down in Brooklyn. Befitting a young man from the Midwest set loose in the big city, the young Stengel was often out of control, constantly brawling with umpires, opposing players, and teammates.

Still, Robinson made him a regular and but for 1915 he performed well. Even then, he wasn't truly terrible: though Stengel hit .237, the National League as a whole batted only .248. Stengel had an OPS (on-base percentage plus slugging percentage) of .647; the National League OPS was .640. This was the dead ball era, when the baseball would not travel in the air when struck, but thudded wetly to the turf, when one ball was used all game long, though it be brown with tobacco juice and lumpy enough for a blind phrenologist to mistake it for the skull of Peking Man. As such, while Stengel's Dodger career batting average of .272, slugging percentage of .393, and on-base percentage of .346 look anemic by today's steroidal standards, they are actually quite good. Hidden in those numbers are a flair for the dramatic—the first home run in the history of Ebbets Field, hit off of the Yankees in a stadium-opening exhibition of April 5, 1913. Later that year, he personally took a game from the Braves at Boston, lining two balls into that team's cavernous outfield that went for inside-the-park home runs.

Off the field he was more troublesome. In addition to general roughhousing, he led a clubhouse cadre known as the Grumblers, discontented Dodgers who agitated for more money. This was always unwelcome in baseball, but was particularly threatening to the bootstrapping Charles Hercules Ebbets, a non–silver spoon owner who had scraped to buy the team and build his ballpark. "You call me grasping," Ebbets once said, "but I am the only club owner in the National League who cannot afford to own an automobile."

Ebbets called for Stengel's salary to be cut from $6,000 to $4,600. This was not only a comment on Stengel's poor 1915 and mediocre 1916 seasons, but also a reflection of the players' lack of leverage once the Federal League threat had disappeared. Ebbets had joined with most of his fellow owners (Connie Mack was a notable exception) in boosting player salaries in the hopes of preventing established stars from defecting to the new league. "I didn't let one of my good players get away," Ebbets boasted. He had had little choice; he was in a tighter spot than most as the Feds had placed a franchise in Brooklyn, the Tip-Tops, at the

Dodgers' old Washington Park home field. Had Zack Wheat, Jake Daub-
ert, or even Casey Stengel provided the invaders with old, familiar faces
for which to root, the Dodgers might have lost their emotional hold on
the populace.

In January 1917, Stengel returned his contract unsigned, suggesting
that he had received the clubhouse man's by mistake. Ebbets called it a
"most impudent letter." Stengel then exacerbated the situation by telling the press, "It seems reasonable that if he charges such high prices to
see his players perform"—this was in reference to the shockingly high
price per ticket Ebbets charged for the World Series—"he should meet
the fans halfway by giving them the opportunity to watch high-priced
players." Stengel's name was pricked. A year later, Ebbets dealt him and
second baseman George Cutshaw to the Pittsburgh Pirates in exchange
for shortstop Chuck Ward, pitcher Al Mamaux, and pitcher Burleigh Grimes.

The Pirates have traditionally been a team of extremes, veering wildly
between years of sustained success and abject failure. Stengel joined
them during one of the latter periods, one helped, or at least sustained
by the Pirates having traded their best young pitcher (Grimes, a four-
time twenty-game winner for the Dodgers between 1918 and 1924) for
him. Stengel was immediately discomfited by this new world of reduced
expectations. Brooklyn had reached the World Series in 1916; Pittsburgh had not won a pennant since 1909. Charles Ebbets had not exactly been tolerant of Stengel's antics or salary demands, but he did not
deal harshly with him either. Barney Dreyfuss, Pittsburgh's owner, was
not known to be nearly as patient. The baseball owner as social Darwin-
ist, he considered himself to be far above the help. In 1904, he tried to
have John McGraw banned from baseball for referring to him by his first
name.

Stengel's most notorious prank occurred on June 6, the day of
Stengel's return to Ebbets Field as a Pirate. The Brooklyn fans, as they
were known to do to former Dodgers who dared to return wearing hostile
colors, unmercifully jeered the "traitor" Stengel throughout the game.
The park was smaller than any park today, the setting intimate; the experience was personal. Undoubtedly the Brooklynites applied their noted
creativity to razzing the young outfielder that summer day.

Stengel did nothing while Pittsburgh took its turn at bat in the top of
the first. Nor did he make any gesture to the crowd when he took his
place in the outfield for the bottom of the inning. Despite the appearance
of inaction, in full view of the Brooklyn fans and both teams he had been
surreptitiously preparing a grand demonstration.

As he came up for his first at-bat in the top of the second Stengel was
welcomed with another chorus of boos. He acknowledged the crowd by
raising his arms. He then turned towards the fans and gave a sweeping

bow. At the low point of his obeisance he doffed his hat and from his head a sparrow rose into the air. He had given the crowd the bird.

Uncle Robbie, who was beyond surprise at this stage of his life, acted as if these kinds of things happened every day with Stengel around. "Well, there's no use getting excited about it," he said. "He's got birds in his garret, that's all."

Stengel spent the rest of his life answering questions about the bird incident, and even reenacted it on two occasions, once for a Dodger Stadium crowd, once for a magazine photo spread. Still, he had cause to regret it as one of the enduring pillars upon which rested his reputation. "I was fairly good at times," he said of his playing days, "but a lot of people seem to remember the stunts I pulled better than they do the ball games I helped win."

Dreyfuss was less than amused. "The higher-ups complained that I wasn't showing a serious attitude by hiding a sparrow in my hat," Stengel said, "but I said any day I get three hits, I am showing a more serious attitude than a lot of players with no sparrows in their hats." Stengel had discovered the problem of perception that was to plague him for the rest of his career. "They didn't see any humor in it," he wrote. "They didn't want you to be a comedian in those days. If you had a bad day, you were wasting your time with comedy, because your manager and your players and the public didn't like it."

Dreyfuss forced Stengel to take a salary cut after his first year in Pittsburgh. Resentful, he played to be traded. He stopped hustling, and did not slide on the basepaths. When Dreyfuss demanded of Stengel why he did not slide, he replied, "With the salary I got here, I'm so hollow and starving that I'm liable to explode like a light-bulb if I hit the ground too hard." One day he dropped a ball in the outfield. When the fans jeered, he turned to the stands and said, "It ain't my fault, fellers. I'm weak. They don't pay me enough to eat with."

To further demonstrate his commitment to the Pirates, Stengel joined the Navy in June 1918, long before the government's "work or fight" order shut down baseball. Stengel's participation in Woodrow Wilson's crusade to make the world safe for Woodrow Wilson did not extend beyond the grounds of the Brooklyn Naval Yard. Stengel was charged with organizing baseball games between returning seamen and sailors working at the naval yard. This early managerial experience was useful to Stengel if only because he learned early how to maximize his advantages: Stengel made sure to play his games against ship-bound crews almost immediately after they had returned to port. In this way his team could beat the exhausted sailors before they found their land-legs.

Then there was this valuable lesson: "My faith in human nature was somewhat upset in the course of those battleship games. At the Prospect

Park parade grounds, I asked a youngster looking on, to hold my wallet. As I slid into second base in the first inning, I caught sight of the kid about a quarter of a mile away, on a bike and pedaling like blazes. That taught me a rule I have followed ever since. I never again will trust my roll to anybody who owns a bicycle.''

When the war ended Stengel returned to the Pirates, but having walked out on a contract it was inevitable that he would be traded. On August 8, 1919, Stengel learned to be careful what he wished for: he was traded, not to a rich contender but to the worst, least competently run team in the National League, the Philadelphia Phillies. He left Pittsburgh with a question that would never be answered. A regular fan at Pirates games had taken to shouting, ''How's Big Bess, Casey?'' Stengel spent the rest of his life wondering who Big Bess was.

The Phillies had been a first-division club as recently as 1917, but having been divested of their best players by their owner (anticipating Harry Frazee's fire sale in Boston, but with less reason), they were in the midst of a slump that would see them lose at least ninety games in ten of the next twelve seasons. (Taking a longer view, they would lose at least ninety games in twenty-three of the next *thirty* seasons.)

Stengel did not want to retreat any further from the spotlight than he already had, at least not without some form of compensation. ''Not enough money here,'' he wired William Baker. ''Will need more to go over there.'' The owner pleaded poverty. Stengel wired back, ''If there isn't enough money in Philadelphia I will be in Kansas City, Missouri.'' He went home.

Stengel's ''retirement'' lasted through the following spring, at which time he gave in and reported to the Phillies. As Stengel discovered in 1918 when he voluntarily relinquished a salary of $4,000 a year in exchange for $15 a month from the Navy, making a point could be very expensive.

The ubiquitous presence of Stengel throughout the history of baseball that was observed by Red Smith was further established during the 1919–1920 off-season. Stengel somehow found himself at Fort Huachuca, Arizona, home of the 25th Infantry. The 25th fielded an all-black baseball team, the Wreckers. Stengel watched them play and was greatly impressed by their skills. In February 1920, Rube Foster proposed the establishment of the Negro National League. Stengel suggested to J. L. Wilkinson, who was going to own the league's Kansas City team, that he sign the players he had seen, among them the pitcher ''Bullet'' Joe Rogan, ''the Negro leagues' Christy Mathewson.'' Wilkinson took his advice and the great Kansas City Monarchs, ''the Yankees of Negro baseball,'' were born.

Stengel averaged .292 in 1920 for a Phillies team that lost ninety-one games and finished 30.5 games out of first place. The outfield unit of Stengel, Cy Williams, and Irish Meusel was the sole bright spot on offense (though centerfielder Williams had to field pretty much everything hit out of the infield), but even so his frustration mounted. The Dodgers, still featuring many of his former teammates, reached the World Series in 1920. For Stengel, Philadelphia was more than ninety miles away from New York. Cincinnati Reds ace Dolf Luque was pitching against the Phillies one day when he grew angry at persistent heckling coming from the Phillies' dugout. He stalked over and punched Stengel in the mouth. Later, Luque was informed that Stengel had not been the guilty party. "Stengel pop off too much anyway," the Cuban Luque said.

He seemed doomed to finish out his career in the second division. On July 1, 1921, he was drowning his sorrows in a Philadelphia speakeasy when the phone behind the bar rang. The bartender answered, listened, and handed the phone to Stengel. Without preamble, the voice on the other end said, "This is McGraw talking. You and [Phillies infielder] Johnny Rawlings report to the Giants in Boston tomorrow. Take the night train." Stengel, dumbfounded and more than a little skeptical that the authoritative voice on the other end of the line was actually the legendary John McGraw, could only manage to say, "Right."

As soon as the voice hung up, Stengel had the operator trace the call back to its source. The veracity of the call confirmed, Stengel beat a hasty retreat from the speakeasy and from Philadelphia itself. He did not bother to wait for the night train, but left immediately. "I got to New York so fast that Mr. McGraw couldn't change his mind," Stengel said. His enthusiasm for the game instantly reappeared, and when he first took the field in a Giants uniform, he was reported to have shouted to himself, "Wake up, muscles! We're in New York now!"

As with many events in Stengel's career, there are multiple versions of his liberation from Philadelphia. Another has him lying on the trainer's table during a rain delay, having the kinks worked out of his muscles. Told of the trade, he leaps off the table, runs onto the field, and slides into every base, muscles no longer sore. "I thought you had a bad back?" someone asks.

"You wouldn't expect me to take that to New York with me, would you?" Stengel replies.

The most important, most successful phase of Casey Stengel's playing career occurred in New York. He reached his peak as a player in his years with the Giants, but more importantly, he came under the influence of manager John McGraw. The timing of the two events was not coincidental.

The modern age of New York City sports began with John McGraw. He came to a city whose upper class affected a placid Victorian gentility and provided it with a class-leveling icon by glamorizing a first-generation American's ceaseless struggle to conquer—in McGraw's case, to strangle—poverty, to rise above the Protestant burghers of Gotham. The mannered world of Edith Wharton had been invaded by something uncouth, unresting, and voracious. What a pity that James Cagney played McGraw's good friend George M. Cohan instead of McGraw himself; one suspects that Cohan's desire to ingratiate himself to an audience and McGraw's hostility were two sides of the same coin.

McGraw was the father of all baseball managers, and all football coaches too. The writers called him "Little Napoleon," and cast him as a field general. In 1902 it was still possible to innocently confuse the manly art of sport and the manly art of war. Then-president Theodore Roosevelt made a career of it in reverse, spending a lifetime treating war as a sport and sport as a war. He was the master, "the czar," as he put it, of the New York Giants, the proudest team in professional baseball.

Prior to McGraw's arrival in New York, the idea of professional sports had not yet rooted itself in the American consciousness. Baseball as an "organized" sport (it was often precisely the opposite) had only existed for about thirty years, and the organizational structure we recognize today had only just begun to emerge. Players and managers were tough characters, undisciplined, lacking regimentation. McGraw had been one of them, and thus he knew firsthand the need to drill his men so they executed plays consistently and all worked together for the winning effort. He was one of the first to put the "professional" into professional sports, in the process giving the game a polished product that attracted the commitment of fans. This is particularly true in New York, where for decades various teams, including the Giants, had been trying without much success to make an impression on the public.

One of McGraw's first moves upon coming to New York was to double the amount of money that was typically spent on players' road accommodations. Charles Ebbets, as always living hand to mouth, assailed him at a meeting of National League owners. "McGraw will break us all. He is going crazy on expenses and giving the players high-toned notions. Ballplayers should not live in high-class hotels. The expense is more than the game can stand, and the players themselves are not happy there."

Any idea that Ebbets had that McGraw's players were pampered was completely erroneous. McGraw gave his players more because he was about to ask more of them. Historian Harold Seymour wrote, "The name McGraw came to symbolize strict discipline enforced by fines and scathing reprimands." He knew how to motivate with the carrot as well as the stick, was as quick to praise a good performance as he was to criticize a bad one, and was given to rewarding excellent play with spontaneous cash bonuses.

Professionalism only went so far with McGraw; if he could not find a strategic edge he would search for a psychological one. If that failed, he would put up his dukes and fight. He only reluctantly accepted that umpires should be safe from physical reprisals after controversial calls. When baseball as a whole made the bodily integrity of the arbiters a priority, McGraw turned to revenge by proxy. In 1907 he was blamed for inciting fans at the Polo Grounds to riot against the umpires. In 1908, he was arrested for starting a riot in Boston.

McGraw was born in Truxton, New York, in 1873, the son of an itinerant railroad worker. From an early age he learned to be self-reliant, determined, defiant; he took more than one beating from his father over his desire to play baseball. McGraw's mother and four of his seven siblings died of diphtheria when he was twelve, and his father, by nature of work and temperament, did not keep the family together. He was mostly on his own from then on, which undoubtedly had at least one positive: his father no longer beat him over his preferring baseball to a steady job. After becoming a professional ballplayer at seventeen, he treated the outcome of each game as a matter of personal survival. They were.

Just a year after getting his start, McGraw became a member of the National League's Baltimore Orioles. The Orioles were the roughest team in a rough age. Honus Wagner, the star shortstop and a contemporary of McGraw's, told of a game when he hit a triple against the Orioles. It would have been a home run, he said, "except that the first baseman bumped him, the second baseman tripped him, the shortstop gave him a couple of shots when he went by and when he got to third, John McGraw pulled out a shotgun." Years later, when Branch Rickey proposed that batting helmets be used in major league play, Stengel remarked, "If we had them when I was playing, John McGraw would have insisted that we go up to the plate and get hit on the head." As Joseph Durso wrote, "Oriole baseball, as it flourished in 1894, was a combination of hostility, imagination, speed, and piracy."

On May 16, 1894, Boston's South End Grounds, home of the Braves, burned down around fans as they watched McGraw scrap with Boston's Tommy Tucker. McGraw had started the fight; as Tucker slid back into base on a pickoff play, McGraw had kicked him in the face. Someone in the stands dropped a lit cigar onto some peanut shells during the excitement and there went the wooden ballpark. One can imagine McGraw and Tucker slugging it out in an empty ballpark, oblivious to the flames shooting up from the grandstand.

The Orioles won National League titles every year from 1894 through 1897 and McGraw was their igniter. A third baseman, he was a patient hitter who twice led his league in walks and runs scored. His career batting average was .334. In 1899 through 1901 he posted on-base percentages over .500. When McGraw was demanding of his players, he was asking them to live up to his own high level of achievement as well as his lack of complacency. McGraw started out with the Orioles as a raw eighteen-year-old with limited hitting and fielding abilities and became an incredibly valuable hitter. Off the field, he recognized that his lack of education might be an impediment to him and spent four winters studying at the future St. Bonaventure University.

At the age of twenty-six he became the player-manager of the soon-to-be-disbanded Orioles. In 1901, McGraw was seduced by Ban Johnson, president of the nascent American League, into managing its new franchise in Baltimore. The two almost immediately clashed. McGraw objected to the poor quality of umpiring in the new league, while Johnson, trying to purge rowdyism from baseball (at this time one attending a baseball game had a chance to experience all the worst elements of a hockey fight, a professional wrestling match, and an urban riot), objected to McGraw's verbal and physical abuse of the umpires. On one occasion in 1902, he suspended McGraw for inciting a bleacher crowd to attack an umpire. (Twenty years later, McGraw would write of "the folly of umpire baiting," admitting that, "Umpire baiting and so-called rowdyism go together." Still, he could not resist getting in a last shot: "Often, though," he wrote, "the umpires themselves are rowdies at heart.")

By the middle of that year it was well known that Johnson planned to transfer the Baltimore franchise to New York, where it would ultimately become the Yankees. McGraw felt certain that Johnson did not intend to take him along. Accepting an offer to manage the National League's New York Giants, a team that had had thirteen managers since 1891 (still at war, the two leagues had little respect for each other's contracts), McGraw orchestrated a deal where, unbeknownst to Johnson, a controlling interest in the Orioles was transferred to the owners of the Giants. All of Baltimore's best players, including future Hall of Famers Roger Bresnahan and "Iron Man" Joe McGinnity, were released by the Orioles and signed by the Giants.

By the time McGraw was finished with his revenge on Johnson, there were only four players on the Baltimore roster. The players he took with him became the foundation of his first great Giants teams, and enabled him to release half of the 1902 Giants' roster, which he considered to be "deadwood." In the meantime, the Orioles, now under Wilbert Robinson, had to forfeit the last games of their schedule. When the team arrived in New York it had to be started from scratch. McGraw's first Giants pennants came at the expense of almost two decades of also-ran status for the Yankees. This was just fine with McGraw.

The Giants found themselves bossed by an unapologetic autocrat, determined to control every aspect of his team. He sought to be the prime mover; the impetus for the team's success or failure would not be with the players on the field, but with him. "Get out there and play baseball as you have all season," he told his players on the eve of the 1922 World Series. "I'll do the directing and if anything goes wrong I'll take the responsibility." This was a recurrent theme throughout his career. Chief Meyers, who played on McGraw's Giants between 1909 and 1915 said, "According to Mr. McGraw his ball team never lost a game. 'Do what I tell you,' he said, 'and I'll take the blame for mistakes.'" After the 1922 World Series, in which Babe Ruth had been held to two hits in five games, McGraw said, "I signaled for every ball that was pitched to Ruth. I think ball players, as a rule, can do a more workmanlike job when they feel that someone else is taking the responsibility."

It was a burden he shouldered with zest. "I think we can win it all," he said in 1921, "if my brain holds out." His megalomania was not unjustified; when it came to baseball, his perceptivity was unrivaled. Where others looked at Christy Mathewson and saw him as a first baseman, McGraw knew he was a pitcher. He knew that Bill Terry was a first baseman, not a pitcher. He knew George Kelly was a good enough defensive player to succeed anywhere on the diamond, and that the same was true of Frankie Frisch. Young Mel Ott was presented to him as a catcher. McGraw moved him to the outfield. He regarded himself as the best teacher for a young player and would tutor a promising prospect himself rather than send him down to the minor leagues. "Ott stays with me!" McGraw declared when seventeen-year-old Melvin Ott came to him in 1926. "No minor league manager is going to ruin him!" The minor league manager in question was Casey Stengel.

As long as the dead ball persisted, McGraw played the game of the bunt and run. When the age of the home run began in 1920, McGraw railed against what he saw as the game being dumbed down, but he also did not hesitate to change his offensive tactics to match the new reality. In the age of the complete game, McGraw used relief pitchers for competitive advantage. In 1909, he put the twenty-one-year-old righthander James "Doc" Crandall into the bullpen, normally the home of the aged and infirm. From then until 1913, Crandall started fifty-two games but relieved in 133 more, compiling a record of 55–24 (.696) and saving twenty-four games. The Giants won the pennant in 1911, 1912, and 1913, in part because McGraw's teams were blowing fewer leads than the competition.

The baseball of McGraw's early years was more dependent on the skill and attentiveness of the manager than in any succeeding era. McGraw managed "inside baseball," a game that counted not on the home run, a rarity until the twenties, but on stealing bases, clutch pitching, and defensive excellence. As games were generally low-scoring, the manager was counted on to glean every possible strategic advantage for his team. He had to know the weaknesses of the other team and possess the sense of timing to take advantage of them. In his time, no one was better at this than McGraw. A mirror image of today's priorities: in McGraw's day, it was the manager who was essential and the players who were replaceable.

This was a concept that neither McGraw nor Casey Stengel ever quite got over. In McGraw's view, a player could negate whatever value his hitting or fielding prowess provided if he was not sufficiently attentive. "McGraw wanted every play executed properly," said Stengel, "and if you couldn't do it after he'd told you two or three times, he figured you were either too stupid or too awkward to play for him." Said McGraw: "I would not have a group of players in whom I did not have confidence. All I want to know is that they are honestly trying to do what I tell them. If they haven't the ability it is my fault if I keep them."

This extended to good things that happened for the wrong reason. "I have made it a point," wrote McGraw, "never to blame a player for failing in a sincere effort to carry out instructions from the bench, but I also have made it a point to censure a player, even if he won the game, by failing to obey orders. That, I regard as necessary to discipline." In 1912 he fined John "Red" Murray for hitting a game-winning home run when he had been ordered to bunt. He insisted that this insistence on precision still gave his players room to make mistakes. "I wouldn't have a man on my team who doesn't make errors," he said. "It shows he doesn't go after the ball."

Yet he would not hesitate to publicly excoriate a player for a mistake, particularly a good player. One of McGraw's enduring contradictions was the quixotic way he chose whom to pity and whom to persecute. Fred Merkle made a right turn at second base during a key game with the Cubs in 1906, McGraw went to his grave defending him. Fred Snodgrass dropped a critical fly ball in the 1912 World Series and he got a raise. Frankie Frisch hit .363 in four World Series and all he got was abuse.

McGraw's faith in his own leadership abilities worked in Stengel's favor. The sour attitude of Stengel's Pennsylvania days would seem a poor fit for a club perpetually in the thick of a pennant race, but McGraw didn't give a damn what a player's attitude was; it was going to be subsumed in *his* attitude. He never hesitated to take on difficult players. He acquired the slick first baseman Hal Chase after Christy Mathewson, the player the manager held in higher esteem than all others, accused him of throwing games, after his indebtedness to gamblers was so well known that fans would chant, "What's the odds?" when he took the field. He picked up Irish Meusel from the Phillies directly after he had been suspended by his manager for indifferent play (Meusel was hitting .353 with

12 home runs in a little over half a season, so one suspects that the real reason for the suspension was not indifferent play, but indifferent pay—that is, Meusel had been asking for more money). McGraw signed Benny Kauff and traded for Rogers Hornsby. Having dealt Edd Roush, he reacquired him despite the fact that the outfielder was a perpetual holdout and made no secret of his hatred of McGraw. Heywood Broun wrote that McGraw "could take kids out of coal mines and wheat fields and make them walk and talk and chatter and play ball with the look of eagles." This applied to the compliant and the recalcitrant alike.

The man for whom Stengel was coming to play was the owner of six National League pennants and one championship. There were also eight second-place finishes; from 1902 to 1920, the Giants had finished out of the first division exactly once. McGraw's record of sustained success, which was only weakly paralleled by Connie Mack in the American League, along with his compelling personality, made him the preeminent figure in the game. It was a position he yielded reluctantly, and not all at once, to Babe Ruth and Judge Landis. Though his star lost some of its luster in the years that followed, the memory of his presence, his unyielding disapprovals and grudging approvals, never lost any power over those who knew him. That is not to say that all of his players liked him. Some hated him, but even for them, years afterward, he was still the focal point of their recollections.

At the time Stengel and McGraw began their association, McGraw, forty-nine years old, in the twentieth of his thirty-one years as the team's manager, was about to begin the last productive phase of his life. Beset by physical and financial problems, his mood was in the process of permanently souring. He was rapidly completing a transformation from provocateur of his players to antagonist. In 1933, F. C. Lane of *Baseball Magazine* wrote, "McGraw was the autocrat of the diamond. His was the imperial purple; his the regal scepter. Players, to him, were little beyond automata who batted and ran bases as he pulled the strings." At the beginning of the century, the players accepted their servility. By the 1920s they were beginning to have doubts.

Nor were the roaring twenties compatible with a man who had lost his sense of fun. "In playing or managing," McGraw said, "the game of ball is only fun for me when I'm out in front and winning. I don't give a hill of beans for the rest of the game" In 1921, the Pirates had a boisterous, all-nickname group of "Jolly Cholly" Grimm, "Possum" Whitted, "Cotton" Tierney, and "Rabbit" Maranville. Grimm played the banjo and the group was as adept at holding a hootenanny as it was playing baseball. On August 23, with just thirty-seven games to go in the season, they led McGraw's Giants by 7.5 games. Over the next four days, the Giants would take five straight games from the Pirates. After a cat-and-mouse chase during the first week of September, the Giants passed the Pirates for good on September 11, ultimately winning the pennant by four games. McGraw's comment: "You can't sing your way through this league." Stengel didn't contribute much as McGraw directed his team down the stretch. His lack of playing time turned out to be one of the biggest breaks of his life—he got to stay on the bench and watch McGraw in action.

Stengel was one of those players who liked McGraw, and the feeling was mutual. After games, Stengel would often go home with McGraw and the two would spend hours eating and talking baseball, a familiarity not awarded by McGraw to many of his players. McGraw's wife Blanche was somewhat nonplussed by the length and frequency of Stengel's visits. "He was a bachelor . . . and treated John as one. They talked through countless nights in the kitchen. What on earth they gabbed about I never learned. Each blamed the other. John confided that Casey could talk your head off. In the morning Casey would pay tribute to John's old baseball stories and how he couldn't get a word in edgeways. . . . Of course, it was just an excuse to stay up all night. They spent most of the time in the kitchen, because it was nearer the food. Casey liked to cook bacon and scrambled eggs, which he did two or three times a night, and John liked to eat them."

As a result of these discussions, which would be suspended whenever Stengel made a mental error on the field, McGraw became well acquainted with the sharp mind that lived beneath Stengel's easygoing demeanor and determined to groom him as a future manager.

Prior to coming to the Giants, Stengel had had only brief flirtations with managing. He had spent an off-season as the baseball coach at the University of Mississippi (as a full faculty member he was called "Professor" for the first time), and there was also his World War I service. Still single, he was too young, too immature, too wrapped up in his playing career to be thinking seriously about his future. McGraw, both by deed and by example, would give him the push and the experience that would allow him to make a commitment.

McGraw was the decisive figure in Casey Stengel's life. He had never applied himself to anything but athletics, laughing his way through school, clowning to the public, having fun. McGraw inspired him in a way no one ever had. McGraw's teams were celebrated by the media as the work of one man, the genius of baseball. It is hard to imagine today, when managers are for the most part an interchangeable, colorless lot who must toady to the multimillionaires who play for them (or pay them), but in 1921, McGraw was as celebrated as any player in the National League. Stengel's years with him were among McGraw's most triumphant. The Giants won consecutive pennants from 1921 to 1924, an unprecedented feat which would not be surpassed for thirty years. In the 1922 World Series, the Giants crushed Babe Ruth and the upstart Yankees, due in part to McGraw's ability to unnerve the great slugger ("Why shouldn't we pitch to Babe Ruth? We pitch to better hitters in the National League—throw a slow curve at his goddamned feet!"). Stengel was viewing "The Mastermind" at his magisterial height.

Stengel idolized him. "McGraw was the best manager I ever knew," he said, but more than admiration was at work. Stengel looked at McGraw and wanted what he had—the admiration, the respect, the chance to be praised by politicians and celebrities. Stengel never made the mistake of trying to *be* McGraw (though as he aged he would display more and more of McGraw's signature impatience), but the accolades he imagined sounded exactly like those that his mentor received on a daily basis.

More than thirty years later, a knowledgeable observer could pick out behaviorisms acquired from McGraw. "Casey . . . has incorporated many of McGraw's mannerisms," wrote Frank Lane in 1954. "Ever notice how Casey erupts from the dugout to protest an umpire's decision? That's pure McGraw. So is Casey's truculent trot to the mound when one of his pitchers gets into trouble. Also . . . those frantic left-handed jabs that punctuate his beautifully staged altercations with umpires are another borrowed McGrawism."

During spring training in 1923, McGraw took Stengel aside and said, "I'm taking an interest in you. Would you like to be a coach on this club in later days?" Stengel responded in the affirmative and McGraw promised he would teach him all he knew. McGraw charged Stengel with managing the Giants' spring training "B" squad (which had the dual function of being McGraw's reserve and his penal colony) during their barnstorming tour north. Stengel recognized the opportunity that McGraw had presented him with, but he could not take full advantage of it. He was still an active baseball player who was primarily concerned with keeping his position on a major league club. He was thrilled that McGraw had chosen him to be coach/manager in waiting, but for all its potential the position was strictly honorary—that is to say unsalaried. His work as an outfielder was still where he earned his money. He was distracted, and he frustrated McGraw with his inability to concentrate completely on his lessons.

McGraw occasionally let Stengel coach first base or work with the outfielders. The neophyte coach would offer McGraw carefully considered evaluations of his players and stratagems. McGraw received some of these cheerfully, but others would inspire him to deflate his protégé's ego. "Did you ever sign a manager's contract?" McGraw would ask him.

As important to Stengel's future was the way that McGraw used him as a player. Stengel, a left-handed hitting outfielder, had a career batting average of .276, with an OPS (on-base percentage plus slugging percentage) of .747 versus a league average of .674 (without making allowances for the parks in which he played, Stengel's OPS was eleven percent better than the National League average). McGraw realized that Stengel was handicapped by left-handed pitchers. Bill Dahlen and Wilbert Robinson had rested him against some lefties, but never religiously; in 1917, Robbie had barely bothered to platoon him at all. McGraw changed all that. When a southpaw started against the Giants, Stengel was benched in favor of Billy Cunningham, a right-handed hitter. This alternating of left and right-handed hitters was called a "shift" at the time, but soon became known as "platooning."

McGraw's strategy combined with Stengel's resurgent enthusiasm to create a career renaissance for the outfielder. "There is one reason why my work this year is better than it has ever been before," Stengel said. "I am satisfied with my job and doing my level best to make good. I have been told that I wasn't straining my suspenders in the service of several clubs with which I have been associated. However that may be, I can say without reservation I am wearing my suspenders threadbare in the effort to do good work for the Giants." In 1922 Stengel registered a career high batting average of .368, and followed that with a .339 average in 1923. Stengel played only about half the time. Injuries, the platoon, and the Giants' defensive alignment limited his opportunities. With Ross Youngs in right field and Irish Meusel in left, Stengel had to be used as a center fielder. He had played nearly his entire career in right field, and at age 31, his lower limbs—Stengel could be identified at a distance by his bowed legs—combined with the huge Polo Grounds outfield (it was 483 feet to the center field wall), restricted him to only 552 plate appearances as a Giant, but they were the best 552 plate appearances of his career: as a Giant, Stengel hit .349, slugged .524, and reached base forty percent of the time (his raw OPS, .937, was 22 percent better than league average).

Though sometimes resentful of being reduced to part-time status, Stengel understood that his hitting had not spontaneously improved. Like any religious convert, he began to wonder if that which had changed his life might be good for everyone. He would write, "My platoon thinking started with the way McGraw handled me in my last years as a ballplayer on the Giants." He would extol the virtues of platooning for the rest of his life.

Stengel's newfound offensive prowess made him a World Series hero. He played only a minor role in the 1922 Series due to—what else—a leg injury. In the 1923 series against the Yankees, the Giants won only two games but both victories were directly attributable to Casey Stengel's heroics. With game one tied 4–4 in the top of the ninth, Stengel caught a change-up from "Bullet" Joe Bush and drove it into brand-new Yankee Stadium's left field gap. The defensive alignment had not been quite right; left fielder Bob Meusel (Irish's brother) was pulled over toward the line, while center fielder Whitey Witt was shaded towards right. With the fences 500 feet from home plate, the ball had plenty of room to roll. Stengel circled the bases at breakneck speed for an inside-the-park home run that gave the Giants the margin of victory. The third game would break a 1–1 tie. The two teams were locked in a scoreless stalemate through the sixth inning. In the top of the seventh Stengel hit a ball over Babe Ruth's head and the right field wall for another home run. As he jogged around the bases, he thumbed his nose at the players in the Yankees dugout. The Giants did not score again, but Art Nehf shut out the Yankees. "That's two for Stengel, one for the Yankees," Stengel crowed.

While Babe Ruth was laughing along with Stengel—"I don't mind," he said after. "Casey's a lot of fun."—and secretly thinking the gesture was directed at him as a reminder that he wasn't the only home run hitter in the game, Colonel Ruppert was less amused, immediately asking Judge Landis to censure Stengel for his gesture. The Judge demurred. "When a ballplayer breaks up a World Series game with a home run like that, he should be permitted a certain about of exuberance and expression." When this failed to quiet Ruppert, Landis added, "Casey Stengel can't help being Casey Stengel."

Leo Durocher wrote that Landis was always on the side of the ball-player, but apparently there were limits to the judge's tolerance for pranksters and cut-ups. Yogi Berra once heard an interview with Ted Williams where he described Judge Landis, Babe Ruth, and Stengel as the three most significant personalities in the history of the game. "I thought it was interesting that Ted put Judge Landis and Casey together," Berra said. "Casey was always on stage, but one time he said, 'Yogi, do you know what Landis said to me?' I had to say no, and Casey said, 'Stengel, you are good for only one thing. Shoveling manure, horse or cow or donkey. That is the one thing you are good for.'"

As for the nose-thumbing incident, Landis may have downplayed it to the offended Yankees owners, but his message for Stengel was altogether different: "If you do that again, I promise you one thing: you won't receive a dollar of your World Series share." Stengel did not challenge him, but then, he didn't hit any more homers. The Yankees swept the rest of the Series for the franchise's first championship.

Although the Giants lost, Stengel was still the hero of the series. This merely added to his popularity, for he was already a star in New York. McGraw had encouraged Stengel to be himself. "There's one good thing about having you around," McGraw said. "This is too dead a ball club.

I'd rather have someone with a little life—somebody that does things a little out of the way." With McGraw's eyes averted, Stengel indulged himself. When playing the outfield he might pick up a stray newspaper and read the sports pages to any fans within shouting distance (and with the sparse crowds some franchise's drew, Stengel could be quite audible), paying special attention to any mention of himself. "Ah, I see where this fellow Stengel had another good day yesterday," he would read. "Quite a hitter, this Stengel. Quite a hitter."

McGraw's indulgence had its limits. On May 7, 1923, Stengel came to the ballpark directly from a haircut, where the barber had liberally dashed him with hair tonic. When Stengel was brushed back by the opposing pitcher he started a brawl and was ejected from the game. McGraw fined him $200. "What do you expect," said McGraw, "when you report to the park reeking with cheap gin?"

There was something about the man himself that inspired others to laugh. He did not have to speak to be funny. His very manner and bearing seemed to suggest humor. Even his on-field actions seemed comically exaggerated, even if comedy was not Stengel's intention at a given moment. If anyone else had hit an the inside-the-park home run in the 1923 World Series, it would have simply been reported as the play that it was. Casey Stengel was a different matter. Damon Runyon, writing for the *New York Sun*, filed this report from Yankee Stadium:

> This is the way old Casey Stengel ran yesterday afternoon running his home run home.
>
> This is the way old Casey Stengel ran running his home run home to a Giant victory by a score of 5 to 4 in the first game of the World Series in 1923.
>
> This is the way old Casey Stengel ran running his home run home when two were out in the ninth inning and the score was tied, and the ball still bounding inside the Yankee yard.
>
> This is the way—
>
> His mouth wide open.
>
> His warped old legs bending beneath him at every stride.
>
> His arms flying back and forth like those of a man swimming with a crawl stroke.
>
> His flanks heaving, his breath whistling, his head far back. Yankee infielders, passed by Old Casey Stengel as he was running his home run home, say Casey was muttering to himself, adjuring himself to greater speed as a jockey mutters to his horse in a race, saying, "Go on, Casey, go on."
>
> . . . The warped old legs, twisted and bent by many a year of baseball campaigning, just barely held out under Casey until he reached the plate, running his home run home.
>
> Then they collapsed.

Ah, the age of the sportswriter/poet. Most contented themselves with an introductory stanza or two, but Stengel inspired grander fare. Grasping for art, Runyan failed to mention that one of Stengel's shoes had come apart as he had run the bases. Heywood Broun was content to marvel. Employing a turn of phrase that easily have come from his fellow Algonquinite Robert Benchley, he wrote, "It would have been a thrilling sight to see him meet an apple cart or a drugstore window."

"I had been married that summer," Stengel said, "and, out in California, my wife's folks, who had never seen me, read the stories of my deeds with interest and then consternation. They saw things like, 'Casey Stengel carried his creaking bones around the basepaths,' and, 'Hauled from the baseball scrapheap, the aged Casey Stengel,' etc. 'What kind of man did our Edna marry?' asked her mother. 'Will he live long enough for us to find out?'" Stengel, the great talker, was unused to being victimized by someone else's hyperbole: "A lot of the newspaper boys have been kind enough to print nice things about me. But I don't altogether appreciate this talk about creaking joints and the rest of it. I am really not old enough yet to go with crutches and I have done fairly good work this season, if I do say it myself."

Runyon's versifying was merely a prelude to a report that speculated that Stengel hit the game-winning home run because he was a funny guy. "People like to laugh at Casey," Runyon wrote, "Casey likes to make people laugh. He has always been a great comedian, a funny fellow, a sort of clown. The baseball land teems with tales of strange didoes cut by Casey Stengel. . . . Who knows but that 'Bullet Joe' may have been thinking of Casey Stengel more as a comedian than as a dangerous hitter when he delivered that final pitch yesterday afternoon?"

Having inflated Stengel's value as a player, McGraw packaged him with his platoon partner, Cunningham, and shortstop Dave Bancroft, ironically McGraw's other kindred spirit on the club, and traded him to the Boston Braves for outfielder Billy Southworth and pitcher Joe Oeschger. "I should count myself lucky I didn't hit a third home run," Stengel said bitterly, "they might have sent me to Topeka." Resignedly he concluded, "The paths of glory lead only to the Braves."

"This trade was unfairly heralded as an example of John's ingratitude to Bancroft and Stengel, but not by the players themselves," Blanche McGraw wrote. "Anyone who had heard Banny's laughter so often in our Pelham home or waited out Stengel's nocturnal visits in the kitchen would know otherwise. To have played for John McGraw now was a badge of distinction, a guarantee of preferred managing or coaching employment . . . the disciples of John McGraw's methods launching forth."

Perhaps this was true for Bancroft, who immediately became the manager of the Braves. Stengel was given a chance to make the team, but that was all. He was not treated as a disciple, but a hired hand.

As his wife did later, McGraw tried to cloak the trade in sentimentality. Christy Mathewson was running the Braves. It was well known that Mathewson was struggling with tuberculosis and could barely keep his breath, let alone do his job. McGraw and others sought to do it for him. "For the good of baseball and with the desire to do something big for my old friend Matty," McGraw said, "and finally to give to Bancroft the opportunity which is due him to become a big league manager." It was all about friendship. "Matty is the only man in baseball who could get Bancroft away from me."

Yet friendship only went so far with McGraw, as Wilbert Robinson had already discovered. So too had Mathewson. Seven years earlier, McGraw had dealt Mathewson, winner of 372 games for the Giants, to the Cincinnati Reds. "He not only was the greatest pitcher I ever saw, but he is my friend," McGraw explained. "He could stay with the Giants as long as he wanted to. However, I'm convinced his pitching days are over, and he is ambitious to become a manager, and I have helped him to gratify that ambition." Key phrase: "I'm convinced his pitching days are over." Had Mathewson something to offer the Giants beyond his name and reputation, McGraw would have held him. Instead, he used that reputation to benefit the Giants.

As with the Mathewson deal, the real issue for McGraw was that the Giants had problems to address. Stengel was not a true centerfielder. McGraw thought Southworth might be able to do a better job, and if he failed, a rookie named Lewis "Hack" Wilson might be able to do the job. McGraw also had a twenty-year-old shortstop, Travis Jackson, ready to replace Bancroft. At thirty-three and thirty-two respectively, Stengel and Bancroft were entering the decline phase of their careers. Having had strong seasons for consecutive pennant winners, they would never look better than they did at that very minute. "Except for Frankie Frisch," wrote the *New York Times,* "Casey Stengel was the most popular of all the McGraw gladiators." It didn't matter, nor did his friendship with McGraw. "Sentiment," McGraw once said, "has no proper place in managing a ball club. I have allowed a good many players to go in my time and regretted the step, but the needs of the moment made it necessary."

This would be an important lesson for Stengel. With a few exceptions, as a manager he kept his players at a distance and dropped them at the first sign of decline. Ironically, for a man who was known as a comedian, Stengel was not about sympathies but results. In 1951, Joe Page, the Yankees' fading relief specialist, was asked about the circumstances of his release. "Shake my hand?" Page responded when asked about Stengel. "He wasn't even there to say good-bye."

"He was not a warm, cuddly manager, like Tommy Lasorda, put his arm around you and hug you. None of that," said Jerry Coleman. "You've got to remember, Stengel hated to be a nice guy, but he was. He was not a guy to get into your life because he knew that he might have to trade you, and do things to you that you wouldn't like. I think that was one of the reasons he stayed aloof."

With this last trade, Stengel had played for five of the eight National League clubs. Quentin Reynolds wrote, "Every time two owners got together with a fountain pen, Casey Stengel was being sold or bought." When this remark got back to Stengel, he added his own interpretation. "I never played with the Cubs, Cards, or Reds. I guess that was because the owners of those clubs didn't own no fountain pens."

Despite his frustration, Stengel retained his affection for McGraw. "McGraw hired me and he fired me," he said, "but he's still the best manager for whom I ever worked." This was a wise posture to adopt, for John McGraw still had plans for Casey Stengel.

CHAPTER 5

CASEY, WHERE ARE YOUR PANTS?

Stengel played regularly in 1924, but not with the same enthusiasm or effectiveness as he displayed with McGraw. He had gone literally from the top to the bottom, from a pennant winner to a last-place team that would lose 100 games in 1924. All of the circumstances of the trade— going from the hitter-friendly Polo Grounds to cold, expansive National League Park, Bancroft's decision to play him every day rather than pro- tect him from certain pitchers, age, being far from the pennant races— were working against him. His time as an active player was clearly drawing to a close, a conclusion forcefully delivered by Bancroft's deci- sion to restrict him to the bench for the first six weeks of the 1925 sea- son. He played only one game in the outfield and made infrequent pinch- hitting appearances.

Stengel's decline as a player coincided with his marriage. Irish Meusel, a Giants teammate, had introduced him to Edna Lawson during the sum- mer of 1923. They hit it off immediately—Stengel was nothing if not mag- netic. He was young then, and quick. He proposed before the summer was out. Now the direction of his career affected more than one person, and it was obvious his playing days were soon to end. Decisive choices about his future would have to be made.

Prior to the season the owner of the Braves, Judge Emil Fuchs, had purchased a ball club in the low minors, Worcester of the Eastern League. When May rolled around and Worcester was mired in eighth place, Fuchs grasped at the owner's traditional quick fix, the managerial change. Casey Stengel was a natural choice to become Worcester's new manager: he was already on the payroll. Judge Fuchs's central motivation was al- ways to do things as cheaply as possible.

McGraw might have had a hand in the move. Fuchs had for many years been the Giants' attorney and was a friend. McGraw had facilitated his purchase of the Braves as a sinecure for Mathewson. His endorsement of Stengel, tacit or overt, would have considerably influenced Fuchs.

Thus it was that on May 21, 1925, the *New York Times* reported that, "The Worcester Eastern League Baseball club was sold today . . . to Casey Stengel, the Boston National League outfielder." Of course, Stengel had not bought the club. The *Times* had been confused by the many titles that he had assumed upon joining Worcester. Besides being the club's playing manager, Stengel had also been granted the additional title of club president. The position had no great meaning. He had been made the head of a very small operation.

Despite what on the surface appeared to be a promotion, Stengel was worried about his career. In the days before players made large sums of money it was commonplace for a veteran player to play his way down through the minors just as he had played his way up when younger. Some players were known to keep playing into their late forties (and in rare cases, early fifties) going down the minor league ladder level by level. Stengel would be a playing manager, and having just left the majors, felt that he should have begun at a level closer to the major leagues, such as the American Association, International League, or Pacific Coast League. The level of competition was closer to what he had become accustomed to and, more importantly, the pay was better.

The route of return to the majors, always a possibility, was also shorter. Stengel had all of an aging athlete's typical anxieties, concerns, and delusions about prolonging his career. He worried that at some point during the season a contender in the higher minors might wish to claim him for help during the stretch drive and his Worcester entanglements might prevent him from going. At the same time, if he was about to begin his managerial career, he did not want to start so far away from the major leagues.

In the end, worrying was all he could do. The Braves owned his contract and that put him at their mercy. In those days before the advent of organized labor in baseball, players were governed by "The Reserve Clause" of the majors leagues' basic agreement. As Harold Seymour wrote, the reserve clause, "gave the club an exclusive and perpetual option on the player's services." Thus a player was bound to his club not unlike a serf was bound to his lord. Prior to the advent of the commissioner system, the reserve clause was combined with the collusive use of the waiver rule to punitively banish players from the majors; the players truly did serve at the owners' pleasure. Even at distant Worcester, Stengel was a puppet on Fuchs's string.

Despite these nagging concerns, Stengel enjoyed his first season as a manager. The Worcester team traveled by bus, and on the long trips over the winding roads of New England he would stand at the front and lecture, debate, and quiz his players on their attitudes and approaches to the game. The "classic" Stengel, the man who would sometimes teach through dialectic, was beginning to take form. He was discovering that his storytelling could be an extension of his deeper talent for teaching.

The Worcester club responded to Stengel. When Stengel came to town, Worcester held last place with a miserable record of nine wins and fifteen losses. Over the rest of the season they won over sixty percent of their games and made a respectable third-place showing. In his first managerial assignment Stengel had shown that he had the ability to lead.

Stengel also got to know the local baseball establishment. He was fast friends with George Weiss, the president of the Eastern League's New Haven, Connecticut, franchise. Born in 1895, Weiss had been running baseball teams since he was eighteen years old. In 1913, his Hillhouse High School team, which starred future major leaguer "Jumping" Joe Dugan, was state champion. It was Weiss's brainstorm to keep the team together and turn it into a semipro barnstorming unit, the New Haven Colonials.

The Colonials were tremendously successful, in part because of Weiss's ability to attract major league ballplayers to New Haven on Sundays. With blue laws in New York and Boston prohibiting Sunday baseball in those cities, idled stars like Ty Cobb and Babe Ruth played for the Colonials. After the 1915 World Series, the champion Red Sox brought their entire roster to Connecticut to play Weiss's team, prompting baseball owners to promulgate stringent rules on post-Series exhibitions that would cost Babe Ruth a month's suspension seven years later.

Weiss had briefly attended Yale University, but left abruptly when his father's unexpected death required him to take over the family grocery business. If his lack of education slowed him down, no one noticed. Weiss's Colonials did so well that they helped put New Haven's Eastern League franchise, the Profs, on the verge of bankruptcy. In 1919, the Eastern League asked Weiss to buy the Profs.

As a minor league owner, Weiss clashed with Ed Barrow of the Yankees. He somehow arranged to play the Yankees at their Polo Grounds home, a game so unsuccessful that it cost the Yankees more to open up the park than they received at the gate. Later, Weiss hauled Barrow before Judge Landis over a $2,000 guarantee the Yankees had forfeited after Babe Ruth failed to appear at an exhibition in New Haven. Landis supported Weiss; Barrow didn't speak to Weiss again until the 1923 party celebrating the Yankees' first World Series victory. "I feel so good right now," said Barrow, "that I'll shake hands even with you."

But for an argument about a train berth, it might have been Barrow's last chance—and Stengel would never have met his best friend in the game. On December 9, 1923, Weiss and his manager, former Yankees manager "Wild" Bill Donovan, were riding the Twentieth Century Limited. The two had a good-natured argument about which of the two would sleep in the train's upper berth. Donovan wanted to defer to his boss and take the upper berth; Weiss insisted that Donovan's age—he had twenty years on Weiss—entitled him to the lower berth. Donovan gave in. That night, the train crashed outside of Erie, Pennsylvania. Donovan and eight others in Weiss' car were killed, all in lower berths. Weiss was severely injured, requiring four months of hospitalization.

Weiss recovered just in time for Casey Stengel to come to town. Weiss's friendship with Stengel provided definite proof of the theory that opposites attract, for Weiss, taciturn, serious, could not have possessed a personality that was more unlike Stengel's. Still, Weiss seemed to recognize in Stengel a superior intellect and an unparalleled knowledge of the game. Like McGraw before him, Weiss would spend late nights with Stengel discussing theories of baseball. In Weiss's case he did far more listening than talking:

> I was impressed with him from the start. We soon got to be good friends and we'd often sit up half the night, at meetings, talking away—Casey, even then, did most of the talking and I did most of the listening. As the years went on we continued to see each other frequently, and my respect for his talents grew. I never felt that his so-called clowning, his great sense of fun, interfered with his managing or affected his remarkable ability to size up a situation, to know when and when not to gamble . . .

> I suppose I have stayed up later and talked longer—or rather listened longer—with Casey than anybody else in baseball . . . He's dedicated. He is all baseball and the way baseball pours out of him, if you know him that way very long you've simply got to respect him as I did. . . . More than 25 years ago I was convinced that here was a great baseball man.

In his autobiography, Stengel stated that after his first season at Worcester he was looking for new opportunities. "I thought I'd fulfilled my obligation to the Braves," he wrote. More to the point, he had received a better offer, the position of manager of the Toledo Mud Hens. Toledo was part of the American Association, a minor league one step below the majors.

Once again, John McGraw had interceded. The Toledo team, just purchased by a group of investors, had been owned by McGraw. The new owners, baseball neophytes, asked McGraw to recommend someone to run the team—McGraw had just canned the incumbent manager due to a so-called administrative error involving a prospect named Lewis "Hack" Wilson, who had just been drafted by the Cubs at the instigation of Joe McCarthy. McGraw suggested Stengel, whom he said, "can handle and develop players, manage the club properly and in addition has business ability." A final endorsement: "He will produce a successful operation for you," and, he added in an allusion to Stengel's comedic reputation, "one that will appeal to the public."

Stengel strained to take the job, but behind him, like a bloated shadow, loomed Judge Fuchs. He still held Stengel's contract and expected him to honor it. Even if Fuchs could be persuaded to release Stengel, that release would have to be bought, something the Toledo owners hoped to avoid.

Stengel never confronted Fuchs. According to Fuchs, he first learned about the Toledo appointment from a newspaper article. He then inspected the Worcester correspondence, finding two letters. The first was addressed to Mr. Charles D. Stengel, President of the Worcester Ball Club:

> Dear Mr. Stengel:
>   Having an opportunity [to] improve my position by going to a higher classification as manager, I hereby tender my resignation as manager of the Worcester club. I cannot leave without thanking you for your courtesy, consideration and advice, which was of great help in running the club.
>
>   Very truly yours,
>   Casey Stengel

Worcester's president responded:

> Dear Casey:
>   Your letter came as a surprise but we realize that ability should be rewarded. Therefore, I join the fans of Worcester in expressing our appreciation for your outstanding services rendered and wish you luck in your new position. We congratulate Toledo on getting your valuable services.
>
>   Very truly yours,
>   Charles D. Stengel

Having accomplished his final task in office, President Stengel sent a letter to Fuchs resigning his position. Stengel was, at least on paper, free to go to Toledo.

Fuchs raged. He brought the matter before Judge Landis, who offered to negate Stengel's actions and return him to the Braves. Fuchs weighed the offer and then turned it down. "Never mind," Fuchs told the commissioner. "If that's the way Stengel works, let him go. We'll be better off without him." Landis would make an identical judgment about Fuchs just ten years later, when he tried to rent out National League Park for dog racing.

Stengel had won, though there were lingering consequences. There would be a persistent rumor that Judge Landis had unofficially banned Stengel from returning to the majors because of his paper maneuverings and overall attitude. The rumor might have scared off more than one potential employer over the next several years.

The Toledo assignment represented the culmination of Stengel's relationship with John McGraw. Even before Stengel had played for the Giants, McGraw had, directly or indirectly, influenced his career. His first manager, Bill Dahlen, had been one of McGraw's most prized players. Wilbert Robinson had been McGraw's best friend and managerial disciple. At the moment Stengel joined the Boston Braves, the owner, team president, and manager were all indebted to McGraw. It was McGraw himself who saw a manager in Stengel when others saw a clown. Stengel and his new wife had even taken their honeymoon with McGraw, accompanying the Giants on a postseason tour of England, Ireland, and France (Stengel, in full uniform, shook hands with King George V) before returning to New York to spend another week as McGraw's guest. Now the Mastermind had placed his pupil one step away from the major leagues.

Toledo was a wonderful place for an aspiring major league manager to be in 1926. The American Association was loaded with future and former major leaguers. Stengel had many players of the latter variety, including (at various times) former Yankees shortstop Everett Scott, who held the consecutive games played record before Lou Gehrig; Bobby Veach, who had played alongside Ty Cobb at Detroit; pitcher Carl Mays, five-time twenty-game winner in the majors (and the man who threw the pitch that killed Ray Chapman, the only fatality in major league history); "Bullet" Joe Bush; and his old Giants teammate Irish Meusel. With real major leaguers and prospects with which to practice, the only significant difference between Toledo and the major leagues was the quality of the restaurants.

Stengel's salary at Toledo was $10,000 a year plus an unlimited expense account with which to entertain major league scouts. Before Branch Rickey, the visionary general manager of the Cardinals, invented the farm system wherein Major League Baseball teams developed exclusive affiliations with minor league clubs for the purpose of developing major league talent, scouting was done from the ground up. Today, the major league teams are involved in every step of the player development process, from locating a young man playing high school or college ball and signing him to placing him on a minor league team and directing his development. The minor league team on which a prospect is placed is either owned by the major league team itself or it has signed an exclusive agreement with the major league team to use players that the organization sends them. Testifying before Congress in 1959, Stengel explained the relationship this way:

> Later on Mr. Rickey came in and started what was known as what you would say numerous clubs, you know in which I will try to pick up this college man, I will pick up that college boy or I will pick up some corner lot boy and if you picked up the corner lot boy maybe he became just as successful as the college man, which is true. He then had a number of players.

During Stengel's time at Toledo, there were three ways for players to advance in baseball. Major league teams were not allowed to own minor league franchises, and in most cases they did not have the resources to scout every promising amateur in the country. Instead, the lowest level of minor league teams would scout and sign amateurs. The next highest level would scout *them*, and the player's contract would be sold to the highest bidder. This process was repeated at each succeeding level until the player either proved himself incapable of advancing or was sold to the majors. Alternatively, some of the higher classification minor league teams had sufficient scouting resources to identify local or regional prospects who would then be placed in the low majors subject to recall by the signing team. Finally, a major league team might scout and sign a player, then place him with one of the independent minor league clubs.

One of the chief ways a minor league team made money was in the profits it reaped from selling player contracts. As manager, part of Stengel's job was to train and promote his players so as to make them more attractive to major league scouts. Stengel was uncommonly successful at this. He considered himself a teaching manager and so it was natural for him to try to improve his players. That this tendency on his part resulted in the frequent sale of his improved players to higher levels was merely a happy coincidence. The sales helped Stengel because it made the club money and endeared him to ownership, but they also hurt him on the field. He often sold players faster than he could replace them with others of equal talent. His teams in Toledo were erratic, up one year and down the next, due to the constant turnover of personnel. As Stengel himself remarked, "I had three teams, one on the field, one coming, and one going."

The presence of so many veterans allowed Stengel to try putting some of his strategic theories into practice. He could bring young players along slowly by blending in veterans against the tougher pitchers. In this way Stengel could protect the young prospects from their own weaknesses and make them more attractive to major league scouts. "You might say I was already platooning," he said.

The process of experimentation had its brutal moments; Stengel found that baseball rules only allowed for so much improvisation. On May 13, 1926, he threw his whole roster into a game, using twenty-one players in the course of a nine-inning game, including himself and a catcher with a fractured ankle. Stengel's everything-but-the-kitchen-sink tactics earned Toledo a one-run victory (the lame catcher delivered the game-winning hit). On other occasions, Stengel found himself with innings left to play and not enough players to cover the field. Once, down by one run in the bottom of the ninth and the bases loaded, he put himself in as a pinch-hitter for his last catcher. His players begged him not to do it. "So what?" he scoffed. "If I get a base hit, two runs come in and the game's over. If I get out, the game's over anyway." He did neither, walking. The tying run was forced in, and the game went into extra innings. A pitcher was made to catch. Stengel claimed he never lost a game using this tactic until 1955 with the Yankees, when outfielder Hank Bauer, pressed into duty behind the plate, allowed a passed ball with the winning run on third base.

Stengel soon extended his role as educator to cover the whole team. Even the veterans came in for correction. Often, he was able to improve them enough to prolong their careers or even earn them a rare second chance at the majors. Ray Hayworth was a catcher who had failed to stick in the majors after a trial with the Tigers in 1926. He joined Stengel at Toledo in 1929 and registered a .330 batting average, earning him a trip back to the majors. "The key to my going back up was my year with Casey Stengel. He was a great teacher," Hayworth told Eugene Murdock. "I used to say that any player who wanted a career in the big leagues should spend at least one year with Casey Stengel." Stengel recalled that not all of the veterans were as receptive as Hayworth. "In the minors, I always liked to work with the young fellows, but it wasn't always possible to do what I liked down there. The old-timers couldn't believe that they still weren't big leaguers."

The manager that Stengel would become was beginning to manifest himself. He had already begun his practice of having long clubhouse meetings, or "skull sessions" as they were sometimes called in those days. He would gather the team in the center of the clubhouse and favor them with long monologues. He would often carry a stick or a fungo bat with him and like a professor striking his lectern with a pointer he would punctuate his points with the dull thud of the bat. "I couldn't keep a straight face," said Hayward. "He was the funniest man I ever listened to. But he'd get his point across."

Jocko Conlan, an outfielder for Toledo in 1930 (later a Hall of Fame umpire), remembered:

Games started at three in the afternoon. He'd call the meetings at ten-thirty, and they were the only meetings I can ever recall in baseball where the players got there early. Not just early, but an hour early, because Casey wouldn't wait until ten-thirty to start talking. He started in the minute he got to the clubhouse and nobody wanted to miss anything . . . he'd say sweetly, "Are all my boys here?" We'd have lost the ball game the day before, and he'd start in on what we had done wrong. He'd give an exhibition of fielding and pitching and hitting and base-running and everything; he would go on and on and on. It was great.

Sometimes he would transmit other things besides his point. While demonstrating to one of his players how to hit the curveball, Stengel accidentally supplied extra emphasis to one of his lectures by striking a spittoon with his bat, splattering his pupil. The player assumed the blow was intentional and became upset.

"Well, that's the way I hit 'em," said Stengel, and rushed out of the clubhouse. As he stepped onto the field, some of the women in the stands began calling to him. "They got some crazy women here in Toledo. . . . What are they hollering about? The game doesn't even start for half an hour yet," he said. Then he stopped, looked down. "Why, I haven't got my pants on." He had been in such a hurry to escape the clubhouse that he had forgotten to dress. For the rest of the season, Stengel was subject to a most unusual kind of jeering: "Casey," the fans would shout, "where are your pants?"

In addition to his veterans, Stengel had the usual collection of prospects, has-beens, and never-weres. An example of the latter, one of Stengel's best players in Toledo was a former Phillies teammate, outfielder De Witt Wiley "Bevo" LeBourveau. Despite four years of occasional use with the Phillies (1919 to 1922) he had not been able to establish himself. In the minors, it was as if he were a different man. In Stengel's first year in Toledo LeBourveau hit in twenty-seven straight games, compiled a .377 average and made over two hundred hits. This stellar performance made him attractive to other teams in other leagues and Stengel sold him. Unfortunately, LeBourveau had some emotional problems. Playing the outfield left him too much time to think. If the game was slow, he would go "almost insane." Off the field, he would get into clubhouse arguments of such intensity that he would have to be moved. As a result, LeBourveau was always returned to Stengel . . . who would cheerfully sell him again. LeBourveau was sold three times by Stengel for a total of $60,000. The men who bought him: John McGraw (who used him to threaten the job security of holdout Edd Roush), Connie Mack, and Branch Rickey. Even geniuses make a few mistakes.

LeBourveau was a player in stasis, an uncommon occurrence. More usual were players on the way up or down. The latter variety was always in greater supply than the former. Among the best of these was Bobby Veach, who at thirty-eight and thirty-nine years old had two seasons for Stengel that were superior to any he had recorded in the majors. He was the driving force behind the 1927 Toledo team, hitting .363 with 145 runs batted in and 133 runs scored.

Third baseman Heinie Groh, thirty-eight, famous for his bottle-bat, had starred with the Giants and the Cincinnati Reds and was a veteran of five World Series. Jeff Pfeffer, thirty-eight, was a teammate and antagonist of Stengel's on the Dodgers. Twice a twenty-game winner in the majors, he became Toledo's pitching ace. Wilbur Cooper, thirty-four, had won over 200 games during fifteen major league seasons. Infielder Freddie Maguire had failed in two trials with McGraw's Giants but Stengel was able to help him back to the majors for a four-season stay. A high concentration of these faded players caused Stengel's 1926 team to be referred to as "Stengel's Ancients."

Among the legitimate prospects, Stengel had high hopes that pitcher Roy Parmalee might be sold for as much as $100,000, especially after he pitched well in an exhibition against Connie Mack's strong Philadelphia Athletics. These hopes were dashed when Parmalee was hammered in a start with John McGraw in attendance. When Stengel went to remove the pitcher from the game he told him to feign injury. "I want to get you out of here gracefully," he said. The deception did not work. Casey had to settle for only $35,000 from McGraw that night. ("The boy's lousy," said McGraw. "A long trip for nothing"). Parmalee would eventually help pitch the Giants into the 1933 World Series. Others to graduate from Stengel's Toledo club to a prominent role in the majors included the shortstop Woody English and the lumbering first baseman Sam Leslie.

The greatest testament to Stengel's abilities as a salesman, or perhaps to the bond of trust between he and McGraw, was sore-armed right-hander Ray Lucas. Lucas, twenty, was 3–10 with a 4.28 ERA when Stengel convinced his former master that the pitcher was a prospect. McGraw bit and bought the youngster for the Giants. There, in a career that began that September and lasted fifty-six innings, Lucas would walk thirty-six batters and strike out five, or 0.80 per nine innings, a record for a career of his length.

Such a disparate group, a microcosm of an America not yet homogenized by mass media and fast food franchises or (momentarily) leveled by New Deal–era redistributions of wealth and educational opportunities, sometimes required Stengel to be not only a manager but a psychologist as well. On one occasion, one of Stengel's more senior players came to him asking for a raise. Toledo had just signed a prospect out of college for more money than the veteran player was making. As he had been around for four years, the player reasoned that he was entitled to more money than the prospect. Stengel's Solomonic reply was that the player had spent four years in college learning to play baseball. "He had to pay his own expenses, and his tuition there, and room and board . . . he must have spent about five grand. Where were you those four years? Getting paid for learning."

"I never thought of that," said the player, and troubled his manager no longer.

During the early part of Stengel's first year with Toledo he contented himself with experimenting and learning the league. Having satisfied himself in this regard by mid-July, Stengel proceeded to rebuild the Mud Hens' pitching staff. The team rallied enough to put pressure on the league's front-runners, going 87–77 to finish in fourth place. The team had placed seventh in 1925, so this was a satisfactory improvement, almost a mirror-image of their 77–90 finish in 1924. The fans responded at the gate. *The Sporting News* noted, "Casey Stengel and his diamond troops are very popular among the rank and file in this city." By July, attendance was up 30,000 over the year before. When the number of players Stengel sold was taken into account with the team's improved standing, 1926 was a great year for the Toledo franchise.

Sometime after the season, Stengel finally accepted that his playing career was over. He had played every day at Worcester in 1925 (hitting .320 with ten home runs), and about half the time at Toledo in 1926. For the next five seasons he took the occasional at-bat in a pinch-hitting role, but that was all; the spotlight was reserved for his prospects.

The next year, 1927, with his platooning in full force, Stengel's Mud Hens exploded on the league, winning 101 games and the Little (minor league) World Series. Toledo had never previously finished in first place, let alone won a minor-league championship. Stengel was the toast of Toledo.

As spectacular as the season was, the victory almost did not happen. Although the team opened the season strongly and led the race from June on, Stengel succumbed to the temptation of adding veteran players as insurance for the stretch run (the theory generally being that more experienced players will be better able to handle the pressures of a pennant race). To this end Stengel signed several major league veterans: Everett Scott, less than a year removed from his last major league action; Irish Meusel, cut by the Dodgers earlier that year; Jesse Barnes, winner of twenty-five games for McGraw in 1919; and pitcher "Bullet" Joe Bush, victim of Stengel's inside the park World Series home run in 1923.

For every action there is an equal and opposite reaction. The addition of veterans to a roster often has the effect of depriving of playing time the very players who propelled the team in the first place. Toledo was no exception. The team plunged into a dramatic slump that coincided exactly with the arrival of the new personnel, losing twelve of nineteen games on its final road trip of the season. Kansas City and Milwaukee passed Toledo in the standings.

Learning on the job, Stengel recognized the cause of the downturn and restored his original players to positions of prominence, even going so far as to release his good friend Meusel, who had hit .354 with power, but was unable to make the plays in the outfield. The team recovered and won the league championship by sweeping a doubleheader on the final day of the season.

Stengel came away with the understanding that the wholesale addition of veterans is not necessarily a beneficial act. Although in the future Stengel did not hesitate to add players late in the season, he was more careful to ascertain the exact needs of his team and then scrutinize whether players available to him fit that niche. The veterans were used to supplement, rather than supplant, Stengel's regulars. In the future, Stengel would occasionally forget this rule and devote too much playing time to veterans like Enos Slaughter—as Billy Martin forcefully reminded him during the 1956 World Series—but for the most part, Stengel went with youth.

Stengel was almost not allowed to participate in his team's revival. In September he was suspended indefinitely by the president of the American Association following an incident with an umpire at Toledo's Swayne Field. The umpire had rendered a decision against Toledo, calling one of Stengel's batters out on a close play at first base. Stengel's protestations resulted in his removal from the game. This in and of itself was not an unusual event for Stengel. The action that resulted in his suspension occurred afterwards. As Stengel left the field, he stood before the spectators, shouting, gesturing, urging, inciting. The crowd came streaming out of the bleachers and onto the field in pursuit of the umpire, no longer merely spectators, but an avenging mob. The umpire escaped, but only after receiving a mild pummeling.

Stengel was accused of inciting the crowd to attack the umpire and was suspended. Strangely, the incident repeated itself in April 1930. With the Mud Hens trailing Milwaukee in extra innings, Jocko Conlan doubled in the tying runs, only to have them negated because, ''Umpire Joe Rue . . . ruled that the Toledo reserves did not move fast enough to allow leftfielder Bennet of Milwaukee to field the ball which landed near or among them.'' Once again Stengel lost his argument, and once again a riot started, though Stengel's role in its beginnings is unclear. Stengel was suspended indefinitely. Judge Landis was consulted by the American Association president, who hoped the commissioner would permanently remove Stengel.

Once again, Stengel was spared the Judge's wrath, but just barely. Called to the judge's Chicago office, Stengel was given a brief, direct hearing. "If you ever behave again like you did toward these umpires," Landis thundered, "I'm going to throw you out of baseball for the rest of your life. Now *get out!*" Subsequently, two of the umpires involved in the incident were suspended for falsely incriminating Stengel. It is doubtful that Landis apologized.

These were not his only suspensions by the American Association during his stay in Toledo. He was frequently in trouble. He had carried down to the minors a hot temper and a penchant for fighting. As a young man, Casey had been quick to his fists. Now he was approaching middle-age, and though still temperamental, he was slowly beginning to see the light: "I got in a couple of fights and the league suspended me a total of twenty-six days. I had to watch my team from the stands. And my owners said, "Look, now, what's the use of having you hired as manager? We'd rather have you become the manager and stay the manager and let somebody else sit in the grandstand."

Following the season it was strongly rumored that he would be leaving the Mud Hens to take command of a National League franchise and would be succeeded in Toledo by former White Sox manager Eddie Collins. The rumor may have been only a rumor. It is also possible that Stengel turned down a job offer. There were three managerial changes made in the National League during the 1927–1928 off-season. One of these open positions, St. Louis, went to Bill McKechnie, a sought after manager who had already won a World Series in Pittsburgh. One of the other two openings was with the Boston Braves. The team was still owned by Judge Fuchs, and it is unlikely that Fuchs would have offered Stengel a job after Stengel's slippery exit from Worcester two years before. The final managerial position was in Philadelphia. It is entirely possible that given Stengel's miserable experience there during his playing days, he might have chosen to pass over this opportunity and wait for one more to his liking—something like McGraw's job in New York. He re-signed with Toledo for another year.

Stengel's championship did not represent the founding of a Toledo dynasty. The next year the team was back down in the standings, finishing sixth. Stengel had sold some players, and the veterans from the prior year also had to be excised. Unlike the younger players who could at least be redeemed for cash, when the older players departed they left nothing but empty lockers. The Mud Hens were victims of their own success.

In 1929 Toledo suffered through 100 losses and landed in eighth place. In 1930 they managed a .500 record and a third-place finish, but in 1931 it was back to 100 losses and last place. The decline of Toledo's fortunes was partially attributable to the volatility of minor league rosters, but the true nails in Toledo's coffin were hammered in by the arrival of the Great Depression in 1929. The most famous anecdote from Stengel's Toledo days has the manager noticing that many of his players seemed to be paying more attention to the stock reports than they were to baseball. Later, while giving one of his famous lectures, he discovered to his chagrin that a few of his players were reading stock quotations rather than following his learned discourse. Interrupting his own comments (something he was used to doing anyway; digressions were his life), Stengel said:

> Now, you boys haven't been playing very well, but I know there's been a lot on your minds. I see a lot of you reading about the stock market, and I know you're thinking about it. Now, I'm gonna do you a favor since you're so interested in Wall Street. I'm gonna give you a tip on the market. . . . Buy Pennsylvania Railroad. . . . Because if you don't start playing better ball there's gonna be so many of you riding trains outta here that railroad stocks are a cinch to go up!

Despite Stengel's protestations, the stock market would finish him in Toledo, though perhaps not in the way he thought. After the pennant in 1927, the Mud Hens' owners borrowed heavily to make improvements on Swayne Field, their home park (ironically designed like Yankee Stadium with a short right field fence). They were still paying off these debts in 1929 when the stock market collapsed. The bank panic that followed stripped the club of its savings.

Stengel could not simply vanish with his team's financial well being. Like a lame duck president he had to finish out his term. The time of Toledo as a credit to his résumé was over, but he could still develop himself as a manager. He could also enjoy himself. Shortstop Dick Bartell, Stengel's contemporary, remembered that Stengel had a unique way of dealing with the effects of the Depression. He gathered his players and said, ''Boys, write down what you think you're worth on a card and put it on your back. We're going to have an auction to meet the payroll.'' The story is outlandish, but not impossible given an economic situation wherein many minor leagues were not completing their schedules.

Stengel was sometimes forced to turn to unlikely candidates to complete his roster. Perhaps imitating John McGraw, who at one time kept

Charles Victory Faust, an untalented tuberculosis patient who fancied himself a pitcher, on his roster as a good luck charm, Stengel carried Al Herman. Herman had showed up for Stengel's first Toledo spring training claiming to be a pitcher. The Mud Hens had never heard of him. Herman's fastball was anything but, and he had a contorted, stunted wind-up, apparently because all of his previous pitching experience had come within the narrow confines of his Bronx apartment. Stengel kept him anyway. "Casey Stengel admits that Al may not win many games as a pitcher," reported *The Sporting News*, "but he is a good luck token on the bench if nothing else."

Early in the 1926 season, in a game against the Minneapolis Millers, Stengel used up all of his pitchers and was forced to bring in Herman to protect the lead (learning to manipulate a pitching staff was the aspect of managing Stengel found most challenging. In later years he would confer part of this responsibility on an experienced pitching coach, such as Jim Turner or Johnny Sain). The Minneapolis batters swung at Herman's pitches and succeeded in hitting the ball for great distances—straight up. It was, as the old baseball saying goes, as if they were hitting in a chimney. Herman retired three batters on three pop-ups and Toledo won the game. As Stengel walked off the field, Mike Kelly, the Millers' manager asked him, "Don't you think, Casey, that you're underestimating this league?" Stengel used Herman eight times in 1926. In fifteen innings he walked eleven batters and struck out only one. He then vanished from baseball.

Accessibility was a constant problem for managers in those days. Almost anybody who thought they had a fastball felt free to show up at the ballpark and demand an audition. Bill Zuber's uncle was an acquaintance of Stengel's When Zuber was seventeen, he and his uncle took a trip to Toledo. "My uncle introduced me to him [Stengel] and he sent me down to third base where I told him I had played around home. He started knocking me grounders. The first nine went right though my legs. I was scared stiff, and that's why I couldn't field the ball. Finally, he hit me the tenth. It bounded off my chest and dropped in front of me . . . Casey looked at me kind of funny and said, 'Why don't you become a pitcher?' It was the best advice I ever got, although I still don't know whether he was kidding or not."

Stengel was always trying to win, even when he must have known that he couldn't, and he resented having it pointed out to him that he was not succeeding. After one Toledo fan who was too vociferous in his criticism Stengel felt compelled to respond to his criticism in a very personal, physical way. "I only won one fight in my life and that was at Toledo. There was a man in the bleachers who was on me very bad one day and after the game was over I hunted him down and pulled him under the stands and flattened him. But I really lost that one too. They fined me a hundred dollars and suspended me for ten days."

When all else failed, there was always the hope that spring training would bring some prospect down from the Giants who might provide a spark for the team, or at the very least be educable. Like all of the best professors, Stengel preferred to work with the most talented students. The young Giants were aware of Casey's covetous eye, said *The New York Times* in 1930: "In addition to Manager McGraw . . . the Giants had Casey Stengel to urge them on. Casey is Toledo's manager and his presence on the practice field symbolized to the Giants Toledo, to which point Giants are sometimes shipped. Often when a Giant felt like standing still . . . the sight of Stengel looking in his direction was enough to send him sprinting after a fly."

The Toledo club struggled with the Depression for two years. All around the country whole minor leagues were going bankrupt and dissolving. The infrastructure of baseball was collapsing as the most local leagues, always chancy operations to begin with, failed to complete their schedules and sent their players home. In 1931 the Mud Hens were finally forced to declare bankruptcy. No longer able to afford Stengel, the club let him go at the end of the season. For the first time since he began his managerial career in 1925, Stengel was without a job. He retreated to his home in Glendale, California (he had relocated to Edna's part of the world) to puzzle out his next move.

In the aftermath of Toledo's failure Stengel was called to Judge Landis's office in New York. The club's financial records were in complete disarray and the commissioner was interviewing the principals of their operation to make sure that improprieties had not been behind the bankruptcy.

Landis asked Stengel if he had in any way unduly profited from his position. "No, sir, I did not," said Stengel. Then, pushing some papers towards the judge he added, "If you want to add this to the list of debts the club owes, here's a couple of personal notes for money I advanced myself."

Judge Landis found no wrongdoing in Toledo—after 1920, he tried to find no wrongdoing whenever possible—but this episode, when taken together with Stengel's slippery exit from Worcester, convinced many baseball insiders that Landis had quietly blacklisted Stengel. There was little room in Landis's conception of the baseball universe for personnel that did not take baseball's rules and scriptures seriously.

Late in 1931, Max Carey, a Pittsburgh teammate of Stengel's, was appointed manager of the Brooklyn Dodgers and Casey applied for a coaching position. There was a slight delay in the Dodgers' answer as they attempted to ascertain whether the return of Casey Stengel to the majors was acceptable to the lords of baseball.

CHAPTER 6

THE NEW RIOT ACT

"Now the best thing I got to go and tell you is my baseball experiences when I had trouble in Brooklyn. They finally said, 'We can't have a comedian running a ball club.' They said, 'Do you know he's running a $600,000 investment? How could you have a simpleton like that run a team?'"

—Casey Stengel

Long before the majestic "Boys of Summer" rose to do battle with Stengel's Yankees in the fifties, there were the Daffiness Boys. Since Brooklyn had gone to the World Series in 1920, it had functioned less as a competitive baseball team than as a home for wayward players. The Dodgers were not a team of losers or underachievers; in many senses they were not a team at all. Rather, they were a collection of individuals who had no idea how to work in concert to achieve success on the baseball field. As an organization, the Dodgers as they were composed in the twenties and thirties frequently made the day-to-day operations of the team itself a rather low priority. Thus, the players who made up the Brooklyn Dodgers were not assembled with any grand plan in mind, but rather with the idea that a product, any product, had to be put on the field for the patrons. It did not so much matter what it was, so long as it was just there. The players, a combination of transients and seemingly permanent inmates (players who were great by Brooklyn standards but would have been unexceptional if ever released to the league at large) were well aware of their status, something that made cohesion, let alone a pretense of optimism, impossible.

Unlike many teams locked in a downward spiral there was something about the Dodgers that lent an air of comedy to what anywhere else would have been an atmosphere of resignation, frustration, and apathy. It was as if the players, freed of the grinding pressure of the pennant race, were able to play a lighter, more carefree brand of baseball. The more they played this way, the more they endeared themselves to their fans, the residents of the borough of Brooklyn. Thus, the Dodgers were known as the Daffiness Boys not because they lost, but because they lost boldly and spectacularly, and because they were loved.

The Dodgers lost in ways that became folklore with countless retellings. It was said that the Dodgers had once tripled into a triple play. They didn't; in reality they only doubled into a double play. This was bad enough, but the Dodgers' reputation for ineptitude was so great that it was believable that they had done something even worse.

Until 1931, the manager of the Dodgers had still been Uncle Robbie, the 1914 incumbent. In his long years in Brooklyn he had grown corpulent, complacent, and profane. The organization feared what the response of the Brooklyn fans might be if Robbie was removed. In those days before national television, the fortunes of a baseball team were heavily dependent on the good will of the localities in which they played. An unpopular change in personnel could translate quickly into a decline in attendance. The Dodgers, never financially sound, could not afford to sacrifice customers on the altar of pragmatism—a misguided notion since the team was losing money anyway.

In 1931 a series of events occurred which changed the Brooklyn ownership and ultimately brought Stengel to the team. The changes stemmed from a business transaction made almost two decades earlier. In order to finance the construction of Ebbets Field, the problematic but soon to be endlessly romanticized home of the Dodgers, Charles Ebbets was forced to sell a fifty-percent interest in his club to Brooklyn developers Ed McKeever and his younger brother Steve. Out of this partnership a dual ownership was created. Charles Ebbets was named president of the Brooklyn Dodgers National League Company, which owned the baseball team. Ed McKeever was made president of the Ebbets/McKeever Exhibition Company, a separate entity that owned the stadium. McKeever was vice president of the Dodgers and Ebbets was vice president of the company that ran Ebbets Field.

Charles Ebbets died in April 1925. Ed McKeever caught pneumonia while attending the funeral—Ebbets's casket was too large for the grave and the assembled mourners had to wait for more than an hour in a driving rain while the site was excavated—and died shortly thereafter. His half of the club passed on to "Judge" Steve McKeever, a less than vigorous old man with a colostomy bag as a conversation piece. Born in 1853, McKeever predated the Brooklyn Bridge and had in fact helped build it, he and his brother having made their fortunes installing plumbing, gas, and steam fixtures on the span.

Ebbets's share went to his daughters, which is to say his sons-in-law.

Unlike their late relatives, the various McKeever and Ebbets heirs could not get along. Each group wanted control of the club. The resultant power struggle, permanently inconclusive, had the lasting effect of subjecting the club to total paralysis. With executive power split fifty-fifty, consensus between the two ownership groups was a prerequisite to any kind of movement.

The animosity between the Ebbets and McKeever families was so great that neither side would approve the other's dealings. The two camps settled into a long stalemate. The Ebbets heirs were willing to sell, but could not find a buyer so long as McKeever would not relinquish his half of the club. "I'm in baseball because I love the game," he said. "I'm going to stay in it until I die. And when I'm gone, my children and my grandchildren will carry on in my place. But I'm here to stay. Make that as strong as you like" (he never did sell—his family owned a piece of the team into the Los Angeles years). Neglected, the club suffered a serious decline both on the field and financially.

The internecine hostility extended to Wilbert Robinson as well. Uncle Robbie's contract expired during the winter of 1929. McKeever, who hated Robbie, refused to authorize an extension, while the Ebbets heirs refused to consider anyone else. John Heydler, the National League president, stepped in to mediate, with the result that Robinson was brought back on a two-year contract.

In an effort to give a semblance of order to the club's day-to-day operations, Robinson was made club president. This was satisfactory to no one. With this so-called promotion, Robinson was placed in the unenviable position of acting as a proxy for two groups which were permanently fractured. Realizing that his promotion did nothing to address the organization's underlying problem, and moreover that being the business head of an organization that was drifting into receivership was beyond his talents, Robinson did nothing. He did, however, enjoy the better office that came with the president's job—until he realized that the path to his office lay through McKeever's office. It was like a junkyard dog had been stationed at his doorstep. After awhile, Robbie gave up on the presidential suite.

Perhaps this state of homelessness contributed to his decision to remain as manager. After half-hearted overtures to Max Carey, who came on as coach, and minor league manager Spencer Abbott (who managed in the American Association, International League, and Pacific Coast League, but never in the majors), outfielder Zack "Buck" Wheat was given the job on a provisional basis. Robinson never left the bench, supervising Wheat in street clothes, inexorably sliding back into the job.

Eventually Heydler stepped in to break the impasse. Robinson was fired, with McKeever finally assuming the title of club president. Robinson's replacement in the dugout was Maximillian Carnarius, better known from his days as a star outfielder with the Pirates as Max Carey. Carey's career had flowered during the dead ball era. His specialty was the stolen base; Carey led the National League in steals ten times. His National League record for lifetime steals, 738, endured for thirty-five years. Where Robinson was felt to be plodding—no Robinson team ever led the league in stolen bases—Carey, forty-two, was expected to be aggressive. It was thought that he would bring the swashbuckling style of his playing days to Brooklyn.

There were good reasons why Robbie's Dodgers did not run. The park was small and favored offense. The home run era had made the stolen base an ancillary tool beginning just twelve years earlier; Robbie had had time to adjust. In 1916, the Dodgers had stolen 187 bases. By 1924 they were down to thirty-four (there was a brief resurgence in 1927 when the team was joined by—who else?—Max Carey). The whole league had had time to adjust; in 1931, the St. Louis Cardinals stole 114 bases. The other seven teams combined to steal 348 bases.

Finally, simply, the Dodgers were slow. "If Carey can make the Brooklyn club, with its present personnel, into a base-stealing aggregation," wrote *Baseball Magazine*, "it will not only help make that team more attractive but it will also stamp the new manager as a magician before whose feats those of Merlin, Hermann the Great, Houdini and Thurston will look like simple card-tricks." Added Dan Daniel, "It is the most intriguing team in the league."

When Casey Stengel was finally "engaged as head coach and first lieutenant" on January 4, 1932, he joined a team that was trying to remake itself all at once. Befitting a fresh start, the club distanced itself from the Robinson era by dispensing with the "Robins" appellation and choosing a new name. Resisting such suggestions from fans as "Canaries" (a variation on Carey's real name), "Speed Boys" (for the strategy that Carey was expected to employ; the fan who suggested the name told the *Brooklyn Eagle* "This is synonymous with Carey as a player, and brother, believe me, if he wasn't the personification of speed I don't know my onions"), "Tip-Tops" (for Brooklyn's 1914–1915 Federal League entry), and a menagerie of other animal names including Carey's own suggestion, the inexplicable "King-Bees," the team chose to revert to its earliest name, the Dodgers.

Max Carey was the wrong man with whom to try to make a clean break from the past. By 1932 the National League was dominated by the power game that Ruth had inaugurated for a number of years (Chuck Klein and Mel Ott would tie for the league lead that year with thirty-eight homers; in 1930 Hack Wilson had set a league record with fifty-six), but it was the antiquated bunt and run philosophy of the pre-Ruthian years that Carey would bring to Brooklyn.

A variety of forces had combined to change the way the game was played since those days. Until 1920, the game focused on speed and place hitting. Batters would choke up on their bats and swing down on the ball hoping to pound it into the ground and then beat out the in-fielder's throw to first. The ball did not carry very well, so pitchers did not try to strike out hitters but instead would attempt to induce fly balls to the outfield. There was little chance of a fly ball leaving the park. Home runs happened only occasionally; fans rooted for doubles and triples in-stead. Whereas today the top home run hitter in a given year might hit fifty or sixty long-balls, a league leader of the National League in the teens might hit only ten. Many of these would result not from balls being hit over the fences but rather from hits that eluded the outfielders long enough for the batter to circle the bases. Final scores of 1–0 and 2–1 were commonplace.

Hereafter this would be known as the "dead-ball" era because the ball was soft and could not be hit for distance. Additionally, only one ball was used per game. This ball would be kicked, cut, and spit on by both sides such that by the second inning the hard white ball with which the game had started had been transformed into a soggy brown one. The crack of the bat was reduced to a dull squish, and when a long game dragged into the late afternoon, the muddy ball blended into the shad-ows and became virtually invisible to the hitter.

Pitchers also had special advantages in this era. They were allowed to deface the ball in a variety of ways. The pitcher was allowed the spitball, the shineball, and the cutball, and might have recourse to the emery ball as well. With any of these an experienced pitcher could make the ball flutter and dive in unpredictable ways.

Two things occurred to alter the situation and bring on the "lively ball" era. In 1920, Ray Chapman, the starting shortstop for the Cleveland In-dians, was killed by a pitch thrown by Carl Mays of the Yankees. In the aftermath of the incident, the only fatality ever to occur as a result of a hit batsman in a major league game, it was claimed that due to the dark-ened condition of the baseball Chapman never even saw the pitch that killed him. The rules governing the condition of baseballs were immedi-ately changed to require the use of multiple balls in one game. As a ball became marked in some way it would be instantly removed from the game. The various trick pitches were also outlawed based on the assump-tion that they were hard to control and might cause injury. Batters could see what they were swinging at for the first time since the game was in-vented. Batting averages rose accordingly.

The second force to reshape the game was called Babe Ruth. In 1919,

Ruth hit a then-astounding twenty-nine home runs. In 1920, the year he was relocated to the Yankees, Ruth nearly doubled that total, hitting fifty-four. Despite Harry Frazee's protestations that Ruth's home runs were, "more spectacular than useful," (antipathy can lead one to say the dumbest things) the owners discovered something new: the public loved home runs and hung on every swing of Ruth's bat. Unfortunately, the rest of baseball could not provide similar attractions. In 1920 Ruth hit more homers than any other *team* in the American League. To compensate, the owners decided to artificially stimulate home runs by introducing a new ball that would fly farther when struck.

The nature of the game did not change overnight, but within a few years a complete transformation had occurred. Rather than trying to bunt or "butcher" the ball (Stengel's term for swinging down on the ball) for infield hits, players took hard, unmeasured uppercut swings in an attempt to hit the ball for distance. The game of John McGraw's early years, "inside baseball," disappeared. It was replaced by a slower game in which runners advanced one base at a time, hit by hit, or rounded the bases all at once, propelled by a home run.

Carey hired Stengel because he thought his former teammate understood what he was trying to accomplish:

> Casey Stengel wasn't with Pittsburgh long. . . . But he cooperated with me better than any other player I have ever known. He would generally wait until the pitcher had two strikes on him before he attempted to hit. That gave me the finest possible opportunity to steal. But it wasn't a one-sided proposition. I helped Casey quite as much as he helped me. I drew him many a pitch-out by taking long leads and then darting back to the bag. I continually worried the pitcher and very often got him in the hole. As a result he would either pass Casey or lay one over where Casey could hit it. We had a neat little combination all to ourselves while it lasted.

In evolutionary terms, Carey's Dodgers were neither fish nor fowl nor duckbilled platypus. They had power, but not quite enough for the park. They had speed, but only enough for Carey to get himself in trouble. Ebbets Field deterred the construction of the Go-Go Dodgers. As originally constructed, the park possessed the spacious pastures that allowed triples and inside-the-park home runs. In the ensuing years, its dimensions were gradually reduced until its close fences favored the power hitter.

Carey didn't notice, but in 1932 the Dodgers' main strength was home run power, epitomized by outfielders Hack Wilson and Lefty O'Doul. The Dodgers rose from fourth place to third but their improvement in the standings was more attributable to improved power production (forty-one more homers than the year before) than to the twelve stolen bases that Carey added over the previous year.

Undeterred, Carey stuck with the running game. In 1933, the team added another twenty-one stolen bases but lost much of its power and dropped from third to sixth place. As Bill James wrote, for Carey, "it was easier to teach his youngsters to run often than to teach them to run successfully." Burt Shotton, then managing the Phillies, once said, "My boys run with all the legs they've got, but I can't run the bases for them." This was a point that Carey had failed to absorb. Second baseman Tony Cuccinello, a fine player despite being a station-to-station baserunner, said, "He wanted everybody to do the things he did as a player, which was impossible."

In line with his philosophy, Carey's first move as Dodgers manager had been to trade offense for defense. Babe Herman's spring 1932 holdout gave him an excuse. On March 14, Herman, a .340 hitter in six seasons with the club, catcher Ernie Lombardi, and third baseman Wally Gilbert were sent to the Cincinnati Reds in exchange for Cuccinello, third baseman Joe Stripp, and catcher Clyde Sukeforth. Herman's power and personality would be missed. Lombardi would blossom into a Hall of Fame hitter. (This trade was cited by Bill James as "The Most Lopsided Trade of the Decade" in his *Historical Baseball Abstract.*)

Carey had wanted to combine Stripp and Cuccinello with holdover power hitters Del Bissonette and shortstop Glen Wright to create a "dream infield." What he didn't know was that at the moment of the trade Bissonette and Wright were essentially finished. After Bissonette suffered a season-ending leg injury, Lefty O'Doul, the team's remaining power threat, had to be traded to obtain a first baseman. Carey's dream infield obliterated the team offense. He later blamed the front office for the trade.

The front office was not about to bail him out, though several of the directors tripped over themselves trying to ensure that it was their faction that helped the team. After O'Doul was traded to the Giants for first baseman Sam Leslie in June 1933, the Dodgers outfield consisted of Johnny Frederick, Danny Taylor, Buzz Boyle, and Hack Wilson—an aggregation that could hit a bit but screamed "triple" when in the field. When Carey asked for help, the best option the team could produce was minor league slugger Joe Hutcheson of the Southern League. A professional ballplayer since 1926, in 1929 he was purchased by Memphis of the Southern League and became a fixture there. Though he had recorded battering averages as high as .380 and slugged up to twenty-three home runs in a season, he failed to advance due to his lack of speed on defense.

Hutcheson enjoyed a torrid first week as a Dodger. In his first game he hit two home runs off of the otherwise invulnerable Carl Hubbell (Hubbell allowed just six home runs all year on his way to a 1.66 ERA in 309 innings). That was the high point of his major league career; pitchers quickly discovered that he was easily fooled by high pitches and breaking balls. He endured an 0-for-37 streak at the plate. Once, after failing to do anything productive with a rainbow curve, he shouted, "Why, these pitchers don't want me to hit!"

"That's about the size of it, Hutch," Stengel said.

That was the best the Dodgers could do, state the obvious. McKeever was full of semi-sincere wishes: "If I had my way I would spend a million dollars to give Brooklyn a winner again," he said. "I would like to see a greater Ebbets Field that would seat 100,000 spectators. Brooklyn has as large a population from which to draw as the Yanks and Giants. We have more actual fans, better fans. A stadium to seat 100,000 would mount up into heavy money. But I firmly believe that the investment would be safe and sound and I stand ready to do my share as a director any time." McKeever knew very well that the Ebbets heirs were not going to be contributing any matching funds. Charles Ebbets's entire worth had been his share of the ball club, and this had already been leveraged by the family.

Not that the board would have known what to do with a million dollars had they been able to spend it. Robbie had once said, "What do you expect of a ball club with a board of directors like ours; a plumber, a hatter, a lawyer, and a butcher? We're lucky to keep out of an asylum." As bankers increasingly came to dominate board meetings, baseball sense decreased proportionately. One banker, upon hearing that a prospect would be signed and sent to a farm shouted, "We want ball players, not farmers."

Carey's personality worked against him almost as much as the front office or his choice of strategies. A stoic, abrasive man who once aspired to the ministry, Carey's seriousness endeared him neither to his players nor to the press. Ironically, this had played in his favor at the time of his hiring. Carey the tactician was meant to contrast with Robinson the jolly buffoon. Unfortunately, the tactician could not be tactful.

In 1932, Waite Hoyt was with the Dodgers. Far removed from his heights with the 1927 Yankees, the future Hall of Fame pitcher had not pitched effectively and Carey decided to release him. The bad news was to be delivered to Hoyt during a workout on a Dodger off-day. Rather than call Hoyt into his office and inform him in the traditional manner, Carey instead turned administration of the workout over to Stengel and left the park.

Approximately thirty minutes later—Carey had apparently left instructions that he be given enough time to get away—one of the Dodger clubhouse attendants approached Hoyt and said something to him. According to Fresco Thompson, who witnessed the event, Hoyt "let out a wild cry of rage. He was practically incoherent, his face was livid." After a few minutes Hoyt recovered enough to utter through clenched teeth, "I pitched nineteen years in the American League and I have to come over here and get my unconditional release from a clubhouse boy. Carey didn't even have guts enough to tell me himself before he left."

The Dodgers board had endorsed Stengel's hiring with the thought that he would take some of the pressures of public relations of off Carey. In addition to providing the baseball skills for which he had become noted at Toledo (developing young players and rehabilitating veterans) it was hoped he would also be cheery and remind enough people of their Uncle Robbie that they would forget Carey's prickliness.

That June, another prickly character departed the scene. On the second day of the month, John McGraw quietly resigned as manager of the Giants, turning the team over to his first baseman, Bill Terry. McGraw was burned out. He was in debt and drank too heavily; his rages had become public and indiscriminate. His health was breaking down. Suffering from a prostate ailment that would eventually kill him, road trips became too difficult, as had coping with the generation of ballplayers who came after Stengel, players like Freddy Lindstrom and, ironically, Bill Terry, who had displaced adulation with open hostility to the old Oriole and his hypercritical style. McGraw was, simply, exhausted. "How do you think Mac really felt about this?" a reporter asked Terry at his inaugural press conference.

"He acted like a man who was glad to get a great weight off his back," Terry replied. "He was the oldest fifty-nine-year-old I ever knew," said Lindstrom. "He was tired and he was angry."

The great weight borne by Stengel was that of trying to counteract Carey's meaner qualities. He partially succeeded, as evidenced by a series of stories by the great Ring Lardner. Written concurrently with Carey's first managerial year, the stories featured Lardner's trademark technique of combining his own invented characters with real baseball personalities. Lardner had used this method to great effect with the 1910s Chicago White Sox in a series of stories called, "You Know Me, Al." This time, in "Lose with a Smile," an epistolary serial for the *Saturday Evening Post*, Lardner used Carey's Dodgers as foils for a fictional rookie outfielder trying to stick with the club.

Stengel was the most prominently featured of the real Dodgers. Described as "a kind of assistant manager and coach of the club," Stengel comes across as a fountainhead of baseball knowledge, a man who has seen and absorbed all there is to know about the game. "Carey has got him rooming with me," says the young, unschooled narrator, "so it looks like there takeing a special interest in how I get a long as Stengel sets and talks to me by the hr about the fine points and gives me pointers about the fine points of the game that comes up durn practice." [sic]

Stengel is both a father figure and a bit of a trickster. In one scene, Lardner has Carey and Stengel try to convince the rookie to switch-hit. Lardner has Stengel reveal the "real" reason that he was platooned and also resolves the mysterious ending of Game Two of the 1922 World Series, which was called for darkness in the middle of the afternoon:

> Stengel says he himself was all so a turn a round [switch] hitter as he use to hit so good right hand it that the pitchers threatened to walk out unlest he would agree to hit left hand it all the time.

> . . . Stengel says well I was so good that they use to pass me on purpose in batting practice and 1 time I was in a world series game again the Giants and the yankees and the empires called the game on account of darkness at 3 pm with the sun shining and judge Landis ast them to exclaim there decision and they said they thought it must be dark because Stengel only hit for 2 bases. [sic]

In a way, Stengel is the hero of the story. It is he who shepherds the rookie through the various pitfalls of life in the majors and brings the player together with his girl (Lardner hung his baseball satire on a conventional love story—the couple's inability to communicate is the main point of the plot). In the most exciting scene of the series, Stengel forcefully chases off a young woman of questionable morals who is trying to take advantage of the ballplayer's innocence.

Lardner's account of Carey's Dodgers is undoubtedly impressionistic. Even so, to Lardner's trained eye, Stengel was the most dominant personality on the club. Carey, when he appears, is depicted as being cold, bland, taciturn, and harsh with his players, whereas Stengel is constructive. As much as he grasped the intricacies of Stengelese, Lardner also understood the real Casey Stengel, realizing that unlike the many coaches who regarded their positions more as comfortable sinecures than actual jobs, Stengel took his role as coach literally. He loved to teach. Al Lopez remembered, "He was warm. I mean, on the ball field he had one great goal: to teach. But as a friend he was simply warm." Lopez thought that Stengel was instinctively drawn to young players through a thwarted sense of fatherhood. "When he got . . . a kid with ability, he wanted to see him make it big," he said. "He'd stick with a young guy and nurse him along. Casey would sit and talk to them by the hour. He never had any children of his own, so he had a lot to give them."

Lardner recognized that Stengel's personality rendered attempts at self-promotion redundant; Charles Stengel could sell himself to others just by being Casey. To endear yourself to others, Lardner told Stengel, do what comes naturally. "Just keep talking," he said, "and I'll get a story." It is interesting to note that Lardner's rendition of Stengelese anticipates and predates Stengel's version, at least as recorded by reporters; sportswriters tended to polish out the imperfections, eccentricities, and crudities inherent in the nonstandardized speech of early twentieth century Americans (the mass media having not yet taught them how to speak "properly"). Stengelese and Lardner's own uniquely idiomatic style bore a strong resemblance to each other, and both made their public debuts at roughly the same time in the 1910s, Lardner's "Busher" stories first appearing in 1914. Confined as he was to the provincial Brooklyn outpost of the National League, Stengel's influence on Lardner-ese was minimal, but it is tempting to see Lardner as a co-originator of Stengelese.

Carey's personality and the team's decline in the standings were not enough to force the Dodgers to seriously consider letting him go, but economic factors were. The Dodgers biggest crowds came when they played their crosstown rivals, the Giants. The National League was comprised of only eight teams, so games against the Giants generated a large percentage of the team's seasonal revenues. As such, how the team performed against the Giants was particularly important to its bottom line. Beating their archrivals was the most direct way to promote local enthusiasm.

In 1932, when Carey brought the team in third, he had done particularly well against the Giants, beating them fifteen times in twenty-two meetings. In 1933, when the team reverted to form and sank to sixth place, they suffered a similar decline in their fortunes against the Giants, winning only eight of their meetings. Dodger attendance, which had peaked at just over one million in 1930, had shrunk to less than half that figure by 1933. A good deal of the decline was due to the deepening economic depression, but the Dodgers directors had even less control over that than they did the direction of their franchise.

Steve McKeever, having finally won his long battle to be rid of Uncle Robbie, did little in the way of aggressively overhauling the club, content to sit back and enjoy a Wilbert-less Ebbets Field. "Every day the Dodgers are home," wrote *Newsweek*, "he clutches his silver-headed cane, walks a few blocks from his ten-room house to the park, and eases himself into a reserved seat directly behind home plate. There he puffs away on black cigars and reaches out his gnarled, jeweled hands for a glass of milk set in a ring built on the arm of his chair. . . . Occasionally the onetime garbage collector, sewer-builder, and asphalt-paver goes to his office and reads the tons of squawks and suggestions that fans send him. He answers most of them with a rubber stamp: 'Good Health and Luck—Steve.'"

Under pressure from Heydler, J. A. Robert Quinn, former operator of the Red Sox ("owner" being something of a misnomer; he was more of a front-man for a group of investors), was hired in September 1933 to act as the Dodgers general manager. Quinn was used to working with impoverished ball clubs. From 1917 through 1922 he had run the St. Louis Browns for the irritable ice magnate Philip deCatesby Ball and was cheered as the architect of a five-year rebuilding program that culminated in 1922's second-place finish, just one game behind the Yankees. Thereafter came the disastrous sojourn in Boston. Quinn took over for Harry Frazee, who everyone was eager to send back to Broadway, only to discover that as bad as things were under the man who sold Babe Ruth, the team still had leagues to fall before it hit bottom. Quinn's main financial backer died before the franchise could be gotten on a healthy footing. Thereafter, Quinn, who had had only $50,000 of his own to contribute to the team's purchase, had to run the club out of profits, of which there were none. Of Quinn's ten editions of the Red Sox, five lost over 100 games, four lost ninety. Desperate to save his life's savings plus salvage additional monies he had secured by borrowing against his life insurance policies, as well as allow his backers to depart with honor if not a profit, Quinn ran through seven managers. Described by *Baseball Magazine* as, "a prince of good sportsmen," Quinn was indefatigable but lacked the perspicacity and the financing to lick the problems of his clubs; three years older than John McGraw, he was already out of date.

As is typically the case when upper management changes in baseball, Quinn began to look for his own man to run the Dodgers on the field. Fortunately for Carey, he was protected by his contract, which was set to run through 1934.

On January 24, 1934, Bill Terry held a press conference at his New York office. Asked to assess the pennant races for the coming season, Terry named the Chicago Cubs and the St. Louis Cardinals as the greatest threat to the Giants' defense of the championship they had won the previous autumn. After Terry had completed his remarks, one of the reporters noticed that the manager had failed to mention Brooklyn in his survey of the league. What about Brooklyn? Terry was asked. The manager thought that the Dodgers' off-season had been too quiet: "Brooklyn?" Terry asked as if he had forgotten that the National League had another entry in New York City. "Is Brooklyn still in the league?"

Terry's rhetorical question was treated with benign indifference by the Manhattan-based papers, and the Brooklyn papers ignored it altogether. Only Marshall Hunt of the *Daily News* decided to get a reaction from Bob Quinn. Predictably, Quinn reacted angrily. More surprisingly, he was honest about the source of his anger: "If Terry persists in ridiculing the Brooklyn club the element of competition will vanish. No one will come to either Ebbets Field or the Polo Grounds if they think the games are a breeze." In other words, pride be damned; it's the attendance levels of the lucrative Giants-Dodgers games that matter.

Quinn's reaction pointed out a money-making opportunity for everybody; the Giants, the Dodgers, and the newspapers. Suddenly, Terry's jibe was played up as an insult. Dodgers fans bought into this "challenge," which had all the veracity and spontaneity of a professional wrestling match. More importantly, the Dodgers front office treated the implications of Terry's question as revealed truth. Steve McKeever, Bob Quinn, and the rest of the Dodger directors seem to have been shocked into alertness, as if they had suddenly realized that it had been years since anything had been done to improve the team's profile. If Brooklyn was to be "in the league," then the status quo had to be disturbed so as to generate interest and optimism. Carey maintained a busy off-season schedule and could not be bothered to participate in this fan-friendly but otherwise empty game of one-upmanship. Quinn fired him.

It says something about the state of the Dodgers operation in 1934 that a simple joke on the part of a rival could cause them to change their plans to such an extent that they would fire a manager they would still be obligated to pay the next year. Such headline grabbing acts of financial imprudence may be commonplace in today's Steinbrennerian baseball, but in the thirties such profligate behavior was shocking.

The first sign that Carey was through came in early February when the Dodgers signed infielder Marty McManus, who had managed the Red Sox for Quinn in 1932 and 1933. At thirty-four, McManus had little value left as a player, and it was widely rumored that McManus had been signed as a manager-in-waiting. Quinn indeed might have intended to go with McManus, but there was a perception around the team that a return to Uncle Robbie-style baseball was needed. "Brooklyn fans had shown they could forgive errors in the field and incompetence, but they wouldn't stand for dullness," wrote Harold Parrott of the *Brooklyn Eagle*, "and Carey had no color, no flair as a leader. The fans were clamoring for a return to the rollicking days of Uncle Robbie." McManus too had nothing of the showman about him. Quinn was either overruled or persuaded to consider a more theatrical candidate.

In late February, Stengel sent a postcard from his home in Glendale, California to a friend at the *Brooklyn Eagle*: "Leaving for Brooklyn on business." He had been summoned to the Dodger offices for what he assumed was a consultation with Carey and Quinn on a trade or some other player-related matter. When he arrived in Brooklyn, Stengel was shocked to find Carey absent and the entire Dodgers board of directors present.

Stengel was tersely informed that Carey had been fired and the job was his for the taking.

It was common knowledge that Carey's contract had another year to run. Stengel's first concern was that Carey's agreement was going to be honored. He was assured that it would be. When Stengel persisted in questioning Carey's fate, he was told, "That's not for you to worry about. . . . If you don't take this job, there are fifty others who will." Even so, he insisted on talking to Carey before accepting the job. A phone call was put through to Florida, where Carey was on a fishing trip. Carey recognized that Stengel would accomplish nothing through a dramatic show of loyalty and urged him to take the job. The next day, February 23, 1934, Stengel signed a two-year contract to manage the Brooklyn Dodgers at $12,000 a year, a $5,000 improvement on his coach's salary. Casey Stengel was now John McGraw's titular equal.

McGraw's reaction, if any, to his protégé's advancement is unknown. On February 23, the Little Napoleon was on his deathbed. He died two days later. Stengel would now have to measure himself against a legend.

Stengel did receive congratulations from Uncle Robbie, who was now president of the minor league Atlanta Crackers. "I am sure pleased you have the position as manager of the Brooklyn Club," he wrote. "I know you will do well, in fact better than anyone I know of, with the material you have." Robinson would join his old friend and rival McGraw on the other side of the veil less than six months later, bringing to a close the age of the Orioles and commending baseball to their heirs, among them Casey Stengel.

Getting Carey's blessing was of utmost importance to Stengel. He was genuinely grateful to Carey for rescuing him from what he called a "life of shame" in Toledo, and did not want anyone to feel that he had been plotting to steal the manager's job. "The most embarrassing moment of my life," he wrote, "occurred when I was offered the managing job, succeeding Carey." The appearance of impropriety disturbed him: "Before I'd accept, I had to be assured that if I didn't take the job some other new man would. I doubt that anyone who knows me thinks that I undermined Carey, but I know that some people think so."

He tried to emphasize that he was more shocked at his elevation than elated. "It might be different if I had been looking for this job and had been trying to get it, but I never dreamed of it." He wanted to stay on good terms with the man who brought him back to the majors. "Max and I are friends. I've played this game square and come in here clean. I think Max knows that too." Carey might not have known the full extent of the lengths that Stengel went to protect him. According to one newspaper report, the club had offered Carey's job to Stengel after the 1932 season, but Stengel refused it.

Carey was bitter, but held no grudge against Stengel. A reporter tracked him down on the fishing trip. "If Casey gets the job I wish him all the luck in the world. He'll need most of it." The stolen base king never again managed in the majors.

The team's public explanation for Stengel's hiring was Carey's inability to get along with the players. *The Sporting News* reported that, "An effort was made to trade one or more of these rude gentlemen during the winter, but these deals failed of fruition and it was decided it would be better to keep the players than the manager." Yet, with Stengel's promotion, the very qualities that caused Dodgers to hire him now seemed to embarrass them. Bob Quinn felt obliged to tell the media that, "Brooklyn fans may be assured that while the club has engaged a colorful personality it has not hired a clown." He added, "I know what a fine job Stengel made of managing the Toledo club when everything was going wrong and the wolf was at the door."

Stengel echoed his employer. "Every one of the gentlemen on this club wanted me to be the manager. I will be the manager too. Darned if I don't know a few things about baseball and I think I can teach baseball." Still, he could not completely suppress his true nature. His reputation was already causing doubts about him, but he had not yet become sensitive about it. "Maybe this means the Dodgers have gone in for the N.R.A.," he said, alluding to the New Deal's National Recovery Administration, "You know, New Riot Act." In a more serious vein, Stengel added, "I know I've got ballplayers who can help the club and help me and I believe I can help them. That's what I want to do."

The manager was given a fairly enthusiastic welcome by the media. Ed Hughes, writing in The *Brooklyn Eagle* under the heading "What Baseball Needs," said, "With the electric personality of Casey Stengel hovering over Ebbets Field, Flatbush fans may enjoy a slice of the old adventurous and romantic days this summer." Harold Parrot, Dodger beat reporter, wrote, "Casey was not always in accord with Carey but was never disloyal. . . . Carey had an unfortunate personality and clicked neither with the players nor with newspapermen." Parrot added, "Biographers have painted this forty-three-year-old funnyman of baseball . . . as the ideal head for the Ebbets Field Daffiness Boys, but the Flatbush fans will come to recognize him as a shrewd baseball man." Joe Williams of the *New York World-Telegram* wrote, "The report that Casey Stengel may replace Mr. Max Carey as manager of the Brooklyn Dodgers is too good to be true. Mr. Stengel is so preeminently the man for this delicate and delicious assignment it just isn't in the cards for him to be named. Just as there is no limit to the obtuseness of a baseball magnate, I have my doubts that there is any beginning to his astuteness, and thus I am not optimistic that plain logic will prevail." Many things in the world have changed since 1934, but even then baseball owners were held in the same high regard that they are today.

Only *The Sporting News* sounded a remotely negative note, observing that Stengel was, "known as a buffoon and a clown," and concluding that, "The jester will hold his own court this year." However, in a separate article in that paper, Daniel M. Daniel, the national correspondent, wrote, "Because of his keen appreciation of fun and frolic and his ready wit, Stengel has acquired a reputation as a comic and a jester. But those that know him well know that Casey is as keen in the ways and the technique of baseball as he is for a joke and a wise crack."

Stengel's first official act as manager of the Dodgers was to respond to Bill Terry. "The first thing I want to say is, the Dodgers are still in the league. You can tell that to Mr. Terry."

Despite this bit of bravado, Stengel was curiously cautious about forecasting his team's chances in 1934. "I am not predicting a pennant for Brooklyn, but that does not mean we're planting ourselves in the second division before the gong rings, . . . I honestly believe that we have a better ball club than most people think. Whether it's good enough to get into the pennant scrap, I don't know." Then, as now, this was an unusual posture for a manager to take. Traditionally, a baseball manager (or a coach in any other sport) will use the inevitable moment when they are asked for the season's outlook to hyperbolize about their team's chances, and in general pump the confidence of the club. Stengel's remarks were realistic and honest.

Stengel was reluctant to promise too much in his first year in any city. He felt that it would take him a year to learn a team and its competition well enough to have a true understanding of its strengths and weaknesses. In the case of the Dodgers, he knew from his time as coach that the state of the roster was such that if he over-promised what his team could accomplish he risked disappointing the fans, ownership, and himself. The team he had inherited from Carey was, in his words, "at the end of its age—you could just see it dropping off."

The club had no promising youngsters and too many over-the-hill veterans. The most prominent of these was outfielder Hack Wilson. Wilson was a strange ballplayer. Journalist Frank Graham wrote that Wilson, "was a colossus from the knees up, but his knees seemed to start at the ground." He was five-foot-six, weighed 190 pounds, possessed an eighteen-inch neck, and wore size five-and-a-half shoes. He had the physique of an inverted bowling pin. Asked to scout Wilson in 1923, John McGraw's succinct observation was, "He ain't got no neck." Another Giant of the time thought that Wilson looked as if he were standing up to his knees in mud. Some teammates called him "Caliban," after the character from Shakespeare's *The Tempest* (Question: Was the average uneducated ballplayer of 1930 better read than the average educated American of 2003? Discuss). There is a photo from around this time of Wilson posed with Babe Ruth and Lou Gehrig. Without a caption, one might guess that the majestic Yankees sluggers are posing with a particularly bulky midget.

Despite a body that bore more than a superficial resemblance to Popeye's, in Wilson's best years he hit like Babe Ruth. Playing for the Chicago Cubs in 1930, he had one of baseball's all-time great seasons, batting .356, slugging a National League record fifty-six home runs, and driving in 191 runs. Wilson's RBI total remains the major league single-season record.

Wilson was also an alcoholic. By the time Stengel took over the Dodgers he was hitting the bottle more often than he was hitting the baseball. His ability to consume was incredible. Glenn Wright remembered, "One time Hack drank a bottle of gin and a bottle of some kind of whiskey and a case or two of beer and then went out and had a couple of hamburgers. . . . The next morning he said, 'I'll be darned if I ever eat anymore of those hamburgers. Made me sick as a dog.'"

Wilson was temperamental and disinterested, but was also the club's main power threat, so Stengel was forced into the difficult position of both stroking him and motivating him. Joe McCarthy had been Wilson's manager in his greatest season and handled him with an uncharacteristically gentle touch. In fact, he disclaimed any responsibility for Wilson's personal habits. "What am I supposed to do?" he asked. "Tell him to live a clean life and he'll hit better?" When McCarthy was replaced by Rogers Hornsby ("He ran the clubhouse like a Gestapo camp"), the bellicose second baseman changed Wilson's program to tough love minus the love with terrible results. Stengel had difficulty finding the middle ground, swinging from the lukewarm, "Hack is alright but he'll have to qualify for his job," to, "Hack's a winning ballplayer—a fellow who still thinks he can do it. I like that kind." As uncomfortable as massaging the misanthropic star's ego was for Stengel, it was probably good practice for the infinitely more complex and sensitive Joe DiMaggio. Prefiguring his later reluctance to suppress critical impulses in regards to his players, Stengel was not above letting his true feelings about Wilson show, so long as the outfielder was out of earshot. When Hack was late for spring training—he held out despite a disastrous 1933 in which he hit .267 with nine home runs—Stengel noted a large tanker truck rolling past the camp. "There's Hack Wilson reporting at last," he said. On another occasion, he told reporters, "We may lose more games than anybody, but we can out-drink anyone in the league."

Stengel might have also been thinking of his ace pitcher Van Lingle Mungo. Now most famous for being the chorus to a Dave Frishberg song,

Mungo was a hard-drinking, temperamental southerner whose fastball was the envy of the league and whose self-control was not (when Bob Feller surfaced in 1936, the initial point of comparison was not to Walter Johnson but to Mungo). By far the most talented member of the team and well aware of it, he was continually resentful of what he felt was a lack of support, and each misplay behind him reminded him that he was a top pitcher on a second-rate team. Mungo had made his major league debut on September 7, 1931, and that game had presaged the rest of his career. He pitched a 2–0 complete game shutout, struck out seven batters, and drove in both runs with a single and a triple.

Periodically the pressure would become too much for Mungo, and he would slip away from the team for awhile, drinking his way back to South Carolina and his wife. These temporary disappearances had been tolerated by the organization, as if they were unavoidable. At first Stengel also seemed inclined to defer to his eccentric star. "Mungo and I get along fine," he said. "I just tell him I won't stand for no nonsense—and then I duck."

They were, in general, rough characters, unused to discipline. Years later Stengel gave a tongue in cheek assessment: "Managing a team back then was tough business. Whenever I decided to release a guy, I always had his room searched for a gun. You couldn't take any chances with some of them birds."

The two best position players were Tony Cuccinello and catcher Al Lopez. The former, a Queens native, was a steady if unspectacular in-fielder who provided better-than-average offense at his position. He was able to reach double figures in home runs at a time when few second basemen, and fewer Dodgers, could provide any power at all. From 1930 to 1937, Cuccinello's best years, he hit more home runs, sixty-three, than any other National League second baseman. "He couldn't hit so good," Stengel reminisced in 1959, "and he manipulated what you would call rather stagnant legs. Whereas he couldn't run fast, he became a player that had to use his shoulders and what was above his shoulders."

"Señor Al" Lopez was respected as the best defensive catcher in the National League. He was also the field leader of the Dodgers. He played the game with a fire and intelligence rarely seen in Brooklyn in those times. So highly regarded was Lopez as a defensive player and strategist that he set the career record for total games caught despite being a weak hitter (after his playing career was over he continued to demonstrate his baseball acumen through a Hall of Fame career as a manager). He was the most professional player the Dodgers had as well as the most popu-lar, and Stengel named him team captain.

The rest of the Dodger roster was comprised of a collection of spare parts that might have made excellent role players on other teams but were stretched as regulars. A chorus in search of a lead actor, the Dodgers featured such players as first baseman Sam Leslie, of whom one writer said, "He could hit if you woke him up at two in the morning but couldn't field if you played him at two in the afternoon," and Nick Tremark, who was so short (five-foot-three) that he was nicknamed "Mickey Mouse." Stengel found Tremark a constant source of amusement, quipping that he could wear shorts and still be in long pants. When Tremark reached base, Stengel would stand in his coaches box and cup his hands like binoculars as if he couldn't quite see his diminutive outfielder. As the smallest member of the Dodgers, he was obliged by Stengel to run a series of races against the Dodgers' largest player, pitcher Les Munns, who was six-foot-five and weighed 212 pounds (Munns won).

These sideshow performers backed up players like third baseman "Jersey" Joe Stripp (notable for the "debatable" habit of sticking his chewing gum to the end of his bat when at the plate, then retrieving it for oral use in the field) and outfielders Buzz Boyle, Danny Taylor, and Johnny Frederick, all journeyman singles hitters who were capable of recording decent batting averages but not much else.

Perhaps the only keeper among the second-line players was Len Koenecke. Billed as "McGraw's last discovery," he would more accurately have been described as one of McGraw's last discards. Signed by the Giants with great fanfare in 1932, he failed to hit and was quickly dismissed. Though already twenty-eight years old, he had gone back to the minors and reestablished himself, hitting .353 with nineteen triples, twenty-four home runs, and 141 runs scored at Indianapolis in 1931. Stengel began blending him into the lineup when Wilson was slow to get his bat started. Koenecke demonstrated power, speed, and good plate judgment. Stengel's first successful major league rehabilitation project, Koenecke's .320 average with thirty-one doubles, seven triples, fourteen home runs, and seventy walks was the team's best offensive performance, and one of the top seasons of 1934.

Asked at his inaugural press conference how fans and reporters should refer to this assemblage, Stengel replied, "I don't care what you newspaper fellows call the Dodgers this year—the Daffiness Boys, the Screwy Scrubs, or anything else—so long as the team hustles."

The Daffiness Boys were the furthest thing from Stengel's mind that February. In fact, with team names being largely informal, Stengel considered changing Brooklyn's name so as to create a new image for the club. *The Sporting News* reported that, "He doesn't like the name and is hoping that somebody will come along with a worthwhile suggestion. Stengel asks only that he be spared the necessity of turning down the name 'Caseys.' . . . It smacks too much of a mythical guy that struck out." Tolerating sloppy or strange ballplaying was a time-honored tradition in Brooklyn. The *New York Post*'s John Lardner (son of Ring) observed that Stengel, "must give Brooklyn a ball club that is both efficient and screwy. Brooklyn fans enjoy a victory, but they enjoy it most with a large dose of what scientists call Flatbush Folly, or Red Hook Raving, or demential greenpantensia, or plain, ordinary, phrenitis."

Stengel knew that the team's longstanding bad habits had been compounded by the feelings of disrespect for the former manager. The trick for Stengel would be to instill discipline without appearing to be cold or aloof, as Carey was. "I am to be neither a slave driver nor an easy mark with my players," he said. "I am going to bring back the curfew on the club. Any ball player who stays out after midnight is going to hear things." He could not resist giving a subtle wink about his own less than disciplined career before finishing up on the subject in his trademarked fashion:

> I believe that's only right. A curfew rule is as much for the benefit of the players as anybody else. You never saw any halos hanging around in my vicinity, but I knew darned well I couldn't stay out late and be at my best the next day. That goes for men in any line. Most ball players are married men. Their wives in more cases than not would raise plenty of hob with them if they made a practice of staying out after midnight. And a wife isn't even a manager. At any rate I've met darned few husbands who'd admit they were managed by their wives.

Thinking back to his playing career, he said, "Since becoming a manager, I have seen the error of those wild days. If any of my boys stays out all night, I will probably fine their ears off. It's all in the point of view."

As these remarks imply, Stengel was challenged to supply discipline without becoming another Carey. He could have gone either way when Jimmy Jordan, a utility infielder, vanished without notice. The club suspended him, but Stengel insisted the player was sick, and when he returned—without explanation—Stengel reinstated him without public penalty.

In more prosaic circumstances, he lacked sympathy. Early in spring training, his infielders complained that the hardness of the infield surface was to blame for the many errors they were making. "Why don't you hit 'em on the ground to the other fellows and get on base that way?" he asked. His outfielders were making mistakes as well. "They don't take bad hops in the air." The *Eagle* reported that the manager called off infield practice, for fear "that the ricocheting ball might lay low another player or two."

"The veterans will be benched plenty in the future," he said early in spring training. "Either they are sadly off form or they are not physically able to do better. Either way you figure it, they don't deserve to be on the field unless they change quickly—they have that Losing Dodger Complex, but they'll have to get rid of that and hustle for me."

The note of discipline struck by Stengel did not alienate his players; he was a better communicator than Carey, and he projected a warmer disposition. He had already demonstrated his character to his players by retaining coach Otto Miller for his own staff. Miller, a former catcher, had been with the team in various capacities for over two decades. It was thought that Stengel should fire him because he was known to be Carey's closest friend. Stengel rebuffed such suggestions. "Loyalty is a hell of a reason to fire anybody. I want all the loyalty I can find." Miller was retained as Stengel's battery coach.

Setting a precedent that would last his entire career, Stengel deferred to a veteran pitching coach. Charles Carrolton "Chick" Fraser was nineteen years Stengel's senior. He had pitched in the big leagues starting at Louisville in 1896, where he played with a young Honus Wagner. He had been a teammate of Cy Young, Three Finger Brown, and Vic Willis, compiling a 176–213 record while watching them win. Stengel wanted the knowledge conferred by Fraser's associations. As a former outfielder he did not pretend to be an expert on the care and feeding of pitchers. Later, with the Yankees, he would employ Jim Turner and Johnny Sain in the same capacity, adopting a corporate style in which the pitching staff was a semi-autonomous department under the coach.

The Dodgers were inconsistent during spring training, and still occasionally daffy. Observing them on April 1, Bill Terry watched two runners land on the same base. "How long have these fellows been down here?" he laughed. "They're in midseason form already!" Stengel was seeing something completely different. "Look—did you see that play?" he exclaimed to a sportswriter. "Those boys of mine look just like professionals out there."

The Dodgers won eight exhibition games on the strength of their hitting and lost ten games due to shaky pitching that allowed almost five runs a game. Despite the confidence of pitcher Walter Beck, who predicted, "I'll win twenty games this year," (he had *lost* twenty the year before) there was no evidence that the pitching would get any better.

There was little that Stengel could do to improve the pitching. The Dodgers had yet to embrace Branch Rickey's farm system method of developing talent—it would take the arrival of Rickey himself in Brooklyn for that to happen—but instead still relied on the purchase of players from independent minor league teams for cash. This was the traditional method of acquiring talent in baseball and it might very well have worked for the Dodgers but for the fact that they had no spending money whatsoever. Bob Quinn wrote, "Our instructions were not to purchase any players without permission from the Board of Directors, not even . . . on waiver, and the waiver price . . . was $6,000." The Board was for the most part loathe to give its consent to any expenditures. Stengel had to make do with what was already on the roster.

Compounding matters, Stengel and Quinn were not on the same page in terms of what kind of players should be added to the team. When the Dodgers opened their spring camp, the team did not have a veteran left-handed pitcher on the roster. Stengel admitted to reporters that he was desperate for one. One was not quick in coming, for Quinn did not place a priority on the acquisition of a portside pitcher. He felt that one of the basic tenets of Stengel's platoon theories, that a southpaw pitcher might be more effective against a left-handed batter, was a "psychological fad."

Before spring training was very old, Stengel had already begun experimenting with this psychological fad. On one occasion in mid-March he held an intrasquad game with one team made up entirely of right-handed batters and the other made up of entirely left-handed batters. In this way Stengel could test each batter against lefty and righty pitchers without making them aware that he was thinking of platooning them.

On the eve of opening day, Stengel participated in a national radio program with all of the other National League managers. Not only did his usual reticence about his team's prospects assert itself, but he took his competitors to task for their willingness to boast. "There'll be about five pennants won over the air tonight and I'm not claiming one for myself. But at the end of the season, I expect to find the Dodgers up ahead of about two or three of these pennant-winning clubs."

When the Dodgers' opening day uniforms arrived, the team name was spelled "Brookyln." No one noticed, but dyslexia was the least of the team's problems. On the basis of spring training, Stengel and Quinn had gone into opening day with the understanding that whatever the deficiencies of the pitching, the team's strong offense could at least keep the team in any given game. Before nine innings had been completed on opening day, this perceived asset had been transformed into a weakness.

Stengel's first official Dodger lineup played as a unit for all of three innings. It performed impressively at first. An "astoundingly svelte" Hack Wilson and fellow outfielder Danny Taylor both hit home runs off of Boston's Ed Brandt to give the Dodgers a short-lived lead. This was to be the high point of the first half of the season. By the third inning, Wilson twisted his ankle running out a single and had to be removed from the game. Wilson's substitute, Buzz Boyle, collided with the centerfielder Danny Taylor. Both had to leave the game. The Dodgers' fatal lack of depth would be exposed almost immediately.

The disabled players would return, but teammates rapidly replaced them on the sidelines. Joe Stripp fractured an ankle on the front end of a double steal, then returned to the lineup only to reinjure the ankle when Dutch Leonard slipped in the dugout and stepped on it. Shortstop Lonny Frey, the club's most promising youngster, was hit in the head by a pitch. As soon as he returned to the lineup, he severely injured his knee when he was spiked by Dick Bartell. His replacement, twenty-three-year-old Jimmy Bucher (In 1933, Bucher had hit .369 with twenty-five home runs for Greensboro of the Piedmont League. The Dodgers rushed him to the majors, ignoring his 176 errors in 485 pro games, as well as the fact that the Piedmont League wasn't Brooklyn), broke an ankle and was lost for the season. Len Koenecke, who had been the team's most productive hitter in spring training, was hobbled by infected feet through April and May. Cuccinello broke his foot. Danny Wilson caught the flu. Pitcher Ownie Carroll had his finger broken by a line drive. The roster became so depleted that Al Lopez had to be used at second and third base. On June 4, the Dodgers dropped an exhibition game to Holy Cross College, 5–4. The amateurs had vitality on their side.

Stengel argued that major league rosters should be restored to twenty-five men from their current twenty-three. They had been reduced as a Depression-inspired austerity measure. "I think it is an injustice to ask the fans to go out to see a big league club play with catchers on duty in the infield and pitchers in the outfield," he said. Desperate to add position players, he cut two pitchers. "I can lose just as many games with eight pitchers as I can with the ten I've been carrying," he grumbled.

With the injuries came poor performance, although other factors contributed to the Dodgers' lack of production. There was early evidence that Stengel and Quinn had misjudged the potency of the offense. In 1934, the Dodgers opened at home and scored runs at a decent, if less than brisk pace. Directly thereafter, the Dodgers were transplanted to Boston where they were immersed in an atmosphere totally opposite that of Ebbets Field. The Braves' National League Park had also been built in an earlier era, and its creator had disdained the home run. The park's huge dimensions and weather conditions combined to create an atmosphere that, more than any other park, favored the pitcher. The deep fences and stiff wind off of the Charles River robbed Brooklyn's hitting of Ebbets Field's added luster. The Dodgers stranded thirty-four runners in three games and were swept by the Braves. This humiliation, climaxed by a shutout loss to thirty-eight-year-old Tom Zachary, an over-the-hill left-hander who, Stengel said, "pitches with an artery, not a muscle—his pulse carries the ball up the plate," convinced Stengel, if not Quinn, that the offense had been badly overestimated. Quinn purchased Zachary from the Braves.

Stengel began to look for ways to improve the offense. Since the budget prevented him from picking up new players, he had to think of manufacturing runs. Whatever method Stengel was to choose, he knew it would not be Max Carey's way. A few years later, Stengel asked Lefty Gomez, who had just come over from the American League, what he thought the biggest difference in the play of the two leagues was. "Over here," the pitcher replied, "they play like they don't know that John McGraw has been dead for five years." McGraw's game of the teens, the "inside baseball" of the bunt and run, had been passed by. Failure to recognize this had been Carey's problem, but it was not Stengel's (nor had it been McGraw's). As a coach he had been loyal to Carey and had adhered to his methods, but he never subscribed to them. In his mind, the introduction of the lively ball had changed everything. "I found out you had to have different methods . . . of how to run a game," he said. That did not stop him from releasing Gomez. McGraw was not to be ridiculed. Besides—Gomez was finished.

Stengel's realization evidenced to his alertness and adaptability. Max Carey was almost exactly the same age as Stengel, and they both played in the National League at the same time. Yet by 1931, Carey was an anachronism and Stengel was just moving into his prime as a baseball thinker. Stengel eagerly embraced the notion that changing times required new tactics. "I could build up the methods they used to play by in baseball and show you that half of them aren't worth a quarter today because the conditions of the game are so different."

As home runs were so prevalent (though not so prevalent as they had been just a few years before—McGraw had complained about the offensive explosion of 1930 and the National League responded by taking the rabbit out of the ball) the conventional wisdom of the day was to play slow, station to station baseball. There was no reason to risk losing a runner on a stolen base attempt when the ball was so likely to go out of the park. Stengel hoped for the long fly ball as much as any other manager, but his lineup seemed incapable of producing one without help. Discarding conventional wisdom that insisted that a manager find a static lineup to play, Stengel tried to maximize his chances though player rotation. "I had to play my own system," he said. "And my system was platooning."

Stengel is often given credit for inventing the strategy of platooning. He did not, of course; McGraw platooned Stengel, and there is evidence that the strategy was used as early as 1887. Stengel often receives credit for it anyway because at the time that he managed nobody else was doing it; like the stolen base, platooning had been temporarily forgotten. But more than reviving the strategy, Stengel improved upon it. Platooning in its most basic concept is the practice of matching left-handed batters against right-handed pitchers and vice-versa. As Stengel said,

"There's not much of a secret to platooning. You put a right-handed hitter against a left-handed pitcher and a left-handed hitter against a right-handed pitcher and on cloudy days you use a fastball pitcher." Generally these match-ups were achieved by platooning players in pairs. If one had a left-handed third-baseman, a right-handed third-baseman would be located to go along with him.

In its most evolved form, Stengel's platooning worked on three axes: left, right, and defensive. He did not platoon fanatically at every position ("Naturally you don't platoon a man like DiMaggio," wrote Stengel) as some later mangers have done, so he had the luxury of platooning players in groups larger than two. His rosters were loaded with multi-position players who would move around the field to accommodate the insertion of another player who was being platooned.

The hallmark of Stengel's platooning was its lack of rigidity. While he understood that lefty hitters, as a rule, did not hit well against lefty pitchers, he also recognized that not all pitchers were created equal. "If [the opposition has] a right-handed hitter who can't hit an overhanded curve ball [at bat], and you've got a right-handed pitcher in there who hasn't got an overhand curve," he said, "Don't you think you might be better off with a left-hander who has?" He put it succinctly: "People alter percentages."

This "3-D" platooning was generally recognized as an innovation of Stengel's Yankees years, but the experimental phase took place in Brooklyn, revealing itself in an early obsession with moving players to multiple positions, experimenting with pitchers as position players and vice versa. Infielder became outfielders, catchers became outfielders, second basemen became third basemen, and so on.

In this way Stengel hoped to gain more flexibility than a major league roster was designed to allow. Some managers have been known to pick nine men and play them until they drop. Stengel understood that the flaw in this strategy was that it left the manager with a bench full of rusty replacements. He knew from his own career that a ballplayer's skills diminish with inaction. Therefore his platoon would by nature rotate bench players in and out of the lineup and keep them fresh and limber.

The system also allowed Stengel more elaborate in-game options. With his carefully cultivated bench, Stengel could, if he felt the situation called for it, pinch-hit for a player in the first inning and suffer no loss of talent. In this way Stengel re-envisioned the position players on the roster as interchangeable parts. Miller Huggins once said, "A manager has his cards dealt to him and he must play them." Stengel's idea was to double the number of cards.

The idea that bench players could be valuable to a team on a day-to-day basis (other than in a time of injury) was a new one. Platooning had previously been considered a tool to cover up a weakness on the part of the batter. The general philosophy was that starting position players should play every day, regardless of who the opposing pitcher was and what hand he threw with. If, in the course of following that policy it became apparent that a player was not capable of this because he could not, for example, hit left-handed pitching, then a grudging effort would be made to find someone else who could hit southpaws and insert him into the lineup. There was an incredible prejudice against players who could not be used on a daily basis; it was if they were deficient in some way (and of course the players themselves fought against being designated as such). The ability to play every day was a manhood issue.

Stengel was not concerned with such matters. Rather than platooning to cover a weakness, Stengel platooned to gain an offensive advantage. From his own experience he knew that that certain players were simply not able to play every day, that the more exposure they received the more apparent their flaws became. It was not an issue of pride but a matter of fact. He had been able to transcend the prejudices of his time.

As demonstrably effective as it was, platooning did not receive much attention prior to Stengel's revival due to the general bias against it—for one thing, there were no statistics to make his point for him. And as Stengel himself pointed out on many occasions, players resented it. They were afraid of being labeled. "In his [the young player's] own head he can hit any pitcher," said Stengel, "so he gives you a great fight at the plate." Again, Stengel's own career gave him insight. "They said I couldn't hit left-handers. Both Robbie and McGraw pulled me out as soon as an opposing left-hander appeared. How was I expected to hit one when I never faced one?"

Stengel may have been sincere in his complaint, but he never hesitated to ignore it when he heard the same grievance from ballplayers under his control. Having been there, Stengel could readily empathize with a player's frustrations at not being able to play everyday. At the same time, he knew that though the experience was painful at the time, its ultimate effect could be beneficial. Whereas a player might see being platooned as an implication of some weakness on his part, Stengel felt that in the long term it would enhance his confidence. "One of the biggest jobs when you're a manager is how to handle the young ball player who has not quite made it, but thinks he has . . . he doesn't realize that he can't hit an expert pitcher yet . . . if he stays in long enough to find that out, then he loses confidence in himself, and that's a terrible thing. I always wanted to prevent that if I could and I would platoon a young man on his mental condition."

In 1934, much of this was in the future. Any team may platoon so long as it possesses depth; healthy bodies are required for each position platooned. Platooning also assumes that each of the players affected actually has something positive to contribute. The Dodgers were not able to consistently meet either requirement. Though Stengel's thinking on the subject first began to express itself around this time, he would not be able to fully implement his theories until some time after.

In addition to trying to improve the Brooklyn club through innovative strategy, he also tried to improve the performance of the players through individual instruction. As coach, Stengel tried to be a positive influence on the Brooklyn players. As manager, he felt that his job should involve not only presiding over in-game decision making, but instruction as well. As he had tried to be in all of his career, Stengel saw in his role as manager as much the teacher as the drill sergeant. This was another inheritance from McGraw, who never considered a ballplayer finished until he had been indoctrinated in McGraw's methods—though Stengel was motivated out of a sincere desire to help rather than McGraw's megalomania.

Like all managers, Stengel's primary concern was providing ownership and the community with a winning ball club. As a competitor, he wanted to win. He also knew that his job depended on maintaining a high level of attendance at the games. But if he could not have these things, he could almost content himself with the education of his ballplayers. "What else are you gonna do when you get a second division ball club?" he wondered. "You've got a couple of young players on it, you work on them. . . . Then for somebody else they turn out to be good players, but what of it? You helped make them good ballplayers, didn't you?"

Stengel's wife Edna said, "He would have liked nothing better than to have ballplayers come home and stay with us so that he could work with them longer." At the same time, like many teachers his expectations were sometimes too great. Stengel maintained a petulant streak that emerged at times of disappointment. His occasionally dashed expectations and continual frustration with losing would sometimes combine to make him appear contemptuous of his players. In reference to one of his pitchers on the Dodgers, Stengel said, "This is what drives managers nuts. As a manager, you work hard, analyze the game, study your players, learn the weakness of every team in the league, and think and sweat all day long. And once every four or five days you have to trust your job and reputation to a lunkhead like that."

For the most part, such frustrations lay in the future. Stengel was still new to major-league managing, and its stresses had not yet begun to wear on him as they do on so many veteran managers. Rather than give in, he attacked adversity. As Tom Meany wrote of Stengel in *The Saturday Evening Post*, "Finding you needed McGraw's players to win with

McGraw's strategy, Casey improvised Stengel's strategy to win with Stengel's players.''

Stengel did not intend to follow McGraw too closely, at least not consciously. He was too much an individualist; if he were to surpass McGraw, he would do so on his own merits. Besides, as much as he wanted McGraw's success, at least part of him knew that he never could be *like* McGraw, at least, not one hundred percent. "Some players, when they get a chance at managing," he wrote, "will copy another manager. That's a very serious mistake. You can take some of a man's methods, but don't ever think you can imitate him. You have to be yourself.''

Unlike McGraw, Stengel was a baseball romantic. "I don't play cards," he said, "I don't play golf, and I don't go to the picture show. All that's left is baseball . . . I have no hobbies. Most of my off-season time is taken up with baseball business. If it isn't, I'd quit and get out of the game. Baseball is my very life, my one consuming interest." When Stengel was an old man, a reporter jokingly asked him if he had known Abraham Lincoln. "No, son," replied the manager, "but you give me his batting average and I'll tell you how to pitch to him.''

Despite his single-minded approach and individualistic philosophy, Stengel was not automatically the perfect manager. He still had much to learn. Stengel's original signals with the Dodgers were perversely simple. "If I'm looking at you," he said to his batters, "you're hitting. . . . If I'm walking away from you and spitting, you're hitting. . . . If I'm looking at you and spitting you're *not* hitting. . . . If I'm walking away and not spitting, you're not hitting." Unlike platooning, this particular innovation of Stengel's did not catch on. He never did change in this regard. McGraw indulged in all manner of cloak and dagger deceptions with his signs. Stengel never bothered.

Van Mungo, who was almost pathologically bitter about being the best player on a poor team, sympathized with Stengel's early troubles. "Casey managed good but he just didn't have the players. I remember Jimmy Bucher at third base one day. He let so many ground balls go through his legs that I sent a telegram to my wife telling her to join the club; she could play third base as well as Bucher.''

Unfortunately, Mungo was far more likely to go to his wife than the other way around, and the team continued to play losing baseball. Mungo was only half right about the source of the Dodgers problems. The team did not lose because of players that were there, such as Bucher; they lost because of players that were not there. The Dodgers were not a good team, but they were not one of baseball's all-time worst either. With Mungo, Lopez, Koenecke, and Cuccinello they had a few better-than-average players. They were not hopeless, only mediocre.

The Dodgers were unique in the National League in not having a single

NATIONAL LEAGUE ALL-STAR SELECTIONS BY TEAM 1934–1936	
St. Louis Cardinals	16
New York Giants	14
Chicago Cubs	13
Pittsburgh Pirates	7
Boston Braves	4
Cincinnati Reds	3
Brooklyn Dodgers	3
Philadelphia Phillies	2

marquee player, top-level pitcher, or run-producer who could not only win a few close games but also become a magnet for fan attention. The Cardinals had a plethora of stars, including Dizzy Dean, Frankie Frisch, Joe Medwick, and Pepper Martin. The Giants had Bill Terry, Mel Ott, Travis Jackson, and Carl Hubbell. The Cubs had Babe Herman, Billy Herman, Kiki Cuyler, Chuck Klein, and Gabby Hartnett. The Pirates had the Waner brothers, Arky Vaughn, Pie Traynor, and Waite Hoyt. The Braves had Wally Berger. Even Cincinnati and lowly Philadelphia, the only two teams to finish below the Dodgers in the 1934 standings, had among their number Dick Bartell, Jim Bottomley, Chick Hafey, and Ernie Lombardi. In all, twenty-five future Baseball Hall of Fame members played in the National League in 1934. Only two of them played for the Dodgers: one, Al Lopez, would be elected not for his abilities as a player but for his managerial career. The other was Hack Wilson, far past his prime.

In the voting for 1934's Most Valuable Player, all seven National League teams, including ninety-game losers Philadelphia and Cincinnati, had players who received MVP consideration above the top-ranked Dodger candidate (Buzz Boyle, four votes).

In May came the first meeting with the Giants, the first chance for revenge. There was momentary excitement, then disappointment and resignation as the Dodgers lost three straight games. Dan Parker of the *New York Daily Mirror* wrote, "It would have been poetic justice had the Dodgers answered Terry's taunts with three straight victories. Instead, the Giants slapped three straight defeats on the Dodgers, which means, 'No, Brooklyn is not in the league.'" The next Dodgers-Giants series, held at the end of the month, saw Brooklyn lose another three straight games to their rivals before finally beating them on May 31.

Although they lost to everyone without prejudice, the Cardinals were a special nemesis for Stengel's Dodgers. The Cardinals were one of the top three teams in the league, vying for the pennant with the Giants and the Chicago Cubs. Known for its scrappy style of play, the "Gashouse Gang" featured Frankie Frisch, Pepper Martin, Joe "Ducky" Medwick, and Ripper Collins on offense, the brains and leadership of shortstop Leo Durocher, and the pitching combination of Arkansas's Jay Hanna "Dizzy" Dean and his brother Paul. Dizzy was the loquacious right hander with an incredible fastball and even more incredible malapropisms. His brother Paul was not nearly as fun, but for the sake of parallelism baseball reporters hung the sobriquet "Daffy" on him anyway. The two were poison to the Dodgers. For example, the day after Dizzy beat the Dodgers on June 21, Paul Dean took the mound and handed them their second consecutive Dean-inflicted loss. "There are too many of those boys," said Stengel.

Sometimes the wounds were self-inflicted. On July 4 the Dodgers played the Phillies at the Baker Bowl, an aging ballpark with an outfield built to the approximate dimensions of a file cabinet. The file cabinet analogy extended to the right field wall, which was forty-feet high, made of tin, and located a short two-hundred and eighty feet from home plate.

Pitching for the Dodgers was Walter Beck, a twenty-nine-year-old who in 1933 had lost twenty games while posting a below-average earned run average of 3.54. (The opposing starter was "Snipe" Hansen. Baseball lost something when the players became too dignified for nicknames.) Prior to the season, Stengel, in either motivational or wishful thinking mode, had listed Beck as one of his staff aces. Once the season started, Beck, like so many Dodgers, only played up to the level of his abilities.

So much for the elements of that day that have not passed into legend. Here is the rest of the story as baseball lore has it: on this particular day Beck continued to pitch ineffectively. Brooklyn's outfielders had run a thousand miles chasing the many long drives the Phillies hit off of him. Hack Wilson, whose lack of conditioning and probable hangover were being continually tested by the barrage of balls being hit to right field, was ready to drop. Between pitches Wilson would crouch down and put his head between his knees, presumably trying to stop the world from spinning.

Beck faced eight batters in the first inning without retiring one. After the first several batters reached base, Stengel went out to the mound and suggested that Beck did not have his best stuff and wondered if he should be removed from the game. Beck replied that his arm was just coming around and that he would shortly commence getting batters out. Stengel left him in.

Beck continued to struggle. Like any pitcher, he was resistant to being removed from the game. Stengel returned to the mound determined to take Beck with him when he left. "No, sir," said Beck when Stengel demanded the ball. "You let me pitch to this next hitter." Stengel was equally insistent: "Walter, let me have the ball." The two argued back and forth. Out in right field, the tug of war on the mound taking place far away from him, Hack Wilson began to doze.

The argument reached its inevitable end. Stengel won. Beck knew that he was done, but he was also angry. He was angry at his manager, angry at the Phillies, and angry at himself. Instead of handing the game ball to Stengel, Beck turned and fired it at the right field wall.

The ball hit the tin barrier with a loud clang and bounced back towards right field. The sound reverberated through the hot afternoon air, and reached whatever world Wilson was currently dwelling in. Wilson awoke, jerked out of his dream by the realization that a ball had been hit to right field. Rising, he charged the wall, fielded the carom, and fired off a perfect throw to second base, holding the runner who was not there to a single.

"A helluva throw," said Tony Cuccinello of Wilson, "best he's made all year." Two Dodgers who were not amused were Wilson and Stengel. Wilson felt thoroughly humiliated. "I hope to hell they send you to Jersey City tomorrow," he said to Beck when he came into the dugout at the end of the inning. He would soon get his wish. Stengel demoted Beck, forever after known as "Boom-Boom," for the sound of the ball hitting the fence. Hack Wilson was gone soon after, sold, ironically, to the Phillies. With his departure, the Dodgers lost their one faded star. Wilson made just two hits in three weeks with the Phillies and was released. Though he was only thirty-four, his major league career was over. His drinking life had just begun, though it was fated to be brief.

Later in July, Steve McKeever, perhaps noting incidents such as the one in Philadelphia, was moved to issue what has come to be known as the "vote of confidence." The vote of confidence is a statement made to the press by the owner or general manager of a losing team indicating the organization's total confidence in, and commitment to, an embattled manager. In general, the vote of confidence should be read to mean exactly the opposite of what it says. McKeever's version stated, "Casey Stengel will be manager of the Brooklyn team so long as I am at the head of it. He's my man for the job."

The writers applauded. Tom Meany wrote, "And now for Stengel, the old professor himself. The Brooklyn owners have no intention of paying off Casey. He has been more than satisfactory to the owners in his development of young players and the gate responses to Casey's efforts have been gratifying. Stengel has restored the personal touch to baseball in Flatbush, something that it lacked after Uncle Robbie moved out. . . . He is aggressive and affable, fighting for his points with the umpires during the game and chatting with fans afterwards.''

The day after the Boom-Boom incident, Bill Terry, who had just been named manager of the National League All-Star team (as this was only the second All-Star Game, the precedent of using last year's pennant winning manager had yet to be set. The first All-Star Game had been managed by Connie Mack and, in a one-time return engagement, John McGraw) announced that Stengel, along with manager Bill McKechnie of the Boston Braves, would be the coaches for the National League. Said Terry of Stengel, "He deserves the honor and I'm glad to show it to him." Dodgers beat writer Tommy Holmes noted in *The Sporting News* that, ''Around the league, the impression persists that Stengel is a canny baseball man and that he will be a successful manager if he ever gets anything worthwhile to manage.''

The All-Star Game, held at the Polo Grounds in New York on July 10, was less of a pleasure for Stengel than Terry might have initially imagined. Stengel witnessed Giant Carl Hubbell strike out five consecutive batters—Babe Ruth, Lou Gehrig, Jimmie Foxx, Al Simmons, and Joe Cronin, future Hall of Famers all—over the first two innings. Stengel was also present for the aftermath of Hubbell's performance, in which his own Van Lingle Mungo entered the game in relief of the Cubs' Lon Warneke.

Mungo was typically wild and he loaded the bases to face Earl Averill. Stengel later recalled that prior to the game Bill Terry had briefed the pitching staff on the American League lineup. "Terry went down the lineup of the American League hitters . . . he told the pitchers what to throw to everybody—except Averill. 'I haven't solved that guy yet,' Bill said. 'He murdered everything we threw him all spring.' '' Averill murdered Mungo too, lining a double off of him to drive in Jimmie Foxx and Al Simmons for what proved to be the winning runs for the American League. Mungo followed the double by striking out Lou Gehrig on three pitches, but it was too late. For Stengel, the All-Star Game would be no refuge from the losing Dodgers.

The All-Star Game also exacerbated the Dodgers' injury problems when Al Lopez further irritated a thumb hurt in an earlier collision by catching in the game.

Stengel was finding that it was impossible to erase years of that "Losing Dodger Complex" in just one season. The team was unable to play with concentration or intensity. Johnny McCarthy, a highly regarded first base prospect, joined the team in September 1934 and made his big league debut on a rainy afternoon in Boston. Late in the game, after a

Boston batter singled, Brooklyn pitcher Ray Benge tossed the ball to Mc-Carthy saying, "Throw it out, John. It's wet."

The rookie dutifully tossed the ball into the Brooklyn dugout. This came as a surprise to the umpires, who had not called time. The Boston baserunner was allowed to advance from first to third on McCarthy's "overthrow." Benge apologized to the rookie. "I forgot to ask for time out." McCarthy tried to explain what had happened to his manager. Stengel shrugged. "Don't let it worry you, kid," he said. "You'll get used to it after awhile."

Stengel's father visited the Dodgers in St. Louis, his first time seeing his son as a major league manager. With the Dodgers up by three runs in the ninth, he left early. The Dodgers blew the lead and lost the game. Unaware, the elder Stengel congratulated his son after the game. "That was a nice job you did," he said, "a most enjoyable afternoon."

The son thought he was being mocked. "So you thought that was a good job," he said. "Well, then, here's what I thought of it." He put his foot through his father's suitcase.

Stengel was not all bitterness over his team's performance. He retained his good attitude, though the sportswriters of the time would have preferred him to have been more traditional, angry and sullen in the face of loss after loss. Stengel hated losing, but he could be philosophical about it. He was bemused when the Dodgers acquired veteran pitcher Rosy Ryan. Ryan had pitched in the majors from 1919 to 1926 (and had been a teammate of Stengel's on the Giants), but had almost exclusively been in the minors since then. Ryan was thirty-six years old, and like Stengel, was puzzled by his return to the majors. "You know my arm's gone," Ryan told Stengel. Stengel was thoughtful. "Well," he said, "You can still sing tenor in the quartet, can't you?"

Finished or not, there was an element of nostalgia to having Ryan around. Stengel well remembered McGraw's aversion to calling for a fastball, which meant that pitchers like Ryan had to rely exclusively on their off-speed pitches. Watching Ryan pitch was like stepping into a time machine. "McGraw is gone," Stengel sighed, "but Ryan's curve ball lingers on."

Stengel once wrote, "Anything you can't do well and don't enjoy you generally fall behind in." There is an underlying premise to this statement: you must succeed at what you do, but there is no need to suffer for your art. The level of your enjoyment and the proportion of your success have a parallel relationship. Stengel was able to put things in perspective. "When I don't win, I'm good and mad at night," he said. "But if you think you're going to do better just by being serious all the time, and never telling any stories or doing any kidding around—why, you're a little mistaken." John McGraw, who sometimes became almost apoplectic on the bench, burned out by his mid-fifties and died at sixty-one. Stengel managed until he almost was seventy-five, and lived to be eighty-five years old.

It was this philosophy that led Stengel into many of his more noted antics and flights of fancy, and earned him a reputation as a clown. It would be an exaggeration, though, to say that it was all premeditated, all designed to take pressure off of the ball club. A lot of it was just Stengel's inexorable attraction to the spotlight. He would amuse fans and annoy umpires by "fainting" in the third base coach's box when one of his players was called out on a questionable third strike. On occasion, he even extended this practice to include keeling over from fake heart attacks while arguing with umpires. Stengel discontinued this stunt when after falling to the ground in a mock-coronary faint, he opened his eyes and saw the umpire lying next to him.

He even adopted a mascot. During an exhibition game played by the Dodgers in Dayton, Ohio, Stengel was gifted with a duck, as was the tradition there. Stengel named the duck "Goldberg," and allowed the fowl to accompany him to the third base coaching box. When the Dodgers won the exhibition, Stengel apparently decided that Goldberg was lucky and brought him to Cincinnati to coach third base there. Unfortunately for Goldberg, the Dodgers were swept by the Reds. Stengel concluded that he was perhaps not so lucky after all. What happened to Goldberg next is not clear, but it is likely that Stengel invited him to dinner.

These gestures were designed to lighten the mood of a losing team and encourage fan support. Stengel believed that it was part of his job to be appealing, especially with the team losing; good feelings about the personnel could deflect fan hostility towards the team's performance and thus encourage attendance. In those days before ball clubs had extra revenue from merchandising, television, and radio, a club's financial status would in large part be dictated by how many paying customers could be brought into the stands. Stengel was well aware that his ability to retain his job was tied to attendance levels. As he said later of another losing ball club, "We are frauds . . . but if we can make losing popular, I'm all for it."

Stengel would go to extreme lengths to make losing popular. In the second game of a Sunday doubleheader against the Giants with National League president Ford Frick in attendance, the Dodgers found themselves trailing by five runs in the second inning. When a Dodger baserunner was called out on a close play by umpire Ziggy Sears in the fifth inning, Stengel took the opportunity to stir up the crowd. Frick remembered, "Casey immediately went into action. He gestured wildly with both arms. He kicked the bag, and the dirt alongside. He jumped in the air. He went down on his knees as if in prayer. Meantime, his jaw was waggling like an unhinged shutter in a strong wind. I couldn't hear what he was saying, but he was saying plenty. I've seen a lot of Stengel demonstrations over the years, but this one was a masterpiece, worthy of Barrymore at his best.''

Frick was astonished that Sears did not eject Stengel. After the game was over, Frick asked his umpire why Stengel had been allowed to remain despite his histrionics. Sears only laughed. "He wasn't arguing or calling me names, Boss. All the time he was saying, 'Don't pay any attention to me, Ziggy. We've got a big crowd, and these guys are kicking hell out of us. I've got to give the people something to cheer about.'" Stengel would sometimes say of a bad performance, "The attendance was robbed," but he always went out of his way to make sure the attendance didn't notice.

Sometimes Stengel had no ulterior motive other than to amuse himself. He loved to rib opposing rookies and would sometimes try to psyche them out by pretending they were ill. "Hey boy," he would yell, "you're as pale as a sheet today. No kidding! You ought to see a doctor. If I was as sick as you look, you wouldn't find me on the bench. I'd be in the hospital.''

As Ring Lardner had understood years earlier, by its very nature, Stengel's public persona would act to ingratiate Stengel and the team with the fans and the writers. In general, the writers treated Stengel very well, recognizing both his ability and the handicap that he worked under. Still, he had the usual manager's complaints about his treatment at the hands of the press. "I have often wondered whether I knew anything about baseball," he said, "after reading the papers the day after I have been trying to beat the Cardinals in ninety-two in the shade with a whole family of Deans throwing balls at my club." In 1949 he reflected on the treacherous nature of the press: "First they want you for radio, then they want you for television, then they want you for luncheons, and all of a sudden, they want you fired.''

The remark about the Deans was only slightly exaggerated. They continued to bedevil the Dodgers on a regular basis throughout the season. The climax came in September 22. In the first game of a doubleheader, Dizzy Dean earned his twenty-seventh victory of the season by shutting out the Dodgers on three hits. In the second game, his younger brother Paul pitched a no-hitter. It was an amazing performance by the two brothers, although Dizzy was not impressed. "If I'd known Paul was gonna pitch a no-hitter I'd have pitched one too," he said. Just before the game he had taken Stengel aside and told him, "You ought to get a pitcher like me and develop a team around him." If Stengel glanced in the direction of Van Mungo and sighed quietly, Dean failed to notice.

With the sweep, the manager was disconsolate. "How would you feel?

You get three itsy-bitsy hits in the first game and then you look around and there's the little brother with biscuits from the same table to throw at you." Still, he was able to find one bright spot in the evening's events. "I didn't see a base-runner for eighteen innings, so I couldn't make any mistakes."

The amazing thing about the Dean sweep was that it wasn't even a unique accomplishment; the brothers had been doing similar things all season long. In their previous joint appearance—each brother had pitched one game of a Polo Grounds doubleheader—the Deans had swept Bill Terry's team, thereby doing inestimable damage to the front-running Giants' pennant chances.

The Dodgers were never in contention and the summer had been filled with long afternoon contests that were, for the Dodgers, virtually meaningless. There were bright spots: Len Koenecke had his breakthrough season. Rookie shortstop Lonny Frey hit .284 and took fifty-two walks, though he was more notorious for the forty errors he had made. One sportswriter had written a parody of a hit song of the day:

> *Lost, a game we should have won*
> *Lost, a fly ball in the sun*
> *Lost, and how the bleacher fans did cry*
> *Lost, and all because of Frey*

Tony Cuccinello hit a career-best fourteen home runs, a total that led major league second basemen (Tony Lazzeri of the Yankees also hit fourteen), though he was puzzled by his failure to hit .300 for the third consecutive season. "A person might think that a hitter would be at least as good, with more experience, as he proved to be at the beginning. In fact, you would think he ought to get better with practice and more knowledge of opposing pitchers and fielders. But I haven't seemed to improve myself." Actually, Cuccinello was roughly the same hitter that he had always been; it was the hare-free baseball that had led the decline in his average.

Sam Leslie hit .330 and drove in one hundred and three runs; Al Lopez provided steady offensive and defensive contributions and field leadership; Joe Stripp hit .315 but missed fifty games, a typical development in a career which had endured a fractured knee, broken wrist, dislocated finger, chronic bad ankles, and a severe case of the flu. Mungo led the league in innings pitched, won eighteen games, and posted a fine 3.37 earned run average. All of these individual accomplishments paled beside a shaky defense and a pitching staff that did not exist beyond Mungo, Ray Benge, and rookie Dutch Leonard.

September offered a chance for redemption. The Giants had been in possession of first place since June, but the scrappy Cardinals had slowly narrowed the gap until there was only one game separating them from the Giants. Inserted into this gap by either fate or the whim of the schedule-makers were the Brooklyn Dodgers.

The Dodgers season, and Casey Stengel's managerial term, began with a wisecrack by Bill Terry. "Are the Dodgers still in the league?" All year long, the Dodgers had failed to answer him. Thanks to the St. Louis Cardinals, the Dodgers would get one final chance to reply. On September 25, the Giants possessed a one game lead over the Cardinals in the National League pennant race. Playing Cincinnati on September 27, a day the Giants rested, St. Louis won to close the gap with the Giants to one-half game with just four games left to play (the Giants were down to only three). On the twenty-eighth, with the Giants again idle, the Cardinals sent Dizzy Dean to the mound against the Reds. Pitching on only two day's rest, Dean spun a complete game shutout. The National League pennant race was now a dead heat. The Giants, comfortable in first place for so long, would have to win the pennant by beating the Dodgers in the final two games of the season.

In Brooklyn, a World Series atmosphere surrounded the games. The possibilities for irony inherent in the confrontation were obvious. Stengel was caught up in the excitement as well. "The Dodgers will be happy to put the Giants out of their misery," he said. To match Terry, who was known as "The Tennessee Colonel," he was commissioned an honorary Kentucky colonel.

The games would be held at the Polo Grounds. Van Mungo was Brooklyn's starter in the first game. Bill Terry went with Roy Parmalee, Stengel's Toledo protégé.

Moments before the first game, as players and reporters milled about the visiting clubhouse at the Polo Grounds, a telegram was delivered to Casey. The message read, "You'll win the undying gratitude of Brooklyn fans if you knock Bill Terry and his Giants flat on their backs." Stengel read the message aloud to his players and then yelled, "This calls for a special meeting!" He chased the reporters out of the clubhouse. In the main, the point he made to his players was, I know Parmelee. He's wild. "Wait him out. . . . Make him give you your ball."

The game remained scoreless for the first four innings as Mungo and Parmalee dominated the opposing team's hitters. In the top of the fifth inning the Dodgers took a 1–0 lead when Mungo scored on outfielder Buzz Boyle's single. They scored another run in the sixth when Mungo, the hitting as well as pitching star of the game, drove in Lonny Frey. Meanwhile, Mungo continued to hold the Giants scoreless.

In the seventh, Lonny Frey singled and Koenecke bunted him over to second. Sam Leslie ripped a ball through Terry at first for an RBI single.

It was a borderline call; to many in attendance, including Stengel, it looked like Terry should have fielded the ball. From the third base coach's box, Stengel's voice wafted across the diamond to Terry at first. "Tough luck, Bill. . . . They're gonna say you kicked away the pennant."

In the bottom of the frame the Giants finally managed to break through against Mungo when George Watkins hit a home run, but for once the Dodgers neither panicked nor fumbled the lead away. They scored twice in the top of the ninth inning and took a 5–1 lead into the Giants' final at-bat.

In the bottom of the ninth, Bill Terry led off with a single and Mungo, fatigued, rattled, and customarily wild, walked Mel Ott. Stengel considered removing Mungo from the game, but stayed his hand; Mungo was uncommonly focused, and he struck out the next three batters to end the game and the Giants rally.

Mungo pitched nine innings, allowing one run (Watkins's home run) on five hits. He walked three and struck out seven. Meanwhile, the Cardinals were in St. Louis, once again playing the Reds. Throwing "biscuits from the same table," as the day before, the Cardinals followed Paul Dean to a 6–1 win. After, the Cardinals sat in their clubhouse and waited for news of the Dodgers game. When news of Mungo's win reached them, a wild celebration broke out. The players danced about the locker room, chanting, "Brooklyn is still in the league! Brooklyn is still in the league!"

The Brooklyn fans were similarly ecstatic. It is easy to be cynical about the amount of posthumous sentimentality heaped on the Brooklyn Dodgers, especially today, when baseball as an organization is disdainful of the fans, when the ballplayers are millionaires, the owners are billionaires, and the lot of them are swathed in corporate logos, but Brooklyn baseball really was a community affair. Stengel was treated like a member of the family, the bar mitzvah boy. The "Section M Rooters Club" of Ebbets Field presented him with a suitcase. Not to be outdone, the corresponding club for Section N gave him a pen and pencil set. It was the Depression; no one had any money. They really cared.

With the Dodgers' victory and the Giants' loss, the Cardinals had passed New York and now resided alone in first place. More importantly, the Cardinals had clinched no worse than a tie for the pennant. They were one game ahead of the Giants with one left to play.

On Sunday, September 30, the Giants and Dodgers once again took the field at the Polo Grounds. With the Cardinals game taking place concurrently, the two teams would not know whether their game had any meaning until it was over.

Stengel's starting pitcher for the second game was righty Ray Benge, a fourteen-game winner. Terry put his hopes on the shoulders of the excellent knuckleballer "Fat" Freddie Fitzsimmons, who had won eighteen games. Meanwhile, in St. Louis, Dizzy Dean had again returned on just two days rest to pitch one more game against the Cincinnati Reds.

The results of the second day's battle were anticlimactic for everyone but the Dodgers and their fans. Benge failed to survive the first inning, allowing four runs on four hits and two walks. Stengel's relievers fared better, holding the Giants to just one more run over the following nine innings. Fitzsimmons could not hold the Dodgers. They scored individual runs in the second, fourth, and sixth innings. Two more runs crossed the plate in the eighth, tying the score and necessitating the removal of Fitzsimmons. With the Dodgers threatening to score again in the top of the tenth, Terry resorted to the expedient of bringing in ace Carl Hubbell to try to save the season. The Dodgers scored three runs off of the veteran left-hander. The Giants failed to score off of Tommy Babich in the bottom of the inning, and the game ended Dodgers eight, Giants five.

Back in St. Louis, Dizzy Dean climaxed his season by winning his thirtieth game, shutting out the Reds 9–0. The Cardinals had won the National League pennant. The Giants were to go home for the winter. Stengel put a final twist on the season's mantra. "The Dodgers are still in the league," he said, "but not very still."

The Dodgers' season ended amidst the chaos of the visitors' clubhouse at the Polo Grounds, with the Dodgers wildly celebrating as if they had won the World Series, rather than simply prevented another team from attending it as a participant. The manager was as caught up in the excitement as any of his players. With the season ended on a triumphant note, a euphoric Stengel sent his players off for the winter. "Farewell, my bonny men! Some of you are off to maim the gentle rabbit. Some of you will shoot the carefree deer. I bid you Godspeed, my lambie-pies, my brave, young soldiers. Go with Casey's blessing upon your sweet heads." Before the final good-byes, Stengel led his team in a salute to Brooklyn. "There isn't a finer, sweeter, better gentleman or lady on God's green footstool than a Brooklyn fan. Three cheers for the Brooklyn fan, and the first mug that doesn't cheer gets a kick in the shins."

A little bit later, after some of the excitement had died down, Stengel was inclined to be charitable towards the Giants. "The Giants thought we gave 'em a beating Saturday and today. Well, they were right. But I'm sorry for them when I think of the beating they still have to take. Wait until their wives realize they're not going to get those new coats. I've been through it and I know." Stengel even considered going to the Giants clubhouse to shake Terry's hand—but thought better of it, and ultimately elected not to. When Terry caught up with him a bit later, he told Stengel that had he gone he might not have made it out alive. The manager also offered a weak compliment: "If your ballclub had played all season the way you did the last two days, you wouldn't have finished sixth."

"And if your fellas had played all season long the way did the last two," said Stengel, offering a last piece of perhaps unneeded gamesmanship, "you wouldn't have finished second." Terry made as if to fight. "I'm sure you can take me, Bill," Stengel said. "But I'll take a piece of you with me." Terry backed down.

The mood outside the Polo Grounds was even more festive than inside the ballpark. Taking the subway back to his hotel in Brooklyn, Casey was recognized by a mob of Dodger fans and not allowed to leave the train. He was forced to make almost a complete circuit of the New York subway system, riding from the Polo Grounds in Harlem to Coney Island, up to Times Square, and back to Coney Island again, before the fans would cease celebrating long enough for Stengel to excuse himself from the train at Borough Hall in Brooklyn. It took him four hours to get home from the game.

When Stengel arrived in Detroit for the first game of the World Series, he was eagerly welcomed into the Cardinals clubhouse. The Cardinals cheered for him; hugged him; patted him on the back. Casey undoubtedly appreciated their gratitude for the Dodgers' role in the St. Louis pennant, but he had his mind on more important matters. Good-naturedly waving off the Cardinals, he said, "Your felicitations are all very well, gentlemen, but I can't deposit them at my bank. You should have voted me a share of that World Series swag."

Stengel need not have worried about money. The Dodgers ownership and executives had been caught up as well. At the end of the 1934 season, Stengel had completed one year of a two-year contract. The Dodgers voluntarily tore it up and gave him a new three-year contract and included in it a raise of $5,000 per annum. Instead of entering 1935 as a lame duck, Stengel would now be employed by the Dodgers at least through the 1937 season. At that moment in October, he was probably the most popular manager ever to work in Brooklyn—including Uncle Robbie.

Stengel was exhilarated. "They have made it clear they believe I'm the manager and I believe it too. If I didn't I wouldn't sign this contract."

The season had been long, difficult, and for the most part, unsuccessful, and yet it had ended on the right note. Much of the year's disappointment had been softened by the enthusiasm generated by two games in September. Next year, it seemed, would be better. For the first time since he played for John McGraw, Casey Stengel could sit back, enjoy a comfortable winter, and regard the coming of spring optimistically.

CHAPTER 7

OUT OF THE
TRENCHES BY CHRISTMAS

"Brooklyn was the borough of churches and bad ball clubs, many of which I had."

—Casey Stengel

A kaleidoscope of wasted time: Stengel's contract is torn up by the Dodgers, extended by two years. He is given a fifty-percent raise, from $10,000 a year to $15,000. He didn't win the pennant, but he beat the Giants when it counted, and now the organization has some momentum for a change. From now on, the sky's the limit, and to prove it, we now have Dazzy Vance.

Wait a minute.

Dazzy Vance had been a great pitcher for the Brooklyn Dodgers. His years there would eventually get him into the Hall of Fame. He achieved seven consecutive strikeout titles, led the league in earned run average three times, and won as many as twenty-eight games in a season. He was the Nolan Ryan of his time. The problem was that his time was the 1920s.

Vance, forty-four, had left Brooklyn after the 1932 season. Max Carey had dumped the pitcher, then forty-one, on the St. Louis Cardinals in exchange for a utility infielder and a journeyman pitcher, neither of whom lasted more than two seasons with his new club. Now Vance was back, the club's only big-name acquisition in its biggest off-season since 1920.

Stengel and Quinn were capable of doing more, but they were still hamstrung by ownership. The club had been in debt since the moment

Charles Ebbets had bought the team with money borrowed from a local furniture dealer. It was rumored that Mrs. Ebbets washed uniforms to save on laundry bills. Now the creditors, principally the Brooklyn Trust Company, had more say in the running of the team than Steve McKeever or the Ebbets heirs. The line of credit would not be extended for player purchases, and so the same year that the Yankees spent $25,000 for a prospect named Joe DiMaggio, the Dodgers brought back Vance for the waiver price of $6,000.

The sports press of the early twentieth century were generally more compliant than those of the present day, allowing perpetual rebuilders such as Connie Mack of the A's to remain beloved civic institutions despite the painful fact that they were perpetrating a kind of fraud, telling the public that their unresolved efforts to build a contender were the result of their own genial incompetence and plain old bad luck rather than being the calculated result of a plan to hold salaries down. Mack once remarked that a perfect Philadelphia A's season was one in which the team opened hot and then gradually declined over the rest of the season. The strong opening satisfied the diehard fans and got the casual buyers coming out, while the losing that followed ensured that there would be no raises that winter. The press let it slide.

The Brooklyn press had generally been easy on the Dodgers, treating the club's foibles as endearing rather than pathetic. However, after the excitement of late 1934 was followed by a complete lack of activity, Tommy Holmes of the *Eagle* blew the whistle:

> Casey Stengel is supposed to be trying to build a winning ball team in Brooklyn. He is also receiving previous little support from the front office. You can check for yourself in the following list of the principal players acquired in the last year, give or take a couple of months.
>
> Tom Zachary, 38 . . . signed as a free agent.
>   George Earnshaw, 35 . . . obtained on waivers from Chicago Cubs. Watson Clark . . . obtained on waivers from Giants.
>   Babe Phelps . . . obtained on waivers from the Cubs. Dazzy Vance, signed as a free agent after receiving his unconditional release from the Cardinals. Zack Taylor, 37 . . . recalled from a Class A league.
>
> . . . The point is that Ebbets Field cannot expect to rebuild with waiver ball players or veteran free agents. The club needs players who are coming and not going. . . .
>
> General Manager Bob Quinn says that the club is willing to buy but doesn't know where ball players in the minors are to be had. And so you can't put the finger on Quinn personally. He isn't scouting himself. But if

Brooklyn scouts can't locate capable minor leaguers, how come other major league clubs come up with them?

Financial realities aside, in taking on Vance, Stengel was encouraged by the example of Wilbert Robinson. "Robbie loved old players," He later recalled. "He loved to get an old pitcher that had a bad arm, because he knew the man was brighter than when he was young and could throw harder . . . he showed them how to take advantage of their experience. And in later years . . . I'd often pick up an old pitcher . . . I'd get the old man to fool the Youth of America." The problem was that Vance had already been an old pitcher when Robbie first discovered him in 1922.

Once, when Vance's stamina was tested, the aged pitcher told Stengel he was "all in."

"All in?" mocked Stengel. "That's just the trouble with you pitchers. Never in shape." Truer words were never spoken. Robinson had intended that his old-timers be used to supplement a pitching staff. Brooklyn was proposing to rely on them. Stengel was consternated. "I've tried a flock of young pitchers. Some of them, like Walter Beck, Phil Page, and Art Herring, are back in the minors. . . . The young pitchers haven't shown me that they're winners. Why shouldn't they show that they can beat out old fellows like Vance and Tom Zachary out of jobs?"

Stengel's question contained a key inaccuracy, "young pitchers." Stengel had failed to succeed with youngsters because he had never had any. Beck was thirty years old in 1934. Page was twenty-nine. Art Herring, the youngest at twenty-seven, was already a veteran of five big-league seasons. As a group, their potential was already in their past.

During the World Series the previous fall, Branch Rickey had invited Stengel into his office. There he had been shown a large map of the United States. Over twenty-five red pins had been stuck into the map. Each of these marked the location of a different Cardinals farm team, part of a vast chain of talent production. This was exactly what the Dodgers needed to compete, yet all Stengel could do was laugh. "I'm going to get some of those pins. I think we'll get good results by sticking them into our guys on the bench." He knew that pins were as close as he was going to come to Rickey's system. Quinn did not believe in farm systems, and there was no money for one anyway. The closest thing the Dodgers would have to a farm team was a working agreement with Sacramento of the Pacific Coast League for a first look at their players.

Therefore, that March saw the same old Dodgers convene in St. Petersburg, Florida, for the annual ritual of spring training. Stengel talked up his players and defended the lack of turnover. "I didn't hear of anybody offering us anything . . . that would help our club. It is the old story of the other fellow being willing to give up a broken bat for a good ballplayer. . . . I guess it's no secret I'd welcome a good pitcher.''

That pressing need aside, Stengel said, ''I'm not particularly worried about the team.'' He was satisfied with the infield, and as for the outfield, ''There aren't any Ruths and Cobbs in the layout and maybe I'd have to do a bit of juggling . . . but I did it last year and I know that I can't let anybody in the list go without getting something pretty darned good in exchange.''

That left the pitching, and as the exhibition season went on he continued to harp on the subject, as if complaining about it would shame the current staff into improvement. ''The Dodgers will have a first division club if the pitching holds up. In fact, give me four pitchers of proved class and ability and I'd say without hesitation that we'd finish one-two.'' This was double-talk, though not Stengelese. Give anyone four pitchers of ''proved'' class and ability and he could finish first or second. Lacking these assets, Stengel knew the team's horizons were limited. Asked where the team would finish as opening day neared, Stengel replied that he thought the team would finish first or second—first or second division. ''I believe we'll finish fifth. If we finish fourth I'll be amazed. If we finish third I will be knocked dead.''

What the Dodgers had in 1935 was what they had had in 1934, Van Mungo and Dutch Leonard. After that it was pot luck. The sensation of camp was left-hander Harry Eisenstat, a nineteen-year-old Brooklyn native. Pitching in relief, he was unhittable in his first few appearances. ''I'm not sure he has enough stuff,'' questioned Al Lopez, ''but he won't make any mistakes. He knows how to pitch.''

Rewarded with a start against the St. Louis Browns, Eisenstat proved Lopez's doubts, giving up seven hits and seven runs in two and a third innings pitched. Clutching at straws, Stengel tried to accentuate the positives. ''I'll rate Harry a real prospect and he's a swell boy too, but we'll all know more about him when we see him react to his first beating . . . no pitcher in the world can continue to pitch shut-out ball indefinitely. Sooner or later they hit 'em all. It's then you can tell something about a pitcher. The good one's are back for more in their next start.''

Eisenstat came back—for more beatings. Such was the dearth of pitching that he made the opening day roster anyway. Stengel hid him until May 19, whereupon he pitched in two games and was banished to Jersey City for the remainder of the year with an earned run average of 13.50.

With the exception of Mungo, Leonard, and sophomore pitcher Johnny Babich (7–11 with a 4.20 ERA as a twenty-one-year-old rookie in 1934), the rest of the staff's spring experience mirrored Eisenstat's. The offense again made a good first impression as almost every regular hit over .300. The only cause for concern was Len Koenecke, who hit only .220 and looked sluggish. He lead the club in runs batted in, so Stengel put aside his doubts.

The writing was on the wall for the offense on March 23, when the Cardinals made 1932 Olympic gold medalist Mildred "Babe" Didrickson their pitcher for an inning during their exhibition with the Dodgers. She walked her first batter, and hit the second, When she grooved a pitch to the third batter, he obligingly lined into a triple play. "My little lambs just couldn't get her," shrugged Stengel. Bob Quinn seemed to be watching a different team. "Unless strange things happen, I don't see how the Reds, Phils, or Braves can beat us out. . . . We're in third place, no less." The Dodgers finished the exhibition season with a record of sixteen wins and eight losses. "That," said Stengel of spring training, "will be that."

The lineup that took the field for the Dodgers opening day was nearly identical to the one the finished the previous season. The one significant change was that Stengel was now platooning the left-handed outfielder Buzz Boyle with the right-handed Stanley "Frenchy" Bordagaray. Frenchy, so named for both his ancestry and his thin moustache, grown in defiance of then–major league convention, had already established a reputation as a free spirit In a short trial with the Chicago Cubs the previous year. "Say, that Bordagaray will be a sensation, I think," observed Quinn. He was correct, but not in the way he meant.

Even with Stengel's first premeditated platoon, it should have been obvious that a lineup of Buzz Boyle, Lonny Frey, Koenecke, Sam Leslie, Cuccinello, Danny Taylor, Joe Stripp, and Al Lopez would be no match for the combined talents of the Cubs' Billy Herman, Chuck Klein, and Gabby Hartnett (all future Hall of Famers); the Cardinals' Ripper Collins, Pepper Martin, and Joe Medwick (the lattor a future Hall of Famer); or the Giants' Bill Terry and Mel Ott (both bound for Cooperstown). Yet the focus remained on the pitching. Prior to Van Mungo's opening day start, Quinn sat him down for a serious talk about his temper. "I told him that I knew of six games offhand he'd tossed away by getting mad last year."

Quinn lectured and the offense was neglected. Stengel, at this early stage of his career, was already delegating the technical aspects of tutoring the pitchers to his pitching coach, but trying to do his bit for the staff helped Mungo's pitching by working on his hitting. "Just meet the ball," Stengel would tell him. "You're trying to hit home runs and you can't. . . . Just meet the ball and you'll get plenty of hits. . . . You'll be a .300 hitter, not just some big monkey up there who's a sucker for any pitcher with an ounce of brains."

Thus Stengel and Quinn, two very able baseball men, tried to make themselves feel useful on a stagnating team. There is no doubt that they believed in their rhetoric and in the importance of their tinkering. These

Dodgers were not the Daffiness Boys. For all of its flaws, the team displayed a consistency of effort and result that tempted the belief that if things broke just right, they could reel off nine or ten wins in a row. Then anything could happen.

Mungo took the lessons of Stengel and Quinn to heart and kept them there just long enough to get through opening day. Pitching at the Baker Bowl on April 17th, Mungo beat the Phillies 13–3, in the process setting a record for pitchers (since broken) by driving in five runs.

The thirteen runs, achieved in the bandbox dimensions of the Baker Bowl, were the season's offensive highlight. Over the course of the year, the team was out-homered by the opposition both at home and on the road. Outside of Brooklyn the lack of offense was especially severe. Opponents hit forty-five homers to the Dodgers' twenty-seven, and overall outscored them 421–362. Away from Ebbets Field's friendly dimensions, the hitting dried up.

Ironically, the pitching, all season the weakness that had kept Stengel and Quinn up at night, was unspectacular, perhaps a bit below average, but only that. Stengel countered their lack of power arms (excluding Van Mungo, the Dodger pitchers struck out 2.7 men per nine innings; the league average was 3.3) by using the bullpen to save twenty victories, leading the league in that category (no one knew it at the time because saves were not an official statistic until 1969. All saves prior to that date were awarded retroactively). The main disappointment was Babich, who showed none of the promise of the previous year. Opposing batters hit .317 against him, resulting in a hypertensive 6.67 earned run average. Scouted personally by Stengel (Babich was a twenty-game winner with the San Francisco Missions of the Pacific Coast League in 1933), Babich would vanish from Brooklyn, shortly to become property of the New York Yankees, where George Weiss would turn him into a suicide weapon.

Slowly, Stengel and Quinn woke up to the problems on offense and began reaching for solutions. With all of the outfielders struggling, minor-league veteran Oscar "Ox" Eckhardt was signed. Playing for the San Francisco Missions of the Pacific Coast League from 1931 to 1935, Eckhardt hit .382. He twice led the league in batting average, hitting as high as .414 in 1933 (315 hits in 760 at-bats over 189 games). Eckhardt was thirty-three years old, and despite his accomplishments his major league opportunities had been limited to spring training auditions with the Cleveland Indians and Detroit Tigers and eight pinch-hitting at-bats with the 1932 Boston Braves.

Before arriving from the West Coast, Eckhardt wired ahead asking for a double room. Players were discouraged from traveling with their wives, but Quinn decided to cater to the new acquisition and allowed the request. Eckhardt arrived not with a woman but with a gigantic St. Bernard. "He always came to camp with me in the minors," said Eckhardt. "I thought he'd enjoy seeing a major league set-up."

Stengel might have been inclined to ignore the dog if Eckhardt had been a more useful player. Cutting corners as usual, the team apparently signed the outfielder on the basis of his statistics without consulting any scouting reports. Had they checked, they would not have been surprised when Eckhardt turned out to be an opposite-field singles hitter who played the outfield and ran the bases like his bovine namesake. "Oscar Eckhardt was the fastest man I ever saw getting to first base," Johnny Babich remembered, "two hops in the infield and he was across first base. But once he got to first base you might as well take him out of there. He was through. He was 'Dumb Old Ox.'"

While a player capable of hitting .367 (Eckhardt's career average in the minors) would have been of great value to the Dodgers, the combination of Eckhardt's inability to pull the ball for home runs and his inadequate defense (not to mention his choice of roommates) were considered too much to ignore when taken with the Ox's intransigence. Stengel begged him to pull the ball. "The third basemen are practically straddling the line on you. You can't get the ball through. Pull it."

"I hit nearly .440 on the coast batting just this way, and the third basemen are just as good as they are up here," Eckhardt replied.

"If they were just as good, they'd be playing up here," Stengel replied. "You don't think all the big-league scouts of America are in a conspiracy to boycott minor league third basemen, do you?"

Eckhardt's audition lasted only sixteen games. He was sent to Indianapolis of the American Association, where he hit .353. His quick disposal suggests that the club was never serious about giving him a chance. Buddy Hassett remembered that the club tried to get rid of the dog before they got rid of Eckhardt. "He said, 'If the dog goes, then I go with the dog.' He did. He went with the dog."

At the same moment the Dodgers were expending their energy on the K-9 Corps, quality major league hitters were changing hands. Kiki Cuyler, a slashing outfielder with high averages and doubles and triples power, was released by the Cubs and could have been had for nothing. Instead he passed to the Reds. Babe Herman, who had had his best years in Brooklyn, was sold to the Reds. Had the club been so inclined, even Babe Ruth could have been signed during the previous winter. The Bambino was an overweight forty-year-old, but would have still been a major power threat in tiny Ebbets Field. More importantly, he would have provided the club with the spark of excitement it was missing. Instead, the Dodgers went for Ox Eckhardt, his dog, and the illusion of activity.

In the place of greatness, or even the residue of greatness, the six-thousand-odd fans that attended each Dodgers game got to see Frenchy

Bordagaray. Bordagaray, twenty-five, had failed to catch on with the Chicago White Sox in 1934 despite hitting over .300 in limited play. In the era of station to station baseball, Bordagaray was noted for his speed and base-stealing ability. The only problem: his instincts for baseball were almost nonexistent or, as Tommy Holmes put it, "Frenchy's speed would have helped them if he'd run in the right direction." Stengel concurred, saying, "Frenchy is the fastest man on the Dodgers—running to the wrong base!"

Bordagaray had a history of eccentric play going back to the minors. Playing for Sacramento of the Pacific Coast League in 1934, Bordagaray apparently forgot to take his position in right field for the bottom of the ninth in a game at Portland. Somehow no one noticed. The game winning hit for Portland occurred when a routine fly dropped into the vacant part of the outfield.

From his first day with the Dodgers, Bordagaray put Stengel on notice that a new showman was in town. In a spring training game against the Detroit Tigers, the Dodgers were trying to tie the game in the last of the ninth. Bordagaray reached base and made it to third with two outs. Suddenly, he took off for home plate. He was out easily, and the game went into the books as a loss for Brooklyn.

Stengel was, for once, nearly speechless. "Are you crazy?" he asked in a tone that suggested that he already knew the answer.

"You ain't seen nothing yet," answered Bordagaray, nodding happily.

Stengel said of Bordagaray, "I aged ten years in one minute the time a fly ball was batted his way. . . . My heart jumps up between my teeth and my veins freeze solid. . . . I collapse on the bench and start counting the new hairs that turned gray and the gray ones that turned white." All that stress for only a routine fly. Imagine the pain Stengel felt when Bordagaray got creative, such as the time Bordagaray literally danced off of second base—he was practicing his soft-shoe—and had to explain to Stengel that he was tagged out because the second baseman got him between taps. Or the time he hit a ball that rolled through the third baseman's legs but only got as far as first base because he stopped to see whether the official scorer called a hit or an error on the play. Stengel fined him twenty-five dollars. Then there was the time when he was chasing a ball in the outfield and his cap fell off, so he chased the cap instead of the ball. "The cap wasn't going anywhere," said Stengel, "but the ball was."

"I forgot," said Bordagaray.

Unsatisfied with being merely a source of frustration, on occasion Bordagaray was capable of causing Stengel physical pain. Catcher Ray Berres remembered an incident that took place just prior to George

Two of the guiding stars of Stengel's professional career, John McGraw, manager of the New York Giants, and George Weiss, future general manager of the New York Yankees. McGraw helped to start Stengel's career, Weiss to sustain it. Stengel called him "That fine fellow . . . who would find out whenever I was discharged and would re-employ me." (National Baseball Hall of Fame Library, Cooperstown, NY)

Friends, teammates, partners, and later bitter rivals, John McGraw and Wilbert "Uncle Robbie" Robinson. Stengel would play for one of the two in seven of his fourteen big league seasons. The intensely focused, hard-bitten McGraw and the acerbic, Falstaffian Robbie would shape Stengel's vision of what a manager should be. (National Baseball Hall of Fame Library, Cooperstown, NY)

Master and student. McGraw and Stengel, freshman manager of the Toledo Mud Hens, confer prior to an exhibition game in April, 1926. It was McGraw who first saw the makings of a manager in Stengel, and his recommendation helped secure the Toledo job for his former outfielder.
(© Bettmann/CORBIS)

Stengel signs the first of his major league managerial contracts, 1934. The player best remembered in Brooklyn for letting a sparrow fly out from under his cap was now expected to run the team and produce a winner—or at least take some headlines away from the New York Giants.
(National Baseball Hall of Fame Library, Cooperstown, NY)

Brooklyn's latest dysfunctional braintrust: first-time major league manager Stengel shakes hands with Brooklyn borough president Raymond V. Ingersoll as owner Steve McKeever (with cane) and general manager J.A. Robert "Bob" Quinn look on during opening day festivities, 1934. (© Bettmann/CORBIS)

The men who hired Casey Stengel, McKeever and Quinn. The elderly "Judge" McKeever had paralyzed the franchise for years due to his unceasing feud with the heirs of Charles Ebbets. Quinn, the architect of the surprisingly successful 1922 Browns, was brought in to reinvigorate the franchise despite ten years of poor results with the Boston Red Sox. (National Baseball Hall of Fame Library, Cooperstown, NY)

Baseball's all-powerful first commissioner, Judge Landis, was at best ambivalent towards Stengel, and it was thought that after the questionable dissolution of the Toledo franchise he might block Stengel's return to the majors. Here, though, he validates Stengel's stewardship of the Dodgers with his presence. (National Baseball Hall of Fame Library, Cooperstown, NY)

Stengel with Philadelphia Athletics owner/manager Connie Mack during spring training, 1934. End to end, these two men were a continuous part of the baseball scene from 1886 to 1975. Mack spent 64 years in the game, Stengel 55. (AP/World Wide Photos)

Stengel the comedian often seized center stage at the expense of Stengel the competitor. In private, or when dealing with his players, the real face would often emerge. This picture was taken during the losing season of 1933, as Max Carey was in the process of alienating his players. (National Baseball Hall of Fame Library, Cooperstown, NY)

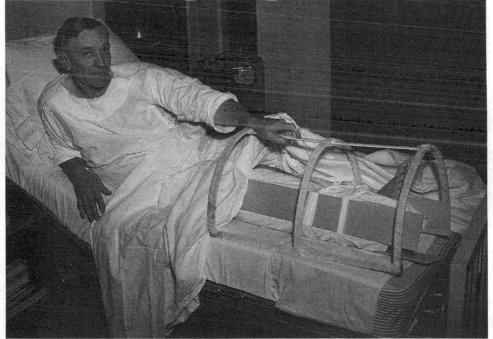

Stengel's leg was shattered when he was hit by a car while crossing Boston's Kenmore Square in 1943. His good friend Frankie Frisch's telegram, "Your attempt at suicide understood," was a comment on the sorry play of Stengel's Braves. With the hospitals full of war casualties, the manager had to recuperate in a maternity ward. (AP/World Wide Photos)

Redemption: Stengel crows as he leads the victory parade for the 1948 Pacific Coast League champion Oakland Oaks. Stengel's success in this nearly major league rehabilitated him in the eyes of the eastern baseball establishment. He likely already knew he would be going to New York in 1949. (National Baseball Hall of Fame Library, Cooperstown, NY)

Out of the wilderness: Stengel, just hired as Yankees manager, surveys Yankee Stadium, albeit one incongruously laid out for football. His decorous posture is diametrically opposed to his clowning reputation at the time. (© Bettmann/CORBIS)

Stengel surveys the possibilities available to a creatively inclined manager within the vast Yankees farm system. In a quarter-century of managing, he had never before had so many options. The Ford listed at the upper left of the blackboard is Whitey Ford, assigned to Binghamton of the Eastern League for the coming season.
(© Bettmann/CORBIS)

Who's sorry? Expressions of fatigue and relief seem to be on the wrong faces as Red Sox manager Joe McCarthy congratulates Stengel on the Yankees taking the American League pennant from the Red Sox on the last day of the season, October 2, 1949. (© Bettmann/CORBIS)

"Moose" Earnshaw's start against the Reds at Cincinnati on May 6, 1936:

> We had been losing, losing, losing. . . . To instill a little life into the guys, Casey decided to hit infield practice and whoop it up a little bit. Casey grabbed an infield fungo stick and he said, "Come on, my little chitlins, let's go." As he ran out of the dugout, Frenchy . . . fired a ball. Casey crossed his path and it hit him in the ear and knocked him out cold. We all ran to see what we could do. And Casey said, "Don't tell me, you don't have to tell me. It was that god-damned Frenchy cracked me in the ear."

It was an eventful day for Bordagaray. The game followed an overnight trip from Pittsburgh, and Stengel had planned on resting some of his players. Thinking he was punishing the outfielder, Stengel put Bordagaray in the starting lineup. "This right field ought to be big enough to prevent you from chipping the concrete with your head," he told Bordagaray. Far from chastened, Bordagaray hit a double, misplayed two flies into triples (of one, which eluded him when the sun ducked behind a cloud and created a momentary shadow, he said, "I lost it in the shade"), made a circus catch of another, and struck out in his last at-bat when he bunted foul with two strikes. In spite of these antics, the Dodgers somehow won a 5–2 decision.

When Bordagaray came into the clubhouse after the final out he confronted two peeved Dodgers—Stengel and Earnshaw. "George," Stengel said, "I'll hold him and you bite him."

"Biting's too good for him," said Earnshaw. For his part, Bordagaray suggested that since the Dodgers had won, he should be allowed to bean Stengel every day as it seemed to bring good luck.

After another particularly egregious series in the field, Stengel took Bordagaray aside. "Tomorrow," the manager said, "I'm going to stand outside the fence and throw balls over to you. You can't catch 'em coming from the plate but maybe you may be able to catch 'em coming the other way."

"Okay, Case," said Bordagaray. "We'll give it a try that way."

Bordagaray's antenna for trouble was his moustache. Ballplayers had not worn facial hair since the 1890's and Bordagaray's only purpose in growing it was to attract attention. "A guy's gotta have color to succeed," he said. "I'm bringing back the good old days. All the great ballplayers used to wear them. I got to thinking that some great modern ballplayer should bring back the mustache, and here it is."

The ploy worked, insofar as Stengel was concerned. Initially he only kidded, "It will only slow you down on the bases," but as his patience with Bordagaray eroded he graduated to threats: "I'm going to tell every catcher in the league to throw at your moustache when you're on the bases." That wasn't often. Bordagaray walked only seventeen times in 422 at-bats, leading to an undersized .319 on-base percentage. "Go shave it off," Stengel grumbled, "before someone throws a ball at it and kills you." Finally, Stengel simply ran out of patience. "I told him, 'They're making fun of you now, and me too, with this mustache.'" Bordagaray shaved.

In June an opportunity to improve presented itself. The Boston Braves were struggling with a winning percentage around .250. Even at that early date in the season it was clear that the team was not going to recover to anything like respectability. Though managed by one of the best ever, future Hall of Famer "Deacon" Bill McKechnie, the team was in complete disarray. Judge Fuchs, the same man who had sent Stengel to Worcester, had finally reached the end of his rope. He had borrowed $200,000 against his interest in the club, and the notes were to come due that August. Desperate for an attraction that would increase his gate receipts, The Judge signed Babe Ruth, promising ambiguously that he would replace McKechnie as manager with The Babe. He had no intention of doing this. Ruth's disillusionment came swiftly; he quit the team in anger. This drama, which played out from March through June, pushed drab issues like winning and losing into the back seat. The pitching staff, averaging a venerable thirty-three years old, packed it in, recording an earned run average that should have been impossible in the pitcher's paradise that was National League Park. It appeared Judge Fuchs was doomed to lose the club.

Fuchs proposed to move his team to Fenway Park and turn Braves Field into a dog racing track. Both the Red Sox and Judge Landis refused. Scrambling, clutching, he picked up the telephone and began the time-honored fire-sale.

The two best players the Braves had to offer were center fielder Wally Berger and lefty pitcher Ed Brandt. The Dodgers seemed a natural fit for both. Brandt, thirty, was a veteran starter who had won at least sixteen games four years in a row, albeit with bulging earned run averages. Berger, twenty-nine, was one of the premier offensive players in the National League, a fact only partially obscured by the offense-damping effects of Braves Field. A career .310 hitter with a .540 slugging percentage, Berger had slugged 135 home runs over the previous five seasons (sixty-six at home, sixty-nine on the road). All Fuchs wanted in return was cash, either $75,000 for both, or $45,000 for either one.

Stengel and Quinn had the same opinion about the proposal: absolutely, positively yes. The Brooklyn Trust Company declined to see things their way. The only way the Dodgers could borrow the money for the transaction was on a personal note from a member of the Dodger board of directors. The signatures of the board members were not forthcoming. Berger and Brandt remained in Boston. No team bit; the National League owners had decided it was time for Fuchs to be starved out of baseball.

Inevitably, the rest of the season was spent treading water as the Dodgers settled into fifth place. The only thing that remained was for mediocrity to be replaced by tragedy. All season long, Koenecke had struggled to replicate his performance of the year before. Mid-September found him hitting .283 average with only four home runs. His attention to defense had declined with his offense, and he had not stolen a single base. He was moody and unfocused. He failed to run after hitting the ball, took the wrong position in the field, and lost track of how many outs had been made. Koenecke's excessive drinking seemed to be a symptom of a larger mental illness, rather than the cause itself.

With the club in St. Louis to play the Cardinals, Stengel decided to make a move, sending Koenecke, Les Munns, and rookie Bob Barr to Jersey City. The other two players were to watch over Koenecke as they made their way back to the East Coast.

Throughout his career, Stengel had a permissive attitude towards his players' consumption of alcohol. "John McGraw used to say, 'Don't drink the water,'" he would say. Well into the twentieth century, players that did not drink were considered to be lacking in manhood. "They say some of my stars drink whiskey," he said, "but I have found that the ones who drink milkshakes don't win many ballgames." At the same time, drinking to excess was frowned upon (Stengel himself was a frequent consumer, but was rarely if ever seen to be intoxication). To Stengel, drinking only became a problem when it affected a player on the field. "No ballplayer should ever get into the habit where he drinks before a ball game. . . . When I had one of those boys, I said, 'Well, this man is limited . . . if he doesn't want to change—why, disappear him.'"

This was one way in which Stengel's handling of players differed from John McGraw's. Wilbert Robinson's Dodgers may have been known as the Daffiness Boys, but it was McGraw, not Robinson, who repeatedly chose to surround himself with a rogues gallery of the greatest drunks, eccentrics, and crooks the game had ever seen. As much as by the tactics of winning baseball, the mind of McGraw was absorbed by cat and mouse struggles with these miscreants. Through a combination of detectives, economic incentives, and verbal (sometimes physical) abuse he connived to stop the drunks from drinking, the obese from eating, and the gamblers from selling out. Robinson had the alcoholic pitcher Phil Douglas and gave up on him after twenty games. McGraw struggled with him for over three years, just as he had with "Bugs" Raymond, "Turkey" Mike Donlin, and countless others.

McGraw's willingness to take on the chronically recalcitrant was partially the result of his longevity in the game. In McGraw's playing days, many of the biggest stars were prodigious consumers of alcohol, and a big part of the manager's job was keeping his roster dried out long enough for them to play the day's game. Ned Hanlon, McGraw's manager with the old Baltimore Orioles, said, "If you tried to run a league with teetotalers alone, the boozers would start a league and outplay and outsell you."

Long after baseball had acquired a greater pride of professionalism, McGraw was still at it. It was a perverse part of his personality, perhaps springing from the egotistical belief that he, the "Little Napoleon," was the one manager who could take baseball's insensate legions and by application of his brand of discipline make useful, winning ballplayers of them. Sometimes he even succeeded, but at a tremendous cost to his own serenity. Donlin was the cause of countless trips to the local police station to post bail. Catcher Larry McLean, a violent drunk, bumped into McGraw away from the ballpark, and without explanation, "calmly picked up his chief and unceremoniously dumped him in a public fountain." Raymond would take the baseballs with which he was supposed to be warming up and trade them for drinks. In 1932, as McGraw's days dwindled down to a precious few, a good many of his remaining hours were devoted to scanning the enormous Shanty Hogan's meal vouchers for signs that he had conned the kitchen into slipping him an extra sausage link at breakfast. "Worrying over Bugs Raymond took five years off my life," McGraw wrote, and he was right.

When Hogan became available to the Dodgers in 1935, Stengel refused to take him. "He can catch a good game for you," Stengel admitted, "and I like his hitting. I managed him at Worcester 19 years ago, and recommended him to the big leagues as a first baseman. That was of course, before he started carrying that duck [a euphemism for gut, apparently] around with him." As such, Stengel was unwilling to carry the player unless he came with his Braves uniform because it was too late in the season "to get another tent made." (Then there was pride. Observed Tommy Holmes of the *Brooklyn Eagle*, "It looks very bad for a club that is trying hard not to slip into seventh place to pretend to strengthen itself by the addition of a player who has been unconditionally released by the Boston Braves.")

Koenecke and his two chaperones began their flight back to New York. Koenecke was put off the plane at a scheduled stopover in Detroit. He had been drinking and became disruptive. He then chartered a plane to take him to Buffalo; he had family there. As the flight neared its destination, Koenecke began harassing the pilots. It is possible he was sexually aggressive towards the pilots. A struggle for control of the plane broke out. Trying to subdue him, the co-pilot struck Koenecke in the back of the head with a fire extinguisher, killing him. Stengel was badly shaken by the news. His decision to demote Koenecke had led indirectly to the outfielder's death. Unable to make a public statement, a writer impersonated Stengel and gave a statement of regret to the press.

The Dodgers' 1935 season, with its record of seventy wins and eighty-three losses, went into the books as a disappointment, a failure to capitalize on the excitement of the previous season's denouement. Ironically, the exciting finish was also blamed for the club's complacency. "Such a strong finish set up a standard of false values in Flatbush," Tommy Holmes wrote. "Nobody's salary was cut, no worthwhile new players were obtained." Harold Parrot blamed the poor showing on an atmosphere that encouraged indolence. "Playing with a lose-always, second-division, also-ran team . . . it kills the incentive, that will to win, makes good ball players into stumblebums who play for 'the first and the fifteenth'—when the paycheck comes. That's Casey Stengel's problem." Stengel concurred. Pointing to one of his players in the dugout, he said, "As smart a player as they come. One weakness—likes to stay out late. Stays out now; but wouldn't, if we were going any place. Get the idea? No incentive to deliver his very best!"

Parrot noted that Stengel had become more insistent on discipline as the players began to drag, keeping them in the lineup when they asked for days off as well as turning his quick wit to sarcasm. "Yesterday," Parrot wrote, "he yanked Frenchy Bordagary out of the game pronto when the fellow didn't slide in the fifth and was out at the plate." "Oh," shouted Stengel, "that man is so fast he doesn't have to slide!"

Stengel was smart enough to know that mere surliness was not going to improve the Dodgers and he searched restlessly for solutions that would be within his means to execute. With expensive acquisitions out of the question, that meant somehow making the current roster into something more than what it was. He grasped onto the idea that he might find a more potent lineup formula if he could move the players to positions others than those at which they had been fixed. "I keep shiftin' 'em around," he said, "working 'em all I can, just to find out who the real deadwood is, so I know where to start next year." In one August game, Koenecke (center) played right. Boyle (right) played center. Bucher (infield) played left field. Cuccinello (second) played third. Frey (shortstop) played second. The winning pitcher was Bobby Reis, formerly a third baseman and outfielder.

Stengel speculated about making even more position changes in 1936. "We could experiment with Johnny [McCarthy, who Stengel had converted from pitching] at first. We can experiment with Junior Frey at second base—when Junie is able to get in there and play. We can use Jordan at shortstop until somebody beats him out of that job. We can use Cuccinello and Stripp at third and shift Jimmy Bucher to the out-field." Just five days after speaking those words, he was pondering yet another alignment. "You have Cuccinello at third base. He is learning to play it better all the time. I will bet you he is my 1936 third baseman. Frankly, I need a shortstop. [Lonny Frey] gets hurt too much in the infield . . . he's too valuable to be out of the game that way. We'll put Frey and Bucher in the outfield." He also thought about moving Joe Stripp, who had played over 700 games in the infield, to the outfield, and putting the burly catcher Babe Phelps in left or right.

He even tried making Frenchy Bordagaray a second baseman, an inex-plicably masochistic undertaking. "I started to study the position," Bor-dagaray recalled a few years later, "just as I had studied the violin. Finally I asked him, 'Do you want me to pivot like Billy Herman does, or do you want me to pivot my own way?' I did not see anything funny in the remark at the time, but Casey was out for a week. . . . Pulled a muscle in his side laughing, he said. . . . Stengel did not trust me after that."

This kind of desperate shuffling was an understandable attempt to react to the team's lack of star power. As with 1934, the voting for Most Valuable Player underscored the Dodgers' lack of top talent. Twenty-seven players representing seven of the eight National League clubs re-ceived votes. No Dodger was mentioned. The Phillies, who finished thirty-five-and-a-half games behind the first place Cubs, and six games behind the Dodgers, had four players receive votes.

That winter, the Dodgers took another step away from professionalism when Judge Landis appointed Bob Quinn to run the Boston Braves. Quinn had shown that he did not possess any insight into how to dispel the team's perpetual malaise, but he was one of the most experienced baseball men in the country with some successes, however remote, on his résumé. His replacement was John Gorman, who had been in the Dodgers organization for his entire professional life, beginning as an as-sistant to the late Ed McKeever. Lately he had been the team's traveling secretary. It was not an appointment that augured a new dynamism in the borough.

At the winter meetings that year, Stengel acted alone in his negotia-tions with dangerous horse traders MacPhail and Rickey and failed to get anywhere. "There's only one way to get the best of that Rickey," Stengel once said. "You let him talk for three hours on the strong and weak points of the players he wants to scoop. Then when Branch says, 'Is it a deal?' you snap 'No!' and walk out on him."

Trade talks conformed to the same pattern they did the previous win-ter when clubs tried to get Mungo for minimal return. "I'll admit that I could have traded Van Mungo," he told Tommy Holmes, "and I'd have been a sap if I had accepted any of the offers that were made for him.

The clubs that want Mungo are first division outfits to which big Van would have meant a pennant. They won't give me a pitcher of his ability alone. They won't give me two regulars. So," he concluded, "you can say that I'd be a complete fathead to shoot the big boy in any kind of deal."

Mungo presented a complicated problem for Stengel to solve. He was too talented to trade lightly, but his talent did not necessarily add up to a good ballplayer. In later years, Stengel would be less hesitant to divorce himself from this kind of player, but by then he had the benefit of being older, more experienced, and in a system that guaranteed he would not be short of talented players. To be fair, Stengel was not the only baseball cognoscenti who failed to get value out of Mungo. After him, Larry Mac-Phail and Leo Durocher were tempted by the great fastball and erratic temper, and they too reaped only meager rewards. They were like Stengel: "I had some sort of an idea of letting my number one man—Mungo—go for general team strength. I couldn't do it."

Stengel had mastered the concept that more is not necessarily more. He knew the quality of the players he had in Brooklyn and had no desire to augment their ranks. Asked why he had passed on outfielders Jack Rothrock and Ernie Orsatti, both released by the Cardinals, Stengel answered, "I don't want them. . . . As Brooklyn manager I'm not interested in spending the rest of my life in the second division. I want to beat the clubs that are on top. St Louis is one of them. How can I beat the Cardinals with ballplayers that can't make the St. Louis team?" Instead, he devoted a considerable amount of time talking to Pittsburgh's Pie Traynor about a trade for future Hall of Fame outfielder Paul Waner. The two could not come to terms, if Waner was in fact available at all.

Meanwhile, Quinn sought to turn Brooklyn's unsettled finances to his own advantage. The Braves organization was at least $233,000 in debt when he took over, but as head of the new regime he had the goodwill of his creditors. For a brief moment Boston was on a better financial footing than Brooklyn. Quinn knew that with their lackluster follow-up to 1934, the Dodgers would be looking to make a splash with a flashy trade. Stengel admitted as much. Armed with this knowledge, Quinn made the Brooklyn Dodger management—not Casey Stengel—an offer they could not refuse. The word came down to Stengel that he had to make a move. On December 12, 1935, over Stengel's protests, the Dodgers sent Al Lopez and Tony Cuccinello, their two best players, and pitcher/outfielder Bobby Reis to the Braves in exchange for Ed Brandt and thirty-year-old reserve outfielder Randy Moore.

Years later, Lopez remembered that Stengel could hardly bring himself to discuss the trade. Stengel showed up at Lopez's hotel room during that winter at three o'clock in the afternoon and stayed until after two in the morning, obviously trying to say something but unable to force it out.

"He became quiet for a few minutes," Lopez told Donald Honig, "and I could see he had something on his mind.

"'Dammit, Al,' he said all of a sudden, 'I'm going to have to make a trade. It's either you or Mungo, and I'd like to keep Mungo because he's younger and because he brings people into the park.' . . . He had been sitting around all afternoon and all night figuring out how to tell me."

The trade refuses to identify itself as anything other than a salary dump. Brandt, who could have been had during the season for only cash, was thirty-one, and had been one of the principle causes or victims of the Braves' 38–115 season. He had lost nineteen games, he allowed five runs per game, and opponents hit .319 against him. Moore had been in the majors for eight seasons and was firmly established as a singles hitter who recorded decent averages but little else—in other words, a clone of Danny Taylor, Buzz Boyle, Joe Stripp, et ceteras ad infinitum.

Stengel, ever the loyal company man, was left to defend a trade he in which he did not believe. "I've been around here for five days trying to make a trade and generally getting the bird. Well, we made this deal and now so far as I'm concerned they can come to me.

"They've already started coming . . . they try to rib me, tried to tell me that there is this and that wrong with the new players I got in the deal. Well, for all they know, there may be something wrong with the players I gave Boston. I know damn well they didn't get my club into the first division."

And with those words, Stengel retired from the field. "I've a couple of theme songs. The first is, 'I'm Out of the Trenches by Christmas.' The second is, 'California Here I Come.' . . . Love to all and if you want to talk trade, wire, write, or come to Glendale, Cal for the next couple of months."

He went home unmolested, as the trade failed to raise much protest. The newspapers were curiously indifferent. Rud Rennie wrote in the *New York Herald-Tribune* that, "Lopez, while not the smartest catcher in baseball, may prove useful if his arm is all right. Cuccinello is an experienced infielder who has slowed up a lot." The Dodger roster was now so bland, so beige, that it aroused only apathy.

In a separate transaction, also achieved without Stengel's collaboration, the Dodgers traded promising outfielder Gene Moore and pitcher Johnny Babich to the Braves in exchange for veteran right-handed starter Fred Frankhouse. The sale of Sam Leslie to the Giants followed shortly thereafter.

A few months later, the Dodgers were still trying to restock an outfield that had been light on power since the now distant days of Babe Herman. The Cardinals offered a promising twenty-one-year-old right fielder named Eddie Morgan. All they wanted in return was Joe Stripp and cash.

At the time, Morgan had hit twenty home runs in 416 at-bats shared between Columbus of the International League and St. Louis. Gorman turned them down. "The Dodgers are tired," he said, "of giving up fifty cents for a dime."

The 1936 edition of the Brooklyn Dodgers had absolutely no power, hitting fewer home runs than any team in the majors, twenty-seven less than the next worst team. When the power outage was combined with an impatient approach—the team was last in the majors in walks—the team struggled to score runs; only the Braves scored fewer. With Bordagaray, Mungo, and catcher Babe Phelps the team had personality, but this did not make up for the lack of excitement on the field. A sense of complacency had overtaken the players, and lackadaisical play was the result. Lonny Frey was the Dodger Defensive Ineptitude poster boy, making sixty-six errors playing shortstop and second base. Buddy Hassett made twenty-six errors at first base. The Dodgers were last in the majors in double plays turned. They were punchless at bat and sloppy in the field.

In this sense they were repulsive even to their own players. They had signed future Hall of Famer Fred Lindstrom, who had spent most of his career under McGraw on the Giants. Dodger first baseman Buddy Hassett recalled Lindstrom's reaction to a particularly hapless loss. "I saw Freddie play his last game. . . . Lindstrom came into the clubhouse and said, 'I'm a son of a gun. I heard about these things that happen in Brooklyn. I never thought it would happen to me, and I'll tell you, it's never going to happen again.' He took off his uniform and never put it on again." Lindstrom left Stengel a "cryptic" note saying he was quitting because he couldn't help the team.

Hassett might have been remembering the game of April 16. The Dodgers had carried a 6–5 lead over the Giants into the ninth inning at the Polo Grounds. With two on and two out, Giants Hank Lieber popped the ball up to Lindstrom in left field. Lindstrom settled under it, only to be run over by shortstop Jimmy Jordan. With both players insensate the two baserunners scored easily to end the game 7–6 in favor of New York.

Lindstrom's departure was no great loss as he had not had an impact season since 1930. What little offense the Dodgers could muster that year was supplied by Ernest Gordon "Babe" Phelps, otherwise known as "The Blimp." As his two nicknames imply, Phelps was one of the greatest hitting catchers of all time, but he couldn't keep out of his own way. (When ball clubs switched their method of transport from trains to airplanes, Phelps refused to fly, and became known as "The Grounded Blimp." Later, when Phelps refused to join the Dodgers on a boat trip to Havana, Leo Durocher concluded that, "he wasn't cut out to be an amphibious blimp either.") Platooning with the punchless Ray Berres, one of the worst-hitting catchers of all time, Phelps hit .367 with twenty-three doubles.

Stengel once asked Phelps why he had not called for a knuckleball at a critical moment in a game. "It's hard to catch," replied The Blimp.

"Did it ever occur to you that if it's hard to catch it might be hard to hit too?" Stengel asked.

"I hadn't thought of that," said Phelps.

The most productive regulars after Phelps were Hassett, who hit a soft (no power, no walks) .310, and Junior Frey, who drew seventy-seven walks. Another way of looking at the situation would be to say that there were no productive hitters after Phelps. Out-homered at Ebbets Field by a three to one ratio, the team did not make for compelling viewing.

On July 11, Gorman finally made a deal with St. Louis, acquiring the rights to Eddie Morgan and left fielder John Thomas Winsett, another prospect the team had coveted. Winsett, twenty-six, had failed to stick in previous trials with the Red Sox and Cardinals, but was in the process of authoring a season at Columbus that was guaranteed to make any baseball man willing to let bygones be bygones: a .354 average, fifty home runs, 154 runs batted in, and 144 runs scored.

Branch Rickey had backed off his earlier demand, yielding the two players and cash in exchange for an initial down-payment of the rapidly failing Moose Earnshaw, now thirty-six and less than a solid citizen in the clubhouse to boot (in 1933, Connie Mack had suspended Earnshaw three times; after a fourth incident he told the pitcher to go home and never come back). This should have been a warning sign: Winsett hit a powerless .237 in the major leagues. Later, Rickey explained why. "Watch that beautiful swing, my boy," he told Harold Parrot. "Mr. Winsett sweeps that bat in the same plane every time, no matter where the ball is pitched! Woe unto the pitcher who throws the ball where the Winsett bat is functioning, but throwing it almost anywhere else in the general area of home plate is safe!" Though taken, the Dodgers were still obligated to make their second payment that December, sending Frenchy Bordagaray, Dutch Leonard, and Jimmy Jordan to St. Louis.

Though it was small consolation, Earnshaw made a point of endorsing Stengel as he left Brooklyn for Rickey-land. "It's the first team I'm sorry to leave. . . . I'd certainly like to work for Casey Stengel on a good club. . . . It's my opinion that he'd rate among the great managers in the game if he had a club with half a chance. . . . I never saw a second division manager make so few mistakes." Earnshaw's previous experience with managers was limited to Connie Mack and Jimmy Dykes.

There was another missed opportunity that year that would have major ramifications for Stengel's future. Brooklyn native Phil Rizzuto, eighteen years old, came to Ebbets Field for a tryout. After an indifferent session in the batting cage, Stengel took the boy aside. "Look kid, this game's not for you. You're too small. . . . Why don't you get a shoeshine box?" Rizzuto would not forget the humiliation he felt in that moment. When Stengel came to the Yankees he would remember his resentment.

In various re-tellings over the years, Rizzuto has ascribed the offending "shoeshine box" comment to others. In Dom Forker's *The Men of Autumn* he is quoted as saying that Stengel thought he was too small to play, but it was Bill Terry, in a separate tryout with the Giants, who flung the insult. In his Hall of Fame induction speech, he mocked "Stengel and Bill Terry, [who] told me I was too small to play baseball." In other published versions, Stengel is not even present at Rizzuto's tryout and it is coach Otto Miller who utters the offending words, or it is Giants coach Pancho Snyder who is the adult with the foot fetish, while Stengel offers the more generic dismissal, "Go peddle your papers, shorty." Or perhaps what Terry said was, "Kid, don't even suit up. But I'll give you a ticket for the game this afternoon." But then, as Milton Gross recognized in 1949, Rizzuto is, "a story-teller of Munchausen proportions." Whatever the truth, from the time of the tryout on, Rizzuto intensely disliked Stengel.

Stengel cut loose when the 1936 season came around. He had always been lively on the bench, a quality he maintained into his old age. Tommy Byrne told Donald Honig, "I really think Casey was at his best when things were tough, when it was close. . . . He'd come off the bench and start yelling and hollering and throwing left hooks into the air and the first thing you know he's got the whole team following suit and everybody is putting out a little more."

In 1936, he carried the act onto the field. Trying to get a game called on account of rain, he coached third base wearing high striped stockings and holding an umbrella. On another occasion, when his suggestion that a game should be called on account of darkness was denied, he signaled for a pitching change using a railroad lantern. "Don't want no trains to run over me in this here darkness," he said before he was thumbed from the game. Stengel was subsequently fined by the league for his dramatization (Al Schacht, the "clown prince of baseball," said of this incident, "That's one, I'll admit, I never thought of"). He "fainted" at close plays and tough calls, had theatrical arguments with the umpires, and made a spectacle of himself as often as possible.

These antics confirmed Stengel's reputation as a clown. The team lacked focus, but Stengel's attention seemed to be focused on getting laughs. It appeared to some that he had ceased to care about winning ballgames. Otto Miller disputed that assessment. "When I think of the players Casey was trying to win with in the Thirties—wow! . . . Yet Casey was always trying something new, always hoping that he would catch lightning in a bottle. He reminded me of fellow who had made up his mind to force a pair of deuces to beat four aces, but he never stopped trying."

One of Stengel's most famous one-liners from this period came when Stengel went for a shave and a haircut. "Don't cut my throat," he told the barber. "I may want to do it myself later." This was typical of the man. He would not express his feelings directly, at least not to the public. But he would allude to them often, in this manner; the public often lost the point in the punch line. Mel Allen once asked Stengel about the act he put on during these years. His response: "With the clowns I had as players, that's the only way you can survive." He did what he could to put fans in the seats, and to boost his own morale. If the ball club was not capable of entertaining then he would. No manager could have won with the 1936 Dodgers. Not every manager could have attempted to bring fans to the ballpark just by giving free reign to his sense of humor. As Branch Rickey said, "Casey was the best link or bridge between the team and the fans in the history of baseball."

Stengel's exuberance in the face of defeat was more than just a ploy. He honestly believed that baseball should be fun, a concept that he later tried to convey to Mickey Mantle: "One time, when I was especially gloomy over the way I was going, he made me a speech about how baseball should be fun, and that a man who did not get fun out the game was not going to stay loose and do his best."

Of course, the Dodger management was in it for more than just fun. After bottoming out in 1934, there had been incremental gains in attendance. The 1936 Dodgers drew 489,618 fans, good for third in the league. This was less than was needed to service the team debt.

Stengel was signed through 1937, but there were signs that his position was slipping. In late August, Gorman told Tommy Holmes that the team was nearing a trade for a second baseman, but refused to divulge any further details. Wanting the full story, the reporter raced to Stengel.

"[What] did Gorman tell you?" asked Stengel.

"No details, but enough to make me think that he is close to some kind of deal."

"Uh-huh," said Stengel.

"But I can guess who it is," said Holmes.

"Who do you guess?" The writer named a name. Stengel shrugged. "You may be right."

"Don't you know?" asked the reporter, incredulous.

"No," replied Stengel. "Gorman won't tell me. He says it's confidential." The reporter rightly concluded that Stengel had been cut out of the loop.

Stengel's fate was sealed when Van Mungo staged a "rebellion" that became public. After pitching and losing a close game in Pittsburgh,

Mungo was consumed by frustration. The club, he felt, had failed to give him adequate support. "I've been the sap for this outfit long enough," he told Stengel. "I've carried this club on my shoulders for years, with nothing but lousy support, and have to make my own hits to win the ones I do. I want to be traded."

Stengel was unsympathetic. "Listen, I just manage the team. I don't own the team. I can't trade you. I couldn't sign a paper because no trade is any good unless it's got the owner's name on it."

Drinking heavily ("He got disturbed that night," as Stengel put it), Mungo decided he would fly back to Brooklyn on his own and present his grievances to Steve McKeever. A writer paid for Mungo's ticket home, hoping to create a scoop. Stengel was informed that Mungo had jumped the team. "Let him go if he wants to," Stengel said. "I can lose with or without him."

Mungo received his audience with McKeever. He complained that there wasn't a professional on the team other than himself. He hung around Brooklyn for a few days after that; nothing was done. This was intentional; in the days when the reserve clause bound players to their clubs in perpetuity, owners were always quick to squelch any suggestion that a player could motivate his own trades. Where the players were allowed to work was the exclusive domain of the magnates. It was quickly suggested that Mungo's dissatisfaction made him morally undesirable. Branch Rickey had been trying to entice the Dodgers to trade Mungo to the Cardinals, but no more. "We don't want him now," said Rickey, "not a man who quits like that."

Stymied, Mungo slunk back to the team. Stengel did not reprimand the pitcher for an act that had the potential to embarrass him before the team ownership, but he did pay extra attention to the pitcher's exercise regimen. "I thought, 'Well, he can't be in too good a shape after laying off like that. I'll just put him to work.' And you can believe I really gave him plenty of work out there in practice to get him back in condition."

The axe finally fell on October 4, 1936. Not much was said to Stengel. "They told me that the club hadn't done so well—hadn't made much money and they decided unanimously to make a change." He seemed more relieved than upset to be finished with Mungo and a few other similarly inclined players. "Them fellas made my life miserable," he said.

His main interest was in making sure that he would be paid off. "What I'm interested in now is the three year contract into which I entered in good faith and the feeling that there was good faith on the other side. I've got a year to go on that, you know, and I'm going to be curious, not only about whether I'm going to be paid off, but how." The answer was, in monthly checks, just as he had been getting paid. For some reason, though, the Dodger front office insisted on mailing them to Omaha, Ne-braska.

Undiscouraged, he turned his back on the Dodgers in characteristic fashion. "So much for the past," he said. "As for the present—I think I have a future."

His faith was strengthened by a farewell party thrown by the Brooklyn sportswriters. Stengel had been three years of good copy, and they genu-inely liked him. The *Eagle* called him the only man in the Dodger organi-zation who knew where first base was. The Yankees and the Giants (with Sam Leslie as their first baseman) played a Subway Series that fall, and so the party was attended by most of baseball's luminaries, in town for the games. One of the guests observed, "This must be the first time any-one was given a party for being fired." It was said that in his five years as coach and manager of the Dodgers he had become personal friends with half the borough. Stengel didn't disagree. "I meet 'em all," he said, "from mugs to millionaires." It took two additional parties to accommo-date all those who wished to give him a proper send-off.

Stengel returned to Brooklyn on opening day 1937, watching the game as a spectator. The Dodgers, crisply attired in new uniforms, held the lead for most of the game, only to fumble it away. Enjoying his paid vacation, Stengel could afford to be amused—and even feel some valida-tion. "The new uniforms fooled me at first, but I recognized the boys in the late innings."

CHAPTER 8

HE CAME TO
SEE POVERTY

"Now, boys, I know you're doing the best you can, and I'm not complaining about losing. But, gee, couldn't you take a little longer doing it?"

—Casey Stengel

For the first time in his adult life the dreaded words "out of baseball" applied to Casey Stengel. The description was only technically accurate. He attended every game of the 1936 World Series (no great inconvenience since the entire Series was set in New York), the major league winter meetings, the minor league winter meetings, the All-Star Game, every game of the 1937 World Series (once again an all–New York affair), an endless series of banquets, and, perversely, many Dodgers games. In short, he went wherever there were baseball games or people were talking baseball.

Having turned down at least one offer to manage in the minors— "You're a big leaguer now," George Weiss advised. "Stick to it."—he and Edna spent the year becoming wealthy. When the Dodgers acquired Randy Moore in the Cuccinello/Lopez salary dump, they had received both a reserve outfielder and a generous Texan with connections to the oil industry. Moore had offered to help Stengel invest in some wells, and Stengel accepted. He and Edna put up $10,000 and began to spend time in Omaha, Texas. The investment paid off, though Stengel was always reticent about his return. It was suggested by some that the wells had made him a millionaire, that he recouped his investment three times over in ten years. He denied it. "The oil well is something like an annuity. It pays a steady income, but nothing sensational." In 1938 *The Sporting News* reported that Al Lopez, also an investor in Moore's wells, was earning $200 a month on an investment of $30,000. If these figures are accurate then Stengel's initial return was somewhat less than advertised.

The point was soon moot: subsequent investments (penicillin, for example) managed by Edna soon gave Stengel financial security independent of baseball. He no longer needed the game to provide him with an income. He could afford to be choosy about taking a job. Instead, he picked the Boston Braves.

The kindest thing to be said about the efforts of those who ran the Boston Braves from 1901 to 1943 was that they sometimes came within spitting distance of basic competence. The team enjoyed near-misses in two World Series, but for most of their half-century of competition with the Red Sox, the Braves were simply not any fun.

When John McGraw (like Chesterton's Sunday, at the center of everything) arranged for Judge Fuchs to purchase the Braves, he hadn't considered Fuchs's lack of capital—McGraw's understanding of financial matters being inversely proportional to his understanding of baseball. Fuchs was a wealthy man but not a magnate. He required additional investment to put up the $350,000 price of the club. Fuchs's lack of financial independence doomed his stewardship of the Braves from the start.

In fairness to Fuchs, he knew that he was in over his head. His initial impulse in buying the club had been a kindly one: the dying Christy Mathewson needed something to do. Mathewson, Big Six, McGraw's greatest pitcher. Mathewson the handsome. Mathewson the honest. Mathewson the dying of tuberculosis complicated by an accidental gassing during the first World War. Mathewson left the planet, and therefore the Braves, less than two years later, his failing health never permitting him to take full control of the club. On the rare occasions he did weigh in, his influence was less than constructive: in 1924 he argued that giving his players more than $4 a day in meal money was overly generous. This had the effect of alienating his players, among them veteran right fielder Casey Stengel. Mathewson died on October 7, 1925. Thereafter Fuchs was on his own, without an experienced baseball man to guide him.

Despite hosting both an American and National League franchise, Boston was never a two-team town. Both the Braves and the Red Sox had their fans, but they seemed to be the same people; each club drew well at times, but almost never simultaneously. If the Red Sox were up, the Braves were down, and vice versa.

Fuchs bought the Braves at the same moment that Bob Quinn took over the Red Sox. That first year, both clubs were so inept that they kept all the fans at home: the Braves were last in attendance in the National League, the Red Sox last (by a considerable margin) in the American League. They swapped places for a few years after that, and the Braves convincingly outdrew their Hub cohabitants from 1931 to 1933. After that it was all Red Sox. Saddled with a mortgage on Braves Field that was extremely favorable to its holders and further handicapped by his own profligate habits in the areas of both business and pleasure, Fuchs struggled even in the years that he had good attendance.

Braves Field itself muted the team's appeal. The man who built Braves Field in 1914 disdained the prosaic over-the-fence home run. With initial dimensions of 402 feet down each of the foul lines and 550 feet to center field and nearly eleven acres of playing surface, Braves Field was intentionally configured so that an inside-the-park home run could be hit in any direction. Ty Cobb dropped in on the ballpark at completion and made a prediction: "Nobody will ever hit a baseball out of this park." He was very nearly correct; it would be ten years before a ball was hit over the left field fence, and that shot came in batting practice.

Braves Field failed to anticipate not only Babe Ruth and the coming prevalence of the home run, but more importantly, that fans would want to see home runs. Faced with the choice of coming out to Braves Field to watch a bad team hit 400-foot pop-ups or staying home by the radio, many opted for *Amos 'n' Andy*.

From time to time, the team tried to drag the park into the present by bringing in the fences, only to find that the stadium's actual location, right on the Charles River, stopped them—pardon the pun—cold. Fly balls would be caught by a stiff, chill wind off of the river and kept in the park. Stengel would call this feature, "Old Joe Wind, my fourth outfielder." The Braves were stuck with a dead-ball game in a lively-ball world.

Fuchs's recipe for drawing fans was to add gate attractions. He tried Rube Marquard, Stuffy McInnis, Jesse Barnes, Dave Bancroft, Rogers Hornsby (who had the best season in Braves' history, .387 with 21 home runs), George Sisler, Rabbit Maranville, "Jumping" Joe Dugan, Burleigh Grimes, Babe Ruth, and even Casey Stengel. These were all fine players, future Hall of Famers in some cases, but the Judge acquired every one of them after they were on the bad side of thirty years old. As ballplayers, their shelf-lives were too limited to build around. Every few years the Braves were forced to burn everything down and start over.

The nadir of this practice came in 1935, when Bill McKechnie (another future Hall of Famer), a manager who liked working with older players, discovered what happened when an entire roster reached retirement age at once. The Braves won only thirty-eight games and lost 115, the worst single-season record of all time. The Braves were so bad that when McK-echnie brought them in fifth in 1937, *The Sporting News* named him manager of the year.

That year, Judge Fuchs, a mostly well-meaning man who had the cards stacked against him, finally lost his team. There was relief at this; Fuchs had failed to make good in twelve years of trying everything from making himself manager for a year to proposing that the Braves Field be vacated for dog racing to making Babe Ruth a vice president. It was time for someone else to have a turn.

The new regime was fronted by Bob Quinn. As he did at Brooklyn in 1934, Quinn tried to drum up fan interest by creating public debate on a new name. Eschewing exquisitely appropriate suggestions such as "Boston Sacred Cods," and "Boston Bankrupts," he changed the name of the team from Braves to B's, and renamed Braves Field "The Bee-hive." Innovative management in Boston had hit the ground running.

When it came to rebuilding, Quinn was lacking in solutions. He did, however, understand the problems. On coming to Brooklyn in late 1933, he described the cycle of frustration that can grip a losing ball club:

A ball club is a machine. On a tail-end club you have perhaps three good players and a collection of Class A, B and C players ranging from mediocre to impossible. Your task is to build a new club around the few good players as a nucleus. You trade here and there, take on young players, grope in the dark. Perhaps you discover two or three. Meantime your original two or three good players have grown old and slipped. You are exactly in the position of a man with a second-hand machine who is rebuilding that ma-chine with second-hand parts. Meantime he must turn out the same grade of work with that machine that a rival does a new, well-oiled and efficient machine. If you have money to buy new parts, you can get somewhere. If you must experiment, you're doomed to a perpetual headache.

What then of the Bees? "They look pretty well shot to me," Quinn said in 1935, "but I've never had a team handed to me yet that wasn't shot." Had Quinn made an evaluation of the Boston situation consistent with his understanding of rebuilding—no money, no progress—he might have stayed in Brooklyn. The position was a promotion in that Quinn went from being answerable to McKeever et al to being the ultimate decision-maker for an entire organization. It is difficult to turn down an opportu-nity to be emperor, even if it is abundantly clear from the start that the emperor will have no clothes. "Better to reign in hell than serve in heav'n," Milton wrote, and Brooklyn was far from heaven. Quinn gave in to the temptation, and so too would Casey Stengel. Stengel missed the baseball life terribly.

Consistent with his Brooklyn stewardship, Quinn undertook a search for a new manager. This time he didn't need Bill Terry to provide him an excuse as McKechnie had resigned to take the same position with the Cincinnati Reds. Quinn received over 150 applications once it was made public that the job was available. Roger Peckinpaugh, Kiki Cuyler, and Rogers Hornsby were among those interested. Because of his past association with Quinn, it was immediately rumored that Stengel was in line for the job. "Nobody has said a word to me," Stengel told reporters. "If any consideration is to be given to me I tell you honestly I know nothing about it now." But when he bumped into Quinn at the World Series the day after McKechnie resigned he told him he would like to be considered for the position. Quinn responded coolly: "I want to give the matter a good deal of thought."

In fact, Quinn had already composed a short list of candidates and Stengel was not on it. Before the Series was over he offered the job to Rabbit Maranville, the former standout at shortstop. A Boston institution for twenty-five years, Maranville had been offered the Braves job once before, by Fuchs in 1929. On that occasion, he had refused to take the position without a five-year contract. He didn't even get that far with Quinn. "When I met him over at New York during the big series, he acted as though he hardly knew me," Quinn sulked.

The next name on Quinn's hit parade was Donie Bush. Bush had played shortstop for the Detroit Tigers in the years of Ty Cobb. Later, he had managed the 1927 Pirates to the World Series, where he was dispatched in four games by the Murderer's Row Yankees. Bush's term with the Pirates ended amidst increasingly self-destructive personality conflicts with his players. In 1927 he benched Kiki Cuyler in a dispute over the batting order. Two years later, he benched Paul Waner, a career .356 hitter to that point, for the punchless Fred Brickell. Stengel was once asked what it was that had made him a great manager. "I don't trip my players on the way out of the dugout," he replied, or as he put it on another occasion, "Don't cut off your nose yourself." As for Bush, asked forty years later to reflect on his managerial foibles, he said, "If I had to do it all over, I would handle it the same way."

In subsequent years, second-division finishes with the White Sox and Reds landed Bush in the American Association. Propelled by two of the greatest minor league stars, Joe Hauser and Buzz Arlett, he had had several good finishes as the manager of the Minneapolis Millers, apparently satisfying Quinn as to his suitability for another major league job.

When a major league job is offered to a minor league manager, a translation to the higher plane would normally be a fait accompli. Bush hesitated. The Boston Braves were the one case where the minors were preferable to the majors. Better to serve in Minneapolis than reign in

Beantown. There were other inducements to stay in the land of a million lakes. Bush told Quinn he wanted to think it over. "Of course, it is a temptation to return to the Major Leagues because it is the ambition of every manager and player to be up there," Bush told reporters, "but honestly I have been so happy in Minnesota it will be difficult for me to make up my mind what to do."

Bush's Midwestern *joie de vivre* was directly tied to his ownership of a beer distributorship, as well as partnerships in a sporting goods store and a hockey club. Managing the Braves would never be that lucrative, or as pleasant. Bush considered for two days, then turned Quinn down. "It was hard to pass up a chance to return to the Major Leagues," he said, "The newspapers and the fans have been so grand to me that I didn't have the heart to leave, . . . Fortunately, I am well fixed financially and can afford to turn down the Boston position."

Knowing that Stengel had five offers to manage in the minors, including rumored invitations from George Weiss to manage at either Newark or Kansas City, Quinn went to still another name on his list, Cubs star catcher Gabby Hartnett. This was pie in the sky stuff. Though Hartnett was thirty-seven years old, he had hit .354 in 1937 and missed out on the Most Valuable Player award by only two votes. Phil Wrigley was not going to part with the best catcher in the National League, who also figured in his managerial plans. By the middle of next season Hartnett would replace Charlie Grimm as manager of the Cubs. Wrigley was about to create for himself the same problem that Bill Veeck inherited when he bought Lou Boudreau's Cleveland Indians: how do you fire your most popular player when you decide he can't manage?

Rebuffed by the chewing gum magnate, Quinn shrugged his shoulders and turned to his Brooklyn discovery, Casey Stengel. On October 25, 1937, Quinn invited a dozen reporters into his office to witness the ceremonial phone call to Stengel. It took over two hours and twenty dollars to get a connection to Stengel in Omaha, Texas. What followed was anticlimactic:

QUINN: Casey, do you want to come with us next year?
STENGEL: I'd be delighted.
QUINN: Okay, you've got the job.
STENGEL: I'm delighted. . . . Thank you. We'll fool a lot of the boys.

As with Quinn's hiring of Stengel in Brooklyn, there was the not-so-subtle denial that Stengel was a clown. "Many of these fellows know you only as you were when you used to pull chippies out of your cap," Quinn said into the phone, "but I know what you really are." Quinn turned to the reporters. "Don't sell him short."

Actually, Quinn was hoping that Stengel would not sell *him* short. Along with Bush, Stengel fit into the limited category of major league managerial candidates who were known to have cash resources. Quinn was looking for more than a manager; he wanted an investor as well. Stengel put at least $20,000 (and possibly as much as $50,000) into the team.

Stengel was always conservative in his predictions for his teams, except with the Mets where everything he did was calculated for comic effect. Asked if the team had overachieved in 1937, he said, "I don't think they were lucky to finish fifth. I believe we can do it again if we do not finish higher." Still, lackluster ball club or not, this was a homecoming. Stengel had been, he said, "fooling around with a little oil—but I'm a baseball man now."

Three days later, Quinn was still apologizing to reporters for the comedic reputation of his fourth choice for manager:

> I know of fewer smarter baseball men than Stengel. . . . Many wise quips are credited to him and over in New York, especially, they have capitalized on every witty remark he makes, but all one has to do to ascertain that he is far from being any buffoon is to sit down and talk with him. John McGraw, a keen judge of men, and a manager who always sought to gather smart men around him, stated more than once that Stengel could do more good just sitting upon the bench than many of the players active in the field. . . . He's a keen judge of a player's ability; no one is any smarter than he when it comes to making trades. . . . With him directing the club— and in this regard I want to state that he will be the one solely in authority—I feel that the interests of the Bees will be in capable hands.

In 1964, President Lyndon Johnson happened to be in Pittsburgh at the same time as Stengel's Mets. "He wanted to see poverty," said Stengel, "so he came to see my team." The comment would have also applied to the Braves, who unlike the Mets were actually poor, and worse, suffered from a poverty of good esteem that the Mets, loved in inverse proportion to the quality of their play, never knew. Nor did the Braves have luck or timing on their side. Whatever could go wrong did go wrong. A butterfly twitched its wings in China, and a hurricane would hit the Beehive.

Stengel surveyed his team at his first meeting with the Boston writers and pronounced himself satisfied. "Our ball club is pretty good right now. The players are satisfactory and the pitching staff is that of a first division club.

"I could tear this club apart tonight and start rebuilding from the bottom, but that's not the way. I'm hopeful that added experience should provide the better batting that we need." That is, his initial thought was to add veterans to the team.

He refused to be drawn into his own "Is Brooklyn still in the league" controversy, deflecting questions about whether the B's would outperform the Dodgers. "Well, I won't say. I don't want to comment too much about the Dodgers right now. We are going to try to take any position that's open. With an average break of luck I expect to do well." And then, as if the reference to the Dodgers had reminded him of his reputation, he added, "I am serious and I am ambitious."

The roster of the 1938 B's resembled nothing so much as those of the Brooklyn Dodgers of 1934 to 1936. There was, happily, no Van Mungo or Frenchy Bordagary, but Tony Cuccinello, Al Lopez, Johnny Cooney, Bobby Reis, Gene Moore, and Joe Stripp had all been imported by Quinn. Why run away from your problems when you can take them with you?

Unlike Stengel's Dodgers, the team's veteran core was supplemented by a few young players that actually had a chance to develop into quality players. First baseman Elbie Fletcher was only twenty-two, discovered when he won an audition in a newspaper contest. The youngster lacked power, but made up for it with a good batting eye. The ability to draw walks was essential to scoring runs in that era of station to station play (in fact, it is essential to scoring runs in any era, a fact not completely acknowledged even by today's managers and executives).

Vince DiMaggio, twenty-five, had ridden his younger brother Joe's coattails to the majors in 1937, ironic since it was his own success with the San Francisco Seals that inspired Joe to play professional ball in the first place. The younger DiMaggio joined the Seals as a shortstop but was quickly moved to the outfield—where he took Vince's job. DiMaggio moved on to the Hollywood Stars where he was an afterthought to scouts until his brother's New York splash.

Less talented than either Joe or his even younger brother Dom, the Beehive was the one place in the majors most likely to smother his one offensive skill, home run hitting. Over his last 1,300 Pacific Coast League at-bats (1936 and 1937) he had socked seventy-nine doubles and forty-three homers, a rate good enough to have landed him among the 1937 National League home run leaders had he sustained it in the majors. Instead, his home park held him to only thirteen home runs in his rookie year. Blessed with the great outfield range of all the DiMaggios, he was an asset in center field even though most of his own best hits were caught at the warning track.

The youngest and most promising prospect was the most important to Stengel, because he was his own discovery. Left fielder Max West was first noticed by Stengel during the winter of 1935. He was nineteen years old, still playing sandlot baseball. Stengel intended to sign him for the Dodgers, but he had been either late in trying or was overruled by the Brooklyn front-office. West signed with the Sacramento Solons of the Pacific Coast League. His numbers that year were not awe inspiring, but his physical tools suggested a coming star. Playing for the San Francisco Missions two years later, he finally capitalized on his talent, hitting .330 with thirty-three doubles, twelve triples, and sixteen home runs. Stengel had kept an eye on him, even tutored him from time to time, and now he had Quinn sign him for the Braves.

The pitching staff was unpromising, despite having led the league in earned run average in 1937. McKechnie had amazed baseball by making twenty-game winners out of two unusually mature rookies, Lou Fette, thirty, and "Milkman" Jim Turner, thirty-three. Along with thirty-three-year-old Danny MacFayden (winner of fourteen games in 1937), these soft-tossing minor league veterans were being counted on to form three-fourths of Stengel's starting rotation. As pitchers in their thirties, the entire trio was at risk for sudden physical breakdown. Their success in 1937 was a surprise. A repeat performance in 1938 would be a miracle. No one talked about this. Baseball statistics had not achieved any kind of currency, and so it was difficult to spot trends that anticipated the peaks and valleys in the career performance of players. It was a time when it was far easier to be optimistic about a fluke year sustaining itself.

There was an air of excitement about the team, despite its obvious shortcomings. Even as the world political situation slid inexorably towards World War II, there was something uplifting about the idea of the Boston Nationals being good for a change. Coming out of a meeting with British Prime Minister Neville Chamberlain, Joseph Kennedy, the United States' ambassador to the court of St. James, tried to explain the average American's isolationism to a pack of reporters. "Right now," said Kennedy, "he's more interested in how he's going to eat and whether his insurance is good than in foreign policy. Some, maybe, even are more interested in how Casey Stengel's Boston Bees are going to do next season." At the moment when the British were looking for American support against German expansionism, the message from the United States' ambassador was, "How can one worry about Hitler when there's a pennant race in the offing?" No wonder Chamberlain opted for appeasement at Munich.

The new spirit of optimism was caught by the Braves' players. When Stengel showed up early for spring training, he found twenty-one men already in camp, anxious to start making an impression on the new boss. Stengel disregarded the chilly February weather and began drilling his men. Mindful of cold related injuries, he warned his men to "make haste slowly."

Stengel addressed the team at the official opening of camp:

You must realize that this club is a new one to me and while a few of you guys have worked for me before, I have an open mind. Just because you fellows all signed contracts before starting south doesn't mean a thing. You are all hustling to make or hold a job. The club has gone to great expense to bring you down here and it is up to me to show that this coin has been well spent. Within the next few days, I'll find out what most of you can do. I have to make good as well as you.

In Boston, Stengel would be able to "make good," free, at least theoretically, of the kind of nagging, niggardly oversight he was subject to in Brooklyn. Anxious to show that with a free hand he could run a professional camp, Stengel began to innovate, improvise, command. He insisted that all his players be awake by eight-thirty. He pushed his pitchers hard, working them out twice a day. "Other outfits may hold but one session daily," he said, "but . . . I'm new to the men and they're new to me. I have to find out the kind of material I have." He pushed the hitters even harder, knowing that the Boston attack was inadequate. He ran "scientific" hitting drills in which a batter was only allowed to pull the ball, or hit to the opposite field. Once he even stood behind the batting cage and called out what pitch the batter was getting as it came in to the plate. The New Riot Act had come to Brooklyn; McGraw's heir came to Bees' spring training at Bradenton, Florida.

Off the field, he remained the irrepressible Casey Stengel. Late one night during spring training, Stengel appeared at the hotel room door of two Bees' beat writers. "Can I come in?" he asked. "I'll only stay a couple of minutes. I'm dead tired." At five o'clock the next morning, Stengel was still there, rolling around the on the floor demonstrating how Uncle Robbie would squeeze into his rubber corset. It was another of Stengel's patented all-night performances, worthy of John Lardner's later remark about him: "He can talk all day and all night, in any kind of track, wet or dry."

Bees' batboy Donald Davidson (who Stengel called "Duckbutt") recalled one of Stengel's first postgame talks with reporters:

Now, you ask me why I pitched this guy today. That's a good question, but it's also a dumb question and I don't ever answer dumb ones. However you guys got a job to do just as I have, so I'll try to cooperate out of the goodness of my happy heart.

I stayed awake most of last night thinking about this game and I made up my mind just before I fell to sleep that this man would not only be pitching this game but win it. I never had any doubts about it and that's why I went to sleep. In order to sleep properly, you have to be relaxed. This pitcher relaxed me last night.

And onward from there, a rain of verbiage signifying nothing except a man enjoying himself. "Well, gentlemen, I hope that answers all your questions."

One of Stengel's main goals for spring training was to replace short-stop Harold "Rabbit" Warstler, whose nickname applied both to his quick fielding and his soft, fluffy bat. Warstler was a former Quinn Red Sox property who had been purchased from the A's to replace the inof-fensive Billy Urbanski. Incredibly, Quinn acquired the flatly punchless Tommy Thevenow at about the same time, thereby endeavoring to re-place Urbanski, an extremely poor hitter, with two players who were his-torically notable for impotence at the plate.

Stengel's plan was to move Cuccinello to third, where his hitting might compensate for his eroding defense. Warstler would be moved to second base, and shortstop would be opened for one of three promising rookies in camp: Roxbury, Massachusetts native Joe "Tweet" Walsh; Harl Mag-gert, son of a former major leaguer who had been banned for accepting a $300 bribe to throw a Pacific Coast League game; or Bob Kahle.

Walsh had the most interesting background of the three. As a child walking home from Sunday school, he passed by Fenway Park and spot-ted Bob Quinn sitting next to an open window. He shouted, "Hey you! Why doncha go get a ball team." Quinn, familiar with the neighborhood kids who frequented the park, recognized Walsh. "I know you, young man, and you'll never get into this park again!" Walsh never did go back to Fenway. Nor did he see Quinn again—until he played for his Braves.

In a harbinger of the season to come, none of the three shortstops was able to claim a job. All three suffered what were essentially career-ending injuries before the end of the training season. Each made token appear-ances during the 1938 season and were never heard from again. The Braves prepared to open the season with the same infield configuration as the year before.

At the start of the season the Bees came whimpering out of the gate, then rebounded. At the Polo Grounds in New York, they dropped their opening game to the Giants 13–1. The team settled into seventh place. A sweep of a strong Pittsburgh Pirates team at Forbes Field sent the Bees back towards the middle of the National League. Still, at the end of their first road trip, Bill Terry, always willing to compliment a Stengel team, remarked that his club, "looked like the same old Bees."

Terry's was an accurate assessment. The Bees could not score. An early series against the Phillies provided what would be a typical experience. The previous week the Giants had visited the Phillies at the Baker Bowl, their cozy home park. The Giants bashed the Phillies mediocre pitching staff for twenty-nine runs in three games. Transplanted to the Beehive to face the Braves, those same inept Phillies pitchers became clones of Cy Young, involving Stengel's team in three pitcher's duels. Through July 10, the Bees outhit their opponents .239 to .204, but had been outscored 278 to 238 due to their lack of extra-base power.

Stengel hoped to press his one perceived advantage, pitching, by exaggerating the Beehive's natural suppression of offense. The infield grass was allowed to grow tall and supplemented with peat moss. Prior to every game, the ground was watered. The Beehive now killed grounders as well as fly balls.

The team's lack of punch stretched back to 1914, so it was no surprise to Stengel. In spring training he had made his players run the bases single-file for photographers. Watching thirty-five players cross home plate, Stengel observed, "That's more runs than the club scored all last year." Now, having failed to make a qualitative improvement in the hitting, he sought to gain a tactical advantage by bunting and stealing bases. He beat the Cubs 1–0 behind Lou Fette when Lopez, Warstler, and Fette bunted for consecutive singles. On May 24, down eight runs to Cincinnati in the fifth inning, the Bees scored in the sixth, seventh, and eighth to win 10–9. Stengel used five pitchers in the game, a high number in an era when managers were reluctant to use their bullpens. The next day, Fette and Brooklyn's Fat Freddie Fitzsimmons hooked up for a thirteen-inning 1–0 duel, won by the Bees. Moving to the Polo Grounds, the Bees shut out the Giants in both ends of a doubleheader. In a victory over the Cardinals, Stengel surprised the opposition by pulling a double steal with Cuccinello and backup catcher Ray Mueller, the two slowest men on the team. There were even a couple of rare displays of power, with Gene Moore and Harl Maggart hitting grand slams to beat the Phillies 16–11. Stengel was also at his most theatrical, provoking confrontations with umpires when he thought it would fire up his team and the crowd to see him get run out of a game.

Nineteen-thirty-eight Bees baseball was not always winning baseball, and it was definitely not home run baseball, but it was exciting baseball. Fans started to come out to see the team, and Quinn began to fantasize about expanding the Beehive by 20,000 seats, and perhaps even adding lights!

With the Bees back in contention, *The Sporting News* ran a headline calling Stengel "Miracleman," an honorific previously hung on McKechnie and the Braves' sole World Series manager, George Stallings. Stengel's reaction was subdued. He had not yet won anything, and the team was substantially the one McKechnie had left him. He was already worrying that the club had peaked.

Despite his ambivalence, Stengel continued to reap accolades. Even when it became apparent that the club was not going to climb any higher than fourth place, his role in bringing the team even that far was celebrated by the media. Gerry Moore of the *Boston Globe* wrote:

> Stengel has refused to bog down with the waning fortunes of his charges. Off the field, he rules his men as if they were only a couple of games out of first place instead of fourth. He has a standing rule that every athlete is out of bed at eight-thirty in the morning. . . . As for himself, Casey has been on the job for twenty-four hours a day from the moment he accepted the job. . . . On the field, Casey's strategy has been exemplary with the result that he has been accountable for many things that do not appear in the box score.

Stengel resisted becoming too enraptured with his own performance. He had been popular in Brooklyn, and all it had gotten him was a year in the oil fields of Texas. During the Bees' hot streak, a photographer came across Stengel lying in the sun at Ebbets Field in the hours before a game. The photographer asked Stengel to pose as if giddy with exuberance. Despite his recent strong showing, Stengel needed motivation, or perhaps he was enjoying the sun. If the photographer wanted Stengel to look happy, he should, "Go up to the front office and find out when it's pay day." Then what, asked the photographer. "Then come back," Stengel replied, and went back to his nap.

Injuries and lack of depth dragged the Bees back to Earth. Al Lopez was lost to a broken finger after being hit in the hand by a Billy Herman foul tip. Ray Mueller, his replacement, suffered the same fate. Max West ran into a wall, a common occurrence in those pre-padding, pre-warning-track days, and suffered a concussion ("You've got a great pair of hands, Max," Stengel said, brimming with sympathy). Gene Moore, who had put together the two best offensive seasons recorded in the 1930s by a Boston Brave not named Wally Berger, injured his knee so severely that he was forced to retire.

By the time the Bees reached St. Louis in mid-July the roster had become so depleted that Stengel found it difficult to field the minimum nine players. He was asked for his probable lineup the night before a game. "I think I'd better wait until we get out tomorrow for fear somebody else jams his foot in a door or something tonight." Even Stengel himself was hobbled by an inflamed toenail. (And like Bordagary, his players kept trying to kill him. During a practice, Elbie Fletcher suddenly whipped a ball into the dugout, missing Stengel by inches. "That will cost you ten,

Sugarbowl!'' shouted Stengel). Stengel had to play one game with only sixteen of his twenty-three man roster available. Afterwards, Quinn vowed to have the roster limit increased. That winter he succeeded in having it raised to the pre-Depression limit of twenty-five men.

With the roster shot, Stengel was forced to depart from his usual way of managing. Platooning requires at least two players for each position. Stengel had matched his third baseman Debs Garms with utility infielder Gil English. Fletcher had been rested against tough left-handers. Now he was forced to play English, Garms, and Fletcher everyday. Ironically, injuries had forced Stengel to play a regular lineup—until Garms joined the legion of the infirmary.

What little offense there was simply stopped. The Bees were already no-hit candidates every time they took the field. On May 17 they were one-hit by Pirate pitchers Russ Bauers and Rip Sewell. On June 30 the Bees were again held to one hit, a Rabbit Warstler double (one of ten he hit that year) by, of all people, Van Mungo. Mungo walked eight Bees, but struck out six and induced three double plays. Consequently, only three Bees got as far as second base. In the aforementioned series against the Phillies, the visitors swept the Bees out of a doubleheader 4–1 and 5–0, with the Bees only run of the day coming on a Harl Maggert homer in the eighth inning of the first game. It would be fifteen innings before the Bees scored another run, coming in the fifth inning of the next day's 2–1 loss to Philadelphia.

Any pitcher who was even above average could shut the Bees down completely. Knuckleballer Freddie Fitzsimmons, a successful but unintimidating pitcher (he struck out all of thirty-eight batters in 203 innings that year), pitched twenty-nine consecutive scoreless innings against the Bees. The Bees accounted for all three of his shutouts that season. Stengel's old nemesis Dizzy Dean, now vastly reduced in potency due to an injury suffered in the previous year's All-Star Game, beat them 3–1 in the opener of a doubleheader. He did not walk a batter, struck out three, and used only one hundred pitches on his way to facing only four batters over the minimum. ''Let me pitch the second game!'' he whooped. Another pitcher was given the task, but it didn't matter; the Braves were shut out 4–0 in the nightcap.

The Bees' June swoon was climaxed by two games against Cincinnati left-hander Johnny Vander Meer. In a June 11 game at Cincinnati, Vander Meer no-hit the Bees 3–0. Stengel sent up three pinch-hitters in the ninth inning (Kuhle for Warstler, Maggert for MacFayden, Mueller for Fletcher) to no avail. Vander Meer's next start came four days later at Ebbets Field. In the first night game played in Brooklyn, Vander Meer no-hit the Dodgers 6–0. This was the first (and to date, only) time a pitcher had thrown consecutive no-hitters.

All eyes now turned to Cincinnati's series at the Beehive. On June 19, Vander Meer took the mound looking for his third consecutive no-hitter. Also at stake was Cy Young's 1904 record of twenty-three consecutive no-hit innings. The seventy-one-year-old master himself came out for the game, as did 34,511 fans. For the entire season, average attendance at the Beehive was about 4,500; in those days when a ball club's primary income was derived from ticket sales, Vander Meer meant real money to the Bees. Prior to Stengel's arrival in Boston, Vander Meer had been Bees property. In a typically shortsighted move, the team had sold him away.

If Vander Meer's opposition had been any team other than Boston, the chance of a third no-hitter would have been automatically discounted. With the Bees woeful offense, anything was possible. Vander Meer did not surrender a hit through the first three innings. As Stengel walked to the third base coach's box for the Bees' at-bat in the bottom of the fourth, he intentionally crossed the mound. Brushing past Vander Meer, he said, "John, we're not trying to beat you. We're just trying to get a base hit." Garms was the next batter. He broke up the no-hitter. Vander Meer won anyway, 14–1. Adding injury to insult, Stengel lost Danny MacFayden to a fractured finger in the nightcap.

On July 9, the Bees christened the second half of the season by beating Bill Terry's ace, Carl Hubbell 7–0. Three consecutive home runs were hit by Cuccinello, West, and Fletcher, chasing Hubbell by the third inning. This was one of two offensive highlights in the second half. The other came at Cincinnati on July 21. With the weight of a seven-game losing streak on them, the Bees were again matched against Vander Meer. Through eight innings, Vander Meer allowed only two hits and struck out seven Bees. In the top of the ninth, Gil English singled, Cuccinello walked, and Max West, a left-handed hitter, hit a three-run homer for the lead. In the bottom of the ninth the Reds loaded the bases with no outs. Stengel brought the infield in. Lou Riggs tapped a grounder to Cuccinello, who forced Frank McCormick at the plate for the first out. Dusty Cooke hit a hot shot between first and second, but Cuccinello snagged it and was able to get it to Warstler in time to turn the double play and save the game.

And that was it. The team drifted down into fifth place and could not get up again. The hitters who had stayed healthy were simply unproductive. Stengel had no choice but to stick with them. Through the middle of July, right fielder Cooney had almost two-hundred at bats, but only two runs batted in. The team's offensive highlight, and simultaneously its greatest disappointment, was Vince DiMaggio. He lacked the fine bat control and plate control of his brothers, and often swung for the fences. Playing half of his games at the Beehive, he was forced to overswing in order to compensate for his environment. Resultantly, he struck out more than anyone else in baseball. He beat the runner-up, Dolph Camilli, by thirty-three strikeouts, 134 to 101. No one else had more than eighty. In an age when the average team struck out around five hundred times, this was a true phenomenon. On September 22, he set a new league record when he whiffed for the one hundred and fourteenth time. The old record had stood since 1914; the new one would last until 1956.

DiMaggio perplexed Stengel. The Californian was seemingly unaffected as his batting average sank into the .220s. "Vince is the only player I ever saw who could strike out three times in one game and not be embarrassed," said Stengel." He'd walk into the clubhouse whistling. Everybody would be feeling sorry for him, but Vince always thought he was doing good." Stengel stuck with him because he was the only real home run threat—he hit fourteen that season (just three of which were hit at home), a reasonable total for a Beehive player—and because he was a ballhawk. "A centerfielder in our park who can't go and get 'em would be a fatal liability even if he got five hits in five times up," said Stengel.

The limitations of players like DiMaggio increasingly frustrated their manager. As opposing teams came in, the real thing, Grade A beef, was all around him. Whereas the Cardinals had thirty-two farm teams and the Yankees had fifteen, the Bees had only six. Talent flowed through the veins of the other organizations, not his. One day in June, with the Bees playing a night game in Brooklyn, George Weiss invited Stengel to watch his top farm team, the Bears, play at Ruppert Stadium in Newark. That day, Stengel saw the Yankees' best prospect, outfielder Charlie Keller, a specimen so impressive that Lefty Gomez had said that he was the first player brought back by Frank Buck. Keller had hit .353 in 1937 and had been named the minor league player of the year, but he had yet to see the inside of Yankee Stadium; the Yankees were that deep. Stengel watched as Keller hit two singles and two homers. After the second shot, Stengel jumped to his feet, shouting, "That's him! That's the guy I want!" There was, of course, nothing Stengel could offer Weiss that would induce him to part with his coming star.

The Bees had one last surge in late August, almost entirely propelled by DiMaggio. Finally listening to Stengel, DiMaggio started to meet the ball and slugged four homers in four games. With this spurt, the team had hopes of making it into the first division, but a Polo Grounds sweep by Terry's Giants put an end to that.

The most dramatic home game of the season took place on September 21, but for all the wrong reasons. A hurricane hit Braves Field with a game in progress. The home plate umpire refused to call the game. "When the advertising signs go down, I'll call it." Shortly thereafter, Cuccinello called for a pop-up on the outfield grass behind second base. The ball was caught by Al Lopez—against the backstop. The umpire called the game. Shortly thereafter the billboards came down on the field.

When it became clear that the Bees would fail to finish in the top four, the writers began to wonder if Stengel's job was in jeopardy. Quinn immediately put those thoughts to rest. "No club in either major league has had such a discouraging list of injuries as Stengel has been forced to put up with, although I imagine Jimmy Dykes with his White Sox runs him a pretty close second." Dykes was so short of players that he had to put himself, forty-one, in the lineup. "Only for these bad breaks, I am convinced that the Bees would still be in the thick of the pennant fight.

"Let me add in conclusion, that Stengel has worked wonders with an outfit that was so badly short in midseason. . . . In short, Stengel is my idea of a clever manager. He has raised the team's morale and made his charges hustle. He has given us unlimited satisfaction and any suggestion that he might be replaced is not worth the trouble of a denial."

The players joined in praising the manager. Danny MacFayden said, "Everyday my respect grows for Casey Stengel as a manager. Some persons are still inclined to think of Case as a clown. Honestly, I think he is one of the greatest students of the game we have in baseball. . . . I thought I had picked up a little pitching knowledge in my twelve years in the big league ball, but Casey has taught me plays this year that no other manager ever attempted. . . . When you consider our weak hitting and injuries, I think Stengel really has been a magician."

Stengel shared the general feeling of optimism, the willingness to attribute the club's shortcomings to injuries. "They had courage," he said of his players. "All you had to do was tape 'em together."

The Bees finished in fifth place with a record of 77–75. This was within two games of McKechnie's record the previous season. Paul Shannon wrote in *The Sporting News*, "In the estimation of Boston fandom, Stengel rates some kind of a super title for his remarkable showing with a badly battered and crippled team during the hectic season of 1938."

Had Stengel somehow proceeded directly from this moment in time to the Yankees, there never would have been any doubt about his abilities as a manager. He would have been remembered for punishing Terry's boastfulness in 1934, and for overachieving with a weak Bees team. His sense of humor would have provided only sidebar material, and he would have retired as the second McGraw.

Unfortunately, the next five seasons in Boston intervened.

CHAPTER 9

GETTING PAID FOR LOSING

As 1938 passed into 1939, few people were aware of a very terrible truth: 1938 would be the last good year for a long time. Not that it had been a great year, with the world still suffering the effects of the Great Depression, but at least it was relatively quiet. On September 29, 1938, four days after the Bees eliminated the Giants from the pennant race by sweeping a doubleheader from them, British Prime Minister Neville Chamberlain returned from Munich, waved a piece of paper at the photographers and announced, "peace in our time."

In the United States, day to day living did not halt just because of some ominous news. Chamberlain's reference to the threatened country of Czechoslovakia as "a faraway people of whom we know nothing," could have applied to all of Europe as far as many Americans were concerned. Though some became increasingly concerned about "preparedness," most went about their business and in their spare time pursued their usual leisure activities. They went to see *Snow White and the Seven Dwarfs* and *Our Town*, both new that year, read *The Good Earth*, God help them, and attended baseball games. With over nine million customers passing through the turnstiles, 1938 was the best season for baseball since 1930.

As the world situation worsened, baseball became ever more important to those who sought to escape the harsh realities of the time. Nineteen-thirty-nine was the beginning of a long road down into darkness, but the gloom was easily dispersed by the bright glare of stadium arc lights. It would not always be thus; the respite was only momentary.

It is 1939, and Casey Stengel is speaking to a reporter: "Well, Fette has a sore arm, Turner hasn't recovered from his broken nose. Errickson's hip pains him. Majeski's stone bruise keeps him chained to third. Warstler's banged up and so is Cuccinello. Posedel has a stomachache.

Hasset's got a cold. West isn't feeling so well. But I guess we can carry on—the batboy's in shape."

In 1939, the song of the Bees was again, "But for injuries . . ." This time, no one was buying, especially not Casey Stengel.

Over at Fenway Park, the Red Sox had Jimmie Foxx, Joe Cronin, Bobby Doerr, Lefty Grove, and a rail-thin rookie from San Diego that Stengel had wanted Quinn to sign, Ted Williams. Utterly lacking in star appeal and playing in an unwelcoming park, there was no reason to care if the reason for the latest Bees setback was injuries. They weren't winning. They weren't exciting. They were, at best, irrelevant.

There was no reason to believe the club was getting better. Over the winter the resemblance to the 1936 Brooklyn Dodgers grew more pronounced, with trades that added pitcher Fred Frankhouse and first baseman Buddy Hassett (the latter acquired in exchange for the recently unretired Gene Moore). In Brooklyn, Larry MacPhail had taken over and was rebuilding at a frantic pace, shaking up the ball club with a plethora of trades, divesting the chronic losers and the role players that for years had been foisted on the public as regulars. It seems not to have occurred to Quinn (or Stengel; he was supposed to have been autonomous) that every time they accepted one of MacPhail's discards they were doing him a favor, helping him improve his club while burdening themselves with a player that he had already condemned as useless.

Putting aside Al Lopez, whose primary role was acknowledged to be defense, the problem with ex-Dodger imports such as Hassett, Stripp, and Cooney was that they had the appearance of major leaguer players, but they made few real contributions to winning. They were ballplaying ghosts, taking up space while having no measurable qualitative density. All they had were intangibles. They hit for averages without power, and sometimes not even that, while eschewing patience, speed, and durability—though some of them were good singers. At the time of Hassett's acquisition he was playing the Strand Theater in Brooklyn with a Vaudeville act that found the first baseman in a tuxedo singing, "When Irish Eyes Are Smiling."

On Stengel's recommendation Quinn purchased outfielder Al Simmons from the Washington Senators. Playing center and left field for Connie Mack's Philadelphia Athletics beginning in 1924, Simmons had been one of the offensive standouts on Mack's last great teams of 1929 to 1931. Beginning with his rookie season he had driven in over one hundred runs in eleven consecutive seasons, averaged .356, peaking at .392, and hit as many as thirty-six home runs in a season.

That was then. Connie Mack contended that the better his clubs played the worse his attendance was, and in 1933 he sold Simmons and two other players to the Chicago White Sox for $100,000. Away from the serene, beatific Mack, whose specialty was handling eccentric ball-players, Simmons' sour personality—"coarse and a little bit ornery"—made him expendable as soon as his bat threatened to slow down. After the 1935 season the White Sox sold Simmons to the Detroit Tigers for $75,000. One season later the Tigers sold him to the Senators for $15,000. Although he hit .302 with twenty-one homers and ninety-five RBIs in Washington's Griffith Stadium (an extreme pitcher's park), his inability to get along with Senators owner Clark Griffith made him available to the Bees for only $3,000. He was thirty-six years old and his marquee value had faded some years before, but maybe, just maybe, he could still hit.

"Now a fellow like that might be a little help to us," Stengel said after watching Simmons lash a double in a spring training game. "We don't get to see many two-base hits on this club. When of our fellows gets a two-base hit we call him the king of swat."

With Simmons and Vince DiMaggio in the outfield, the Bees could hope to have more than their usual power quotient. Another forty home runs would put the team among the league's power-hitting elite.

At least, that would have appeared to be the plan. Just prior to the start of the season, DiMaggio was packaged with four other players and cash (one of the players was pitcher Johnny Babich, consigned by the pre-Stengel Bees to the minor leagues) and traded to the Yankees' Kansas City Blues farm team in exchange for shortstop prospect Eddie Miller. Though DiMaggio was the club's main power threat, if the outcome of the trade meant that Rabbit Warstler was out of the infield then anyone was expendable. Besides, DiMaggio had threatened to hold out, and Stengel had grown tired of him. "I give up," said Stengel. "All I can say is I helped Vince set a new strikeout record. Maybe somebody else can make him a hitter." Perhaps Simmons could have accomplished what Stengel failed to do; Simmons's hitting philosophies, formed in collaboration with Ty Cobb, might have calmed DiMaggio.

Miller, twenty-two, was a gift to Stengel from George Weiss, who owned his contract through the Kansas City club, the Yankees' top Midwestern farm team. With an even better prospect named Rizzuto a year behind him in the system, Miller had been made redundant. Rather than trade him for real value, Weiss gave him to Stengel. The players the Bees contributed to the Yankees were regarded as filler and rapidly passed out of the system. Nor was Weiss tempted to put the two DiMaggio brothers in the same outfield, even for a day, despite the obvious publicity such an event would bring. Though Miller was "the most sought after prospect in the minors," friendship had brought him to the Bees for practically nothing. Weiss even allowed the cash included in the deal to be paid in installments.

Miller did have one drawback, a reputation for temperamental behavior. Despite his youth, the Bees were his fourth organization, a sign that in his previous homes he had worn out his welcome faster than his talent could sustain him. Still, for a shortstop he could hit. Playing for Kansas City in 1938, he averaged .290 and slugged .473 on thirty-three doubles, eleven triples, and fourteen homers. Although his power promised to be reduced by the Beehive, he would still provide more thump than Warstler. But then, a cantaloupe provided more thump than Rabbit Warstler. Acknowledging that, "They say he's hard to handle," Stengel's plan for handling Miller was simple: "I'm going to leave him alone."

With Miller, Simmons, Hassett, rookie third baseman Hank Majeski, and pitcher "Sailor" Bill Posedel all expected to play major roles, it was as if Stengel had received a new club. "We're not saying a great deal this spring," he said, "but by next fall I think we will have done a lot of talking in the percentage tables. Last season we had more injuries than any other big league team; at one time I was down to thirteen able-bodied players. For weeks, two of my best pitchers were incapacitated. . . . But with it all we were one of the hardest National League teams to beat, and for the second straight year we won more games than we lost, had a better percentage at home than any club in our league and kept pushing the contenders around all season."

In conclusion: "No matter how I line up my present material, I am bound to get more hitting than I had last year. Our defense should be as good as last season, if not a little better." Then, as if by habit, he added, "There is nothing funny about this ball club."

Stengel was asked if he would succeed in getting along with Simmons where so many had failed. From Stengel's point of view, the question was irrelevant. "I know Simmons used to be a big shot in the other league, but his only desire is to get in shape and help us win games. These players realize that we've been a second division club, a club . . . which hasn't scored enough runs to go places. They know their own future is hooked up with the future of the club. For that reason I have to lay down few training rules, and there isn't a fellow on the club that needs watching. With that kind of spirit, why, this club is bound to improve."

Jim Turner derived inspiration from Simmons. "If we had Simmons last year, I honestly believe we'd have won the pennant. His presence in the line-up can't help but make us fellows who did most of the flinging the past two seasons better pitchers than we ever were before."

It was strange logic to expect a former slugger to improve the pitching with his hitting, but it must have been tempting for the Bees to cling to whatever small bits of cheer they could conjure. In fact, Simmons's arrival had little immediate impact, and the Bees won only six of nineteen spring training contests. Things were a little better with the start of the season. The opener was rained out, a Boston tradition. ("Well, here it is," said Stengel. "The usual opening of the season.") The Bees came back the next day to beat the Phillies in the first game of what was now an opening day doubleheader, 7–6. The second game was rained out. Between bursts of precipitation, the Bees started out with three straight wins.

The high water mark of the season rushed up quickly after that. On May 17 the team record stood at twelve victories and ten losses. They were a game and a half out of first place. Stengel shook up his lineup, looking for extra punch. He benched Elbie Fletcher, who had started slowly, moved Hassett from right field to first base, Garms from third to right, and put Majeski in at third.

The new lineup marked the beginning of the end of Elbie Fletcher in a Bees uniform. A month later he was traded to the Pirates. Opting for Hassett over Fletcher was one of Stengel's few mistakes of evaluation. Still only twenty-three, Fletcher would develop into an all-star with Pittsburgh. Though he never hit for high averages or great power, in his years with Stengel his hitting had improved to the point that his early label, "the kid who will never hit," could have been revised to "the kid who generally hit." Fletcher had excellent plate judgment, and drew over one hundred walks four times in his career.

Hassett had no power and no patience. His .290 batting average was deceptive, full of empty calories. Here was one of the few times that Stengel selected flash over substance. Fletcher thought the decision was personal. "When Stengel made that decision to take Hassett over me, with the record that I compiled against what Hassett had, I think there was a little bit of a buddy relationship there." That seemed to be the most likely explanation, given that Stengel second-guessed the trade before Fletcher was out the door. "He talked to me just like a father," Fletcher said. "After giving me plenty of sound, common sense advice, he wound up by saying, 'If you do what I tell you, you'll show me up for letting you go.' "

The new lineup had little impact, and was coincidental to the tailspin that followed. The Bees had played weaker teams like the Phillies early on (the Phillies were still in the midst of their century-long slump), but once the Reds, Cardinals, Dodgers, and Cubs began appearing on the schedule the club's weaknesses—lack of power, lack of defense, and a terminal lack of patience (the Bees drew fewer walks than any major league team)—became apparent.

In the first game with the revamped attack, the Bees took their now customary loss at the hands of Vander Meer. From there it was all losing. By the end of the month the Bees were 15–21 and nine games out of first, having lost twelve of fifteen games.

The pitching was at fault as much as the hitting. Fette was good and Posedel unexpectedly terrific, but nearly everyone else was ineffective. On the rare occasions the pitching held up, the batters failed to respond. Typical was an early June game against the Cardinals. With the Bees trailing 2–1 late, Fletcher hit a triple to lead off the ninth inning. The next three batters failed to hit the ball out of the infield.

Injuries were again a factor in the Bees' poor showing, and were again singled out for a large portion of the blame. Simmons suffered from a concussion after being beaned early in the season, and after that from a chronically sore throat. Turner's nose was broken by a line drive. The most devastating injury was to Cuccinello, who was lost when Cubs shortstop Dick Bartell tore up his knee on what Stengel and the Bees perceived to be a crooked slide. By then, Stengel and Bartell had a long history going back to a similar takeout of Lonny Frey in 1934.

The one bright spot among the carnage of the position players was Max West. At twenty-two, he had begun to find his potential. He hit .285 with nineteen home runs, an impressive total given that only two of his round-trippers were hit at the Beehive.

Cuccinello returned to play the Dodgers at the Beehive on Tuesday, June 28. He should have waited one more day: the game was a twenty-three inning 2–2 tie that took a then-unheard-of five hours and fifteen minutes to play. The Bees could have won the game in the thirteenth, but rookie Otto Huber tripped rounding third on Al Lopez's apparently game-winning hit. The game went on and on. "Night baseball in the daytime," said Stengel, whose team had taken the field at 3:00 PM and was still playing at eight, "I think I'll start batting practice right now for Wednesday's game."

Huber offered Stengel a lame excuse for falling. "I guess I didn't have the right kind of shoes," he whined. Other versions of the tale have Huber replying that his spikes had worn out on the dugout concrete from too many weeks of sitting, or that he had assumed that Stengel would not use him so he switched to an old pair of comfortable shoes. "Well, get yourself a pair if you want to play on my club!" snapped Stengel without his customary humor. Huber had little future with Boston after June 28. "For the next three years, whenever I wanted to use a hitter or runner," Stengel would say when recounting the story, "I'd call him over first and make him show me his spikes." As for the newly reinstated Cuccinello, he couldn't play again for three days.

Perhaps Stengel was still over-tired four days later when in the eighth inning of the July 3 game against the Phillies he was ejected for starting a brawl. Pinky May hit Eddie Miller with a hard slide trying to break up a double play. Miller went down. Stengel was out of the dugout before the play was over, visions of Bartell's crippling of Cuccinello in front of him.

Miller was uninjured, but before departing the field, Stengel took the opportunity to tell May that had Miller been injured, he would have punched him in the mouth. May rose to the challenge, responding, "Why don't you do it on your own account?"

"I think I will," said Stengel, and the melee ensued. Stengel was restrained and taken out of the game. "Lucky for that kid I wasn't ten years younger," he muttered. Ford Frick fined him $25 for fighting.

Miller was not to survive the rash of injuries, despite Stengel's protection. In mid-July the shortstop collided with Simmons on a play in short left field. Simmons came away unscathed, but Miller had a hairline fracture of the left ankle and missed most of the rest of the season.

Al Lopez remembered, "Everybody went running out there to see how Miller was. He was the bright young ballplayer, the one they had the investment in. Hardly anybody paid any attention to Simmons."

For Simmons, the accident served as a reminder of how far he had fallen as a thirty-seven-year-old player on the Boston Bees. Afterwards, he approached Al Lopez. "You know something Al? Ten years ago, when I was playing for Mr. Mack, if that collision had happened, they would have sent a goddamned kid shortstop nine hundred miles from Philadelphia for running into me."

It was Simmons's intensity that provided the team with some excitement. Losing didn't affect him; every at-bat was equally important. When Ty Cobb visited the team on the road in Chicago, it was like Christmas. "I'll have Ty look me over and there may be just some little thing he can tell me about what I'm doing that will help me. There weren't many smarter in this business than the Old Peach and I'll take the chance he can help me." It was age and the Beehive that had stopped Simmons's hitting cold. There was nothing Cobb could do about that; he had already diagnosed the problem back in 1914.

With the team obviously doomed, Stengel began acting out again. He was ejected from several games for arguing too vehemently. The stunts returned as well, and with them came the props. On July 19, the Bees commenced a string of nineteen close games. They lost thirteen of them, nine by just one run. Four of the wins were also carried by the same thin margin. On August 9, the Bees appeared at the Polo Grounds to play a doubleheader with the Giants. New York took the first contest 5–4— another one-run loss for Boston—and Stengel's patience became strained. After trying and failing to get the second game called on account of rain in the sixth inning, he looked on as the contest was knotted at five runs apiece and stretched into extra innings. At 7:45 PM, Stengel took a last stab at having the game suspended, this time for darkness. Refused, he called to the bullpen for Fred Frankhouse, signaling him to the mound with a flashlight.

Frick hit him with another $25 fine. "Casey was very funny and got his share of laughs in using a flashlight to signal his players. However, he can pay $25 for his laughs as his tactics unnecessarily slowed up the game." Stengel didn't care. "That's all right with me," he said. "If I had not had that old magic lantern, [umpire] McCurran would never have found us at all." On entering the game, Frankhouse immediately wild-pitched the winning run home for the Giants for one last one-run loss. No one talked about this, and perhaps it didn't matter. Stengel had literally taken the spotlight off of the team's performance and put it on himself.

Temperamentally, he was not well equipped to handle a club out of the pennant race. As with his years in Pittsburgh and Philadelphia, when he was far from the first division he became bored, angry. He was a little bit like McGraw in this way, although he was more complicated than his role model. His anger, mixed with bitterness and self-pity, was moderated by a healthy self-awareness. Stengel could laugh at his situation and himself.

One way he kept himself interested was by teaching. One of the beneficiaries that year was Bill Posedel, a thirty-two-year-old sophomore in the big leagues. "That fellow is a wonder, no fooling," he said of Stengel. "If his club is seventh, it must be because of our injuries. He really is one of the greatest managers I ever have played for. He has taught me how to make plays that I didn't even know were in the book. I felt the confidence he had in me and tried to live up to it." After winning only eight games against an earned run average of 5.66 in his first season, Posedel would finish 1939 with fifteen wins and a 3.92 ERA.

Sailor Bill's turnaround was a minor victory in a losing campaign. Disillusionment spread from the team to the fans, who stayed home. In a year in which the National League as a whole improved its attendance, the Bees were down by sixteen percent. Symbolic of fan dissatisfaction was a late July game in which the Bees had made six errors through six and a half innings. When Al Lopez dropped a foul pop in the bottom of the seventh for his second error of the game and the Bees seventh overall, spectator Ferdinand Brabant, thirty-eight, jumped out of the stands and made for Lopez with both fists raised. Brabant was intercepted before he could reach Lopez, but he later explained that it had been his intention to pummel the catcher for his sloppy play.

And still nothing changed. When the Bees beat the Giants 4–3 on September 7, it was their forty-third one-run game of the season, representing one-third of their games played to that point. They had won only eighteen of those contests. Another galling loss came on September 9 at the hands of Walter "Boom-Boom" Beck. Beck, who would finish the 1939 season with a record of seven wins and fourteen losses, held the Bees hitless until the sixth inning. After Lopez lead off that frame with a double, rookie Sibbi Sisti bounced out to the pitcher. Lopez, who ran like the catcher he was, failed to advance and was ultimately stranded. In the eighth, after another Lopez hit scored Majeski to make the score 2–1, Sisti bounced into a double play to kill the rally.

After the game, Stengel admitted that he had made a mistake allowing Sisti to hit in the sixth and the eighth innings. This lesson, derived from this moment and others like it, stayed with Stengel for the rest of his career. Later, he would not hesitate to pinch-hit for his weaker hitters early in the game if he perceived that a timely hit could make the difference between a win and a loss. He was known to pull players even as early as the first inning, a practice his players found confusing and embarrassing.

The day before, as the Bees and Phillies watched the autumn rains wash away their game, President Roosevelt declared a state of limited national emergency due to threats to the neutrality of the United States and the resultant need to strengthen the national defense. At a press conference, Roosevelt insisted of the declaration that, ''it is not exactly a startling thing to do; it is an ordinary precautionary measure.''

Having nothing to lose but more games, Stengel began giving more playing time to youngsters who had been called up from Hartford. Majeski got more time at third, Sibby Sisti replaced Cuccinello at second base, Whitey Wietelmann took over at short for the injured Miller, and Bama Rowell logged some time in the outfield. Trying to build them up, Stengel called the players his Young Turks.

The last step in this process was the disposal of Al Simmons. He had played ninety-three games, and hit .282 with seven home runs in 330 at bats. These were respectable totals for an aged player in an immense park, but with the Bees solidly out of contention there was no longer a need for either his personality or his salary. McKechnie's first-place Reds were in town and happened to be looking to buy an outfielder. Just like that, Simmons was sold. The transaction was carried out so impulsively that Simmons could not be found in time to join the Reds in Boston and had to be sent on after them.

At the end of it all, Stengel and Quinn shrugged their shoulders and agreed to try it for another year. While the club was on the road, Quinn announced from Boston that Stengel would be returning to manage the team in 1940. He held the press conference while Stengel was away, he said, in order to quell ''much loose gossip'' that suggested Stengel was ''going to another major league ball club.'' The owner insisted that he was ''perfectly satisfied'' with Stengel's work, and said he realized that the team had been hampered by injuries.

There were some observers, albeit from outside of Boston, who agreed with Quinn that Stengel had done a fine job. *The Detroit News* called Stengel the ''Manager of 1940'':

It is impossible to ignore Stengel and difficult to name anyone else. . . . Stengel has one of the least desirable jobs in baseball. The Boston club controls so little money . . . that only Bob Quinn's personal popularity has kept the sheriff from taking over. . . . Because he lacked funds, Stengel had to get rid of his high-salaried stars . . . he had to develop new ones, and he did. He made Ed Miller into one of the best two shortstops in the National League, developed Carvel Rowell into one of the leading hitters and has elevated Sebastian Sisti and Chester Ross into headliners. Taken, all in all, Stengel performed a masterful feat.

Yet, however well Stengel disguised his disappointment, "feats" were no substitute for victory. Earlier that season, when the Bees visited New York, Bill Terry asked the Boston writers how Stengel was holding up emotionally piloting a seventh-place team. "He's fine," said a reporter.

"Gosh," said Terry, "What does it take to get him down?"

But it did get him down. Out to dinner that year, someone offered to pick up Stengel's check. He would not have it. "It's on me," he grumbled. "I'm getting paid for losing." Over the course of his career, it was in one-liners such as this one that he would express his bitterness. That he was not throwing tantrums outwardly did not preclude his throwing them inside; this was a subtlety missed by some members of the press, who chose to take Stengel's funny remarks as funny remarks.

CHAPTER 10

TRYING TO KEEP MY BOYS

On September 1, 1939, Adolf Hitler's Nazi hordes invaded Poland and conquered the Boston Bees. At least, that's how things worked out, though it wouldn't be obvious for a while. The Bees would not surrender until 1943; the Poles surrendered on September 27. On September 3, England and France declared war on Germany, commencing what the writers called "The Phony War." On October 8, the Yankees completed their World Series sweep of the Cincinnati Reds. Hitler took no notice. On October 9, Hitler issued Führer Directive Number Six, which stated, "Should it become evident in the near future that England, and, under her influence, France also, are not disposed to bring the war to an end, I have decided, without further loss of time to go over to the offensive." The Yankees did not interrupt their celebration. Baseball went into its winter quarters. The Phony War prepared to shed its skin.

At the winter meetings that year, Brooklyn's Larry MacPhail offered $55,000 and four players for Max West. It wasn't that the Dodgers had become flush with money since Stengel's years there; the team was still deeply in debt. Not only did MacPhail simply not care, but he was more successful than previous regimes at badgering the Brooklyn Trust Company for extensions of credit. Quinn had to refuse; trading West would have been both a public relations disaster and a personal relations disaster with Stengel.

At one point during the meetings, Stengel went looking for MacPhail's room so they could discuss the proposed deal. Baseball men correctly thought of MacPhail as dangerously unpredictable. These qualities were apparently on Stengel's mind as he wandered into an opulently appointed suite that he took to be MacPhail's. As he passed through the door, two Chinese men approached him, bowed severely, and went out. "Gosh," wondered Stengel, "is that guy gonna play Chinamen now?"

Moments later Stengel discovered he had mistakenly entered the apartments of Dr. Ho Chih, Chinese ambassador to the United States.

In January 1940, Stengel announced a change of philosophy for the Bees. The import of veteran retreads like Stripp and Simmons would cease. He would build with prospects. "I've made up my mind that from now on we're going to have a team of young players and now that West would appear to be the most improved player in the league, if you believe what is being said, it seems that we can start with him as a nucleus. We've monkeyed around with older players in the belief that they would help us while we were finding young stars. Where do you get, sticking along with the veterans? The second division."

Adding an exclamation point to his pronouncement, Stengel announced his first baseball "school." Since he had begun managing he had toyed with the idea of an early spring training for prospects. Free of the need to pet the veterans, Stengel could spend time teaching the game the way he wanted it to be played. McGraw had tried the same thing, though the rules of the time concerning spring training reporting dates forced him to disguise his purposes.

That spring, two dozen prospects were brought to Bees' camp in Bradenton, Florida two weeks early to participate in what *The Sporting News* called a "kindergarten class." Stengel had no real farm system through which he could supervise the education of his prospects, as Branch Rickey did, no channel to convey something akin to "The Oriole Way," the development philosophy which propelled Baltimore in the 1960s and 70s. Had he written an organizational manual, as Buck Showalter did for the expansion Arizona Diamondbacks in 1997, it would have been a curiosity piece; there would have been no one to receive it. Stengel could not send his wisdom to the prospects. The prospects would have to come to him.

Auditioning for the Bees that spring were a cavalcade of youngsters, the outcomes of whose stories will be obvious from the obscurity of their names: Chet Ross. Carvel "Bama" Rowell. Sibby Sisti. Les Scarcella. Manny Salvo. Al Javery. Bob Loane. Phil Masi. Whitey Wietelmann.

None of them made it. Sometimes it was injuries that did them in, as with Chet Ross, or personality, as with Bob Loane. Some could hit but not field, like Rowell; Masi could field, sometimes hit well for a catcher, and even made a few all-star teams, but was never anyone's idea of an impact player. As a group, the young Bees had the representative strengths and weaknesses of any crop of untried players one could randomly select. Later, some in the Boston press would argue that young players might have fared differently under another manager. They were mistaken; their futures were preordained. If the newcomers failed to make a lasting mark, it was not because of their manager, and not even due to a paucity of talent. Mostly, it was the war.

The story of the Bees' 1940 season is very quickly told. Prior to the season, the dimensions of the Beehive were reduced. Left field shrank from 368 feet to 350 feet, centerfield from 408 to 385, right field from 378 to 350. The intention, Quinn said, was "Not to make cheap home runs, but to make our park chummier. People want to get close to the playing field and we're going to make our park lots closer than it has been." The chummier Beehive hosted only 241,616 fans as attendance dropped for the third straight season.

Quinn admitted that shortening the fences had something to do with inflating the offense. "Our own players have been under a psychological handicap with such distant targets." With the new park and the new players, the team did creep within hailing distance of the league average for runs scored, though it didn't help much. Although the number of home runs hit by the Braves in the park increased from thirteen to twenty-five, the number hit by the opposition jumped from fourteen to thirty.

In spring training there was the usual fuss about trying to move Tony Cuccinello, stiffening at thirty-two, to third base. This time Stengel succeeded, replacing him with Rowell, a converted outfielder. Rowell was yet another of those singles hitters who are supposed to be "pesky" but really don't accomplish very much. Rowell would hit .305 in 1940, but lacking the two other traits essential to scoring runs, power and selectivity, he didn't contribute a great deal offensively, while his defense was what one would expect from an outfielder playing the infield.

Stengel had players of this nature by the score in his early years: Rowell, Buddy Hassett, Joe Stripp, Debs Garms. The standard-bearer for the group, in that he was the longest lived and the least successful, was Johnny Cooney. Cooney had pitched in the majors from 1921 to 1930. He suffered a serious arm injury in 1926 and was so butchered by the sports medicine of the time that his left arm wound up three inches shorter than his right.

Going down to the minors, he landed at Toledo, where Stengel masterminded his career-prolonging position change. As a pitcher, he was good enough to lead the American Association in earned run average. As an outfielder-first baseman he hit .289, no great shakes in a league that hit .300, but good for a sore-armed pitcher.

When Stengel went up to the Dodgers in 1932, Cooney hung around the minors, gradually metamorphosizing into a full-time player. In 1935 he hit .371 for the Indianapolis Indians and Stengel brought him to the Dodgers. He became a full-time player in 1936.

After that there was no getting him out of the lineup despite the fact that he was virtually useless. Though Cooney was able to hit in the low .300s from time to time, he had no power, never walked, and didn't run the bases. "I don't care what any body says," Stengel said, showing an uncharacteristic loyalty to a poor player. "Cooney played ball for me at Toledo and he's the smartest ballplayer I've ever seen."

Stengel was not alone in this estimation; in his autobiography, Dick Bartell called Cooney, "the best left fielder in the league," an extraordinary statement given that Cooney played center field, not left, and that Joe Medwick was among the left fielders of the time. In fairness to both Stengel and Bartell, the class of National League center and left fielders in the years of Cooney's second career (1935–1942) was unusually weak, a situation that would change with the arrival of Stan Musial in St. Louis at the end of the period.

Cooney's first career home run was hit on September 24, 1939. His second and last home run was hit the next day, on September 25. After that Cooney's stars went out of alignment: In 3,372 career at bats, those would be Cooney's only home runs.

Stengel liked Cooney enough to make him a player-coach in 1940. Stengel also took him to Kansas City in 1945 and made him a coach there as well. In later years, friendship would not dictate his lineup selection. At this time, players like Cooney cost him runs in a run-scarce environment.

At least Cooney was a decent fly-catcher, whereas Bama Rowell was far below average at second base. He had little ability there, and even less confidence. When Rowell failed to take a single chance during either game of a doubleheader (in itself an indictment of his range), he simply shrugged his shoulders. "Maybe it's just as well I didn't," he said. He committed a league-leading forty errors at second during the 1940 season.

Every spring boasts at least one phenom, and that year it was infielder Sibby Sisti, nineteen, who had been rushed to Boston the previous year when Miller got hurt. Promising rookies were a rare thing for Bees camps, and several individuals stepped forward to take credit for the discovery of Sisti. "It took one Italian to discover this whole country," Stengel laughed, "and now it takes two dozen baseball scouts to discover one Italian. Once I thought I knew who discovered him but now I don't know anything about it. I'm confused." With Cuccinello injured, Sisti played third, joining Eddie Miller (twenty-three years old), Rowell (twenty-four), and Hassett (twenty-eight) to complete the youngest infield in the majors.

Another highlight of the spring was Miller's healthy return. He showed no ill-effects from his broken leg of the year before. Miller hit .276 with thirty-three doubles and fourteen homers, trailing only four future Hall of Fame shortstops—Arky Vaughan, Luke Appling, Joe Cronin, and Lou Boudreau—in productivity.

Rookie Chet Ross had impressed Stengel by hitting .323 during the previous season's September showcase. Only twenty-three, he took over for Garms in the outfield. Although he led the league in strikeouts with a Vince DiMaggio–like 127, the pulled-in fences at the Beehive helped him compensate in ways denied to the lesser DiMaggio. His twenty-three doubles, fourteen triples, and seventeen home runs in 1940 represented the best offensive season during Stengel's tenure in Boston.

Max West was still with the team, retained despite the tempting entreaties from MacPhail. He was only twenty-three and coming off his best season. As spring training opened, Stengel praised his protégé. "They said he was my boy and that I was stuck with him. For awhile it looked as though I was stuck with him too. But he came through for me—and I'd like to be stuck with a few more like him."

Stengel never had any children, and sometimes became attached to special players. He was not looking for sons in the literal sense, a foster child on whom he could bestow thwarted paternal feeling, but for a son in the game, a great player who he could teach and mold into a monument to himself. West was the first player to be chosen, the first "Casey's Boy." It was a double-edged sword; the father could be a harsh, unsympathetic taskmaster who quickly became impatient when his lessons were not executed properly.

Once again Stengel was emulating the Mastermind. McGraw too had had his legacy in the diminutive outfielder Mel Ott, who lead the National League in homers the year West joined the Braves. Ott became a Giant at the age of seventeen, and McGraw nursed him along for two years before granting him a starting role. "Into the ears of Mel Ott, McGraw poured all the wisdom he had gained down through the years," wrote Jack Sher in *Sport* magazine. "The growth of Ott as a slugger and outfielder was a monument to the genius of John McGraw." Ott and McGraw were together for almost seven years. Ott hit 511 home runs and was elected to the Hall of Fame in 1951. That same year Stengel brought a nineteen-year-old rookie outfielder named Mickey Mantle to the Yankees.

Stengel had known West since the latter was a high school junior in California. He noticed him, as he had so many players, by going to neighborhood sandlots to take in the local talent. "He used to like to get together with young players," West remembered. "He had balls and bats. He'd hit balls to us and throw and we'd throw." Stengel immediately knew that West was something special. "I was almost his adopted son before we got through."

West was not the best candidate to become the vessel for Stengel's knowledge. He had an unmeasured approach to the game. He ran into walls, knocking himself unconscious. He overslid and underslid the bags when running the bases. He drove himself hard in all the wrong directions.

An oft-repeated story about West, Stengel, and their love-hate relationship concerns an occasion when West came to bat in a game against the Phillies with men on second and third and nobody out. Overanxious to score the runners, West popped up the first pitch thrown to him. After running to first, he began the long walk back to the dugout, head down, muttering and cursing. Paul Waner stepped in to hit.

The first pitch was wild and rolled away from the catcher; the runner on third broke for home. The ball rolled directly into West's path. At that moment West occupied a world very much like our own except angrier. Not really seeing anything except his own failure to get two RBIs, he casually picked up the ball and tossed it to the Phillies catcher—who tagged the runner out at the plate. Buddy Hassett called to Stengel, who was staring dumbly from the third base coach's box. "Casey, do you think they'll give him an assist on the play?"

Now West was really angry. He strode up and down the dugout, berating himself. As he bent over the water cooler, Waner stepped back in. The first pitch resulted in a wicked line drive into the Bees dugout. It struck West on the side of the head, loosening several teeth and knocking him unconscious.

The players ran over to their fallen comrade. Stengel pushed through the crowd, shouting, "Don't anybody touch him! Don't anybody touch him!" The players backed away. Stengel looked down dismissively. "Let him lay there. It might drive some sense into the son of a bitch."

Be it a result of insult or injury, West went backwards in 1940. He failed to take advantage of the reduced dimensions at Braves Field; his home runs dropped from nineteen to seven. His season had one highlight: on July 9, he hit the only home run of the All-Star Game, a game winner, off of Yankees ace Red Ruffing. The problem might have been Stengel, who was eager for West to cut down his swing and put more balls in play. "The move was a ghastly mistake," Al Hirshberg wrote. "It transformed West from a pretty consistent home run slugger into an inept bat-waver . . . and wrecked his confidence." "He wanted me to do so good," said West, "he hurt me."

This scenario would repeat itself a decade later when Stengel attempted to restrain Mickey Mantle's constant pursuit of the home run. Though throughout his career Stengel frequently decried the deadball tactics of the reactionary managers of the 1930s and 40s, he retained an appreciation of the more conservative batting approach of the time. This is what Tommy Henrich meant when he said that Stengel was more attuned than either Bucky Harris or Joe McCarthy to the "more subtle forms of attack." Stengel had no hesitation about constructing his lineups for power—five Stengel teams led their league in home runs, six in slugging percentage, whereas no Stengel team led in sacrifice hits—but he also saw the value of applying power selectively. Swing for the fences on the hitter's counts, cut down your swing at other times. This made instinctive sense to him.

West was unable to comply, Mantle unwilling, and as a matter of baseball evolution Stengel's point has largely been forgotten. Even on a noballs, two-strike count, or one-ball, two-strike count, modern hitters routinely swing for the fences. Most fail miserably in these situations (in 2003, major league batters hit .159 hitting 0–2, .198 when hitting 1–2).

For a true power hitter, the unfettered approach makes some sense, as one at-bat in ten or fifteen may result in a home run. For everyone else, the players who might boost their home run total from ten to fifteen but drop their on-base percentage by fifty points, it's a sheer waste.

The only good news on the Bees pitching front was twenty-two-year-old Al "Bear Tracks" Javery. Said Stengel, "A fastball with a hop on it is a wonderful thing. It doesn't matter where you come from just so long as you have it, and the greatest minds in the world can't hit when it hops." Stengel mixed Javery in slowly, giving him time in the bullpen before giving him a shot at the rotation.

One episode during the spring showed off Stengel's softer side. The Bees had seven catchers in camp that spring. Seventh on the depth chart was Eddie Antolik. His chances for a major league career were acknowledged to be remote; he was in camp as a warm body, an extra pair of hands to warm up the pitchers. He should never have gotten a chance to play. Stengel gave him one anyway. In an exhibition against the Yankees, he started Antolik. He wanted the boy to have his one moment of glory. "Dignity be damned!" Stengel shouted at suggestions that Antolik was not up to the champion Yankees. "You'll get all you want of that at the opera, or even at John and Mabel Ringling's art museum. Maybe this game's getting a little too dignified.

"There's a paper in this town called the *Bradenton Herald*. Tomorrow afternoon, they'll carry a box score of this game. If that kid's name is spelled wrong, I'm going to take a baseball bat over to that office and I'm going to beat the brains out of the editor. And I'll call him tonight and warn him. How do you spell that kid's name?

"No matter how long he lives, no one else will ever look big to him."

Dave Egan, the self-styled "Colonel" of the *Boston Daily Record* (in all likelihood he wasn't one), though a dedicated, vituperative Stengel critic wrote, "I must cast a hurried ballot on behalf of Professor Casey Stengel. . . . Not as a baseball manager, you must understand. . . . No, this ballot is marked and stuffed into the box where go the votes for men with human and lovable traits.''

Those were the players; this was their season: the Bees barnstormed north with the Washington Senators. The Senators were not a good club that year; they would lose ninety games in 1940. The two teams played five exhibitions. The Bees lost all five games to a team even younger than themselves.

Reaching Boston, Stengel was asked to speak on his team's prospects for the coming season. Although he was always conservative in these predictions, his answer on this occasion was jaded, rote, as if he was doing an imitation of a Casey Stengel monologue. ''Ah, there's no place like home. From here in there'll be no place like home plate. We've got an improved ball team here. The fans will take note of this today, and the rest of the league will catch on commencing Tuesday.''

Youth movements mean inconsistency: periods of growth, failure, frustration. Young players can be stubbornly insistent on sticking with methods that got them through the minor leagues even when it is clear that those methods will not serve them in The Show. Going into his sixth season as a major league manager and third with the Bees, it was difficult to generate the same excitement for a season of rebuilding, even if rebuilding was the right move. Stengel was aware the club was out of money, so he knew that the rebuilding had not even started yet, that there was no bottom to the trough the team was in.

After losing opening day, Boston rains forced the Bees into five straight postponements. Finally resuming the season in Brooklyn, they were thumped eight to three, the second loss in what proved to be six consecutive defeats. Stengel became uncharacteristically sullen. The *Boston Globe* reported, ''Since the Bees began losing consistently in spring training, it has been pretty much 'silent' Casey Stengel.'' During spring training he had amused himself by giving writers ''scoops'' on fictional trades (announcing on one occasion that the depressed Phillies had sent their fireballing right-hander Kirby Higbe to the Dodgers, a move that would have significantly altered the balance of power in the National League—in this Stengel was not only humorous, but prescient. The trade actually happened that November) and by spending time with George Weiss, in camp with the Yankees. Now it was just him, the Bees, and losing.

Stengel's depressed state took a heavy blow when his father died on April 7. Stengel went home to Kansas City for the funeral; George Kelly, his coach and former Giants teammate, ran the team in his absence.

He returned to a team that had improved offensively over the year before (if only thanks to the changes made to the park), but was still far behind the rest of baseball. Other managers found they could use unconventional tactics against the Bees because of their weak bats. On July 5, Dodgers manager Leo Durocher put Bees runners in scoring position three times by issuing intentional walks with a man on first. Each time, the subsequent Bees batter grounded into a double play. The game went twenty innings; Stengel was not on the field for much of the extra play as he had been run after expressing his frustration to the umpires. He was fined $75 by President Frick for using abusive language.

The occasional good days only made the surrounding misery stand out even more. On July 17, the Bees swept Frankie Frisch's Pirates in a doubleheader at Pittsburgh. Mike Kelly, a Pirates coach and old friend of Stengel's, expressed frustration and disbelief that the Pirates had been beaten by an inferior team; the Pirates had the best offense in the league. Sadly for Stengel, a good deal of Frisch's attack was built on a foundation of former Bees, including Elbie Fletcher, who would total sixteen homers, 104 runs batted in, and a league leading 119 walks; Vince DiMaggio (nineteen homers, .289 average in 356 at–bats), whose strikeouts no longer hampered him; and Debs Garms, who would lead the league in batting with a .355 average, an unforeseen development for which— adding compliment to injury—the lefty swinger credited Stengel, saying the manager had taught him to hit to the opposite field instead of trying to pull the ball ("Casey told me to make the third baseman my target, and hope that I missed him. . . . Yes, I owe Casey a great deal for the way . . . he always tries to help you improve yourself").

"I know just how he feels," Stengel said of Frisch. "In fact, I should know better than anybody else in the world, because up until today I'd taken more lickings than any other manager in the league." After the twin defeats, Frisch went home to sulk, leaving Stengel calling up to his window from the street, begging him to keep their dinner date.

Despite feelings of negativity, Stengel railed against the sell-off that he knew must follow the team's bad record. Once again, he blamed injuries. "I've got a great young club in the making and if [pitchers] Jim Tobin and Lou Fette hadn't become crippled and spoiled my pitching plans, we'd be in the first division now, so I'm trying to keep my boys."

I'm trying to keep my boys, a public plea to Bob Quinn. The season was no longer about winning or losing; it was about ownership quitting on the team. Unsuccessful and undercapitalized going into the third year of the regime, it was decided to burn everything down and start over. Jim Turner had been traded to Cincinnati and Debs Garms sold to Pittsburgh (where he would win the National League batting title) before the season had started. Now a parade of veterans followed them to the exits. Lou Fette was sold to the Dodgers. Al Lopez was sent to Pittsburgh for $40,000 and the offensively impotent catcher Ray Berres (also the replacement for Lopez in Brooklyn). Tony Cuccinello, converted to third at last, was sent to the Dodgers for pitcher Manny Salvo, who Stengel had seen, and coveted, at Sacramento back in 1935, and utility infielder Al Glossop. Even inoffensive Rabbit Warstler was sent packing, sold to the Cubs at the waiver price.

Trimming away the deadwood was not necessarily a bad idea. Rookies are cheaper than veterans, and have a chance at growth and development. Every man listed above had long ago established the upper level of his talents. In various Brooklyn and Boston combinations they had played together for years and had amply demonstrated that without star support they were not pennant-winning material. Even away from Stengel and the poverty of his ball clubs they failed to win; among them, only Turner and Garms would see the postseason as a player. Undeservedly or not (and it was undeserved, for all were bound by the reserve clause and had no say in where they would spend their careers), they were second-division ballplayers, and the sooner the Bees could shed them the better.

The moves were ill-timed. The Bees were facing the one moment in the history of baseball when a team would have been better off standing pat, even at the cost of stagnation. On September 16, 1940, the United States Congress approved the Selective Service Act. The first peacetime draft in the history of the nation, it called for 900,000 selectees to be enrolled in the military.

Nineteen forty-one was coming.

CHAPTER 11

IT'S A GRAND WORLD— IF ONLY IT WOULD STOP RAINING

"And of course, you've heard of the guy who wrote Casey Stengel asking for a tryout with the Braves and explained that he was not only a pitcher, but 'also a first-class futility player.'"

—J. G. Taylor Spink, April, 1943

"Next time a ball is hit towards you, don't touch it, because then my left fielder can come in and hold it to a single."

—Casey Stengel to a Boston Braves third baseman

Our memory of the year 1941 is dictated by the voice of Franklin Delano Roosevelt—for some witnessed, for most received—echoing out of the dark of the past. More than half a century later, the words still retain the drama of the moment. Listening, we cannot see him before Congress, but in the rich tones of that patrician voice, we can feel the president's righteous anger, his firmness of purpose, his confidence: "Yesterday, December 7, 1941—a DATE which will LIVE in INFAMY—the United States of America was suddenly and deliberately ATTACKED by naval and air forces of the Empire of JAPAN."

With those words, all of 1941 disappeared except for twenty-five days: Pearl Harbor and the weeks that followed. But Pearl Harbor had come late in the year. The sneak attack was preceded by Lend-Lease, the Atlantic Charter, the *Reuben James*, price controls, the Four Freedoms, Rudolf Hess's bizarre parachute ride to Winston Churchill, the sinking of the *Bismarck*, and a thousand other baleful events.

Pearl Harbor was preceded by Ted Williams and Joe DiMaggio.

The 1941 baseball season could be a book in itself, and it has been. Trying to make the epic succinct, in 1941 Joe DiMaggio hit in fifty-six straight games, becoming in that moment, and for the rest of his life, America's greatest living ballplayer (a title conferred on him by fan poll on the occasion of baseball's centennial in 1976—for the rest of his life he clung to it as if it were a peerage). Everything he did on the baseball field that summer was informed by his innate grace and reserved silence. DiMaggio had always been a great player, but his popularity had been attenuated by holdouts and other public relations missteps. His mystique, taken for granted by subsequent worshippers, was created in 1941.

Sparked by DiMaggio's streak and a fortuitous bit of second-guessing by Joe McCarthy—he reconsidered his springtime decision to move acrobatic second baseman Joe Gordon to first base at about the same time the Yankee Clipper began hitting—the Yankees won 101 games and the American League pennant. They were a classic team, with six future members of the Hall of Fame (DiMaggio, Phil Rizzuto, Bill Dickey, Lefty Gomez, Red Ruffing, and McCarthy). The outfield of DiMaggio, Tommy Henrich, and Charlie Keller was quite possibly the greatest of all time. Even the presence of Frenchy Bordagaray on the bench could not detract from the team's excellence. More so than the 1927 Murderer's Row edition and the 1961 Mantle and Maris record-setters, this was the quintessential Yankees team.

History was also made in Boston, though not by the Bees. Left fielder Ted Williams, who had grown up wanting nothing more than to be remembered as the greatest hitter of all time, was making his case, putting together a remarkable year in which he would hit .406, slug thirty-seven home runs, and draw 145 walks.

Like DiMaggio, Williams could capture the imagination. Having already reached the .400 mark, Williams was invited by his manager to sit out the last day's doubleheader rather than risk a bad day and the loss of his historic achievement. Characteristically, Williams refused. The "Splendid Splinter" made four hits in six at-bats to put his final average at .406.

In the National League, Larry MacPhail's rebuilding of Brooklyn paid off in a one-hundred-win season and the first Dodger pennant since 1920. The Dodgers were fueled by the aggressive, dangerous manager Leo Durocher, the daredevil outfielder Pete Reiser, and the pitching of Kirby Higbe, who was traded to Brooklyn less than a year after Stengel joked that it would happen.

These two testaments to intelligent team building and charisma played a classic World Series, highlighted by game four at Brooklyn. Down by a

score of 4–3 with two outs in the top of the ninth, the Yankees took advantage of Mickey Owen's dropped third strike by scoring four runs and
winning the game. New York celebrated both its teams. Pearl Harbor was
still eight weeks away.

During all of the excitement of that last good summer, the Bees had
been where they always were. The most they had in common with DiMaggio was a fading acquaintance with his older brother. The most they had
in common with Williams is that they were also in Boston. The Bees had
less to do with the pennant race than Hermann Goering, the machinations of whose government began to draw baseball players into a different kind of uniform that summer.

Very little had changed for the Bees over the winter. All of the 1940
regulars had returned to their same positions. Babe Dahlgren, who had
replaced Lou Gehrig as the Yankees first baseman in 1939, had been
purchased from New York over the winter. When Stengel learned that Joe
McCarthy had soured on Dahlgren because, "his arms are too short,"
he once again activated the Weiss connection, this time to add a platoon
partner for Hassett. Dahlgren had more power than the average Bee,
though not much else; he had replaced Gehrig, but there was no confusing him with Gehrig. Despite some early success, especially in the annual
city series against the Red Sox at Fenway Park, Stengel refused to ex-
pand his role. "I wanted some right-handed hitter with power to take
advantage of that chummy left field fence," Stengel explained. "Dahlgren took advantage of that short fence and really exceeded my fondest
expectations. But since we can't very well cart that Fenway Park wall
around the circuit with us, I've decided to leave Babe where he was when
he joined us." Which meant, on the bench.

Stengel tried, gamely and lamely, to explain the lack of turnover from
the previous year. "I realize Dahlgren will be the only new player in our
opening line-up but several other members of our team really are different ballplayers even though they are the same guys." That was weak,
and he knew it. So did the mechanical recitation of baseball platitudes
that served as his season's forecast: "Well, I see by a popular poll they
have consigned us to seventh place. That's okay with me, because I think
we're going to be able to surprise a few of the boys. As long as they're
doing the picking I won't say a word. But just keep your eyes on the Bees
this summer."

Stengel's career managerial record now stood at 413 wins and 501
losses. This placed him in an impossible position. It had now been so
many years since a Stengel team had done something positive that if he
left Boston he might not get another job. Logically, his only option was
to stay and try to force something positive to happen. Given the club's

circumstances that was highly unlikely. He was frozen. That April, his affairs would become more, not less, entangled with those of the club.

Stengel was also alone. Edna was off in California tending to her invalid mother. His first year in Boston he had been able to spend time with Frankie Frisch, then in-between managerial assignments and working as a Bees broadcaster. Now there were only the writers, some of whom, like Dave Egan, were beginning to be critical.

How many managers have won pennants with bad teams? Disqualify those winners that were less than great, such as the 1973 Mets or 1988 Dodgers, teams with weak hitting and great pitching. The defining line is "bad," or "without redeeming features." The correct answer is "none." No team in the history of baseball that should have lost ninety games has ever won ninety. Now and then a *weak* team (as opposed to a *bad* team) will rise up, contend very briefly, and sink back into the mire. In 1976, the Chicago White Sox lost ninety-seven games and finished last in their division. In 1977 (an expansion year) they won ninety games and finished third under manager Bob Lemon. In 1978 they were back to ninety losses. In the twentieth century, only eight teams finished with a record at or above .500 after losing 100 games the year before. These were aberrations.

In the era of free agency and the amateur draft, rebuilding can sometimes pay off quickly. In 1990 the Atlanta Braves, future incarnation of Stengel's team, lost ninety-seven games and finished last. Through free agency they added a new first baseman, third baseman, and centerfielder, promoted two of their former first-round draft picks to full-time roles, and went to the World Series.

In Stengel's time, there was no free agency. If the Bees had wanted to acquire Joe DiMaggio, the only method available to them was kidnapping. There was no amateur draft that rewarded teams for poor finishes. All amateur talent went to the highest bidder. If one could not outspend the MacPhails and Rickeys on signing bonuses, or serenade teenagers with tales of guaranteed World Series shares, as Weiss's scouts did (cynically using that as an excuse to offer them a lower bonus), then building through the minors was a long and arduous process that counted on developing a few good players out of the prospects left behind after the great ones had signed elsewhere. The Phillies did not lose one hundred games a year for thirty-five years purely due to their own incompetence (though surely that had a great deal to do with it); they were in a system which made getting out of the hole very difficult once you were in it. Boston was in the same position. Stengel had signed Max West, but he had also scouted Ted Williams, Ralph Kiner, and Gus Zernial. He was not given the money to sign them.

Stengel was fifty-one years old and the idea of the waiting game was terrifying. The team would continue to lose, his reputation would continue to suffer. The players he had were, in his opinion, poor, and yet he had to maintain the illusion that the club was trying to win. In doing so he justified the team's meager attendance and the faith of the fans, while issuing an indictment of himself. "We're really trying," was the message he had to convey, even though it provoked the inevitable question: If you're really trying, why aren't you succeeding? He couldn't say, "Well, the truth is that we really *aren't* trying," because that would destroy the team's credibility with the fans. He couldn't denigrate the quality of the players because that would destroy his credibility with his team. The only person left to take the blame was the manager.

Here was the midlife crisis: at fifty-one McGraw's triumphs were already behind him. Stengel might have little time left. Shepherding a parade of minor prospects before crowds of 1,200 people held little appeal. Being a full-time comic held little appeal either. Having no control over his relationship to either aspect of his career, he tried for a sullen compromise between the two.

This meant that the commitment to youth was out, or at least compromised. The Bees would once again try to catch the last spark of energy from veteran players. The positive aspect to this, and it was an improvement, was that they would try not only Dodger veterans, but those of other teams as well.

The first candidate for reanimation was Earl Averill, thirty-nine. Averill had been the centerfielder for the Cleveland Indians from 1929 to 1939. In his prime, he had been a six-time All-Star, consistently delivering .300 averages and thirty-homer power. Averill peaked in 1936, hitting .378 on 232 base hits. He was thirty-four then, and his time as a top hitter was nearly over. That is the way the aging process works in so many things. One day you can do it, then, gradually, you can't.

Still, he was a Hall of Fame–level player (enshrined in 1975), the man who had beaten Mungo in the 1934 All-Star Game. Starved for talent, Stengel looked at the shadow of Earl Averill and saw only the positives, what remained of the great player: the focus, the poise. It made him angry with what he had: "When I see him take some of those close pitches, I half expect to see the umpire call him out, but he never does. West, on the other hand, swings at some balls that almost get by the catcher." Even so, West remained in the outfield and Averill was gone after seventeen at-bats. As art cannot exist without commerce to support it, talent without production is merely an empty promise.

Pitcher Wes Ferrell, a six-time twenty-game winner with the Indians and Red Sox, stopped by on his way out of the majors. So too did Lloyd Waner, who was acquired from the Pirates on May 7, given fifty-one at-bats (in which he hit .412), and traded on to the first-division Cincinnati

Reds. Three days after Waner departed, Dahlgren was sold to the Cubs. He had hit seven home runs in 166 at-bats, a very respectable total for the Beehive. Only Max West would hit more home runs for the Braves that year.

Dahlgren's departure was problematic. He was an excellent defender at first base and one of the few Bees who appeared to be doing something positive with the bat. Stengel's financial interest in the team was first rumored at this time, and clubhouse scuttlebutt had Stengel pushing for the trade because he didn't want to pay Dahlgren's Yankees-inflated salary (some things are eternal). Though he vigorously denied the accusations, the trade of a popular and able player opened management to charges that it wasn't really trying to win, charges that were very difficult to refute. Stengel's standing with his own players was slow to recover.

Meanwhile, West and the old-timers proved incapable of shielding Braves Field's expansive outfield grass from falling baseballs. Stengel's defensive alignment featured West in left field, the forty-year-old Cooney or the thirty-five-year-old Waner in center, and the hobbled Gene Moore in right. Waner's stay with the team was concurrent with a 9–20 stretch, the nadir of the season. "Fly balls fall like raindrops," Stengel said wistfully. "If only I had a long-ball, draft-exempt right-handed hitting outfielder with power."

When Stengel listed his all-time team for his autobiography, he cited Lloyd Waner's older brother Paul as the best National League right fielder of the period 1912 to 1960. "For a little man, he was the greatest hitter I ever saw. . . . Waner could hit the ball to all fields and he was a good little fielder in the outfield." In 1941 he had the chance to judge the future Hall of Famer up close. From the beginning of his career until 1940, Waner had held down right field for the Pittsburgh Pirates, hitting .340 in over 2,000 games. The Pirates cut him after 1940; Brooklyn signed him but found that he had a thirty-eight-year-old's legs. Naturally, he was signed by the Bees, last refuge of the aged and the cheap of wage.

In fairness to Stengel and Quinn, there was an emergent reason behind this particular signing. Chet Ross, who had been so spectacular the previous season, had severely hurt his leg in a baserunning accident and a replacement was needed.

In his prime, Waner was indisputably a great ballplayer. He was a master of bat control, almost impossible to strike out (it must have been genetic, as Lloyd was the same way. In 1941 he would have 219 at-bats spread among three teams and not strike-out a single time). It would have been contrary to his finely tuned handling of the bat to be a home run hitter. Instead, his precision stroke allowed him to aim his hits at the outfield alleys and the foul lines, resulting in large numbers of doubles and triples. He had over six-hundred two-base hits in his career, and nearly two-hundred three-baggers. His single season batting averages included years in the .360s, .370s, and .380s.

It's a shame that the Bees had not acquired Waner in his prime, because he was one of the few hitters that might have been capable of putting up strong numbers at the Beehive. The distance to the fences would not have been important to him. The wind off of the Charles might have turned some of his doubles into singles, but he would have succeeded in the same way that Hornsby had succeeded.

As it was, he had just enough left to be competent. He hit only .279 with the 1941 Bees, but he was patient, drawing forty-seven walks in only 341 plate appearances. Sadly, this made him the most patient hitter on the club; with the exception of Max West, who had 219 more plate appearances, Waner walked more than any other Bee.

The Bees' record in 1941, incidentally the last season of the "Bees"— Quinn would revert to "Braves" the next year (the immediate consequence of which was that Stengel would no longer have to dread receiving actual beehives from oh-so-clever well-wishers)—was a meager 62–92, good for the predicted seventh-place finish, thirty-eight games behind the Dodgers. In his four years, Stengel had overseen a decline of seventeen games from McKechnie's last finish. In defense of his regime, Stengel could point to the youth movement begun in 1940, his "up and coming" players like Miller and West, both of whom had made the All-Star team. As long as nothing happened to derail their development, the Boston Nationals had a future.

There was no way Stengel could have anticipated Pearl Harbor and what it would mean to his career. From the moment on the evening of December 6 when President Roosevelt finished reading a packet of intercepted Japanese transmissions breaking off negotiations with Washington, turned to Harry Hopkins and said, "This means war," Casey Stengel was finished in Boston.

The news was a bit late in reaching Beantown. That April, Stengel had joined with eleven other investors to purchase the Bees for $350,000. Quinn was part of the syndicate and remained club president. Max Meyer of Brooklyn, a Stengel friend, held the largest share of the club.

Stengel had plenty of time to contemplate the impact of the world situation on his personal fortunes on May 27, when his club was subject to one of the most unusual game delays in the history of the sport, one which spoke volumes of the anxieties of the time. The Bees were playing the Giants at the Polo Grounds. With the score tied 1–1 in the seventh inning, the umpires halted the game, just as they would have had it been raining. For the next forty-five minutes, the two teams and the 17,009 fans in attendance listened to the president of the United States make his first substantive remarks on the European war since the enactment of the Lend-Lease program back in March.

Actually, the president said, it wasn't a European war. "The first and fundamental fact is that what started as a European war has developed, as the Nazis always intended it should develop, into a world war for world domination. It is unmistakably apparent to all of us that, unless the advance of Hitlerism is forcibly checked now, the Western Hemisphere will be within range of the Nazi weapons of destruction."

The president's goal was to make the threat posed to the United States by German aggression overseas unmistakable and undeniable, even for the isolationists and America-firsters, the Bundists, and the black shirts. He painted a picture of a Nazi-dominated America that included the abolishment of labor rights. "Trade unions would become historical relics, and collective bargaining a joke." Ironically, the ballplayers listening to the speech had neither a union nor the right to collective bargaining nor even individual representation.

The president said that the country was rearming itself only "to repel attack," but he also insisted that "attack" had to be loosely defined to allow for the speed of modern warfare. "Some people seem to think that we are not attacked until bombs actually drop in the streets of New York or San Francisco or New Orleans or Chicago. But they are simply shutting their eyes to the lesson that we must learn from the fate of every nation that the Nazis have conquered . . . it would be suicide to wait until they are in our front yard. When your enemy comes at you in a tank or a bombing plane, if you hold your fire until you see the whites of his eyes, you will never know what hit you. Our Bunker Hill of tomorrow may be several thousand miles from Boston, Massachusetts."

So far so good: the Beehive would not be shelled. Roosevelt's wrap-up was more direct, more chilling: "We will not accept a Hitler-dominated world. We will accept only a world consecrated to freedom of speech and expression, freedom of every person to worship God in his own way, freedom from want, and freedom from terrorism. . . . We in the Americas will decide for ourselves whether, and when, and where, our American interests are attacked or our security threatened. . . . We will not hesitate to use our armed forces to repel attack." And then, in case the point was somehow *still* not clear, the president declared a state of unlimited national emergency. It was beginning to look like a very bad time to invest in a baseball team.

After the speech, the president welcomed Irving Berlin to an informal gathering in the Monroe Room and listened to an impromptu concert of "Alexander's Ragtime Band" and other hits. The Bees resumed their game with the Giants, and lost.

When America joined the first World War in 1917, the young men of the nation were given a "work or fight" order by the government. All men of military age were to find work in some war-essential industry or be subject to the draft. The baseball owners implored the government to spare the players, for which they incurred a great deal of negative publicity. "Entertainers" had been exempted for their morale value. Baseball had a good argument for exclusion on the same grounds. Provost Marshal General Crowder turned the owners down, giving his name the same sort of cachet in baseball that Vidkung Quisling would have for the Norwegians. Baseball was declared nonessential, given a few weeks to wrap up its season, and shut down.

After Pearl Harbor there was some question as to whether this would happen again. Judge Landis appealed to the White House for instructions. Fortunately, World War II found no professor in the White House but a millionaire career politician and sportsman (albeit a disabled one) whose sense of fun rivaled his sense of duty. On January 15, 1942, President Roosevelt issued a "green light" to baseball. "I honestly feel," he wrote, "that it would be best for the country to keep baseball going. There will be fewer people unemployed and everybody will work longer hours and harder than ever before. And that means that they ought to have a chance for recreation and for taking their minds off their work even more than before . . . if 300 teams use 5,000 or 6,000 players, these players are a definite recreational asset to at least 20,000,000 of their fellow citizens—and that in my judgment is thoroughly worthwhile."

There was a "but." "As to the players themselves, I know you will agree with me that individual players who are of active military or naval age should go, without question, into the services. Even if the actual quality of the teams is by the greater use of older players, this will not dampen the popularity of the sport."

Baseball would continue, though not at the same level of quality. The military would make good on the president's suggestion that players should be drafted just like anyone else (though for a long time they would not receive the same treatment as everyone else). The drain on personnel started slowly, then picked up speed as the demands of the African, European, and Pacific campaigns took their toll on the military. In 1942, there were only seventy-one major league players in the military. The Yankees won a pennant with DiMaggio, Rizzuto, and the rest of their usual stars, and Ted Williams won the Triple Crown. The next year they would be gone, as would many others as the planned invasion of France began to put incredible demands on manpower. By 1945 there would be almost 400 major leaguers in military uniform.

What was then offered as Major League Baseball was often not pretty. That baseball managed to put its product on the field during a war was in itself a success, but the results were not artistic. As Bill James wrote,

"With the good players in the service, a collection of old men and children and men with one arm and seven dependants gathered regularly and battered around a dull spheroid and this was called major league baseball for four years." Two-thirds of 1945's starters lost their jobs when the big leaguers returned in 1946.

The government had taken not only the major league stars but the minor league prospects. In 1941 there were 5,298 players reserved to the major league clubs. In 1944 the number had shrunk to 1,753. With most minor league teams unable to fill their rosters, only ten circuits remained in operation throughout the war.

Though the big leagues sometimes made up the shortfall with novelties, such as fifteen-year-old pitcher Joe Nuxhall of the Reds or one-armed outfielder Pete Gray of the St. Louis Browns, in most cases they simply asked players who would have normally aged themselves out of the league to hang on a little bit longer. Inactive stars like Babe Herman, Al Simmons, Jimmie Foxx, and Pepper Martin made comebacks. Forty-year-olds like the Braves' Waner and Cooney found themselves pursued by the Yankees. Almost every major league team had at least one player over forty on the roster.

The first star to go was Hank Greenberg, slugging first baseman of the Detroit Tigers, followed by young fireballer Bob Feller and a parade of others. For the Braves, the names were not as big but no less devastating. Bill Posedel, a veteran of the Navy, disappeared with the first call-ups. Bama Rowell followed shortly thereafter.

Like all the teams, the Braves found it increasingly difficult to replace the players called to military service. Because they lacked depth, specifically, because they had failed to invest in a farm system, the quality of their replacements was a step down from those of the top teams, like the Yankees and Cardinals. When the Cardinals needed to promote an outfielder to regular play in 1942, they were able to reach into their system and come up with Stan Musial. When Musial was drafted in 1945, they reached down again and pulled up Red Schoendienst. Such was the foresight of Branch Rickey that his creation resisted even the entropic power of a global war.

For the Braves, the youth movement was over. It had to be. Youth was now under the German and Japanese guns and could not be had at any price. If Stengel had retained any hopes that he was building towards the future in Boston, those illusions were swept aside by the war.

The question that remained was how to get out, and when. The shares Stengel purchased gave him job security, but also bound him to the club; like the captain of the *Titanic* he would go down with the ship.

The 1942 Braves featured thirty-nine-year-old Paul Waner in right field, thirty-four-year-old Ernie Lombardi behind the plate, and forty-one-year-old Johnny Cooney (finally) on the bench. Even Tony Cuccinello was back. Stengel did not even pretend that his players were not re-treads. With tongue firmly in cheek, he admitted the Braves' roster was seventh-place material. "I've got what you might call a well seasoned club. They're settled family men for the most part and right in their base-ball prime, though Cooney probably isn't as good as he should be in an-other four or five years at the rate he's developing. . . . I've got pretty good age behind the plate in Ernie Lombardi. He's thirty-four and well out of the rookie class. And at second I can play Tony Cuccinello to steady the infield. Tony's going on thirty-five."

He seemed bored. Still, if the team won a game, as they did the season opener against Philadelphia (one of 109 losses for the Phillies), the com-petitive juices began flowing, the wit became jolly instead of sardonic. "As long as I've been in baseball they told me never to break up a win-ning combination"—this was after one win—"but I intend to tempt the fates this afternoon. . . . Before game time I might get so hungry to win that I'll start nine right-hand hitters against [Phillies' southpaw] Blanton."

Platooning would have been a nice solution to the subpar production of the replacement players, but platooning required more than one player for each position being platooned. "Casey did not platoon the Braves," Dick Donovan wrote. "Casey had a good day when he could locate nine able-bodied players."

Surprisingly, the Braves of 1942 were a substantial improvement over any previous Stengel edition. It took some looking to see it, but the growth was there. In February, the Stengel-Weiss connection was used to their mutual advantage. Four years had passed since Lou Gehrig's premature retirement and the Yankees had yet to find a replacement. Stengel made Buddy Hassett available in exchange for Tommy Holmes, a young center fielder whose path to the majors had been blocked by Joe DiMaggio. Holmes had been in the Yankees' system since 1937 and had hit .326 in 702 games. As a singles hitter who was far from the prototypi-cal slugging Yankees outfielder, he had little hope of displacing any of the Yankees' outfield trio or rising in the esteem of Joe McCarthy. The trade would later redound to the Yankees' discredit, but for the moment Holmes seemed excess baggage (though only in a postwar sense; Holmes was invaluable in that he could not serve in the military—apparently Uncle Sam liked singles hitters even less than did the Yankees).

Through Stengel, who brought the two together, Holmes fell under the influence of Paul Waner and adopted his approach at the plate. "Now, he will take a drink once in awhile," Stengel told Holmes, "but he can hit the lines. Listen to him and you might learn six or eight things." Holmes would hit .278, strike out only ten times in 558 at-bats, and twice break up no-hitters. The rookie also drew sixty-four walks; if the Braves were ever to develop an offense, it was not only power that they had to add, but baserunners. Of equal importance were two final qualities: Holmes could not serve in the armed forces, so the Bees could count on his continued presence, and he was likable. Over time, he would help to give the bland Braves an identity.

When Holmes arrived in Boston, he asked Stengel how the Bees knew to ask Weiss for him; he had not been greatly heralded as a prospect. I scouted you personally, said Stengel. Asked where he found the time, Stengel replied that day games against the Dodgers left him plenty of time to go over to Newark at night. "I'm going to build the ball club around you," Stengel told Holmes. That was Casey Stengel: after a day with his baseball team, he spent the evening watching more baseball, dreaming about a better baseball future.

Also in February, the five-time All-Star catcher Ernie Lombardi had been sold to the Braves. Lombardi was an unusual acquisition for the Braves in that he was a great player who still retained many of his peak abilities. In this the Braves had simply been lucky. Lombardi's previous team, the Reds, had been willing to part with him cheaply because his 1941 season was so far below his usual standards that they assumed he was washed up at thirty-three.

When the greatest hitters in baseball history are mentioned, Lombardi is often a footnote. Every reference is exactly the same: Lombardi was the slowest player in the history of the game. Lombardi would have hit .400 annually if only he had the speed to run out his own base hits. Infielders "cheated" against him, setting up in the short outfield to snare his grounders, knowing they would still have the time to throw him out.

He was a huge man, six-foot-three, with gigantic hands and a nose which by itself would have qualified for the heavyweight division. The proboscis caused Lombardi to be popularly referred to as "The Schnozz." Lombardi was probably not born to be a catcher, but that was the position that required the least mobility. He would have made a great designated hitter. He would have made a terrific wall. If a modern analogue is needed, imagine a cross between Mike Piazza and a St. Bernard.

Lombardi was an offensive force whenever he was able to get the ball past the infielders. Despite being a total stranger to the concept of momentum (it was once reported that he "beat out a hit to deep center"), Lombardi's incredible strength allowed him to hit the ball hard enough and far enough that he still reached base a great percentage of the time. His best season was probably 1938, when he hit .342 with nineteen home runs and ninety-five runs batted in. Lombardi's batting average led the National League, and he was honored as the league's Most Valuable Player. Only twice in modern history has a catcher won a batting title. On both occasions the honor belonged to Lombardi.

The downside was double plays, twenty or more a season, one every twenty at-bats. Lombardi led the National League in hitting into double plays four times, and would have hit into even more if the rigors of catching had allowed him to play every day.

Despite his strengths, Cincinnati ownership was not disappointed that Lombardi hit only .264 in 1941 as they were looking for an excuse to get rid of him. He had two strikes against him with the Reds: money and history. The former pertained to his annual holdouts for more money. In the days before free agency, a player's club unilaterally decided whether a player deserved a raise or a pay cut from the previous season. There was always a limited degree of negotiation, in that a player could make his case to management, though management was under no obligation to seriously consider the player's proposal. The possibility of compromise existed, if only to preserve good will, but the final decision was in the hands of the club. Players that resorted to holding out, which was their only real leverage, were considered troublemakers. In the thirties and forties, the most prominent player of this class was Joe DiMaggio. Lombardi was right after him.

The burden of history was a more intractable problem. Lombardi had been, unfairly, the goat of the 1939 World Series against the Yankees. In the tenth inning of the fourth game, the Yankees had Frank Crosetti on third and Charlie Keller on first. DiMaggio singled, scoring Crosetti. When the Reds' left fielder bobbled the ball, Keller raced for home. The throw came in at the same time as Keller. As Lombardi lunged for the ball, there was contact with Keller; the big man took either a knee to the head or a foot to the groin. Lombardi momentarily blacked out, the ball lying beside him. DiMaggio never stopped running. As Lombardi finally emerged from his stupor, DiMaggio executed a beautiful hook slide to evade Lombardi's tag. The Yankees won the game and the Series, which would come to be remembered for "Lombardi's Snooze."

That the Reds had been swept in four straight games was lost in the rush to make a goat of Lombardi. The fans had forgiven him—it was said that Lombardi was the most popular player in club history—but ownership never did.

Lombardi was re-energized by the sale. Though he missed time due to injury, he hit .330, the highest batting average in the league. Despite some controversy over his low at-bat total (309), it was a successful comeback season.

Stengel enjoyed having Lombardi on the team, a man he had known and admired since Lombardi's minor league days at Oakland (Stengel had assisted the Oaks in the sale of Lombardi to the Dodgers). On one occasion, Lombardi was standing on first when Stengel suddenly shouted, "Steal it, Lom!" Two teams watched in stunned silence as the lumbering behemoth took off for second base. Lombardi slid; the earth trembled. There was no throw. The opposing catcher had been too shocked to make a play.

Waner was still with the team, and though he hit only .258, most of the year's excitement revolved around him. He was a strange man, a combination hitting guru and drunk. Buddy Hassett recalled that Waner "had remarkable agility, like an acrobat." Stengel agreed. "He had to be a very graceful player because he could slide without breaking the bottle on his hip."

At this late stage of his career, Waner would have been ideally utilized as a pinch-hitter. The war pushed him into a greater role. In a double-header at Pittsburgh, Stengel was forced to use Waner in center field. Even in his prime, Waner had been strictly a right fielder. The pastures at Pittsburgh's Forbes Field were large enough to host a herd of bison (at the smaller Baker Bowl in Philadelphia, the owner settled for sheep). There was enough ground for two center fielders to cover; a thirty-nine-year-old corner outfielder with bad legs didn't stand a chance.

On this particular day, ball after ball was hit at Waner, and his body was letting him know that he had already left his youth on the field, and had no more left to give. Perhaps like Hack Wilson that hot July day in Philadelphia he was still feeling the effects of the previous evening's over-indulgence.

One ball was hit over his head, a triple. Waner ran it down. Another shot up and over, another triple, more miles on Waner's odometer. As he walked back to his position his legs were shaking. The next batter popped up to short centerfield. Waner charged in, stumbled, fell. The ball hit the ground next to him. He tried to get up, and could not. He lay helplessly until one of the other outfielders could retrieve the ball and help him up.

Still, Waner knew his role, worked with the younger players, and was fun to be around. After his Braves career he moved on to the Yankees. A fan once shouted, "Hey Paul, how come you're in the outfield for the Yankees?"

"Because Joe DiMaggio's in the army," Waner replied. "Big Poison" had no illusions.

Waner also provided a historic moment, earning his 3,000th hit in a Braves uniform. In actuality, he earned it twice. His first 3,000 hit was a ground ball that bounced off of a fielder's glove and was ruled an infield single. Waner gestured angrily at the press box to have the hit changed to an error—he wanted his milestone safety to be a clean hit. The scorer obliged, and Waner got number 3,000 on a clean hit to the outfield.

Though no one, not even Stengel, knew it at the time, the Braves received a hint of the better world to come after the war. Two rookie pitchers had managed to survive the initial military call-ups and reach the Braves. One was Warren Spahn, the other Johnny Sain. At the outset Stengel was an enthusiastic believer in Spahn, predicting future greatness "if nothing happens to him," but changed his mind when refused to hit Pee Wee Reese when Stengel ordered him to. "Young man, you have no guts," said Stengel, and sent him back to Hartford. Shortly thereafter, Spahn was inducted into the armed forces and was lost for the duration.

Though Stengel immediately recognized Spahn's ability, he could not have known that Spahn would establish himself as one of the greatest pitchers in the history of baseball, a winner of 363 major league games. Nor could he have foreseen that Spahn would have a heroic, action-filled military service, earning a Purple Heart and a Bronze Star and seeing action in the Battle of the Bulge. Still, for the rest of his life he readily admitted that he had been too hasty with the twenty-one-year-old southpaw, calling the demotion the worst mistake he ever made as a manager. "I said 'no guts' to a kid who wound up being a war hero and one of the best pitchers anybody ever saw. You can't say I don't miss 'em when I miss 'em." Spahn never did like to hit anyone. In 5,245.2 career innings, he hit only 42 batters.

Spahn joined Stengel's Mets at the end of their careers and famously said he was the only player to work for Casey Stengel before and after he was a genius. He also said that no one knew more baseball or cared more passionately about the game than Stengel. Perhaps that's why Stengel never pointed out that he was the only manager to work with Warren Spahn before and after he was a great pitcher.

Sain, twenty-four, spent most of the year in the bullpen. He hit five batters, which may or may not have had something to do with his staying power. He also pitched fairly well, though he struggled with his control at times. He was a bit thin-skinned as well. "I led the Reds three to two, going into the eighth and was lifted when they got two men on bases. Tost relieved me—allowing the tying run to score. . . . The next day the Boston headlines read: 'Sain blows up—fails to last.' When I saw that I really blew up, and enlisted in the Naval Air Corps with Ted Williams, Johnny Pesky, and the rest."

When Sain and Spahn returned from war they would become the aces of a resurgent Braves team, prompting the verse, "Spahn and Sain and pray for rain." Like Spahn, Sain would work with Stengel again, albeit with much better results.

The future receded even more than it already had on December 4, when Eddie Miller was sent to the Reds in exchange for infielder Eddie Joost, pitcher Nate Andrews, and $25,000. Miller had become one of the top defensive shortstops in the game, a fielder with good range who didn't make a lot of errors. In 1940, he fielded 251 consecutive chances without an error, and his overall fielding percentage was .970, both National League records. In 1942, he fielded .983 (thirteen errors in 142 games) to break his own record. In the 1939 twenty-three inning game, he accepted twenty-one chances, a record for a single game.

Now he was gone, though not without some reason. His offense had slipped in 1941 and 1942. Over the two seasons he had hit .241 with only fifty-seven walks, leading to a .284 on-base percentage (against a National League average of .332). His power had disappeared with his patience, leaving only twelve home runs—six a season—over 1,119 at bats.

Miller's prickly personality had taken its toll on his relationship with Stengel, who was becoming more irascible with each losing game. The two had become locked in an unproductive cycle of open disrespect and punitive benchings. Long after his departure, Miller was tossing veiled invective Stengel's way from Cincinnati, saying that the Braves did not have "the victory complex," by which he meant that they did have Stengel. "It wasn't that we didn't have good players," he said. "One year Ernie Lombardi was burning up the league at bat and we finished seventh. Then Babe Dahlgren came over . . . and we still floundered around."

Most importantly, Miller had committed the cardinal sin of holding out. His batting slump, clubhouse problems, and financial intransigence made other clubs reluctant to deal for the player widely perceived as the Braves' best. The money received by the Braves was $15,000 less than they had paid Weiss to acquire him.

Boston fans were conditioned to be suspicious of sell-outs, going back to the Intolerable Acts—not to mention the sale of Babe Ruth and the rest of the early Red Sox stars to the Yankees. There was a bad backlash. Dave Egan was furious that the popular infielder had been let go. "His chief eccentricity," he wrote, "was that he asked for more money, so that each spring he was described in the papers as a hold out. It was my opinion each April that the Braves were holding out on Miller, instead of vice-versa. . . . He erred only thirteen times during the course of the entire season, and I wish Perfesser Stengel, who is also eccentric, could say as much for himself."

Stengel sounded almost maniacal defending the trade. "I've got to have some more pitching. The Red Sox could get into second place with Ted Williams, but I couldn't seem to get out of the second division with Miller at short. I had to get some pitching. I'm looking for still more pitching."

It was a stretch to place the failures of the entire regime on the head of a twenty-five-year-old shortstop, but that was the state of things with the Braves and a tired Casey Stengel. With the Reds, Miller recovered some of his offensive productivity and made the All-Star team in 1943, 1944, 1946, and 1947. His Braves replacement, Whitey Wietelmann, hit much like the former batboy that he was.

It would seem to be self-evident that all managers are not equal. This statement applies not just to "good" and "bad" managers, but to all managers and the kind of teams that their individual personalities and talents allow them to succeed with. Stengel's own protégé, Billy Martin, was much better restructuring a losing team into a contender than he was with the contender itself. With the Mets in the 1990s, Bud Harrelson took over a contender from Davey Johnson and helped run it into the ground. Stengel would later prove to be an engineer, a man who could take a machine that was in danger of breaking down and not only restore it, but fine-tune it until it worked even better than it had before. Had the machine had already broken down, it might have been better to call someone else.

Stengel's critics have said this reflects badly on his case for managerial greatness, but it is no great criticism to say that he was limited in this regard. He shares that limitation with almost every manager in history. It is the rare artist indeed who can paint with a dull brush. Given the proper tools, Stengel was a master at utilizing them. Stengel's Yankees had a great deal of talent to draw upon, but talent is not enough. Many managers have failed to succeed with talented teams. Sometimes even talented managers fail with talented teams, as with Leo Durocher and the Chicago Cubs of the late sixties.

It was Stengel's ability to work with the talent he was given, to integrate the new with the old, that allowed him to stay at the top of his game for so many years, as the fortunes of other managers rose and fell around him. With the Yankees, George Weiss kept the team supplied with fresh, though often flawed, talent. Stengel kept stretching his roster to accommodate it, creating ever more complex platoons and defensive alignments in order to disguise those flaws.

This ability sets Stengel apart from most managers, even those with winning records. Consider Cito Gaston, manager of the Toronto Blue Jays from 1989 to 1997. Gaston took over a talented team that was underperforming and immediately restored it to the pennant race. After a second place finish and two playoff losses, he won the World Series in 1992 and 1993.

Almost immediately, the Blue Jays began to slide. Gaston was slow to move young players into the lineup. He had personality conflicts with some of the team's most promising prospects, including John Olerud and Shawn Green, and seemed to rejoice in their failures. He made a point of sticking with several veterans past their prime and often seemed to forget he had a bench or that his team could manufacture runs. Bill James called him the "most conservative, virtually inert manager in baseball." His record for the four seasons after the second championship was 261–322 (.448).

Casey Stengel would never have put himself in that position. He would have traded the unproductive veterans, or failing that, forced them off of the team (as he would do to Phil Rizzuto in 1956, and as some say he did to DiMaggio before that). The young players would have been platooned at first, then given full-time jobs if their performance warranted it. The Blue Jays would have stayed in the thick of the pennant race.

After Gaston was fired, the Blue Jays followed Stengel's prescription, purging the veterans and replacing them with younger players. The next year they finished over .500 for the first time since 1993.

From Bob Quinn's office the greatest disasters of World War II must have looked like, in order: Dunkirk, Pearl Harbor, the Rape of Nanking, and the Rape of the Braves Roster. By 1943 there was simply no one left. Braves in the service included Posedel, Spahn, Sain, Rowell, Sibby Sisti, Chet Ross, and Max West. Johnny McCarthy (another former Stengel-Quinn Dodger) had been acquired to play first base. McCarthy had been the subject of one of Stengel's first manifestations of the McGrawish syndrome that said that a prospect's place was with his manager. "He's mine," Stengel said in 1934, "and I'm going to have him playing in Brooklyn. . . . Nobody can convince me that he's not the goods until I've had a chance to see him up here where something can be proved." McCarthy had hit all of .218 in two short trials before being sold to the Giants for $40,000. Stengel's second chance with the one-time prospect, now thirty-three-year-old veteran began well, with McCarthy's .304 average somewhat offsetting his fanatical resistance to taking ball four. He was drafted halfway through the season, and it all came to naught.

Waner and Cooney had moved on to the Yankees. Lombardi was a holdout, and that meant he had to be disposed of. The Braves did not even pretend to deal with holdouts. Rather, they pretended that there was no holdout, circulating a rumor that Lombardi was going to skip the season to be with his sick father, and had taken a job at a defense plant. Eventually, the Braves signed Lombardi to a contract calling for a large raise, then immediately traded him to the New York Giants. That was one more player gone.

Spring training 1943 was held in an unusual location, Wallingford, Connecticut. Wartime restrictions on travel had eliminated Florida and the usual barnstorming tour north, so the Braves had taken up residence at the exclusive Choate boarding school. Stengel, who never refused a chance to look silly, posed for photographers in a professor's robes and mortarboard, lecturing his players.

Stengel opened spring training with a hole at short that he had no way to fill. The Miller trade had been completed without much thought being given to who would replace him. "I'd sell a catcher for a shortstop or third sacker," said Stengel, "But nobody seems to want to deal these days."

Stengel knew that teams might have been willing to deal if they had any players to trade. "It's impossible to make predictions this year," he said, "what with players being called into the armed services almost daily, there's no telling what any club will do in the coming year. If we happen to hold the players now on our roster we should be fairly strong everywhere." In the midst of the carnage that was his roster, he could still laugh, at least occasionally. "We look better on paper than we really are. Fellows who should be pitching well by now have sore arms and my team is riddled with injuries. And one of the darndest things you ever heard of happened to one of my young outfielders. . . . A catfish chawed off a hunk of his foot." This last was rookie outfielder George Metkovich, whose injury, the result of an ill-fated fishing trip, earned him the sobriquet "Catfish."

What remained on the roster was exceedingly thin, strong neither on paper or in practice. Catcher Phil Masi, first baseman Kerby Farrell, second baseman Connie Ryan, shortstop Wietelmann, third baseman Eddie Joost, and outfielders Chuck Workman, Butch Nieman, and Tommy Holmes, combined to make the lowest scoring lineup in the majors. It was a low-scoring year in general; substitute baseballs were now in use to conserve war materiel, and the new "balata" ball (featuring a core covered in balata, the material used for golf ball covers) had far less life in it than the standard model. The change exacerbated the Braves' lack of punch, but the weak lineup was really at fault. Only Masi, Ryan, Joost, and Holmes would have significant postwar careers. In replacing the record-setting Miller at short, Joost set a record of his own: his .185 batting average was the lowest mark ever recorded for a full season (in later years, Joost would become an expert at drawing walks. As with his contemporaries Ed Yost and Eddie Stanky, the walks made him a valuable hitter despite his low batting averages).

Unable to match the offensive firepower of the other National League teams, who still retained some very potent bats in players such as Stan Musial, Bob Elliot, and Bill Nicholson, Stengel tried diplomacy. In 1943 the Cubs' right fielder "Swish" Nicholson defied the balata ball, batting .309 with twenty-nine home runs and 128 runs batted in. Prior to a Braves-Cubs contest at Wrigley Field, Stengel approached Cubs manager

Jimmie Wilson and pointed to Nicholson. "Take that guy out of there," he said.

Wilson was unused to other managers passing judgment on his lineups and merely blinked stupidly. "Take him out," Stengel expanded, and I'll let you play two men in his place, and I'll agree to use only eight men against your ten. Just take him out."

Stengel's suspicion of his pitching staff is proof that the concept of parks affecting players' statistics had not yet been imagined. Braves pitching was reasonably good in 1943. The team earned run average was 3.24. The National League ERA was 3.38. Al Javery and his hopping fastball won seventeen games. Nate Andrews, the other player acquired for Miller, did nothing to make the trade look good, losing twenty games on the season—not that it was his fault; his 2.57 ERA lead the team. Even Lefty Gomez, four-time twenty-game winner with the Yankees, could not make the team—though his attack on the memory of John McGraw had something to do with the timing of his release.

Stengel tried improvising to deepen his roster, revisiting his old fascination with converting pitchers into position players and vice versa. In addition to Bobby Reis, who went from a utility player to a pitcher and then back again, Stengel considered making Jim Tobin, an excellent hitter for a pitcher (his three-homer game on May 13, 1942, had been the offensive highlight of the year), into an outfielder or first baseman, and floated the idea of Johnny Cooney returning to the mound after more than a decade in the field. When Johnny McCarthy left the lineup (first because of injury, then because of Uncle Sam), his replacement at first was former pitcher Kerby Farrell.

These were desperation moves, though with a hint of method to the madness. There were several forces at work on Stengel's thinking. There was the manpower shortage caused by the war, which made the idea of having several jobs embodied in fewer players more appealing. He was also still thinking about the way players could be used if only they were more versatile. Assigning a player one defensive spot from which he could not be moved was too limiting, especially in a talent-deprived atmosphere. Stengel began to see his players as pieces in a three-dimensional puzzle. If you shift the right-fielder to third base against left-handers, you can get an extra right-handed outfielder into the game. If your second baseman can also play short, then you can pinch-hit for your shortstop early in the game. By experimenting with radical position shifts, he was testing the limits of his theories.

At the same time, Stengel's simultaneous frustration and desperation at his own plight meant that more than ever he was hoping to force his way into an improved roster. There was a recognizable aspect of escapism in this; managers who need relief from their jobs but cannot bring themselves to quit will often act in outlandish ways. A quintessential example of this was supplied by Chicago White Sox manager Eddie Stanky in May 1968 when he chose to bat pitcher Gary Peters ahead of, among others, Luis Aparicio. In Stengel's case, he chose in one 1942 game to bench all of his outfielders and start catcher Phil Masi and infielders Sibby Sisti and Nanny Fernandez in their places. This was not experimentation, but a cry for help.

The spring ended auspiciously enough, with a 7–5 exhibition game victory over McCarthy's Yankees at Yankee Stadium on April 13. It was a rare Yankee Stadium appearance for Stengel, and he enjoyed himself thoroughly, cracking, "The Yankees ain't the same without Gomez; they've lost their punch."

Stengel was nearly permanently relieved of his punch and all of his other worldly possessions on April 20. Crossing Kenmore Square in Boston one rainy evening he was the victim of a hit and run accident. Stengel suffered a severely broken right leg. On May 15, 1928, John McGraw left the Polo Grounds so angry at a Giant loss that he stepped into traffic without looking and was hit by a cab. McGraw too fractured his leg. It was said that Stengel had been hit by a cab as well. Stengel disputed this. "It wasn't a taxi driver that hit me," he said. "It was a Spanish fella, and he didn't have any insurance."

Stengel was taken to St. Elizabeth's hospital. The facilities were crowded with wounded soldiers that had been shipped stateside, so Stengel was placed in the maternity ward. The doctors had to wait until the swelling had receded before they could work on his leg, and by then a ghastly knot had formed. Billy Martin later said that Stengel's leg looked like a sock that had had a ball stuffed into it. Already bowlegged, Stengel would walk with a limp for the rest of his life. "Goddamn doctor," he said, "put my leg on backwards."

He would be in traction, immobile and away from the Braves, until June 12. Two fans sent Mother's Day cards. Stengel's friends were not much better. Frankie Frisch wired, "Your attempt at suicide fully understood. Deepest sympathy you didn't succeed." Sloppy Thurston, a pitcher with Brooklyn when Stengel coached for Carey, wrote in a note cosigned by Pittsburgh coach Jake Flowers and addressed to St. Elizabeth's psychiatric ward, "I always knew you couldn't take it. You took one look at your team and threw yourself in front of an auto." They concluded affectionately, "Things are tough, but suicide is not the answer. Next time you feel the urge to jump in front of a car, please remember we'll gladly come off the retired list to help an old pal."

Stengel bore his wounds well, his sense of humor insulating him from shock and pain. He told Edna not to leave her mother. "Don't come unless you know how to set a broken leg," he wired her. She stayed in California. A reporter who visited tried to cheer him with news that Lombardi's holdout had come to an end. "Yeah," sighed Stengel, "but I'll probably still have to run for him."

Visitors to the hospital were not there to provide sympathy but to act as straight men. Tony Cuccinello visited and said that the manager was looking better, Stengel said, "Yeah? It must be because I've just shaved." When Frisch, whose Pirates were struggling, visited, the one-man show blossomed into a full-fledged comedy act. "Move over and share that hospital cot with someone who really needs one, Casey," Frisch said.

"Just a bed won't do you any good," Stengel replied. "The way your Pirates are going, you need at least an operating table."

"That's really quite a cage they've got you in, Case. Will you give it to me when they let you out? You know, they'll be putting you in a much bigger one when you get back on your feet."

Even when Frisch had left, Stengel was still on a roll. Frisch too had recently been hospitalized, providing his old Giants teammate with a raft of material. "They noticed his head was egg-shaped, because of the wicked way the infielders used to tag him when he did that head-first slide into a base. The docs wrote it up in the medical books when I told them about how Frank's cap always blew off when he ran, all on account of his head being tagged out of shape. . . . The doctors said they had never seen such a specimen. I, having studied dentistry two years, was able to discuss things scientifically, while Frisch couldn't understand, he having majored in gymnasium etiquette while he was at Fordham."

Even a visit from Frenchy Bordagaray was an opportunity for some—a little—amusement. Bordagaray used the visit to remind Stengel that he had never returned one of the fines that he had levied for kamikaze base-running back in the Brooklyn days. "Howsa 'bout that fifty bucks you owe me?" Bordagaray asked.

"Yeah," Stengel said. "I'll buy you a War Bond."

Although Stengel could not watch the team play under his substitute, Bob Coleman, he could still get the games on the radio. When a group of New York writers reached the bedside just after the Giants had swept a twin bill from the Braves, Stengel said, "I believe I suffered a relapse when the curtain went down on that second defeat. And on your way out tell 'em at the desk if Lefty Gomez visits, I can't be seen." Coach George Kelly visited him prior to a road trip. "When you get back," Stengel told Kelly, gesturing to the radio, "I'll either be out of the hospital or out of my mind."

He seemed to feel no anxiety about the contrast Coleman provided to his own stewardship of the team after the Braves got off to a strong 14–8 start, propelled by a seven-game winning streak. Playing the Cardinals,

Reds, and Pirates at home, the Braves received strong starting pitching in every game and outscored their opponents 25–9 during the streak. "Lying here and listening to the radio tell me about those seven straight they've just won has been wonderful, and don't sell the Braves short. Everybody on our team wants to be on it, and that makes a lot of difference. It's a grand world—if it would only stop raining."

He returned to the Braves too soon for either health or peace of mind. The leg had not healed, and he was forced to sit on the bench in street clothes. Quinn had not gone out of his way to keep him up to date while he was incapacitated. Lombardi had been traded while he was gone, and on his first day back he failed to recognize the catcher who was warming up his pitcher. He asked a bystander, and was told that the catcher's name was Hugh Poland. "Oh," he said. A moment later he turned again. "Who's Hugh Poland?"

Despite his isolation, his instincts were still intact. On June 18, the Braves hosted the Giants. It was Stengel's first day back on the job. Since the conclusion of the seven-game win streak, the Coleman Braves had gone 7–17 and were in desperate need of an infusion of energy. The day before, player-manager Joe Cronin of the Red Sox had given some lift to an otherwise lackluster season by hitting his third pinch-hit home run in two days. On-field heroics had been beyond Stengel since the Toledo days—he was a month from turning fifty-three—but as the Braves took the field he found himself thinking about what Cronin had done.

Al Javery started and pitched excellently, carrying a 3–0 lead into the top of the seventh inning. Without warning, the Braves' defense fell apart. The Giants plated six unearned runs, four in the seventh and two more in the eighth. The Braves scratched back for a fourth run of their own in the bottom of the seventh, but with two out in the bottom of the ninth inning, the Braves were still looking at the wrong end of an 6–4 score.

The Braves found life when Chuck Workman hit a double over Mel Ott's head and Butch Nieman singled him home. Johnny McCarthy followed with another single, moving Nieman to third base. It was now 6–5, but there were still two outs and Hugh Poland was due to bat. Once identified, Poland had proved to be a backstop of the catch-and-throw type, which in baseball's lexicon is code for a receiver with no bat. He had yet to hit a major league home run, and in a career that spanned 83 games and 218 plate appearances, he never would.

A pinch-hitter was clearly needed. Stengel had a brainstorm: "I should send for Cronin." Unfortunately, Cronin was the property of the Red Sox, not the Braves. Mentally conceding the point, Stengel sent the right-handed outfielder Chet Ross to the plate to face the right-handed pitcher Bill Lohrman.

Ross had looked like a coming slugger in 1940, but after multiple injuries he was just hanging on to the Boston bench. Stengel was hoping he could recapture his power swing for just one at bat. "See if you can get a ball through that wind and bring a run in," he told Ross.

Ross took a ball and a strike, then swung. The ball not only went through the wind, but over the wind. The three-run pinch-hit homer won the game 8–6.

Dave Egan was still not satisfied. "Would it be indelicate to suggest that a day be run at Braves Field in honor of the guy who ran over Perfesser Stengel? And that the local chapter of the Baseball Writers' Ass'n present him with a plaque as the man-who-has-done-the-most-for-Boston-baseball-in-1943? The Perfesser himself, having a sense of humor, probably will be the first to second the motion."

Actually, no. "I think Casey cried when he read that," Edna Stengel told Maury Allen. "He was flat on his back, he was worried about his health, and he cared about the club. That was cruel. Why would somebody write that?"

Egan had an honest answer: because it sold papers. "No one pays any attention to a 'goody-goody' writer. You can praise a guy all over the sports page and you won't draw so much as a ho-hum from your readers. When you start belting someone, you attract attention. There's nothing like controversy to catapult a writer into the spotlight."

This was what passed for sportswriting in Boston in those days (in a few years the writers would turn on Ted Williams), and the rest of the season went on this way, with the team losing, Egan laughing, and Stengel in pain. "A fellow has to write the facts regardless of who is hurt," Egan said. "I owe my allegiance to the man who plunks down a nickel to buy a copy of the paper for which I work, and as long as I'm working for a newspaper, I'll print all the facts and let the pieces drop where they may." When Egan said "facts," he meant "character assassination."

Contrary to his wife's intimation of emotional distress, Stengel ignored Egan, at least in public. "I didn't care about that," he said. "They also said he [the driver] could manage the club better than me." Later he claimed that the *Daily Record* had wanted to fire Egan for his below-the-belt attacks and excessive drinking. Stengel supposedly intervened to save his job, an unaccountable act of selflessness. Had Ted Williams, another favorite Egan target who considered the writer "the busiest dispenser" of "garbage" among Boston sportswriters, known of Stengel's generosity, he might have been less thrilled to share the dais with him at Cooperstown.

To paraphrase another California resident, Egan would not have Stengel to kick around for much longer. In January 1944, controlling interest in the Braves was purchased by a trio of Boston contractors. Quinn stayed on the board of directors, but he was merely a figurehead. The real power belonged to the contractors—the "Three Steam Shovels" as they came to be called—and their front man, Louis R. Perini.

With the new ownership came rumors that Stengel would be replaced. "Perfessor K. C. Stengel, if current reports are to be credited," Egan gloated, "will live the whole year 'round in the remarkable climate of California and spend his declining days second guessing the weatherman instead of himself."

Perini felt the team had grown used to losing, and Stengel had not made a good impression in his few contacts with the new owner. It's hard to imagine that the former complaint was much more than an excuse, as most of the players had not been in a Braves uniform long enough to get used to Boston itself, let alone losing. Thanks to the war, the starting lineup had been turned over completely since 1940. It was, however, probably true that Stengel had grown numb to losing. After five years in the second division he was tired, and the broken leg merely served to sap the rest of his energy.

As for Perini's latter point, the traditional story is that he had found himself on the receiving end of one of Stengel's monologues and made a snap judgment that his manager was a buffoon. The specifics of the conversation do not survive, so it is not clear if Perini objected to a Stengelese obscuration of a baseball point the manager had not felt like answering, or if Stengel had been too direct, telling the neophyte owner to let him, as Joe McCarthy might have said, do the worrying and stick to steam shovels. Either way, Stengel's name was pricked.

Quinn told Stengel of the new owner's feelings. Stengel's response was that if he was bought out he would resign. On January 27, 1944, not having bothered to consult Edna, he sent a letter to Quinn:

Whenever a new group purchases control of a corporation they have the right to dictate the policy of that corporation. In order that there be no embarrassment for the new group, I hereby tender my resignation.

I am sure that the city of Boston and the Braves will profit by the young players I have developed. Many of the players are now in the service.

I want to thank you and, believe it or not, my many friends in Boston . . . particularly the newspaper men who were kind to me while I was trying to win and develop young players for the future of the Boston club. I sincerely hope the new owners have every success and Boston will have a first-division team.

He repeated: "I do not want to embarrass the new group of stockholders who have taken over control of the Braves."

Egan was exultant. "The discharge of Stengel, I suppose, is a belated confession that Bob Quinn . . . made a slight error back in 1937 when he encouraged Bill McKechnie to resign from the Braves. I have suspected ever since . . . that Mr. Quinn wants to and does run the team from the front office, and that the nominal manager, down on the field, is a mere figurine whose chief duty is to nod and say yes at suitable intervals." Egan was setting up Quinn as a new target, now that Stengel was gone. "So long Perfesser!" wrote Egan. "You were great when you had it."

Egan would not find the new Braves' management such an easy target. In Perini and his partners he was dealing with a type of character that Braves management had never been associated with—the professional businessman. A few years later, once Perini had concluded he could do better elsewhere, he moved the Braves, by then a good team, to Milwaukee where the fans, and presumably the media, would be more supportive. It worked for awhile, directly inspiring the relocation of several eastern franchises.

Other writers were more kind to Stengel. George Carens of the *Boston Traveler* wrote, "Only good wishes go from this corner to Charles Dillon Stengel, who has resigned after a long and honorable career in the big leagues. Months ago Casey confided to close friends that the leg broken on the eve of the 1943 campaign was not healing properly. It was only a matter of time before he would seek surcease from the mental torture of trying to manage the Braves while suffering physically. Those post-game sessions in the Braves nineteenth hole won't be the same without Stengel throwing ideas around. My only regret is that he didn't have much luck here."

Quinn, who remained in the employ of the Steam Shovels (ultimately yielding administration of the club to his son John), said of the man who he had employed for seven years, "All Casey had to do was to be furnished with a half-decent, respectable club and he could get more out of it than any other manager I ever had." But Quinn could never supply Stengel with even a half-decent team.

Despite these encomiums, the dominant depiction was that Stengel had failed to prove his worth as anything but a whimsical figure who still had more in common with the young man who let a bird fly out from under his cap than he did with John McGraw. What was not generally understood, except by the writers who covered the club on a daily basis (as opposed to the columnists), was that the Stengel of the clubhouse was much more in the McGraw model than was the public Stengel. As for the latter facet of the manager, it represented more than just the manifestation of a man in love with his own sense of humor—he was trying to distract the public from the team's failure. As Jimmy Breslin said, "If you didn't have Stengel talking, you would have had silence."

It is written in one of the early Stengel biographies that after Stengel's reemergence with the Yankees that Perini came to recognize Stengel's quality, that he and Stengel became friends, and "now laugh" about his resignation. It must have been a bitter laugh for Stengel, who left six wasted years behind in Boston.

CHAPTER 12

WHERE I'LL BE
A YEAR FROM NOW

"I have been discharged fifteen times and rehired. . . . As far as I'm concerned, from drawing a salary and from my ups and downs and being discharged, I always found out that there was somebody ready to employ you, if you were on the ball."

—Casey Stengel

In 1958, Stengel was in the midst of a typically rambling testimony before the Senate subcommittee on antitrust and monopoly when he gave a surprisingly candid description of some of his experiences in baseball prior to coming to the Yankees, disguised as a throwaway line. "I have been through two or three depressions," he said, "in baseball and out of it." Here was an epigram for the Braves years, and their immediate aftermath.

Leaving Boston, Stengel went home to Glendale, California, and began exercising his leg. The gadfly who had spent his previous vacations rushing from one baseball event to another was gone, replaced by a tired old man with a limp. He had no plans other than to sit by his swimming pool and heal. Though he received a few offers to coach or manage in the minors, he turned them all down. The ghost of McGraw was secure in Cooperstown.

The conventional wisdom was that he was gone for good, retired. His reputation, which had survived Brooklyn, had been destroyed by the Braves. Back in 1932, when Max Carey had given him his return ticket to the major leagues, Dan Daniel had written, "Those who really know Stengel know him for a baseball anomaly. He is a clown—one of the funniest men connected with the game. And yet he is a wise, crafty leader, sound strategically, and keen in the development of young players."

Time had chipped away at Daniel's description until only "clown" remained. When Stengel was fired by the Dodgers back in 1936, many people had said nice things about him. Columns were written deploring his removal. Banquets were held in his honor. No bonfires were lit when he resigned as Braves manager. He quit by mail, as if delivering a ransom note saying he was kidnapping himself, quietly disappearing so he would not have to "embarrass" his new employers. He had surrendered the field to Dave Egan, whose venomous prose followed him even into exile:

> He's a great guy except to those who work for him. He's a funny guy, too, but he's always funny at somebody else's expense, and the somebody else is usually within hearing distance. So he wound up with a sullen ball club, there in Boston and the majority of members of that ball club hated him then and hate him now, so that I laugh a sour laugh each time I read in the papers that Stengel is a great man on developing young ballplayers . . . yet he always remained funny, in his cruel and malicious way.

Egan was vicious, and Egan was unfair (for what executive in any field does not alienate some of his underlings by the very act of pursuing his duties?) but Egan was a perceptive man in that he knew precisely the wounds on which to throw salt. Keywords: "sullen," "malicious." Those terms, or similar ones with different shades of meaning, might have described Stengel in his last years at Boston. Is it likely that, as with Max West, his wit found a few targets who would have rather not been stung? Of course. If Stengel gave up on his team after Bob Quinn gave up on it, he would have been only human. No manager in the history of the game could have dug the Boston Braves out of their doldrums without a change of ownership, and when that change finally came it was too late for Stengel.

But Stengel at Boston was just one facet of the man, one moment in a long professional life. It was not representative. The difference between Stengel at Boston and Stengel at Brooklyn was that in the latter case he was having fun. The Dodgers were never an afterthought with their fans. They supported the team even when it was losing. The players he had were not very good, but they were always colorful. From 1934 to 1936 he projected the image of a man who loved what he was doing. From 1938 to 1943, he blended in with the drab gray world of the Braves: gray team, gray stadium, endless gray days of gray rain delays, and eventually, gray Casey Stengel.

His negativity was not only a result of constant losing, but of frustration at having spent nine years as a victim of undercapitalized ownership. His precipitous resignation of early 1944 was actually opportunistic; he wanted to get his money back and invest it elsewhere. Max Meyer had what looked like a solid chance to purchase the Dodgers. Stengel intended to be his partner. Had this not been the case, Stengel said, he and his Braves co-investors would have refused to be bought out by Perini. "Guys with all the confidence in the world in me," Stengel said, were ready to ante up to keep him employed. "They treat me like Joe McCarthy. You'd think I had won a world championship, and made a bundle of money for all of them."

Meyer's Brooklyn deal collapsed when the prospective investors got a look at the team's books and found that satisfying the Dodgers' many debts would have left no money to operate the club. Stengel decided to go home. In his present mood, if he wasn't buying, he wasn't working.

What had to happen if he were to come back—not necessarily to baseball, but to himself—was that he needed to rediscover his joy of living. The first step in that process was to heal his leg. He vigorously applied himself to this task. The second step in his process of recovery was furnished, appropriately, by a man known as "Jolly Cholly."

Charlie Grimm was known, among other things, as "baseball's only left-handed banjo player," by which it was meant that he was something of a free spirit. He and Stengel had briefly been teammates at Pittsburgh in 1919. Though managed by the football coach Hugo Bezdek, the two Pirates teams Stengel was halfheartedly a part of in 1918 and 1919 were nonetheless a hotbed of future managerial talent. In addition to Stengel and Max Carey there was Bill McKechnie and Billy Southworth, both of whom won World Series, and Grimm. The first baseman had taken over the Cubs in 1932 and taken them to the World Series, then repeated the trick in 1935.

Lately, Grimm had been in the minors managing the Milwaukee Brewers of the American Association, sharing the ownership of the team with young Bill Veeck, the freewheeling son of the late president of the Cubs. The enterprise was successful, particularly for Grimm. Since taking over as manager of the team in 1941, he had guided the Brewers from eighth place to second in 1942 and then to first place in 1943.

The 1944 Cubs had started out with a 1–9 record under the temperamental Jimmie Wilson. Owner Phil Wrigley decided to make a change. As is typical in these situations, teams shift from high-pressure to low-pressure managers. The "high-strung, noisy, openly critical" Wilson was pushed out to make way for the "Jolly" Grimm.

Grimm hesitated to accept. He wanted to go back to the majors, but the Brewers were doing very well. In those days, prior to television and the complete absorption of the minors into the farm system, there was no shame in being the manager of a top minor league franchise. Locally, a league championship had tremendous cachet. If one was called to the majors to work with a chronically down team (as Donie Bush was by

Quinn), it was conceivably better to stick with a sure thing in the minors than to risk one's reputation and security in the major leagues. The pay was often better in the minors too.

These were the Chicago Cubs, and their owner was not only a baseball magnate but a chewing gum magnate. The ball club would be well supported, could logically be counted on to improve, so that was alright for Grimm. The real problem lay with Bill Veeck. He was in the Marines, somewhere in the Pacific. Veeck was not a wealthy man. His entire financial well-being was dependent on the success of the Brewers. Grimm did not want to simply abandon the club.

Grimm had to think fast; Wrigley had given him only a few days to consider his offer. Unable to contact Veeck, Grimm decided that his best hope was to find a trustworthy, experienced manager to take over the team. The name that came to mind was Casey Stengel.

Since Grimm had been given little time to make his own decision, Stengel had even less time to make his. He hesitated at first; Boston's wounds—psychological as well as physical—had not yet healed. Grimm was persistent and Stengel agreed to come to Milwaukee. In May 1944, at the age of fifty-three, he was starting over. After thirteen years away, he was back in the American Association.

For once he had picked the right assignment. The Brewers were a veteran club (with the war on they had to be) with the kind of players he could work with and would respond to his philosophies. They were, as a group, patient, disciplined hitters. These were not young men hitting fly balls into the teeth of the Charles River winds.

The Brewers had finished 90–61 (.596) the year before. Stengel's team improved on Grimm's record by better than ten games, taking first place with a record of 102–51 (.667). More importantly, Stengel had been able to showcase fifteen of the players for sale to the majors—among them several who had failed in previous trials. He had put a new luster on some known commodities. The season was a rousing success. "I had the horses," Stengel said of the American Association pennant. He was announcing to his critics that given the proper tools he knew how to utilize them.

At the same moment that Stengel was celebrating his triumph, his former boss, Max Carey, was celebrating one too. "Right here in this room," he said, staring at a collection of women whose short skirts showed off their scabby knees, "is the greatest girls' ball club in the world." Carey had just guided the Milwaukee Chicks to the championship of the All-American Girls Professional Baseball League.

The only individual closely connected with the Milwaukee Brewers who was not enjoying the 1944 season was Bill Veeck. One of his legs had been shattered by the recoil of an artillery piece at Bougainville. Now he rested in a military hospital as the doctors tried to convince him to have the leg amputated. At that moment he had every reason to be miserable, and his feelings were compounded when he finally received the news that Stengel was his manager. His partner had deserted him, he had not been consulted, and he had the same low opinion of Stengel's managerial abilities that was apparently shared by everyone but Charlie Grimm. His forebodings were confirmed when he received two letters from, respectively, a Brewers coach and his team vice president, telling him that Stengel was, "a bum."

Veeck fired off a furious letter to his business manager in Milwaukee, who had been acting as his proxy. The letter was chiefly an indictment of Casey Stengel's career. "He has been closely connected with Bob Quinn and the operation of the Boston Braves. This in itself is enough to damn him. . . . From my observation, Stengel is mentally a second-division major leaguer. That is, he is entirely satisfied with a mediocre ball club as long as Stengel and his alleged wit are appreciated. . . . I have no confidence in his ability and rather than be continuously worried, I'd rather dispose of the whole damn thing."

It was as if some copies of the *Boston Daily Record* had found their way to the Pacific theatre. Not that it would have made a difference. As Veeck later admitted, he was unable to view the situation rationally. His emotional state had been dictated by his wounds, his loneliness, and blind panic.

When Veeck returned to the United States and was able to have closer contact with his operatives, he realized that his assessment had been mistaken. Stengel had become immensely popular with the fans and the players, had won the pennant, and the fifteen ballplayers sold for, in Veeck's opinion, "outrageously high prices," was the clincher. Veeck's feelings for Stengel had turned around 180 degrees.

It was too late. Stengel had become aware of Veeck's original letter and decided his position was untenable. At a banquet celebrating the Brewers' championship, he dramatically announced his resignation. Confidence restored, he went out boldly. This time there was no quiet letter to Bob Quinn.

Veeck had been shipped stateside and was hospitalized in California. He urged Stengel to come see him on his way home to Glendale. Veeck apologized for his letter and asked Stengel to reconsider his resignation. Stengel refused. He knew about the letters from the coach and the vice president; there were just too many people to reconcile. He did try to cheer Veeck by showing him how well his own leg had recovered from its injury.

With the American Association championship, Stengel knew that he now had momentum on his side for the first time since 1934. George

Weiss now reappeared. Stengel had been sufficiently rehabilitated—at least in Weiss's eyes—that he could now be considered for a job in the Yankees organization. His name was floated as a replacement for Earle Combs, the longtime Yankees player and major league coach who was retiring due to family considerations. When Weiss suggested to Ed Barrow that the Yankees would do well to position Stengel "one heartbeat away," so to speak, from the fading Joe McCarthy, Barrow condemned the idea with a two-word question: "That clown?" Johnny Neun got the job.

With a large degree of autonomy when it came to running New York's minor league operations, Weiss was still free to offer Stengel a job within the Yankees farm system. It was rumored that Stengel would get to captain the Yankees' top team at Newark of the International League. In fact, the only managerial position open was that of the Kansas City Blues of the American Association, a club that had finished last in 1944 with a record of 41–110, sixty games behind Stengel's Brewers. It was not much of an opportunity, but it was a job, and Stengel wanted to repay Weiss for their years of friendship, not to mention Buddy Hassett, Eddie Miller, and Tommy Holmes.

Stengel's Blues had been hit hard by the war, and lacked almost anything in the way of potential major league talent. Weiss had concentrated what talent he had at Newark. "I guess he had about the poorest material in the whole farm system," Weiss said. He repeatedly promised to transfer quality reinforcements, but none were forthcoming.

With no stars and few victories, the Blues drew fewer than 40,000 spectators for the season. The team was so bad that when Milwaukee visited, Veeck (recently discharged), who loved to tease the Yankee organization and specifically George Weiss, both of which he regarded both as having an undeservedly snobbish and superior attitude, stood in front of the gate and gave each attendee his dollar admission back, saying, "It's a shame you have to pay to see a team as bad as this." Still, Stengel managed to promote three players and the club moved up in the standings to seventh place.

At the end of the season, Stengel resigned. "I had paid off my obligation to Weiss," he said. More significantly, Weiss had been unable to interest Larry MacPhail, who was in full Durocher-obsessed mode, in the manager's services. Stengel did not have another job lined up, but having already faced retirement, he was now playing with the house's money. In fact, it was money that had given him the idea for his new career paradigm.

Stengel once said, "If you're playing baseball and thinking of about managing, you're crazy. You'd be better off thinking about being an owner." This had been his thinking at least as early as his dismissal from the Braves in 1943. With his increasing financial resources—not only were the oil wells still pumping, but the death of Edna's mother had meant a large inheritance—he was through applying for jobs. From now on, he wouldn't ask, he would buy. "I won't be out of baseball this year," he told Dan Daniel shortly after resigning from the Braves. "You see, I have a strange slant on the game. I have a private angle on baseball jobs. For one thing, I am one former player who is willing to back up my confidence in baseball with dough. My own dough. All the dough I have."

After the failing to become owner/manager of the Dodgers, Stengel turned his attention to the minor leagues. Though in the interim he had worked for Veeck and Weiss, these were time-fillers while he looked for a chance to buy.

On September 2, 1945, General Douglas MacArthur stood on the deck of the battleship *Missouri* and signed the instrument of Japanese surrender. "These proceedings," he said, with equal application to the ceremony on the ship and the entire war, "are closed."

The soldiers began returning home. The drafted ballplayers, many of whom had spent the war playing exhibition games for the benefit of servicemen, came home with neither shrapnel wounds nor hamstring pulls (some ballplayers, like Warren Spahn, did see action). Joe DiMaggio resumed his place in center field for the New York Yankees. Throughout the country, the minor leagues once again swelled with young men bursting for a chance to make it to the major leagues. Baseball as a whole experienced an attendance boom, as the national pastime shared in the national prosperity.

The new exuberance was particularly felt in the Pacific Coast League. Major League Baseball stopped at St. Louis, but there was a huge, untapped audience West of the Mississippi hungering for baseball. They flocked to PCL games in great numbers. At the league's best it was just a shade removed from major league quality. The teams had a good mix of still-vital former big-leaguers and prospects. The clubs were managed by experienced hands like Jimmy Dykes (Hollywood Stars), Lefty O'Doul (San Francisco Seals), Jim Turner (Portland Beavers), and Dick Bartell (Sacramento Solons). The crowds were enormous. In 1946, San Francisco drew 670,563 for a 186-game schedule, a minor league record. Seven games between the Seals and the Oakland Oaks that year were attended by 111,622 fans. By way of contrast, the 1946 Philadelphia Athletics drew only 621,793 for their entire home schedule, while the St. Louis Browns suckered in only 526,435 paying customers.

At that moment in time, just before television and expansion forever diluted the appeal of minor league baseball, the Pacific Coast League was the closest thing to being in the major leagues without being there. Given the enthusiastic following its teams attracted, the PCL was probably a better place to be, emotionally speaking, than several major league cities. Only lack of leadership among the league's owners and the recalcitrance of American and National League owners, already thinking of the west as their escape hatch from the northeastern cage to which they had been confined, prevented the PCL from claiming its rightful status as a third major league.

Stengel was home in Glendale looking for offers when he was contacted by Cookie de Vincenzi, a longtime friend and former owner of the Oakland Oaks. In 1943 de Vincenzi had sold the Oaks to Brick Laws, a veteran baseball operator. Laws was looking for a manager and had come to de Vincenzi for help. De Vincenzi had recommended Stengel. Endorsements had also come from the president of the league, another acquaintance of many years, and George Weiss, whose Yankees had a working agreement (and therefore input) with the Oaks.

Everything was perfect geographically. The league had outposts in Hollywood and Los Angeles, which meant that Stengel could live at home for a good portion of the schedule and enjoy something of a year-round relationship with his wife. He accepted the job.

After his previous experiences, Stengel was reluctant to promise his new employer too much. Asked how long it would take him to develop a winner, he estimated three years. "It will take me a year to learn the league, another year to develop and buy players to compete, and then with a little luck I can win it in the third."

Stengel enjoyed managing at Oakland. For the first time in over twenty years of marriage, he and Edna could live relatively close to home. The PCL also had the kind of media buzz that stimulated him. He set out to charm the writers. The playful air had returned to his gibes as he stopped feeling sorry for himself. He took a look at the Bay Area and imagined it in baseball terms. "I like the idea of bridges," he said. "Every manager wants to jump off a bridge sooner or later, and its very nice to know the doesn't have to walk fifty miles to find one." Unlike Boston, everyone laughed. Even the park was beautiful. Laws had recently invested $250,000 in its renovation, and it was worthy of major league play.

The old man and the team clicked. Stengel nearly outdid his prediction in 1946. Fueled by minor league veterans Les Scarsella (who had failed to catch on with Stengel's Braves), Brooks Holder, and Bill Raimondi, and the pitching of two youngsters sent by the Yankees, "Spec" Shea and Gene Bearden, Oakland went 111–72 (.607) to finish in second place, four games behind first place San Francisco. The league had a tiered playoff system in which the top four finishers qualified for the postseason. The Oaks beat the Los Angeles Angels in the seven-game opening round, four games to three, but lost the finals to the Seals, four to two. It was the Seals' fourth straight championship.

Shea was with the Oaks only because of a dispute with Larry Mac-Phail. Just as spring training had started he had suffered a burst appendix. MacPhail had the hospital bills forwarded to the pitcher, a gesture that did little to suffuse Shea with that warm and fuzzy pinstriped "I want to thank the good lord for making me a Yankee" feeling.

When Shea had healed, Weiss sent him to Stengel. When MacPhail saw he was pitching well, he tried to recall him. Stengel advised Shea not to report until he had received the money for his operation. With the manager's encouragement, Shea sent a letter to MacPhail in New York: "I know you want to win the pennant with the Yankees next year. Here's the way to do it: Besides bringing me up to pitch for the team, you can also hire me as the new manager. That way you can't miss. You know my record. I'll handle both jobs for $25,000 and we'll forget about the bill the team sent me after I had to have my appendix removed." Reading the letter, MacPhail had one of his trademark meltdowns.

The ploy worked for both Shea and Stengel; Shea was paid off, and Stengel got to keep his ace for the rest of the season. Fortunately for Stengel, MacPhail didn't take the part about making the pitcher manager seriously.

Though Stengel had an interest in not antagonizing the Yankees, it was not unusual for him to side with his player in a dispute with ownership. One way that he liked to motivate his players was to use his influence with ownership as leverage. When it came time for the next year's salary to be negotiated, the player could count on a good word from Stengel if his performance had been good. This was not entirely noble: in those days when players had little leverage in salary matters, the manager's ability to influence ownership was used as a motivational tool.

Both Shea and Bearden were moved to the majors by Stengel. Shea would join the Yankees rotation and be a key factor in Bucky Harris's 1947 title. He won fourteen games, made the All-Star team, and beat Brooklyn twice in the World Series. Bearden was a southpaw of questionable ability due to weak stuff and a wartime injury that altered his delivery. After Bearden pitched well in an all-star charity game in Hollywood, a "small gent" with a listing stride hobbled up to him and asked to what team Bearden belonged. Bearden replied he was to report to Newark the next spring.

"So the Yankees own you, huh?" the man said. "I like your hustle. I like the way you backed up those plays. My name is Casey Stengel. I manage Oakland. How would you like to play for me?"

Bearden's in-laws lived on the coast and he was happy to stay. "I think I can swing it," Stengel said. "Larry MacPhail and George Weiss are good friends of mine. I used to manage Kansas City for them. Maybe I can get them to option you to me at Oakland.''

Bearden's transfer was accomplished just in time for Stengel to save his career and make him, momentarily, a star. As with most knuckleball pitchers, the fluttery pitch was something that Bearden began throwing as a pregame lark. Stengel noticed and encouraged him to throw it in games. It rapidly became his new out pitch. "Casey was like a second father to me," Bearden remembered. "He got me a raise and kept talking baseball to me all the time. That's the way to learn. Talk the game, think the game and live the game.''

Late that year, the newly attractive Bearden was used by MacPhail to entice Bill Veeck into parting with some depth behind the plate—Yogi Berra having not yet convinced anyone he was a major league catcher despite a fine season at Newark. MacPhail coveted Sherm Lollar, a twenty-one-year-old catcher who had just hit twenty home runs in 222 at-bats for Baltimore of the International League. He was offering pitching in return.

Veeck asked Stengel, now "my man from Milwaukee," which of his pitchers would be worth acquiring. Stengel suggested Shea, but Veeck knew that MacPhail was not inclined to part with him. Bearden then, Stengel said. "He isn't ready yet but he will be in a year or so." In case Veeck wasn't clear, Stengel added, "Get him before MacPhail regains his sanity.''

The trade led directly to a championship for Cleveland. In 1948, Bearden would have one of the great rookie seasons of all time. He won twenty games and led the American League in earned run average (2.43). Manager Lou Boudreau chose him over the vastly more experienced Bob Feller and Bob Lemon to pitch against the Red Sox in a one-game, pennant-deciding playoff, a choice that was infinitely more fortuitous than Joe McCarthy's selection of Denny Galehouse. Bearden and the Indians won the game 8–3 and advanced to the World Series. Bearden started the third game against the Spahn and Sain Braves and threw a five-hit shutout, then came out of the bullpen in the deciding sixth contest and saved the game and the Series for the Indians.

Stengel's advice would be generously rewarded. Veeck's pennant started the chain reaction that led directly to Stengel's hiring by the Yankees. Demonstrating that loyalty in baseball lasts only as long as the consanguinity of uniform colors, when Stengel reached the majors he destroyed Bearden. He taught the Yankees to lay off of Bearden's knuckler, knowing that the lefty could not reliably throw it for strikes. Bearden was never effective again. "Casey giveth," wrote Veeck, "and Casey taketh away.''

The 1948 championship might have been belonged to Stengel instead of Boudreau had the population of Cleveland been more pliant. Veeck had inherited player-manager Boudreau when he had purchased the team. Veeck thought Boudreau's approach to managerial decision-making too casual and was determined to undo his 1944 mistake by replacing Boudreau with Stengel.

Boudreau, however, proved difficult to get rid of. He was immensely popular in Cleveland, and rumors that he might be traded caused a great outcry. Rightly so: Boudreau was the best combination offensive/defensive shortstop in baseball. Veeck hadn't given much thought to how Boudreau would be replaced, not that he could have been.

In the history of baseball, no one was more aware than Bill Veeck of fan loyalty, and how easily those feelings could be wounded or alienated. He asked Stengel to take a front-office position and wait until Veeck found a more propitious moment to replace the shortstop. Stengel refused. A rumored invitation to manage the Pittsburgh Pirates also failed to materialize.

As Stengel promised, 1947 was a year of retrenchment for the Oakland Oaks. He added Dario Lodigiani, a five-year major league veteran second baseman, and Vince DiMaggio —there were a number of former Stengel players in the league that summer, including Bill Posedel, Manny Salvo, Chuck Workman, and Max West, who hit forty-three homers for San Diego. DiMaggio hit twenty-two homers for the Oaks, but the team as a whole declined to 96–90. With Shea gone the pitching was not as effective as it had been. Hugh "Losing Pitcher" Mulcahy, formerly of the Phillies, was added to the staff to make the decline official.

Stengel had made former Dodgers washout Johnny Babich his pitching coach, placing him in George Weiss's service, an ironic position given that since leaving Stengel in 1935 he had twice been a source of extreme frustration to the Yankees. After the Yankees acquired Babich in the Eddie Miller deal, Weiss had sent him to Kansas City where he was teammates with Phil Rizzuto, Tommy Holmes, and the ubiquitous Vince DiMaggio. Babich pitched well there in 1939, reestablishing his bona fides as a prospect. With a minor league draft upcoming, Weiss knew that Connie Mack was going to select one of the pitchers he had contracted out to the Blues. Thinking he could save a better prospect, Weiss tried to convince Mack of Babich's possibilities.

Mack bit. In 1940 Babich became a Philadelphia Athletic and had the only good season of his major league career, going 14–13 with a 3.73 earned run average for an A's team that lost 100 games. It was the Yankees that allowed him to rise above his team; Babich beat New York five times, including the September 27 game that eliminated the Yankees from the pennant race. "Babich . . . Babich . . . BABICH! Who in hell ever heard of Babich?'' Joe McCarthy screamed. Weiss blamed himself for giving away the pennant.

The next year, Babich made himself a footnote to Joe DiMaggio's record-setting consecutive-games hitting streak by threatening not to pitch to the Yankees center fielder in the streak's prospective fortieth game. The two Californians had a history. Playing for the Seals in 1933, DiMaggio hade hit in sixty-one consecutive games. Babich, pitching for the intracity rival San Francisco Mission, had almost stopped him at thirty-six games, surrendering a game-winning triple in DiMaggio's last at-bat. On June 28, 1941, the Yankees visited Philadelphia's Shibe Park for a tilt with the Athletics. Babich, starting for the A's, had made it clear he would not give DiMaggio anything to hit. Babich retired DiMaggio on a pop-up in the first inning. In the fourth, Babich threw three balls wide of the strike zone. The fourth pitch was also outside, but DiMaggio reached across the plate and ripped it up the middle on a line, nearly carrying off Babich's genitals in the process. Not long after, the pitcher and his privates were back in the Coast League.

Despite the shortcomings of the pitching staff, the Oaks' record was good enough to make the playoffs. A measure of revenge on the Seals was gained by knocking them out of the first round, four games to one. A Los Angeles Angels team with superior pitching then defeated the Oaks by an identical number of games to take the league championship. Stengel had fallen short of a title, but he had succeeded wildly at the box office. The Oaks sold 590,327 tickets. Once again, the Oaks outdrew the St. Louis Browns' 1947 attendance of 320,474.

Stengel developed a method of motivating his players that was unavailable to less financially successful managers. ''After each game the Oaks won, I had a few cases of beer delivered to the dressing room. The more the players drank, the more they won.'' Eventually, he rewarded them with $3 dinners, and then $10 dinners. ''With twenty-five or twenty-seven guys on the team, that came to some money too,'' said catcher Bill Raimondi. After the Oaks rallied to win a playoff game 23–15 after trailing 9–2, Stengel said, ''Every man here rates a ten-dollar dinner from the old man.'' Charlie Metro remembered, ''He would make a statement: 'If we win [this series] five games to two, the dinner will be on me.' We'd get out there and hustle like a son of a gun and beat them.'' The next day he gave each player a ten dollar bill out of his own pocket. ''You could have a fine dinner on that,'' said Metro. ''No wonder,'' said another Oak, ''we played our heads off for him.''

At the end of the season, Stengel would have a big send-off for the Oaks at his Glendale home. ''His wife, Edna, would have a big barbecue there,'' remembered pitcher Rugger Ardizoia (another erstwhile Yankee). ''If you drank beer, he'd give you quarts of beer, or if you wanted drinks, he'd give you a half-pint. . . . When we got through, about 8:30, he'd have a line of taxis to take us down to Glendale to pick up the train to come home. They were real, real nice people.''

McGraw had also given out spontaneous cash bonuses, but he was even quicker with fines, and as an inveterate gambler and poor investor he could not have kept up with Stengel in terms of either consistency or largesse. As for visits to McGraw's home, they were limited to a privileged few.

The year 1948 changed Casey Stengel's life. It was the year of "The Nine Old Men." The nickname had originally applied to the Franklin Roosevelt–era Supreme Court, but now it came to refer to the veteran team that Stengel fielded in 1948. He added first baseman Nick Etten, who had started for the Yankees from 1943 to 1945. A star of war-depleted baseball, Etten had led the American League in home runs (with twenty-two) in 1944 and RBI in 1945 before being dismissed by Bill Dickey in 1946. Stengel platooned him, never letting him see a left-handed pitcher. Etten responded with forty-three homers and 155 RBIs.

Stengel also added George Metkovich, the man who had "a hunk of his foot chawed off by a catfish" back in Boston; Cookie Lavagetto, Brooklyn's 1947 World Series hero; and inveigled Ernie Lombardi to come out of retirement and catch one last season. Metkovich was terrific, demonstrating power that would completely elude him in the major leagues. In 1948, the former catfish victim hit .336 with twenty-three home runs (.548 slugging)—in over 1,000 major league games, he would hit just forty-seven round-trippers.

The Nine Old Men were actually comprised of eight old men and one kid, appropriately called "The Kid." Alfred Manuel Martin, better known as Billy, had been forced on Stengel, but like Dr. Seuss's protagonist in *Green Eggs and Ham*, the manager grew to enjoy the experience. Martin, twenty, was a native of Berkley, California, a star of his high school baseball team—until he was kicked off for fighting. Earlier, he had befriended Augie Galan, the talented Cubs left fielder who was also from Berkley. Galan introduced Martin to Red Adams, the Oaks' trainer.

Beginning in the spring of 1946, Adams began bringing Martin to Oaks camp so Stengel could see him play. Stengel hit grounders to the seventeen-year-old and was impressed with his resilience and tenacity. Later that year, Stengel came out to watch Martin play in a high school all-star game. Martin did not play very well. Stengel appeared in the locker room to cheer him. "You had a bad day, son, but keep on playin' ball. I think you have a future."

Stengel later remembered Martin as, "a young man that came out of a neighborhood, which we have in every city, which they try to watch. He'd had a stepfather." By this Stengel meant that Martin was a juvenile delinquent from a broken home. Still, the more he looked at Martin, the more he admired his pugnacious attitude. "I swear when I first laid eyes on that skinny, funny-looking kid, I looked and watched and the more I watched him, the more I saw myself as a fresh young ballplayer . . . I saw Old Casey once again 'fighting for a place in the sun.'" The Oaks signed Martin and sent him to Idaho Falls of the Pioneer League for a little seasoning.

Stengel was greatly impressed by the young man's attentiveness. "He was anxious to learn and he was very smart," Stengel said, "but not too smart that he couldn't listen and pick it up if you gave it to him." Charlie Metro remembered Stengel urging his players to keep their wits about them. "Now take a look at those outfielders, every pitch," he'd say. "See if they moved around. Get in the game. Someday you're going to be a manager." Martin clearly got the message. As early as 1949 he was displaying the compulsions that would make him a great but tormented major league manager. "I must remember," the twenty-year-old told *The Sporting News*, "to always think correctly and quicker than the other fellow." From there it was but a short leap to the fifty-three-year-old who told Roger Angell, "Managing takes a lot out of you. You can be so high one day, and so down the next that you don't want to eat. . . . I go over something in my mind before I talk to a player—I'll go over it twenty or thirty times, rehearsing it, so I'll do it the right way when I talk to that player."

Sometimes that extended to thinking quicker than Stengel, at least in Martin's opinion. At times he acted as if he were the master and Stengel the student. By spring training of 1947 he felt free to question the manager's every decision. When Stengel tried to refine Martin's approach to turning the double play, the tyro snapped, "What's the matter with the way I do it?"

"You're not on the dance floor jitterbugging, kiddo," Stengel answered.

"Don't knock it if you can't do it," Martin replied, reaching for the generation gap comeback.

For Stengel, what would have been irritating coming from another player became endearing when Martin was concerned. "If that was any other kid, I'd tell him to take off his uniform and clear out of the park. Not this kid. He wants to play ball so bad, it sticks out all over him. And I love him for his lip."

Not that Stengel failed to be objective where Martin was concerned. At the end of camp he optioned him to Phoenix of the Arkansas-Texas League. "You sure blew one," Martin said angrily.

"Prove me wrong," Stengel said. Martin did. In 130 games he batted .392, scored 141 runs, and plated 174 baserunners. The only downside to his record was the fifty-five errors he made while playing third base. In 1948, Martin made the Oaks roster out of spring training.

He still lacked a position, something that nettled Martin more than it did Stengel. At season's outset, the old man seemed content to keep Martin on the bench like a third-string quarterback and have him learn by watching. Martin nagged him constantly. Stengel responded by deflating Martin's ego. "Grab your glove, kid," he shouted at Martin during one game. Thinking he was finally going to play, Martin bounced out of his seat. Stengel blinked languidly. "Stick around," he said. "I made need you to umpire."

Carefully moderating his approach, he also took pains to build Martin up. When the Oaks veterans mocked Martin because his big season had come in a lower league, Stengel jumped in. "Goddamnit, I don't care if he done it in Africa. It's still .392 and a lot of you guys ain't never hit that in any league."

Stengel seemed to enjoy having the volatile youngster mix with the grizzled veterans. "Now you take Lombardi, who's a big man and has a big nose," he said, "and you take Martin, who's a little man and has a bigger nose. How do you figure it?" Martin's nose, which inspired one of his initial baseball nicknames, "The Horn," was a frequent source of amusement for Stengel. After Martin had minor surgery on his olfactory organ, Stengel told him he was worried that Martin had suffered a reduction of his "biggest asset." The veterans were used more for just anatomical juxtaposition; Stengel assigned Cookie Lavagetto to be Martin's roommate, defensive tutor, and all-around role model.

Ultimately, Martin became Stengel's prototypical everyday utility player, a fielder with no set position who nonetheless started daily. Stengel was now actively cultivating the kind of versatile players he had tried to force into existence in Brooklyn and Boston. Not that Martin was satisfied. "What do you think I am, the grounds-keeper?" Martin asked on one occasion when Stengel batted him eighth. In keeping with his pay-for-performance strategy, Stengel would pay Martin $25 to go to the plate and get hit by a pitch. For Stengel, there may have been a dual motive involved in the transaction.

If there was a bit of pleasure in Martin's pain, it was only momentary. Stengel rarely held a grudge. Over the course of his career he had many arguments with players, but he was usually willing to forgive and forget. "I saw the way he treated each player differently," Martin wrote. "He never had a doghouse. If you got in a fight with him, by the next day it was forgotten. And he would talk to me all the time, even when I wasn't playing. He made everyone feel right at home." He also impressed upon Martin how a manager could change the course of a game if the conditions were right. "Keep that game close," Martin remembered him saying, "give me room to operate and we'll beat 'em."

This was, of course, how Stengel had always envisioned himself. "He would get a young fellow and sit with him by the hour and talk to him about baseball," Al Lopez told Donald Honig. "I think he tried to pattern himself after McGraw in many ways. Of course, he was a different personality from McGraw, though he could eat you out on the bench if he had to. The difference between them was at that a little while later he'd be kidding with you, which I don't think McGraw would ever have done."

For the first time in Oakland, Stengel emphasized platooning—in part because the fragile "Old Men" suffered injuries ranging from fractures (Scarsella) to cigarette ashes in the eyes (Ray Hamrick). Stengel's pitching was not any better than the previous year, but the offense responded to the mixing and matching. Though a dominant club—the Oaks won 114 out of 188 games (.606), the best record in the league—the race for the pennant with the San Francisco Seals went down to the last day of the season, with Stengel using four pitchers in the clinching game. A 29–11 record down the stretch was just barely good enough.

"We had to battle all the way for it," Stengel said. "The pennant wasn't handed to us and we didn't back in. Winning the pennant meant more to me than anything that's ever happened to me in baseball.

"They called us the 'nine old men' . . . well, we showed them, didn't we? I've managed three pennant winners now—Toledo in 1927, Milwaukee in '44, and now you fellows. And I want to say right here that this is the best bunch I've ever managed anywhere and any time."

It was Oakland's first pennant in twenty-one years. Incredibly, Ernie Lombardi had played on the last winner in 1927. In the playoffs, Oakland beat Los Angeles four games to two in the first round, then defeated Seattle four games to one in the league finals. Given a talented veteran club, Stengel had again demonstrated that he could execute. He was named Pacific Coast League Manager of the Year. Oakland fans chipped in and bought him a $6,000 car.

On August 18, *The Sporting News* reported, "You can bet all the tea in China that Charles Dillon (Casey) Stengel will return to manage the Oaks in 1949." The announcement was as premature as "Dewey Defeats Truman" would be later that year. By October, the baseball situation had changed dramatically. In New York, superannuated Ed Barrow had retired, Larry MacPhail had popped his last cork and had gone, and now George Weiss was in charge, answerable only to co-owners Del Webb and Dan Topping. After some internal wrangling, Weiss received approval to offer Stengel the manager's job.

As Webb came to tell the story, the clincher apparently came sometime during the season when he observed Stengel holding court at a party late one night in Los Angeles. Webb had to leave early, but the next morning he passed near the location of the party and saw Stengel on a sandlot, instructing several youngsters on the finer points of the game. He had never gone home, and was still talking—talking baseball. Webb admired Stengel's indefatigability, and his dedication.

Stengel and Weiss held some informal discussions; Stengel was enthusiastic. He told Martin that he would be managing the Yankees the next season and that he would take the second baseman to the majors with him.

The offer to manage the Yankees was formally tendered by Del Webb on the same day that the Oaks won the Pacific Coast League title. "I at once commenced not thinking of retirement," said Stengel.

Stengel came East and was announced to the press. He was excited, but nervous. Sportswriter Grantland Rice rode the train back to California with him. "His previous managerial experience had been slightly on the melancholy side. 'I wonder how things will be next season,' he said, 'where I'll be a year from now.'"

CHAPTER 13

GRADUATION DAY

"I was the best manager I ever saw, but I tell people that to shut them up quickly and because I also believe it. But John McGraw was an enjoyable man, too."

—Casey Stengel

At the 1949 season's halfway point the Yankees stood atop the American League with a .657 winning percentage and a 4.5-game lead on the second-place Philadelphia Athletics. Though the reputedly unsinkable Tommy Henrich had confessed to a reporter that, "Without [DiMaggio], we are sunk," the Yankees had not sunk. The Red Sox were buried in fifth place, twelve games back.

Despite their many injuries, by late September the Yankees' winning percentage had slipped only slightly, to .636. In fact, but for five days, the Yankees were in first place for the entire season. The only problem was that those five days were some of the last of the season, September 26 to September 30, a problem that threatened to undo a season of hard work and fulfill the skeptics' predictions for both Stengel and his team.

In 1949, Casey Stengel had a response for every situation that occurred. Each of the seventy-plus times the trainer walked through his office door and told him that this or that star player would be unavailable to him for a week, a month, or forever, he found solutions. In the end there was nearly one injury too many to survive. Even then, Stengel proved himself to be the most versatile thinker in baseball. He had played in or managed over 5,000 games. He had at his fingertips the lessons of them all. One of the great contradictions of his character was that though he was an indefatigable talker, he also had fantastic powers of observation. "I can read the temper of friends, the whims of women, and the changes of weather," he once said in a moment of knowing hyperbole. He was no savant. He had, as his favorite player Yogi Berra once said, observed a lot by watching. As his 1949 troubles multiplied, he could channel John McGraw and he could call upon the spirit of Uncle Robbie. Most of all, though, he could call upon himself, a more flexible, more able personage than either of them, or indeed anybody else.

In the immediate aftermath of DiMaggio's spring training disappearance to Johns Hopkins for treatment on his bad heel, Stengel asked his players for just a minimal commitment to the sans-Clipper winning effort. "Let's hang on until Joe gets back," he said, "and then we will breeze by the field." Once the initial shock had passed, he sought to recast the team's identity and confidence as something independent of stars, DiMaggio or otherwise. "Look, you fellows, you've been waiting for this opportunity. How good do you know you are? Maybe you are better than you think. Now is the time to find out." Later, during a four-game losing streak, he kept the players "after school" so they could watch film of the 1947 World Series and "The Making of a Yankee," a kind of propaganda piece about the glory of the Yankee uniform. The players reacted emotionally. "Like it?" Stengel shouted. "Well, go then and do likewise. The opportunity is wide open. The pennant is yours for the hustling and the fighting."

And if they threatened to come around the Henrich's point of view, the deferential Stengel of spring training suddenly vanished. At Philadelphia on May 15, the Yankees lost both ends of a doubleheader to the Athletics. It was the team's fourth consecutive loss. As the Yankees embarked on their train ride back to New York, Stengel found the players in entirely too light a mood. Interrupting a game of twenty questions he said, "I got a question. Which one of you clowns ain't gonna be here tomorrow?" There was a sudden, sharp sobering of ballplayers.

As of mid-June, DiMaggio was still MIA, while Berra had suffered several injuries (including being steamrollered by his own first baseman, the hapless Dick Kryhoski), Jerry Coleman had been hospitalized with an infected sinus, Johnny Lindell had torn up his knee, Bob Porterfield's elbow had imploded (again), Tommy Henrich was acting like a car whose warranty had just expired with nearly every moving part threatening to quit at once, Allie Reynolds went out with tape burns after flensing his own ribs by ripping off adhesive bandages too eagerly, not to mention countless other cuts, scrapes, aches and pains. "I'm not a manager," Stengel complained. "I'm a hospital attendant." As the injuries mounted, there was a proportionate lessening of Stengelian jocularity.

"It was plain," John Lardner wrote in *Newsweek*, "that, whether his Yankees won or lost . . . this man, once gay and happy on the wrong side of the tracks, had taken sudden success very hard . . . he talked and acted just like the president of a bank. Conservative and solemn, if you know what I mean. On bank presidents, such traits look fine. On C. D. Stengel, they make you stop and think.''

October, 1948 was a long way in the past now, Dan Daniel recalled:

You know what they said . . . ''Casey will clown his way through the schedule, into third place, and have a lot of fun.'' Casey hasn't been clowning. Even though he has won, he has had no fun. It turns out that Stengel is no different that the rest. He is a worrier, by nature, just like all other major league managers. He worries if he wins and he is distraught if he loses. He has uttered no quips. . . . Stengel reminds me of a juggler on a tight rope. You figure that one of these days Casey will drop all six of those Indian clubs and fall off the rope. But, meanwhile, he still is up there, putting on a terrific act.

Daniel's juggling analogy was apt. In 1943, Stengel had joked that working over his lineup card was an exercise in futility. ''Ya know, there just ain't any way in the world to juggle this lineup so I can hide my bad hitters.'' Still, juggling was what he did, day after day.

Flash forward to the penultimate game of the 1949 season, a literal must-win-or-go-home contest against the Red Sox, who had a one game lead with two games to play. That morning, Del Webb went to Stengel's hotel for a breakfast meeting. When Stengel opened the door, Webb observed crumpled pieces of paper all over the floor. ''What in the hell is that mess?'' asked Webb.

''Line-ups,'' said Stengel. He had been up all night, juggling holes. Like a magic fifteen puzzle, Stengel's season-long challenge was to keep relocating the spot vacated by DiMaggio to a place where it didn't do the team any harm. DiMaggio was impossible to replace, so Stengel didn't bother looking for a single replacement. He replaced him with everybody, boosting their production to DiMaggio-like levels by using them only in situations in which they were likely to excel. That meant riding an early hot streak by Gene Woodling, unless there was a lefty on the mound, and promoting Jerry Coleman to the top of the order when the rookie hit a hot streak. He rescued Phil Rizzuto from the eighth spot in the batting order where Bucky Harris had buried him so Snuffy Stirnweiss could lead off, and batted the Scooter first or second all year long. Most important of all, he made Yogi Berra the focal point of the offense.

All of this worked very well for awhile. Woodling slumped, then got hurt. The first base platoon, of which Stengel was quite proud—between Kryhoski and Phillips the Yankees had two men who had battled the position to an offensive draw—fell apart when Kryhoski hurt his knee and Phillips developed shoulder bursitis. Stengel kept juggling. The team then had an apparent coup, buying first baseman Johnny Mize, the major league's active home run leader, from the Giants. The original "Big Cat," the left-handed Georgian had launched 315 home runs since 1936, a huge total given that he had lost three seasons to military service in World War II. A patient hitter with outstanding control of his heavy bat, Mize had career averages of .320 (batting), .577 (slugging), and .405 (on-base). He had become available when Giants manager Leo Durocher, focusing on Mize's one identifiable weakness, decided that the plodding first baseman did not fit in with the dashing ballclub he was hoping to build.

The first base situation had finally been solved, and with a future Hall of Famer at that. Stengel was able to enjoy the notion for only a few days; in Mize's first week he dove after a ball and badly injured his shoulder. More holes; Stengel juggled again. Stengel had sworn he would not move Henrich, "the greatest right fielder in the game," to first base (Harris had had him there for the last forty-six games of 1948) unless an emergency developed. On June 23, Stengel broke the glass on Henrich's first baseman's mitt.

After each new improvisation, he restlessly anticipated the next disaster. "I believe we need a shakeup very badly," he said on July 5, just after the club had taken two of three games from the Red Sox. The Yankees had won seven of its last nine games and held the top position in the American League. "Sure we are four games in front. But I think we are about to slip. I may send Billy Johnson to first base during the series with Detroit. I may use him at second." And on he went, dreaming an endless series of line-up permutations, none of them anticipated by the players or the sportswriters, who had been raised to believe that a third baseman was not a second baseman, that your everyday player was morally superior to your part-time player, even if playing every day exposed the everyday player's weaknesses, and that it was teams who trod the same tired players out day after day that won pennants.

Each day brought a new batting order. Rizzuto batted first or second. Coleman batted first, sixth, eighth. Woodling batted third, sixth, eighth. Henrich batted second, third, fourth, fifth. Berra batted third, fourth, fifth, and seventh. Bobby Brown batted second, third, fifth, sixth, seventh. Mapes batted second, third, seventh, eighth. Billy Johnson hit third, fourth, fifth, sixth. Bauer hit first, third, fourth, fifth, sixth, seventh, eighth. Kryhoski batted second, seventh, and eighth.

Lineup rotation was a controversial idea, and it remains one to this day. "He has changed his line-up almost daily as the opposition started a left-handed or right-handed pitcher, playing the 'percentage up' for every last smidgeon of power," Red Smith wrote. "Slavish devotion to the 'percentages' exasperates many observers, who contend the strategy makes it impossible to develop complete ball players like DiMaggio.'' Today sportswriters keep track of lineups and cite too many as a sign of instability. Players complain that it is difficult to perform in an "unstable" environment in which they have to check the lineup card every day to see if they are playing. In 2001, the Red Sox fired manager Jimy Williams in the middle of the pennant race because of either his frequent lineup changes, his poor communication, or his poor communication about his frequent lineup changes. They would like you to believe that. Stengel proved it to be a myth in 1949. Necessity, not consistency, is the mother of tailored batting orders.

"I realize people have been puzzled," Stengel said of his lineup cards, "especially the Yankee fans. I don't blame them. They were brought up on steady line-ups. In the days of Ruth, Gehrig, Dickey, and fellows like that, there was no sense in switching a man when the other team switched a pitcher. Our ball club isn't like the old Yankee teams. We've got a lot of new players. It seemed to me in spring training that the best plan would be to get two men ready for every position."

A note to present-day managers: the reason Stengel was able to do this was because he didn't overstuff his bullpen at the expense of position players. Stengel was no less aware of the realities of individual pitcher-batter matchups than Tony LaRussa is today, but unlike that manager or his many imitators he did not carry as many pitchers as he could fit on a charter plane, failing to discriminate between quality arms and disjointed appendages so long as they threw from the requisite side of the rubber. Stengel restricted himself to the live ones, lefty, righty, or other, knowing that his if his best pitcher was a righty and his fourth-best pitcher was a lefty, he'd better leave the righty in the game even if Ted Williams was coming to the plate. In August, at the height of the dog days, the Yankees roster was comprised of ten pitchers, three catchers, six infielders, and six outfielders. "It would be nice to be able to carry twelve pitchers," Stengel once said, "but you've got to leave room on your bench for some pinch-hitters too." On a club that had enough injuries to fill a good-sized hospital ward (Del Webb, a contractor, joked he might have to build one for the team), Stengel had more depth than most present-day managers have on their team's healthiest days.

To a large extent he was unfazed by the injuries as they gave him the opportunity to do what he had planned to do all along, use that depth. In July, *after* DiMaggio had returned, Stengel said, "The reserve strength of the Yankees is going to be the dominant factor in their pennant victory." Fred Lieb once asked him about the number of players he was running in and out of games. "None of these players board here," he replied. "That's why they give us twenty-five players—to let managers play games with them." To him, the injuries were fortuitous, revealing that the club had strength hidden in the dugout:

> Folks were saying what terrible luck we were having. Actually it was one of the luckiest breaks I ever got. It taught me that if you've got a number of good players sitting around in the bench you'll do yourself a favor playing them, because every time one of my front players got hurt I noticed the feller I stuck in his place would bust out with hits all over the place. Then just about the time he started to peter out he'd oblige me by stepping in a hole or something and another guy, rarin' to go, would take over.

He was uncharacteristically coy about this, a consequence of the muted, introductory-basis tone he had adopted. "I don't like shifts," he lied, "but I have to like them on the basis of what they have done for us. Between Kryhoski and Phillips we have a first baseman hitting around .330 and driving in more runs than any first sacker in the league. Between Brown and Johnson, we have a third baseman of similar rating and similar comparison with the rest of the field. In short, the shifts have been the making of us, and I am especially glad because two of the players involved are rookies, earnest, hard-working kids who deserve every point of their batting averages and every run they have driven in."

As Henrich was the key part in so many of Stengel's plans, it was paramount that he stay healthy. Stengel told Henrich to drive carefully, avoid drafts, and "under no circumstances are you to eat fish, because them bones could be murder. Sit quietly in the clubhouse until the game begins. I can't let anything happen to you."

Naturally, Henrich got hurt. Constantly. "We must be the most-injured first-place club in baseball history," Henrich said in September. He was speaking from bitter personal experience. "According to my lists," said Red Patterson, the team's public relations director, "Henrich was injury number twenty-seven when he hurt his knee; injury number thirty-eight when he bruised his ribs and fragmented his knee; injury number forty-five when he broke his toe, and injury number sixty-one when he received his back injury August 28."

The last injury on the list came in Chicago. Playing behind the star-crossed Fred Sanford, Henrich ran into the unpadded wall chasing a ball hit by Charlie Kress. He fractured two lumbar vertebrae and displaced a third. Henrich had already been counted out several times on the season, only to stage miraculous returns. He was supposed to have been gone for an extended period when he broke his toe on July 25, but cut a hole in his shoe and played the next day. This time it seemed impossible that he would recover in time to rejoin the team before the end of the season.

The team's pennant hopes seem to fade away as he did. The sage Red Smith wrote:

> [I] declare, without reservation or equivocation, that the Yankees lost the 1949 pennant . . . when Tommy Henrich plastered himself against a concrete wall and dislodged an assortment of vertebrae. . . . There is no better time than now, when he has sustained what may be an irreparable loss, to applaud the performance which Stengel has given this year. . . . He brought genuine humility to this job. . . . "I never had good ones like this before," he kept saying during the training course in Florida, and all he asked was the opportunity to do the best he could with them. His best has turned out to be very good indeed."

Smith was premature; Stengel wasn't yet done. Even as Henrich's body crumpled to the Chicago turf, he was already calculating. The manager rushed out to right field. "Lie down," he said to Henrich. "Don't get up. Take it very easy." It was all very soothing to Henrich until, just as he was about to think something akin to, "He loves me! He really loves me!" Stengel said, "Lie down and give me a little more time to get someone warmed up and get this clown [the pitcher] out of here."

It would be difficult to argue that Henrich was not one of the most dedicated ballplayers of all time. He would miss most of September, then get fitted with a corset and return to the lineup. Though clearly debilitated—he hit only .200 with two home runs and nine runs batted in after the injury—his presence was inspirational.

Henrich's crippling came at the worst possible time, as Berra was out of the lineup with a fractured thumb. Henrich had had an accident, but Berra was the victim of an assault. On August 7 he was hit by St. Louis Browns' pitcher Dick Starr in what was clearly an act of retribution for the way that the catcher had been hitting the weak pitchers of that perpetually also-ran franchise. The Browns were at Yankee Stadium for a crowded five-game series. It was to be played in three days by way of two doubleheaders. The Yankees won four of the five—the fifth game was called with the game tied—destroying the Browns by a combined score of 49–17. In the first game, Berra hit a grand slam home run off of Cliff Fannin. The next day, Browns manager Zack Taylor, who had worked with Stengel in Brooklyn, brought back Fannin to face Joe DiMaggio. The result was another home run. In all, the Yankees hit four home runs in the first two games and five in the third game, including two by Rizzuto, two by DiMaggio, and one by Berra.

In the fourth game of the series, the Yankees destroyed Ned Garver—a pretty good pitcher, actually—20–2. Berra hit another home run. Starr came in and nailed Berra on the hand, breaking his thumb.

Just in case anyone missed the point, Karl Drews, grandfather of future Yankees' pitching prospect Matt Drews, came in and hit Coleman, Henrich—who had to leave with a bruised ulnar nerve in his right forearm— and Niarhos. Efforts to draw Drews into a retaliatory collision by way of a drag bunt, a legendary play that no one has ever seen work, were fruitless. Tommy Byrne threw at both Starr and Drews, but with his historically awful control was unable to hit either.

Berra had been hitting .293 with sixteen home runs and a team-leading seventy-five runs batted in. Though reserve catcher Charlie Silvera would play well in his absence, he was a singles hitter. Berra's power would be greatly missed. Though he would return just in time for the season's climactic days, like Henrich the productive portion of his 1949 campaign were over; he would hit just .218 after the injury.

Both Starr and Drews had been failed Yankees prospects. "Just imagine two crows like that. They couldn't make good on this club for four years and they haven't made good on the Browns," Stengel said. "They're getting their ears pinned back so they take that way of getting even. Were they throwing deliberately? Are you kidding? I can't read a player's mind, but I can see. There wasn't any reason at all for it, with us so far ahead. They just couldn't take it, that's all." Taylor insisted that the multitude of beanballs had been accidental. Stengel didn't care. "That does not give me back Berra, at a time when we need him most."

The need was indeed acute, for though the sun had finally risen on Joe DiMaggio's season, it was about to set again. The Yankees had survived DiMaggio's loss before, but that was when Henrich and Berra were still vital. Phil Rizzuto was the only healthy star left (though Rizzuto had played with bone chips in his throwing elbow all season long, his only concession to injury had been a brief absence after a Johnny Pesky takeout slide had left him with a serious concussion), and though the Scooter was an excellent player having one of his best years, his main contribution was to the defense, not the offense. "Rizzuto is the greatest shortstop I ever have seen," Stengel said. "Miracles every day." But if Rizzuto's glove was saintly, his bat was agnostic.

Throughout the first two months of the season, DiMaggio would periodically test his heel, come away discouraged, and slink back to his Manhattan hotel room. He and Stengel did not communicate directly; publicly the manager took the position that when and if the Clipper was ready to play he would be welcomed with open arms. Until then, he had other things to worry about, like whether Gene Woodling could hit lefties in the majors as well as he did those in the Pacific Coast League, and if his Oakland Oaks closer Ralph Buxton could be an asset to the Yankees bullpen.

Early in the season he periodically would suggest that he could use

DiMaggio as a pinch-hitter until he was sufficiently healthy to play the field. On further consideration he rejected the idea as too dangerous to DiMaggio and too dangerous to himself. "I now want all of DiMaggio or nothing. That is, I do not want to risk using him as a pinch-hitter. I am willing to wait until he is ready to return to full-time service. If I sent him in to hit, and he suffered another bad reaction in his ailing right heel, or he got a pulled muscle in his leg. I would be labeled the man who had crippled a marvelous player for the sake of a time at bat. I am not in a position to take that chance. We will just have to go along as best we can until DiMaggio comes to me and says, 'Casey, this is the day.' Until that happens, Joe will continue to run his own affairs."

On June 28, the Yankees traveled to Boston to play the Red Sox. It was, as they say, a key series. The Red Sox came in hot, having shaken off a three-game sweep at the hands of Cleveland to win ten of eleven games. Though they were in third place, five games behind the Yankees, a strong showing would throw the race open. Given the precarious state of the team, the Yankees couldn't afford open.

Had DiMaggio's life been analyzed by Joseph Campbell, the June Boston series would represent the hero's acceptance of the call. In every heroic tale, there is a moment where the protagonist must rise above self-doubt and claim the mantle of hero for himself. For DiMaggio, that moment came on June 28, 1949.

On June 27, DiMaggio played in an exhibition against the Giants for New York City's Mayor O'Dwyer trophy. He walked once and popped up four times. More importantly, his heel didn't trouble him. He would take the night to rest. If the heel was still quiescent in the morning, he would play against the Red Sox. "Hurrah," said Stengel. Bob Quinn, now president of the Hall of Fame, had been on hand to accept the lockers of Babe Ruth and Lou Gehrig for the museum. Despite his presence, nothing went wrong. The Yankees even won the game. It was a very good day.

The next day there was a wild scene in the visitors clubhouse at Fenway Park. The story has been told often. The nuances differ, but the basics remain the same: sportswriters buzz around Stengel. It is late, and he has not yet posted his line-up card. In the background, DiMaggio laces up his shoes. "I can't give you the line-up yet," says Stengel. The reporters protest. Stengel casts an eye towards DiMaggio, who pulls the laces tight. Stengel vamps for a moment, checks DiMaggio again. The man of the hour slowly rises to his feet, catches Stengel's eye, and gives a thumbs up. Stengel smiles. "*Now* I can give you the line-up," he tells the reporters. DiMaggio will play centerfield and bat cleanup.

What came next was the apotheosis of Joe DiMaggio. More than his 1941 hitting streak, it was this moment that framed his memory for all time. What DiMaggio did after returning to the lineup had a certain inevitability about it; once he committed to rising to the occasion something was freed within him. His pain was gone, his fear was gone, and all that was left was the pent-up energy of the greatest ballplayer on Earth. He was like a force of nature in the three game series, hitting four home runs and driving in nine runs in only eleven at-bats. As DiMaggio circled the bases after his fourth home run, a biplane suddenly appeared in the sky over Fenway. It was trailing a banner that read, "THE GREAT DI-MAGGIO."

The Yankees won all three games, dropping the Red Sox to eight games back. They were finished, or so it seemed. DiMaggio had killed them. "Babe Ruth alone could match Joe's flair for drama, for putting on a show and responding on occasion," said Stengel. "And not even Ruth would have put on the kind of demonstration DiMaggio staged here. Eight workouts and then socko. Four homers. The answer is this man is a pro." After DiMaggio's home run in the second game, Stengel came out of the dugout and salaamed.

The Yankees played very well with DiMaggio in the lineup, though they were only about a game better with him than without him as the compromises Stengel had made to keep the team in contention, particularly the punishing use of Vic Raschi, began to take their toll. Then DiMaggio was gone again, the victim of pneumonia. "They told me he'd be back in two days and now it's four," Stengel said on September 21. "Pretty soon it'll be a week, and then in another week the season will be over. But then there's always another Joe—Joe Page." But like Raschi, Page was tiring and would lose four decisions in September.

This last illness demonstrated the limits of Stengel's inventiveness. He had shown that a team could lose its best player and with creativity could survive. With two stars out of the lineup, you could still get by provided you had a third. Three, however, was the limit. With DiMaggio, Henrich, and Berra diminished or absent, the Yankees were just an average team, and no amount of platooning or perspicacious pinch-hitting could mask that. At the same moment that healthy Yankees were becoming rarer than a respirating thylacine, the Red Sox had kicked it into gear, winning two-thirds of their games and rising to second place. The new disparity between the two clubs was readily apparent during the last two weeks of the season. The Yankees became merely average, going 6–6. The Red Sox went wild, going 8–1, overcoming their tiring pitching by battering opponents by an average score of 8–5. It was that last surge, including a three-game sweep of a series geographically split between Boston and New York (two games at Fenway Park, a make-up game at the Stadium) on September 24, 25, and 26 that allowed them to catch and pass the Yankees.

Looming before both teams was the reality that unless either gained a three-game lead on the other, the pennant race would not be decided until the last game of the season, possibly even later. There were two last games to be played, on October 1 and 2 at Yankee Stadium. If two games behind, a sweep by the underdog could force a playoff. In the trailing club was only one out, a sweep would win the American League.

On the September 27, Joe McCarthy took time away from his team to attend the unveiling of a monument to Hack Wilson in Martinsville, West Virginia. Wilson had died November 11, 1948, alcoholic and nearly destitute. There had been no money for a headstone. The monument, a ten-foot high column of granite, said, "One of Baseball's Immortals, Lewis R. (Hack) Wilson rests here." Speaking at the ceremony, McCarthy said, "To me, along with the sorrow I feel in thinking of Hack, comes the pleasant memory of happy days with him." Stengel did not attend.

Neither the Yankees nor the Red Sox were able to pull away, in part because the limited time remaining worked in the Yankees' favor (there weren't enough games left to play down to their injury-diminished level), in part due to a quirk of the schedule that had the Yankees playing the mediocre Philadelphia A's while the Red Sox toyed with the execrable Washington Senators. By September 28, the Yankees had tied up the race by beating the A's while the Red Sox were losing a 2–1 decision to the weak Ray Scarborough. Two days later, the Yankees blinked. Eddie Lopat, who would win just three of eight decisions over the season's final weeks, engineered a 4–1 capitulation to A's junk-baller Dick Fowler. Simulataneously, the Red Sox outlasted the Senators 11–9, barely holding on to win a game that the Senators were desperately trying to give away by spotting the Red Sox fourteen walks and three errors. The Yankees would now need to sweep both of the final two games; one win by the Red Sox would send Boston to the World Series.

"We're just gonna win two straight," said Stengel. "We did it in the spring and I think we can do it now. It's up to us to prove ourselves." He had intentionally kept Page out of the last game with the A's to rest him for Boston. As for his other big weapon, "If DiMaggio feels a little better tomorrow than he did today he may start. I don't know how long he'll play. No sense leaving him out there if he's weak." Stengel shrugged. "Anyway, I feel that now we're going to go out and beat the tar out of the Red Sox tomorrow and Sunday. I really feel it."

Along the way to the final confrontation an amazing thing happened: the Yankees had become popular. After six years with the Braves, Stengel had become used to New England apathy. "I've never seen anything like it. Every day I get calls, telegrams from all over. Everybody's pulling for us and it helps. The fans are showing almost as fine a spirit as our players and, brother, that's wonderful." As usual, Red Smith had the reason for the outpouring of affection:

"The old Yankees were a team of matchless skill. The current Yankees are a team of incomparable spirit. And that is the difference. Although they have been in front every day since the season began, they have never been easy front-runners. Every game has been a few problem for Stengel and a new challenge to the players; Mr. Stengel has faced and solved his and the players have risen to theirs."

Stengel's problem-solving was not limited to roster management. His in-game tactics were masterful, displaying the sure touch of good instincts informed by experience. "I never," observed Connie Mack, "saw a man who juggled his lineup so much and who played so many hunches so successfully." Ah, but they weren't hunches, as Bill Veeck realized. "You can ask Casey Stengel why he made a certain move," he wrote, "and he will tell you about a roommate he had in 1919 who had demonstrated some principle which Casey was now putting into effect." It turned out that the class clown had been paying attention. "I am the same kind of manager I always was, but nowadays I seem to get a little more assistance from my help," Stengel said.

He simply ran rings around other managers. On July 28, the Yankees hosted Lou Boudreau's Cleveland Indians. Allie Reynolds had nursed a 3–2 lead into the ninth inning. The first two batters of the frame reached on a single and a walk. Boudreau sent Jim Hegan, a light-hitting catcher, up to bunt. Hegan took a called strike, then fouled a bunt. Boudreau played one of his patented hunches, the kind that made Bill Veeck cringe, and called for switch-hitting pitcher Early Wynn to complete Hegan's at-bat.

With the bunt off, Stengel made some moves of his own, first calling in Joe Page to turn Wynn around to the right side, then, taking account of Gene Woodling's weak arm in left field—"He couldn't throw from here to that wall," Jerry Coleman said. "If he did it once he did it fifty times. He'd try to get a guy at third and the guy who hit the ball would go to second. He'd do it over and over and over. He had no arm at all, and he never knew it. But Casey knew it."—Stengel pulled Woodling out of the game, shifted Hank Bauer from left to right, and put Cliff Mapes, his best outfield arm, in right field, reasoning that Wynn was not going to pull Page's fastball.

Wynn fouled a pitch, then drove Page's second offering to right field. Mapes' throw to third baseman Billy Johnson, himself a ninth-inning defensive replacement for Bobby Brown, barely beat the runner. Double play. Page then retired Ken Keltner, Boudreau's third pinch-hitter of the inning, for the win. Wrote Ed Sinclair of the *New York Herald-Tribune*, "In their best days, Hannibal, Napoleon, or Eisenhower had nothing on Casey Stengel."

Such victories were routine, but Stengel disclaimed responsibility.

After Page escaped a similar jam in September, Stengel said, "When I thanked Page, I told him, 'You made me look good.'"

A reporter interrupted. "They've made you look good all summer," he said, "which suggests they've been managed some."

"Thanks," said Stengel, "but it's a hustling team."

Stengel's use of Page has often been cited as a decisive moment in evolution of the modern closer, but in actuality the manner in which Stengel deployed Page is now an anachronism. His use of Page made "The Gay Reliever" far more valuable to the Yankees of 1949 than any closer is to his club today, including Page's spiritual descendant, the much celebrated World Series hero Mariano Rivera.

The modern closer pitches only the ninth inning, only with a lead. Although the closer is theoretically the best pitcher in the bullpen, he is rarely used with the game on the line. This dangerous work is left to the set-up men, who are, paradoxically, considered to be lesser beings than the closer. Resultantly, many games are lost in the sixth or seventh inning by a team's third- or fourth-best pitcher while the highly paid closer naps in the bullpen.

Joe Page was called an "emergency" reliever, which meant that he could be used at any time, ahead, behind, or tied. Stengel understood what Leo Durocher meant when he said, "You don't save a pitcher for tomorrow. Tomorrow it may rain." The same thinking applied to a critical situation early in the game—there was no reason to save your best weapon for the ninth inning when you might not get the lead to the ninth. "Joe Page," Stengel said with deceptive simplicity, "is a relief pitcher who provides relief." In this he was unlike today's closers, who provide managers with a sense of security.

With Tommy Byrne in trouble at home on April 26, Page entered the game with one out in the seventh inning and the Yankees trailing 4–3. He pitched an inning and a third of hitless baseball, keeping the game static until the Yankees could rally. Stengel pinch-hit Bobby Brown for Page in the bottom of the eighth inning. Brown singled, bringing Jerry Coleman to the plate. Coleman launched a two-run home run, giving the Yankees a 5–4 lead. Stengel then called upon Frank Hiller—literally any old pitcher—to close out the victory in the ninth inning.

On May 28, Page entered in the ninth inning in relief of Vic Raschi, who left trailing 1–0. The Yankees tied the game in the bottom of the inning and Stengel, apparently seeing no one better, let Page stay in. And stay. The Yankees finally pushed ahead the winning run in the fourteenth inning. Page's line: six innings pitched, four hits, no runs, two walks, two strikeouts.

On June 2, Page was called upon with one out in the fifth inning. Though the Yankees were leading 9–6, the bases were loaded. Page walked the first batter, but after that he was untouchable, pitching four-and-two-thirds innings for the win. Stengel also used Page leading 7–1, losing 10–5, literally anywhere he thought he might help. If Stengel could help it, he would call on Page in the seventh inning and let him pitch the last three innings of the game, but sometimes emergencies forced the same kind of improvisations o the pitching staff that Stengel was making daily with the position players.

There were occasional days when Stengel did not call on Page in situations that would have been consistent with his normal usage. These seemed to follow appearances in which Page faltered, though there were also days of planned rest in response to fatigue or minor stiffness. At St. Louis on June 5, Page was asked to hold the Browns to a 4–1 lead in the fifth inning with two outs and two on. The slugging phenom Dick Kokos hit a three-run home run. Three days later at Detroit, a chastened Stengel allowed Byrne to go all the way in a 3–2, 11 inning loss. Byrne's line: ten innings pitched, four hits, three earned runs, thirteen walks, six strikeouts, one hit batsman. Byrne walked the bases loaded with two out in the eleventh inning. Stengel made no move. Page next appeared on June 9, trying to protect a 5–4 lead with two outs in the sixth inning. Two errors and four hits later, Page was a loser. Two days later, at Cleveland, Raschi took a 3–0 lead into the ninth inning. Raschi allowed two runs, reducing the lead to 3–2 before finally closing the door on the Indians. Stengel did not call Page.

Despite these periodic lapses, Page did not suffer for work. He pitched 135 innings, more than any other pure reliever in baseball. Because of his heavy workload, Page saved the team more runs than many a modern closer who is artificially capped at sixty or seventy innings a year.

Midway through the season, Bob Cooke of the *Herald-Tribune* asked Stengel what he thought about in his spare time, "Baseball A guy can't think about anything else when he's up here in the majors. He can't afford to. After all, if you have a bad year, you're generally gone, and then you've got nothing but spare time, and worse yet, nothing to think about."

Actually, it was remarkable how little the other managers made him think, how one-dimensional their thinking was compared to his. One of the risks to platooning is that a manager can, at selected moments, force his opponent to make changes by using his bullpen, but since most bullpens were an afterthought to their managers, few availed themselves of this tactic. On July 24, the Tigers took a 2–1 lead into the top of the ninth at Detroit. Detroit had started the excellent Hal Newhouser, a left-handed pitcher, which meant that Stengel had Woodling on the bench and Johnny Lindell in left field. Tigers manager Red Rolfe left Newhouser in to face Lindell, who couldn't do anything on a ballfield *except* hit left-handed pitchers. Lindell hit a home run, tying the game. The Yankees won in eleven innings.

At Yankee Stadium on July 31, the young lefty Billy Pierce started against the Yankees and could still be found on the mound in the bottom of the ninth inning, protecting a 2–1 lead. Up came Lindell, out went another home run. With the game tied and one out, Stengel let Ed Lopat hit for himself. He singled, and Stengel pinch-ran with Jack Phillips. Bauer hit an easy double-play grounder to shortstop, but second baseman Cass Michaels dropped the relay from Luke Appling. There were now two on, one out. Phil Rizzuto walked, loading the bases. Leo Durocher used to say, "I'm not glued to the bench." Sox manager Jack Onslow was glued to the bench. Tommy Henrich drove in the winning run with a single. On August 13 at Philadelphia, Stengel called on Page in the seventh inning to stifle a rally that had turned Vic Raschi's 5–3 lead into a 6–5 deficit. When the Yankees rallied in the ninth, Connie Mack could only call on Joe Coleman, who had pitched nine innings the night before.

Stengel did make his share of mistakes, chiefly the way he drove Vic Raschi throughout the first half of the season. As of June 1, Raschi was 7–1 with seven complete games. One-third of the season had not yet passed, yet Raschi was well on his way to 100 innings pitched. Part of the problem was that Raschi was pitching too well to be relieved; three of the seven complete games were shutouts. Still, the burden was on Stengel to preserve the pitcher for the entire season. Such things were not spoken of openly in 1949, yet his ready use of Page demonstrated that he had outgrown the traditional view of durability as a test of a pitcher's courage, resourcefulness, and virility. As of July 4, Raschi was 13–2 with 143 innings pitched. He was 7–8 from that day until his starting assignment on October 2.

Stengel tried to laugh off Raschi's slump. "Vic dislikes the heat," he said. "Given a cool spell, he will recover his stuff and come through just when we need him most." On August 4, Raschi lost an eleven-inning complete game to the Detroit Tigers. It was his third straight loss. Stengel's witticism was hopeful, rather than an evasion of responsibility. "There are not many managers who would walk into the clubhouse and say, 'Okay, I blew that. I did it. I blew that one. It was my fault,' Jerry Coleman remembered. "I heard him say that two or three times. Very few managers would ever admit that, that they had made a mistake."

That September, Brick Laws, owner of the Oakland Oaks, told the press that Stengel would quit the Yankees at the end of the season:

He has more money than he'll ever need and he is becoming a weary old gentleman. I'm sure Casey positively will hang up the spikes if his Yankees win the American League flag. And if he wins the World Series too—wow!

He'll not only quit but fly home on clouds. . . . He didn't want to return to the majors in the first place. I had to talk to him like a Dutch uncle, had to make him so he was drooling to go East and show those bums he could manage an inning or two.

All his life, Stengel has dreamed of skippering a major league pennant winner. He never had a sold team during all those years with the Boston Braves, and we all know you can't make chicken salad out of kippered herring. . . . I pleaded with Casey to go back up there just to show some of those wise monkeys . . . that Stengel was more than just a funnyman, a clown.

Stengel should have had his final confrontation with the perceived clown on October 1 and 2, just as the Yankees had their final confrontation with Red Sox. Before the first game, Stengel looked across the field at his opponents and said, "I think we've got 'em. I can feel it in my bones." In the penultimate game of the season, officially "Joe DiMaggio Day," Stengel was able to start Joe DiMaggio, always an unexpected pleasure. DiMaggio was eighteen pounds underweight due to his bout with viral pneumonia, but, he said, "If the Yankees are going down, I'll go down with them."

Stengel sent righty Allie Reynolds to the mound to face lefty twenty-five-game winner Mel Parnell. Reynolds always issued a lot of walks, but on this day he was out of control. Already down 1–0 with one out in the third, Reynolds walked the first three men he faced, then allowed a single for another run. With the game on the line, Stengel called for Page. "How far can you go?" Stengel asked Fireman Joe.

"A long way."

"Then get going."

The move seemed to blow up in Stengel's face when Page walked the first two batters he faced to put the Yankees in a 4–0 hole, but Page came back to fan the next two hitters. After that, he was untouchable, allowing only one hit in six-and-two-thirds innings of relief.

The offense took care of the rest. DiMaggio was the key figure in two rallies that tied the score. In the eighth, McCarthy relieved Parnell with one of his starters, Joe Dobson. McCarthy had no pitcher comparable to Page. Essentially, he did not have a bullpen. With the Yankees, McCarthy had been something of a bullpen trailblazer himself, getting excellent relief work from Johnny Murphy. With the Red Sox he had not been able to find a pitcher to fill that role and lapsed into riding his starters. Though Stengel had pushed Raschi, his pitchers had thrown only fifty-nine complete games. Red Sox pitchers completed eighty-five of their starts.

Dobson was a right-hander. Stengel gambled again. All season long he had platooned righty outfielder Johnny Lindell, reserving him for use against left-handers. According to his own practices he should have called for Woodling. He let Lindell hit. Lindell rewarded his confidence with a game-winning home run.

The Yankees had earned one more day of life. The final day of the season featured a matchup of two twenty-game winners, Raschi and Ellis Kinder. In his previous start against the Yankees, he had shut them out on six hits. Rizzuto led off the game with a triple. With McCarthy playing his infield back, Henrich purposefully tapped a grounder to the right side to drive in the run. The score remained 1–0 through the eighth. In the top of that frame, Joe McCarthy pinch-hit for Kinder, once again exposing his team's weak bullpen. First came Parnell, who had pitched the day before. Henrich put his second pitch in the seats. Berra followed with a single, and McCarthy called for Tex Hughson, a formerly great but sorearmed right-hander who had last appeared on the mound in times beyond memory. The Yankees pounced on the opportunity, scoring another three runs (Jerry Coleman's double in front of right fielder Al Zarilla was the killing blow). Boston staged a late rally when DiMaggio's legs gave out in pursuit of a fly ball, but Raschi, knowing that Page could not come to his rescue, held fast. The Yankees were the winners of the American League pennant.

In the clubhouse after the game, Stengel was effusive. "I want to thank all you players for giving me this, the greatest thrill of my life," he said. When the players thanked *him*, he was modest. "Hell, you fellas got me up there. I didn't do it." Tearfully he shouted, "And to think they pay me for managing so great a bunch of boys."

McCarthy came to congratulate him, saying, "You did a fine job, Casey." Here was a benediction from the establishment, and Stengel was appropriately gracious. "Joe, you're a great manager, too," he said, "and you know, having won so many times, it was nice of you to let me have this one."

After the celebration died down, reality and exhaustion set in. The Yankees were going to play the Dodgers in the World Series. "We'll probably play them thirty-six games right though until spring, and we will never get home." A writer asked if he'd be coming to the ballpark for the next afternoon's workout. "Of course," he said. "I've been showing up all year, haven't I?"

Among the congratulatory telegrams Stengel received after winning the pennant, he found an invitation from Branch Rickey to attend a reunion dinner for the pennant-winning 1916 Dodgers and watch the World Series as a guest of the team. Stengel went to the dinner, but watched the Series from the dugout. He was greatly amused that destiny intended him to be at the Series one way or another.

After the tension of the pennant race, the World Series was, as Stengel put it, an anticlimax. The Yankees won four games to one, dominating with Raschi, Reynolds, and Page. On the occasion of his greatest triumph, Stengel was, for the first and perhaps only time in his life, reduced to monosyllables: "I won one! I won one!"

The first game had been a scoreless tie until Henrich hit a home run in the bottom of the ninth ("Tommy Henrich hit a home run for the Yankees to win the opening game of the 1949 season," said sportswriter Tom Meany. "Tommy Henrich hit a home run to win the pennant for the Yankees in the closing game of the season. Tommy Henrich hit a home run for the Yankees to win the opening game of the world series. What's the matter with the guy? Is he in a rut?") There is a wonderful picture from that day in the *New York Times*. It is of Stengel, moments after Henrich's ball landed in the seats. He is on the field, facing away from the viewer. His arms are spread wide, his cap in his outstretched left hand. He is balanced on one leg, as if he were about to click his heels. Casey Stengel, dancing for joy. A journey of twenty-five years had ended. He was out of the wilderness, seeing the promised land. "They're pretty nice, these players I've got," he said.

After the final game of the World Series, Jerry Coleman felt compelled to speak with Stengel. "I was just thanking him for giving me a chance to play, because if Harris was there who knows what would have happened. He always went with veterans. The year that Casey came, you got Bobby Brown, a young guy, you got Berra, they made a catcher out of him, you got Coleman at second base, they got Woodling, they got Bauer, Mapes, who was a young guy—all these young guys."

Coleman said, "Thanks for giving me the chance to play, Skipper. I hope I never disappoint you."

"You're thanking me? I gotta thank you. I gotta thank [scout Joe] Devine for talking to me about you. I gotta thank myself for listening to him. Disappoint me, kid? You made me the manager of the world champions. Nobody ever did that kind of a favor for me before."

He was uncharacteristically modest that fall. "I didn't catch a fly ball, make a base hit, or strike a guy out all season. So why should I take any credit?" Nor would he name a most valuable player, for the same reasons. "Gee! Most valuable? Most valuable! How much guts did they have? I don't know. Their guts were scattered all over the field all year and they still had enough left to win it. They did it . . . their guts did it." Nevertheless, as he posed for photographs after the last game of the World Series, he held tightly to a baseball. Someone asked Stengel to give it to him as a souvenir. "Not this one," he said. It was the ball with which Joe Page had struck out Gil Hodges for the final out of the Series. Yogi Berra had given it to Page, and Page had given it to Stengel. "I don't know of any manager who could have done a better job with us," Henrich said. "I rank him right up there with Joe McCarthy, and you know what I've always thought of Joe."

Stengel was sixty years old, yet he felt that he was just beginning to make his reputation. After a quarter century of being called a clown, one victory did not feel like a vindication. "That victory was sweet, very sweet," he told Fred Lieb, "but I've got to win some more before I convince some people that I'm a real manager." Contrary to Brick Laws's assertion, Stengel was already planning another championship. The writers thought he was crazy; there was no way this team of brittle veterans could be nursed through another race. The Yankees, they thought, would return to third place.

Stengel knew about three things that the writers did not: a teenage shortstop with Independence of the Kansas-Oklahoma-Missouri League named Mantle, a southpaw pitcher with Binghamton of the Eastern League named Ford, and that the day the Yankees eliminated the Red Sox, Billy Martin had been purchased from Oakland, along with another fine looking prospect named Jackie Jensen. The pieces were in place. The dynasty had begun.

The Yankees won the World Series again in 1950, 1951, 1952, and 1953. The five consecutive championships were a record, breaking the mark held by Joe McCarthy. John McGraw had won only three of his World Series. Stengel further surpassed his mentor by winning additional pennants in 1955 (missing in 1954 despite winning 103 games), 1956, 1957, 1958, and 1960. In twelve seasons with the Yankees, Stengel won ten pennants. In thirty seasons with the Giants, McGraw won only ten. By all measures, Stengel had surpassed his master. He was widely acclaimed as a genius, the mastermind behind the Yankees dynasty. "That's a lot of bunk about them five-year building plans," he said in 1955. "Look at us. We build and win at the same time."

Yet the old memories were never far away. He never completely escaped his comedic reputation. Page, who blamed Stengel for his rapid decline after 1949, said, "He's nothing but a clown. He was a clown when he came and he'll be a clown when he goes." If people believed, it was his own fault; he was simply too funny to be thought of as a serious figure. He could never be treated with fear and reverence, as McGraw had been. Stengel would receive respect and *ir*reverence, difficult attitudes to rationalize. In this sense McGraw remained his rival. Late in his Yankees career, a writer asked Stengel if he had patterned himself after McGraw. Stengel became visibly angry. "He was a great man in this town . . . but Stengel is in town now, and he's won a lot of pennants too." He stormed off, ending the interview.

NOTES

Key To Abbreviations

AI: Author Interview
BBM: *Baseball Magazine*
BDE: *Brooklyn Daily Eagle*
BDR: *Boston Daily Record*
BG: *Boston Globe*
BH: *The Boston Herald*
NWK: *Newsweek*
NYDN: *New York Daily News*
NYHT: *New York Herald-Tribune*
NYT: *New York Times*
SAM: U.S. Senate Subcommittee on Antitrust and Monopoly
SBE: Sabermetric Baseball Encyclopedia
SEP: *Saturday Evening Post*
SI: *Sports Illustrated*
SNBR: *Sporting News Baseball Register*
TSN: *The Sporting News*

Chapter One

"Bartlett's Familiar Quotations": Kaplan, 680.
"The Smithsonian Institution": See National Portrait Gallery,
   Washington, D.C., particularly Accession Number NPG.81.67 (bronze
   sculpture).
"It seems to me": Red Smith, *The Red Smith Reader*, 134.
"Only superficially . . . Sanskrit": Red Smith, *Views of Sport*, 3–4.
"I have been up . . . ladder": Stengel, SAM, 11.
"I've learned a lot": Lieb, *Baseball*, 279.
"Americans . . . change class": Vidal, 725.
"Our ball club . . . 1776": Stengel, SAM, 11.
"He had . . . come back": Mantle, *Quality of Courage*, 107.
"I have been discharged": Stengel, SAM, 19, 21.
"The most widely known": Lieb, *Baseball*, 277.

"Whitey Herzog said": Herzog, 31–32.

"Around here you are measured": Michael O'Keefe, *NYDN*, July 14, 2003

"Casey Stengel . . . America": Anderson, 102–103.

"On October 9, 1970": Casey Stengel, *NYT*, October 9, 1970.

"If You Live Long Enough": Richard Norton Smith, 15.

"Certainly Casey was one": Robinson, 50–51.

"You or I could have managed": Golenbock, *Dynasty*, 76.

"Fell into it": Fokker, 50.

"Stengel might have been": Peary, 106.

"Stengel was never a good": Peary, 106.

"In nine years of managing": Werber, 134.

"That's why I don't go": Jerry Coleman, AI, August 4, 2003.

"A man that's been around": Dickson, 416.

"What does it do to a man": Bouton, 79.

"Don't give up": Creamer, 292.

Chapter Two

"Rooting for the Yankees": Dickson, 245.

"A self-effacing star": Barrow, 194.

"A second division manager": Veeck, 96.

"The same writers": Allen, "You Could Look It Up," 5.

"Nice guys finish last.": Durocher, 5.

"They never doubted": BBM

"The Yankee Way": Bouton, 221.

"You're a Yankee": Halberstam, 21; Mead, 172.

"Then he would go off": Halberstam, 102; Bouton, 234; Kahn, 165.

"I hope the pride": Dan Daniel, *TSN*, May 4, 1949.

"Yankee fans were refined": Frommer, *New York City Baseball*, 128.

"What does that guy expect": Henrich, 6.

"Subject to harassment": Dan Daniel, *TSN*, May 11, 1949.

"Excuse to abuse alcohol": Jerry Coleman, AI, August 4, 2003.

"Through the years McCarthy": Gross, 55.

"He was probably . . . dissipater": Cairns, 4.

"Barrow looked on him as a son": Barrow, 188.

"It was about time": Robinson, 261.

"A souvenir of the time": Rosenthal, 38

"At the left side of his mouth": Felker and Havemann, *Life*, September 29, 1952.

"This here pair of palm-leaf fans": Tommy Holmes, *BBM*, May 1934.

"He looked more like a horse": Tom Meany, *SEP*, March 12, 1949.

"No typewriter has yet": Peter Williams, 162.

"Casey Stengel's change of face": Allen, "You Could Look It Up," 7.

"Casey Stengel actually . . . dignity.": Rosenthal, 23–24.

"Sea captain or a range rider.": Allen, 139.

"The old man has the face": Cannon, 82–83.

"Casey Stengel is a white": Light, 692.

"There is an oft repeated": Okrent and Wulf, 193.

"Don't rush me": Light, 692.

"Perfectly clear": Berra, 42–43; Coleman, AI, 8/4/03; Ryne Duren, AI, July 20, 2003.

"That jargon of yours": Wells Twombly, *TSN*, October 18, 1975.

"They're so slick": Steve Jacobson, *Newsday*, October 29, 2000.

"It never fails": Tom Meany, *SEP*, March 12, 1949.

"The general attitude": Lieb, 279.

"When Casey Stengel . . . job": Holtzman, 12.

"Ole Case had better": Arthur Daley, *NYT*, March 16, 19498.

"Why, he won't even": Jerry Mitchell, *TSN*, May 4, 1949.

"Casey may not win the pennant": Washington *Post*, May 8, 1949.

"When the rumor that Stengel": Red Smith, *NYHT*, October 14, 1948.

"Let me worry about that": Stan Baumgartner, *TSN*, April 25, 1946.

"Lefty you go in and stay in": J.G. Taylor Spink, *TSN*, February 18, 1943.

"Well, sirs and ladies": Dave Egan, *BDR*, October 14, 1948.

"Egan speculated that Stengel": Robert Smith, *Baseball*, 1970 ed.

"Lucifer Sulphurious": Parrott, *Lords of Baseball*, 79.

"They always said this": Durocher, 105.

"Borderline criminal personality": Auker, 24.

"Larry could have been": Stanley Frank, *SEP*, July 24, 1948.

"Leo Durocher . . . forth": Dewey and Acocella, 257.

"The extra-colossal": Red Smith, *SEP*, March 29, 1947.

"One of Barrow's cardinal rules": Barrow, 138.

"In late May . . . stay": Goldman, *Yankees Magazine*, May 1999.

"Had let it be known": Durocher, 215.

"Asked to evaluate the team": Warfield, 117.

"The talents of . . . Myer": James, *New Historical Baseball Abstract*, 499.

"Harris clashed . . . Collins": Golenbock, *Fenway*, 88.

"If there is any jerk": *TSN*, November 26, 1977.

"My offer didn't hurt you": Barber, *1947*, 79.

"Dressen had a guaranteed": Barber, *1947*, 88.

"MacPhail denied": Barber, *1947*, 90.

"Chandler owed his job": Barber, *1947*, 67.

"He reluctantly agreed": Frommer, 87.

"Got a little drunk last night": Durocher, 135.

"Lindell, Johnson, Stirnweiss": Stanley Frank, *SEP*, July 24, 1948.

"A toast to Joe Page": Joe Page, *SEP*, May 22, 1948.

"The Yankees have often been": George Weiss, *SI*, March 6, 1961.

"I have no objections": Graham, Jr., 107.

"McCarthy is the strict commander": Dan Daniel, *TSN*, May 4, 1949.

"When to change pitchers": Frommer, 182.

"I really don't care": *TSN*, November 26, 1977.

"Very quiet, very lenient": Peary, 52.

"The four hour manager": Frommer, 219.
"Leave them alone": Henrich, 198.
"He treated you": Dan Daniel, *TSN*, May 4, 1949.
"It was up to him.": Henrich, 204.
"You're likely to get sunburned": *TSN*, March 15, 1934.
"Go on up there": Nathan, 186.
"Under Bucky we were": Henrich, 205.
"If a guy blew a play": Durso, *DiMaggio*, 163.
"They thought all you": Red Smith, *Views of Sport*, 3–4.
"Page burned himself out": Jerry Coleman, AI, August 4, 2003.
"You can't relax": Forker, 3.
"He did fine Page": Kaiser, 102.
"I felt like Lincoln": Frommer, 85.
"Joe, whatever happens": Golenbock, *Dynasty*, 32.
"Lindell Bombers": Hank Bauer, AI, August 23, 2003.
"He's lost control": Kahn, 166.
"DiMaggio and Henrich": Stanley Frank, *SEP*, July 24, 1948.
"Preferred to work with veterans": Jerry Coleman, AI, August 4, 2003.
"God gets you up": *Time*, November 11, 1946.
"It's all depends on the big fellow": Whittingham, 533.
"It was like being socked": Sullivan and Powers, 102.
"Though he had known": Linn, 192.
"He came back for the knife": Orodenker, 251.
"The Fifty-seven-year-old Stengel": John Drebinger, *NYT,* October 13, 1948.
"The Yankees executives": *TSN*, January 15, 1949.
"The great Joe McCarthy": Graham, 175.
"Now I must study": Kahn, 169.
"This is a big job, fellows": DeGregorio, 180.
"There is always some kid": Dickson, 113.
"I cannot tell you very much": Kahn, 169.
"I didn't get this job": Tom Meany, *SEP*, March 12, 1949.
"Somebody asked a question": Graham, Jr., 105.
"Because I can make people laugh": Lieb, 279.
"Let them think it's a joke": Allen, *Now Wait a Minute, Casey!*, 3.
"The old Yankee tradition": Red Smith, *NYHT*, October 14, 1948.
"When I heard that old Pepper": *NYT*, October 14, 1948.

Chapter Three

"I still recall the headline": Jerry Coleman, AI, August 4, 2003.
"It was a shock": Frommer, 221.
"He interceded with Weiss": Dan Daniel, *TSN*, January 26, 1949.
"I know little about this league": Rizzuto, 60.
"It's like this": Schoor, 122.
"The two-a-day training scheme": James P. Dawson, *NYT*, March 2, 1949.

"He didn't tell us": Kahn, 183.
"Behind his back": Golenbock, *Dynasty*, 26.
"Collared his teammates": NWK, July 28, 1947,76.
"I've never seen": Halberstam, 32.
"DiMaggio was the last": Rudd Rennie, *NYHT*, March 12, 1949.
"News for the papers.": Red Smith, *NYHT*, March 13, 1949.
"I will handle this": DeGregorio, 190.
"Stengel had tried to treat": Hirshberg, 102.
"No sense fining a player": Rudd Rennie, *NYHT*, March 12, 1949.
"DiMaggio admits he feels": DeGregorio, 190.
"Bobby reminds me": Sullivan and Powers, 39.
"I ask him if he's ready": Milton Gross, *TSN*, October 12, 1949.
"Slipping on a cake of soap": Dan Daniel, *TSN*, June 1, 1949.
"Stengel didn't think he": Stengel, 178.
"We're all set except": Bob Cooke, *NYHT,* April 24, 1949.
"He pulls a miracle": Meany, 128.
"Bill James has compared": James, *Historical Baseball Abstract*, 382.
"The big man of our team": NWK, September 12, 1949.
"My best pitch": Madden, 4.
"Hands, accuracy, and quickness": Jerry Coleman, AI, August 4, 2003.
"By Berra's own estimation": Lopate, 2003; Berra, *Ten Rings*, 40.
"My catching was awful": Berra, *Ten Rings*, 25.
"We'll make him a catcher": Berra, *Ten Rings*, 34.
"As early as spring training": Berra, *It Ain't Over*, 104.
"They would scratch": Golenbock, *Dynasty*, 227.
"Did you see The Ape": Berra, *Ten Rings*, 22.
"You're not really thinking": Berra, *It Ain't Over*, 100.
"In 1946, Mel Ott": Arthur Daley, *NYT*, March 20, 1949.
"During the same period": SBE
"Lefty Gomez quipped": Dickson, 161.
"To suit McCarthy": Karst and Jones, 564.
"I have been trying": John Lardner, *NWK*, October 17, 1949.
"The next Charlie Keller": Meany, 144.
"Jan Murray said": James, *New Historical Baseball Abstract*, 835. Commonly
    credited to columnist Jim Murray, apparently inaccurately.
"DiMaggio candidly accepts": Whittingham, 559.
"He does everything better": Daniels, *SNBR*, 1950.
"Joe DiMaggio had an imperial": Jerry Coleman, AI, August 4, 2003.
"There was an aura about him": www.baseball-almanac.com.
"DiMaggio was so impressive": Broeg, 118.
"I saw today why you": Red Smith, *SEP*, March 29, 1947.
"The Pride of the Yankees": Page, *SEP*, May 22, 1948.
"Hot condition": Whittingham, 525.
"DiMaggio did not believe": Whittingham, 559.
"Doing a little dancing": Daniels, *SNBR* 1950.

"I suppose I look": James P. Dawson, *NYT*, March 4, 1949.
"It is doubtful that the fans": Red Smith, *NYHT*, May 19, 1949.
"Henrich never volunteers advice": *Time*, June 13, 1949.
"He's a fine judge of a fly": Einstein, *Second Fireside Book of Baseball*, 37.
"Henrich had rolled back his age": Allen, *Where Have You Gone*, 67.
"Lean and lithe as a greyhound": Milton Gross, *TSN*, October 12, 1949.
"Expression of Weiss's commitment": Meany, 91.
"Wads of tissue paper": Berkow and Kaplan, 62.
"When you are ready to blow": Karst and Jones, 574.
"69–58 support-neutral": *SBE*. Support-neutral refers to the number of wins
    and losses the pitcher would have had given an average amount of offensive
    support.
"Every time he wins a game": Berkow and Kaplan, 62.
"Support neutral 73–75": *SBE*.
"Rightly or wrongly": Meany, 77.
"The Vanishing American": Meany, 85.
"They told me": Golenbock, *Dynasty*, 95.
"His 'baseball age' ": Meany, 81.
"He made you want to pitch": Frommer, 89.
"Thumbing his nose at Weiss": Linn, 191.
"Tommy Byrne would rather strike": Charlie Silvera, AI, July 2001.
"Look . . . don't watch him pitch": Halberstam, 235.
"He had a good fast ball": Weiss, *SI*, March 14, 1961.
"You know, Marshall": John Drebinger, *NYT*, March 3, 1949.
"The Naugatuck Nugget": Kaiser, 29.
"Bovine looking," and *"bloated"*: Gross, 28, 32.
"Duane Pillette had caught": Kelley, 154.
"Page had no buddy among": Gross, 21–22.
"They tried to take my slider": John Drebinger, *NYT,* March 1, 1949.
"I don't have to have my hair": Tommy Holmes, *BDE*, December 13, 1935.
"What do I care . . . didn't we?": Berkow and Kaplan, 40.
"No more of this stuff": Golenbock, *Dynasty*, 227.
"Phil is the one man": Dan Daniel, *TSN*, June 8, 1949.
"I figure that Bobby Brown": Rudd Rennie, *NYHT*, April 8, 1949.
"With Johnson in action": James P. Dawson, *NYT*, April 8, 1949.
"Johnson . . . hasn't looked graceful": Joe Trimble, *NYDN*, April 15, 1949.
"Johnson proved too green": Dan Daniel, *TSN*, April 27, 1949.
"He professed to dislike platooning": Dan Daniel, *TSN*, June 1, 1949.
"No better or worse": Rudd Rennie, *NYHT,* April 9, 1949.
"I certainly am not": Rudd Rennie, *NYHT*, April 13, 1949.
"Go fly a kite": Red Smith, *NYHT*, April 14, 1949.
"Leave me alone": *NYHT*, April 15, 1949.
"DiMaggio appears phlegmatic": Whittingham, 533.
"In the spring of 1949": Jerry Coleman, AI, August 4, 2003.
"Joe won't be with us": Sullivan and Powers, 102.

"There is no reason he should": Dan Daniel, *TSN*, April 27, 1949.
"Lindell looks better in center": Joe Trimble, *NYDN*, April 15, 1949.
"You cannot take Henrich": Dan Daniel, *TSN*, April 20, 1949.
"Keller hits the ball": Rudd Rennie, *NYHT*, April 6, 1949.
"I don't want to take him out": Bert Gumpert, *NYP*, April 27, 1949.
"206 baseball writers were asked": Stengel, 173.
"Good pitching generally": Rudd Rennie, *NYHT*, March 27, 1949.
"Let's face it chums": Jimmy Powers, *NYDN*, 4/14/19.
"Well, the way things shape up": Dan Daniel, *TSN*, April 27, 1949.
"There should be a wreath": Rudd Rennie, *NYHT*, April 19, 1949.
"You're the luckiest stiff": Red Smith, *NYHT*, April 16, 1949.
"At Washington, trailing 4–1": Rudd Rennie, *NYHT*, July 2, 1949.
"McCarthy and Harris . . . power": Dan Daniel, *TSN*, May 4, 1949.
"Last night Casey Stengel": Rudd Rennie, *NYHT*, April 29, 1949.
"Stengel's idea of heaven": Rudd Rennie, NYHT, June 3, 1949.

Chapter Four

"Could be I was born in Brooklyn": Daniels, *SNBR* 1959.
"This was the same Kansas City": Fjellman, 170; Disneyland, 16.
"I wasn't cut out for that work": Daniels, *SNBR* 1959.
"G'wan, Stengel, your old man": Anderson, 114.
"Handicap of being left-handed": MacLean, 9.
"I remembered of course": Fitzgerald, 74.
"The Swede was a hard guy": Asinof, 209.
"The Dullest Sport in the World": Furnas, 391.
"Ruth and modern technology": Goldman, "The Monument Park Project" 3,
    www.yankees.com, September 9, 1999.
"When the battle ceased": *TSN*, September 13, 1945.
"When I broke in as a rookie": Tommy Holmes, *BBM*, May 1934.
"Play the angles!": MacLean, 3.
"It's only a matter of time": Henrich, 218.
"So I got out of Kankakee": Stengel, SAM, 16.
"You'd better be good": Carmichael, 220.
"I was not so successful": Stengel, SAM, 7.
"I broke in with four hits": Dickson, 416.
"He also lost the name Dutch": Lieb, *Baseball as I Have Known It*, 278.
"Hands-on advice on sliding": Stengel, 87.
"John McGraw . . . of Dahlen": McGraw, 136; Graham, *Brooklyn Dodgers*, 28.
"It has always been my ambition": Hynd, 122.
"Well, Bill, I hear you're losing": Red Smith, *NYHT*, September 27, 1949.
"This early experience . . . child labor": Lieb, *Connie Mack*, 6
"Every game was like a wake": Robinson, 149
"I do not say my players did not try": Alexander, *John McGraw*, 193–194;
    Seymour, 287; Goldstein, *Superstars*, 120.

"Old Robbie was the manager": Ritter, 179.

"He has grown in grace": Robinson, 154

"St. Louis roughs . . . 'Falstaff' ": Graham, *Brooklyn Dodgers*, 57.

"A fat, witty, good-humored": Harvey, 291.

"Look, Robbie, if I'm so dumb": Thompson, 12–13. Thompson's reminisces are spectacularly inaccurate; he remembers himself as a teammate of Stengel's despite his major league career having started after Stengel left the majors to manage Worcester.

"Like Falstaff . . . witty himself": Kavanaugh and Macht, np.

"Taking him circumferentially": Peter Williams, 102.

"Robbie played from day to day": John Lardner, *NWK*, June 3, 1940.

"Most of these fellows": Robinson, 138

"Jesus, I'm killed! I'm dead!": Creamer, 87

"Well the fella I got on there": Okrent and Wulf, 198.

"Everyone was 'Hey you,' ": Hank Bauer, *AI*, August 23, 2003.

"Robbie always had trouble": Meany and McCullough, *SEP*, March 6, 1937.

"Joe, go out there and run for Pete.": Thomas J. Connery, *BBM*.

"There's nothing to be gained": Lane, 166.

"No man has a right": Kuenster. 71.

"George, I'm trying": Lieb, 290.

"Stengel was suffering from typhus": Creamer, 83.

"He led a clubhouse cadre": Allen, *You Could Look It Up*, 22.

"You call me grasping": Tommy Holmes, *TSN*, July 13, 1949.

"Ebbets called for Stengel's salary": Koppett, *The Man in the Dugout*, 141.

"I didn't let one of my good players": Goldstein, *Screwballs*, 106.

"Most impudent letter": Goldstein, *Screwballs*, 124.

"The higher-ups complained": McMane, 45.

"How's Big Bess, Casey?": Tommy Holmes, *TSN*, July 13, 1949.

"He somehow found himself": Holway, 6; O'Neil, 79; Shatzkin, 932–933.

"The Negro . . . Christy Mathewson": O'Neil, 82. Rogan was named to the Baseball Hall of Fame in 1998.

"The Yankees of Negro baseball": Holway, 31.

"Stengel pop off too much": Tom Meany, *Look*, June 6, 1961.

"On July 1, 1921": Howell Stevens, *TSN*, December 28, 1939.

"I got to New York so fast": Broeg, 453.

"You wouldn't expect me": Carl Felker, *TSN*, August 25, 1945.

"He took more than one beating": Koppett, *The Man in the Dugout*, 30.

"Honus Wagner, the star shortstop": Bill James, *Let's Not Eat the Bones*, 120–121.

"Oriole baseball, as it flourished": Dickson, 122.

"John McGraw would have insisted": Dickson, 419.

"Off the field, he recognized": Koppett, *The Man in the Dugout*, 37.

"McGraw's teams were blowing": Bill James, *Managers*, 56.

"The name McGraw came": Seymour, 140.

"I think we can win it all": Nathan, 45.

"His ball team never lost a game": Ritter, 174.

"Stengel would often go home": Creamer, 140.
"He was a bachelor": Blanche McGraw, 283.
"Which would be suspended": Stengel, 114.
"Incorporated many of McGraw's": Frank Lane, *Colliers*, May 14, 1954.
"I'm taking an interest": Stengel, 112.
"McGraw occasionally let Stengel": Creamer, 156.
"There is one reason why my work": Lane, 165–166.
"My platoon thinking started": Stengel, 17.
"I don't mind . . . Casey's a lot of fun": McMillan, 179.
"Secretly thinking the gesture": Ruth, 123.
"It was 483 feet to the . . . wall": Lowry, 196.
"I thought it was interesting": Berra, 167.
"There's one good thing": Stengel, 3.
"I see where this fellow Stengel": Kaese, 240.
"A lot of the newspaper boys have": Lane, 200.
"People like to laugh at Casey": Johnson, 75.
"The paths of glory . . . to the Braves": Kaese, 195.
"This trade was unfairly heralded": Blanche McGraw, 290.
"Sentiment . . . has no proper place": Lane, 212.
"He was not a warm, cuddly": Jerry Coleman, AI, August 4, 2003.

Chapter Five

"I feel so good right now": Stanley Frank, *SEP*, July 24, 1948.
"I was impressed with him": George Weiss, *SI*, March 14, 1961.
"I thought I'd . . . my obligation": Stengel, 140.
"Stengel letters": Fuchs, 51.
"The best man . . . for you": Ibid.
"England, Ireland, and France": Durso, *Casey*, 74.
"To spend . . . McGraw's quest": Stengel, 135.
"So-called administrative": Parker, 43.
"Landis would make an identical": Pietruscza, 322.
"Later on Mr. Rickey came in": Stengel, SAM, 17.
"You might say I was already": Stengel, 143.
"So what? If I get a base hit": Tom Meany, *Look*, June 6, 1961.
"The key to my going back up": Murdock, 193.
"Games started . . . afternoon": Conlan, 47.
"Off the field": Stengel, 142.
"I want . . . out of here gracefully": Harold. Parrot, *BDE*, April 1, 1934.
"Sore-armed righthander . . . Lucas": Kenneth S. Conn, *TSN*, August 22, 1929.
"Getting paid for learning": Graham, Jr., 71–72.
"If you ever behave again": Pietrusza, 501. Emphasis from source.
"My uncle introduced me to him": John Drohan, *TSN*, September 4, 1946.
"In addition to Manager McGraw": William E. Brandt, *NYT*, April 15, 1930.
"Boys, write down what you think": Bartell, 97.

Chapter Six

"I'm in baseball because I love": Harold C. Burr, *BBM*, June 1932.

"After half-hearted overtures": *BBM*, September 1932; Tommy Holmes, *TSN*, July 13, 1949.

"If Carey can make the Brooklyn": James M. Gould, *BBM*, January 1932.

"It is the most intriguing": *Daniel M. Daniel, BBM*, 2/1932.

"Casey Stengel wasn't . . . long": Lane, 156.

"It was easier to teach . . . youngsters": Bill James, *Historical Baseball Abstract*, 399.

"My boys run with all the legs": F.C. Lane, *BBM*, January 1932.

"He wanted . . . impossible": Westcott, 96.

"The Most Lopsided Trade": Bill James, *Historical Baseball Abstract*, 155

"He later blamed the front office": Graham, *The Brooklyn Dodgers*, 134.

"A professional . . . 1926": Minor League Stars, 148.

"Why, these pitchers don't want me": Meany and McCullough, *SEP*, March 6, 1937.

"If I had my way I would spend": Harold C. Burr, *BBM*, June 1932.

"What do you expect of a ball club": MacLean, 55.

"We want ball players, not farmers": Meany and McCullough, *SEP*, March 6, 1937.

"According to Fresco Thompson": Thompson, 36.

"His rages had become public": Durso, *Casey & Mr. McGraw*, 184–185.

"How do you think Mac really felt": Graham, *The New York Giants*, 200.

"Stengel says he himself was all so": Bruccoli, 489.

"Every day the Dodgers are home": *NWK*, June 20, 1936.

"A prince of good sportsmen": F. C. Lane, *BBM*, September 1932.

"Brooklyn fans had . . . dullness": Parrott, 103.

"Carey's team . . . humorless": *NWK*, June 20, 1936.

"Leaving for Brooklyn on business": Parrott, 104.

"Entire Dodger board of directors": Graham, *Brooklyn Dodgers*, 134.

"That's not for you to worry about": Stengel, 149.

"I know what a fine job Stengel": Harold Parrott, *BDE*, March 22, 1934.

"The Dodgers . . . for the N.R.A.": Durso, *Casey*, 93.

"With the electric personality": Ed Hughes, *BDE*, April 1, 1934.

"Casey was not always in accord": Harold Parrott, *BDE*, March 22, 1934.

"The first thing I want to say": Creamer, *Stengel*, 182.

"A colossus from the knees up": Graham, *Brooklyn Dodgers*, 126.

"He ain't got no neck": Mead, 57.

"Caliban": Mead, 9.

"One time Hack drank a bottle": Langford, 34.

"What am I supposed to do?": Parker, 94.

"Stengel noted a large tanker truck": Bartell, 112.

"We may lose more games": Durso, *Casey*, 92.

"Mungo and I get along fine": Dickson, 421.

"He couldn't hit so good": Stengel, *Life*, October 12, 1959.

"The most popular": Clifford Bloodgood, *BBM*, May 1933.

"He could hit if you woke him": Shatzkin, 620.

"Nicknamed 'Mickey Mouse'": Goldstein, *Superstars*, 178.

"When Tremark reached base": Graham, Jr, 85.

"Why don't you hit 'em": Harold Parrott, *BDE*, April 5, 1934.

"The ricocheting ball might lay low": Harold Parrott, *BDE*, April 6, 1934.

"The veterans . . . benched plenty": Harold Parrott, *BDE*, April 4, 1934, 20.

"Dodgers' opening day uniforms": Goldstein, *Superstars*, xi.

"Stengel's first . . . Dodger lineup": Allen, *The Giants and the Dodgers*, 157.

"Astoundingly svelte": *BDE*, April 15, 1934.

"Notable for the 'debatable' habit": Edward J. Wilkinson, *BBM*, December 1932.

"He ran the clubhouse . . . camp": Light, 348.

"The initial point of comparison": *NWK*, May 15, 1939.

"Our . . . were not to purchase": Stengel, 149.

"I could build up the methods": Stengel, 23.

"I had to play my own system": Stengel, 172.

"There is evidence . . . 1887.": James, *New Historical Baseball Abstract*, 117.

"Can't hit an overhanded curve ball": Linn, *The Great Rivalry*, 237.

"People alter percentages": Tom Meany, *Look*, June 6, 1961.

"What else are you gonna do": Creamer, 185.

"Some players . . . they get a chance": Stengel, 120.

"Casey Stengel will be manager": Tommy Holmes, *BDE*, July 10, 1934.

"He deserves the honor": *NYT*, July 6, 1934.

"Terry went down the line-up": *NYT*, July 12, 1934.

"You know my arm's gone": Joe Durso, *NYT*, October 1, 1975.

"McGraw . . . curve ball lingers on": Tom Meany, *TSN*, February 10, 1944.

"Casey . . . went into action": Frick, 147–48.

"You're as pale as a sheet today": Howell Stevens, *TSN*, December 28, 1939.

"First they want you for radio": *NYHT*, April 30, 1949.

"One sportswriter had written": Bob Cooke, *NYHT*, September 25, 1949.

"A person might think that a hitter": John J. Ward, *BBM*, December 1934.

"A typical development in a career": F.C. Lane, *BBM*, December 1934.

"Wait him out . . . away the pennant": Al Lopez, December 30, 1943, 9.

"I'm sure you can take me": Broeg, 454.

Chapter Seven

"It was rumored that Mrs. Ebbets": Harold C. Burr, *BBM*, June 1932.

"Casey Stengel is supposed to be": Tommy Holmes, *BDE*, August 8, 1935.

"He loved to get an old pitcher": Stengel, 125.

"That's just the trouble with you": Furman Bisher, *SEP*, August 20, 1955.

"I've tried . . . young pitchers": Tommy Holmes, *BDE*, April 8, 1935.

"Over twenty-five red pins": *Total Baseball*, 497.

"I'm going to get some of those": Graham, Jr., 85

"I didn't hear of anybody offering": Tommy Holmes, *TSN*, November 29, 1934.

"The Dodgers . . . first division club": *NYT*, April 14, 1935.

"First or second division": J.G. Taylor Spink, *TSN*, April 4, 1935.

"I'm not sure he has enough stuff": Tommy Holmes, *BDE*, April 2, 1935.

"I'll rate Harry a real prospect": Tommy Holmes, *BDE*, April 2, 1935.

"My little lambs . . . couldn't get her": Gregory, 126.

"Unless strange things happen": Harold Parrot, *BDE*, April 5, 1934.

"Bordagaray will be a sensation": Harold Parrot, *BDE*, April 5, 1934.

"I told him . . . I knew of six games": Harold Parrot, *BDE*, April 5, 1934.

"Just meet the ball": Tommy Holmes, *BDE*, April 17, 1935.

"He always came to camp with me": Graham, Jr., 84

"Oscar . . . was the fastest man": Dobbins, 175.

"The third basemen are practically": Tom Meany, *Look*, June 6, 1961.

"Frenchy's . . . would have helped": Graham, Jr., 82.

"Frenchy . . . man on the Dodgers": J.G.T. Spink, *TSN*, July 13, 1944.

"From his first . . . with the Dodgers": Stanley Frank, *SEP*, July 24, 1948.

"We had been losing, losing": Goldstein, *Superstars*, 178.

"This right field . . . for him": Tommy Holmes, *BDE*, May 7, 1936.

"I lost it in the shade": Arthur Daley, *NYT*, March 3, 1948.

"Tomorrow . . . to stand outside": J.G.T. Spink, *TSN*, July 13, 1944.

"I'm bringing back the good old": Creamer, 188.

"sixty-six at home": James, *All-Time*, 177.

"National League . . . had decided": Hirshberg, 65; Kaese, 228.

"He failed to run . . . hitting the ball": Dewey and Acocella, 229.

"John McGraw used to say": Broeg, 453.

"No ballplayer should ever . . . habit": Stengel, 19.

"If you tried . . . teetotalers": John Lardner, *The New Yorker*, May 12, 1954; Robert Smith, 156.

"Calmly picked up his chief": Stetson Palmer, *BBM*, March 1933.
   McLean died in a gun fight a few years later. There is no truth to the rumor that it cost McGraw a year's salary to pay for the hit.

"Worrying over Bugs Raymond": Gallen, 234.

"He can catch a good game for you": Harold Parrot, *BDE*, August 6, 1935.

"It looks very bad for a club": Tommy Holmes, *BDE*, August 8, 1935.

"I've been the sap": NWK, June 20, 1936.

"We don't want him now": NWK, June 20, 1936.

"Nobody's salary was cut": Tommy Holmes, *BDE*, August 15, 1935.

"Playing with a lose-always": Harold Parrot, *BDE*, August 6, 1935.

"That man is so fast": Ed Hughes, *BDE*, August 10, 1935.

"I keep shiftin' 'em around": Harold Parrot, *BDE*, August 6, 1935.

"We could experiment with Johnny": Tommy Holmes, *BDE*, August 1, 1935.

"McCarthy . . . had converted": Halsey Hall, *TSN*, August 21, 1946.

"Just five days after speaking": Harold Parrot, *BDE*, August 6, 1935; *BDE*, May 7, 1936.

"I started to study the position": J.G.T. Spink, *TSN*, July 13, 1944.

"Stengel admitted as much": Tommy Holmes, *BDE*, December 13, 1935.

"He became quiet for a few minutes": Honig, 632.

"Morgan had hit twenty home runs": Wright, 234.

"The Dodgers are . . . giving up": Tommy Holmes, *BDE*, May 4, 1936.
"I saw Freddie play his last game": Honig, 280.
"Lindstrom . . . Stengel a 'cryptic' ": Meany and McCullough, *SEP*, March 6, 1937.
"The game of April 16": http://www.baseballlibrary.com.
"A .354 average, fifty home runs": Wright, 234.
"Mack had suspended Earnshaw": *BBM*, September 1932.
"On July 11, Gorman finally": Tommy Holmes, *BDE*, July 12, 1936.
"What that beautiful swing": Parrott, *Lords*, 100–101.
"The Dodgers were still obligated": http://www.baseballlibrary.com/baseballlibrary/teams/1936dodgers.stm.
"It's . . . team I'm sorry to leave": Tommy Holmes, *BDE*, July 17, 1936. Earnshaw was also briefly managed by Lew Fonseca.
"His Hall of Fame induction speech": Stout, 118.
"He is quoted as saying that Stengel": Forker, *The Men of Autumn*.
"Go peddle your papers, shorty": Arthur Daley, *TSN*, September 8, 1948.
"Kid, don't even suit up.": Ira Berkow, *NYT*, July 31, 1994.
"A story-teller of Munchausen": Milton Gross, *TSN*, October 12, 1949.
"One time . . . especially gloomy": Mantle, *Education*.
"That's one, I'll admit, I never": Schacht, 146.
"When I think of the players Casey": Graham, Jr. 81.
"Them fellas . . . life miserable": *TSN*, October 18, 1975.
"I meet 'em all, from mugs": *NWK*, June 20, 1936.

Chapter Eight

"Now boys, I know . . . doing it?": Dickson, 421.
"You're a big leaguer now": Weiss, *SI*, March 14, 1961.
"The oil well is something like an annuity": Tom Meany, *SEP*, March 12, 1949.
"Tom Meany . . . speculated": Tom Meany, *SEP*, March 12, 1949.
"Lopez, also an investor in Moore's wells": *TSN*, September 8, 1938.
"In 1924 he argued . . . $4 a day": Robinson, *Matty*, 212.
"Nobody will ever hit a baseball": Reidenbaugh, 40.
"A ball club is a machine": F.C. Lane, *BBM*, December 1933.
"Stengel missed the baseball life terribly": Allen, *You Could Look It Up*, 125.
"Quinn received over 150 applications": *NYT*, October 26, 1937.
"Nobody has said a word to me": *NYT*, October 10, 1937.
"I want to give the matter . . . thought": *NYT*, October 10, 1937.
"He offered the job to Rabbit Maranville": *TSN*, October 28, 1937.
"When I met him over at New York": *TSN*, October 28, 1937.
"The next name . . . was Donie Bush": *NYT*, October 22, 1937; Kaese, 239.
"In 1927 he benched Kiki Cuyler": Kuenster, 134.
"He benched Paul Waner": Bartell, 70.
"I don't trip my players": Dave Ulrich, Jack Zenger, Norman Smallwood, *Results Based Leadership*, Harvard Business School Press, 1999.
"If I had to do it all over": Kuenster, 134.

"It was hard to pass up a chance": *NYT*, October 23, 1937.
"Knowing that Stengel had five offers"TSN, October 28, 1937.
"The Cubs' star catcher Gabby Hartnett": *NYT*, October 26, 1937.
"Casey . . . come with us next year": *NYT*, October 26, 1937.
"Many of these fellows know you"BDR, October 12, 1937.
"I don't think . . . lucky to finish fifth": *NYT*, October 26, 1937.
"I know of fewer smarter baseball men": *TSN*, October 28, 1937.
"He wanted to see poverty": Dickson, 415.
"Our ball club is pretty good": *NYT*, November 23, 1937.
"Over his last 1,300 Pacific Coast League": Snelling, 179.
"Blessed with the great outfield range": James, *New Historical*, 726.
"Right now . . . how he's going to eat": *BDR*, March 5, 1938.
"Make haste slowly": *TSN*, March 3, 1938.
"You must realize that this club": *TSN*, March 10, 1938.
"Other outfits . . . one session daily": *TSN*, March 17, 1938.
"Can I come in . . . stay a couple of minutes": Kaese, 243.
"Duckbutt . . . I pitched this guy": Davidson, *Caught Short*. 23.
"Why doncha go get a ball team": John Brooks, *BDR*, March 3, 1938.
"Looked like the same old Bees": Waite Hoyt, *SEP*, March 31, 1938.
"That's more runs than the club scored": *BDR*, March 5, 1938.
"Quinn began to fantasize about expanding": *TSN*, June 16, 1938.
"Miracleman": *TSN*, June 9, 1938.
"Stengel has refused to bog down": Gerry Moore, *BG*, July 14, 1938.
"You've got a great pair of hands, Max": Kahn, *The Era*, 163.
"I think I'd better wait until we get out": *BG*, July 13, 1938.
"That will cost you ten, Sugarbowl!": *TSN*, August 4, 1938.
"Let me pitch the second game!": Gene Moore, *BG*, June 30, 1938.
"Vander Meer had been Bees property": Allen, *Cincinnati Reds*, 261.
"John, we're not trying to beat you": Creamer, 192.
"Vince is the only player I ever saw": Sugar, 85.
"A centerfielder in our park": J. Cashman, *BDR*, April 3, 1939.
"That's him! That's the guy I want!": *TSN*, July 7, 1938.
"Bought back by Frank Buck": Dickson, 161.
"No club in either major league": *TSN*, September 1, 1938.
"Everyday my respect grows": Fred Lieb, *TSN*, September 22, 1938.
"They had courage": Kaese, 243.
"In the estimation of Boston fandom": *TSN*, September 8, 1938.

Chapter Nine

"Well, Fette has a sore arm": *TSN*, December 28, 1939.
"At the time of Hassett's acquisition": *TSN*, December 15, 1938.
"I give up . . . set a new strikeout record": Kaese, 245.
"The most sought after prospect": Hirshberg, 86.
"Now a fellow . . . a little help to us": Williams, 165.
"They say he's hard to handle": Kaese, 245.

"We're not saying a great deal this spring": Fred Lieb, *TSN*, March 23, 1939.
"I know Simmons used to be a big shot": Fred Lieb, *TSN*, March 23, 1939.
"If we had Simmons last year": Joe Cashman, *BDR*, April 3, 1939.
"Well, here it is": Joe Cashman, *BDR*, April 3, 1939.
"When Stengel made that decision": Kelley, *The Early All-Stars*, 34.
"He talked to me just like a father": Howell Stevens, *TSN*, June 19, 1941.
"Night baseball in the day-time": *BG*, June 28, 1939.
"I guess . . . right kind of shoes": J. O'Leary, *BG*, July 4, 1939.
"Other versions of the tale": Hirshberg, 96.
"For the next three years": Koppett, *All About Baseball*
"He couldn't play again": Westcott, 98.
"Why don't . . . do it on your own account?": J. O'Leary, *BG*, July 4, 1939.
"I'll have Ty look me over": Jack Malaney, *TSN*, June 29, 1939.
"Casey was very funny": *TSN*, August 17, 1939.
"That fellow is a wonder, no fooling": *TSN*, August 31, 1939.
"Bees were down by sixteen percent": *Total Baseball*, 76.
"When Al Lopez dropped a foul pop": *TSN*, August 9, 1939.
"President . . . national emergency": www.presidency.ucsb.edu.
"Young Turks": *BH*, September 1, 1939.
"It is impossible to ignore Stengel": *TSN*, September 5, 1940.
"He's fine . . . take to get him down?": Howell Steven, *TSN*, December 28, 1939.
"It's on me . . . I'm getting paid for losing.": Howell Steven, *TSN*, December 28, 1939.

Chapter Ten

"Gosh . . . Chinamen now?": *TSN*, December 14, 1939.
"I've made up my mind . . . young players": Jack Malaney, *TSN*, January 4, 1940.
"McGraw had tried the same thing": James, *New Historical Abstract*, 757-758.
"Kindergarten class.": Jack Malaney, *TSN*, January 11, 1940.
"Not to make cheap home run": Hy Hurwitz, *BG*, April 15, 1940.
"So butchered by the sports medicine": Bartell, 75.
"I don't care what anybody says": Tommy Holmes, BDE, 5/8/36.
"The best left fielder in the league": Bartell, 75.
"Maybe it's just as well I didn't": Gerry Moore, *BDR*, July 18, 1940, 10.
"It took one . . . discover this whole country": *BDR*, March 5, 1940.
"They said he was my boy . . . stuck": Grantland Rice, *BG*, April 10, 1940.
"He used to like to get together": Cataneo, 6.
"An oft-repeated story about West": Cataneo, 163.
"Casey . . . an assist on the play?": Honig, 281.
"The move was a ghastly mistake": Hirshberg, 85.
"He wanted me to do so good": Cataneo, 57.
"More subtle forms of attack": See chapter three.
"Bear Tracks": Howell Stevens, *TSN*, June 10, 1943.

"A fastball with a hop on it": Dave Egan, *BDR*, April 13, 1940.
"Constructing his lineups for power": James, *Managers*, 280.
"Dignity be damned!": Dave Egan, *BDR*, April 25, 1940.
"Ah, there's no place like home": Joe Cashman, *BDR*, April 13, 1940.
"Since the Bees began losing consistently": Melville Webb, *BG*, April 6, 1940.
"He had amused himself . . . scoops": *TSN*, April 11, 1940.
"Casey told me to . . . improve yourself": Ed Rumill, *TSN*, December 7, 1944.
"I know just how he feels": Gerry Moore, *BG*, July 18, 1940.
"I've got a great young club in the making": *TSN*, April 11, 1940.

Chapter Eleven

"And of course, you've heard of the guy": J.G.T. Spink, *TSN*, April 14, 1943.
"Next time a ball is hit": Clay Felker, *Life*, September 29, 1952.
"His arms are too short": Mayer, 117.
"He . . . scouted Ted Williams": Allen, *You Could Look It Up*, 127; Williams, *My Turn At* Bat, 223.
"Fly balls fall like raindrops": Bob Broeg, *TSN*, November 1, 1975.
"Quinn would revert to 'Braves' ": Hirshberg, *92–93*.
"Receiving actual beehives": *TSN*, April 10, 1941.
"Stengel had joined . . . other investors": Kaese, 248.
"Max Meyer of Brooklyn, a Stengel friend": Hirshberg, 101.
"This means war": Davis, 338.
"The umpires halted the game": Creamer, *1941*, 169.
"His first substantive remarks": Sherwood, 292.
"The president's goal . . . the threat": Davis, 184–185.
"The first and fundamental fact": http://www.fdrlibrary.marist.edu. The next day the president took back everything he said, but that's another story.
"The president welcomed Irving Berlin": Sherwood, 298.
"I honestly feel . . . for the country": Dean Sullivan, *Middle Innings*, 182.
"With the good players in the service": James, *Historical Baseball Abstract,* 180.
"In 1941 there were 5,298 players": Kolbert, xx.
"Stengel-Weiss connection . . . advantage": Spatz, 76–77.
".326 in 702 games": Spink, *Baseball Register, 1949*, 85.
"Through Stengel": Cataneo, 8.
"Now, he will take a drink": Allen, *You Could Look*, 129.
"Holmes fell under the influence": Honig, 412.
"Twice broke up no-hitters": Pietruscza, 509.
"Holmes . . . serve in the armed forces": Hirshberg, 108.
"He was likable": Hirshberg, 104.
"I'm going to build the ball club": Westcott, *Masters*, 32.
"Lombardi was the most popular player": Allen, *Cincinnati Reds*, 262.
"Steal it, Lom!": Honig, 413
"The owner settled for sheep": Ritter, *Lost Ballparks*, 12.
"If nothing happens to him": Meany, *The Miracle Braves*, 87.
"I said 'no guts' to a kid": Bak, 84.

"I led the Reds three to two": Stan Baumgartner, *TSN*, April 25, 1946.
"More irascible with each losing game": Kaese, 251.
"The two . . . in an unproductive cycle": Peary, 99; Hirshberg, 101.
"The victory complex": Jack Malaney, *TSN*, January 13, 1944.
"Most conservative, virtually inert": James, *Managers*, 308.
"He's mine, and I'm going to have him": Tommy Holmes, *TSN*, September 6, 1934.
"Take that guy out of there": Gilbert, 105.
"White Sox manager Eddie Stanky": Lindberg, 129.
"He chose . . . to bench all of his outfielders": Kaese, 251.
"The Yankees ain't the same": *TSN*, April 22, 1943.
"It wasn't a taxi driver that hit me": Anderson, et al, *The Yankees*, 116.
"Goddamn doctor put my leg on": Cataneo, 94.
"I always knew you couldn't take it": Kaese, 253.
"Things are tough . . . an old pal": *TSN*, April 29, 1943.
"Yeah . . . still have to run for him": *TSN*, April 29, 1943.
"It must be because I've just shaved": Kaese, 253.
"Move over and share . . . with someone": *TSN*, 5/27/43, 12.
"They noticed his head was egg-shaped": Ed Burns, *TSN*, May 27, 1943.
"Howsa 'bout that fifty bucks": *TSN*, May 20, 1943.
"I believe I suffered a relapse": *TSN,* May 14, 1943.
"Lying here and listening": Ed Burns, *TSN*, May 27, 1943.
"I should send for Cronin": *TSN*, June 24, 1943.
"I think Casey cried": Allen, *You Could Look It Up*, 133.
"No one pays any attention": James O'Francis, *TSN*, April 17, 1949.
"I didn't care about that": Allen, *Now Wait a Minute*, 3.
"Stengel supposedly intervened": Allen, *You Could Look It Up*, 133.
"The busiest dispenser . . . garbage": Williams, 125.
"He might have been less thrilled": Williams, 223.
"Not having bothered to consult Edna": *TSN*, February 3, 1944.

Chapter Twelve

"I have been discharged fifteen times": Stengel, SAM, 19, 21.
"Those who really know Stengel": Dan Daniel, *TSN*, January 28, 1932.
"Stengel intended to be his partner": *NYT*, January 28, 1944; Dan Daniel, *TSN*, February 22, 1944.
"High-pressure to low-pressure managers": This is one of many concepts that Bill James first pointed out. Two excellent New York examples are Bob Lemon for Billy Martin in 1978 and Art Howe for Bobby Valentine in 2003.
"Highstrung, noisy, openly critical": Bartell, 109.
"Right here in this room": Tom Haudricourt, *Milwaukee Journal Sentinal,* August 26, 2000.
"He has been closely . . . with Bob Quinn": Veeck, 95–97.
"As Veeck later admitted": Ibid.
"Outrageously high prices": Ibid.

"Veeck apologized for his letter": Ibid.
"His name was floated": Dan Daniel, *TSN*, March 2, 1944.
"It was rumored . . . at Newark": *TSN*, December 21, 1944.
"Stengel felt that he had to repay Weiss": Stengel, 164–165.
"I guess he had about the poorest material": Schoor, *Casey Stengel*, 113.
"If you're . . . thinking of about managing": Dickson, 419.
"I won't be out of baseball this year": Dan Daniel, *TSN*, February 22, 1944.
"Athletics . . . paying customers": *Total Baseball*, 76.
"It will take me a year": Golenbock, *Wild*, 45.
"With the manager's . . . pennant": Gross, 30–31.
"After Bearden pitched well": *SNBR*, 1949.
"Casey was like a second father to me.": IBID
"My man from Milwaukee . . . year or so": Frank Graham, *TSN*, October 20, 1948, 7.
"Get him . . . regains his sanity": Veeck as in Wreck.
"Casey giveth and Casey taketh away": Veeck, 145.
"Veeck thought Boudreau's approach": Veeck, 94.
"He asked Stengel . . . front office position": Veeck, 97.
"A rumored invitation . . . Pirates": *TSN*, August 28, 1946; September 11, 1946.
"St. Louis Browns' 1947 attendance": *Total Baseball*, 76.
"Babich pitched well there": Wright, *American Association*, 253.
"Weiss blamed himself . . . the pennant": Stanley Frank, *SEP*, April 16, 1960.
"After each game the Oaks won": Frommer, *Managers*, 219.
"With twenty-five or twenty-seven guys": Falkner, *The Last Yankee*, 63.
"Every man here rates a ten-dollar dinner": MacLean, 86–87.
"He would make a statement": Metro, 109–110.
"His wife . . . would have a big barbecue": Dobbins, 147.
"Dismissed by Bill Dickey in 1946": Red Smith, *SEP*, March 29, 1947.
"You had a bad day, son": Falkner, *Last Yankee*, 43.
"I swear . . . a place in the sun": Schoor, *Billy Martin*, 21–22.
"He was anxious to learn": Allen, *Damn Yankee*, 33.
"Now take a look . . . other fellow": Metro, 111; John B. Old, *SN*, May 4, 1949.
"Managing takes a lot out of you": Angell, 243.
"Don't knock it . . . I love him for his lip": Schoor, *Billy Martin*, 29.
"You sure blew one": Falkner, *Last Yankee*, 47.
"Grab your glove, kid": Martin, 147.
"Goddamnit, I don't care": Allen, *Damn Yankee*, 33.
"The Horn": Clyde Giraldo, *TSN*, June 9, 1949.
"Biggest asset.": *TSN*, March 17, 1948.
"What do you think I am": Golenbock, *Wild, High, Tight*, 45.
"I saw the way he treated each player": Martin, 148.
"Keep that game close": Billy Martin, *Sport*, March 1961.
"He would get a young fellow": Honig, 631.
"We had to battle all the way for it": Darrell Dreyer, *TSN*, October 6, 1948.
"Oakland fans chipped in": *TSN*, October 6, 1948.

"He told Martin . . . with him": Golenbock, *Wild, High, Tight*, 46.
"Stengel would pay Martin $25": Golenbock, *Dynasty*, 177.
"You can bet all the tea": *TSN*, August 18, 1948.
"His previous managerial experience": Rice, 294.

Chapter Thirteen

"I was the best manager": Joe Falls, *TSN*, October 18, 1975.
"Without Joe . . . by the field": Dan Daniel, *TSN*, September 27, 1949.
"I can read the temper of friends": Frank O'Neill, *TSN*, September 20, 1945.
"I just said, look, you fellows": *NYHT*, August 30, 1949.
"He kept the players 'after school' ": *TSN*, June 8, 1949.
"I got a question": Al, Jerry Coleman. August 4, 2003.
"I'm not a manager": Arthur Daley, *NYT*, August 30, 1949.
"It was plain . . . won or lost": John Lardner, *NWK*, October 17, 1949.
"You know what they said": Dan Daniel, *TSN*, May 25, 1949.
"There just ain't any way": Robinson, 48.
"The greatest right fielder": Dan Daniel, *TSN*, July 6, 1949.
"I . . . shakeup very badly": Ibid.
"He has . . . line-up almost daily": Red Smith, *NYHT*, June 28, 1949.
"Fired manager Jimy Williams": Tom Verducci, sportsillustrated.cnnsi.com, July
    9, 2001.
"I realize . . . been puzzled": Bob Cooke, *NYHT*, July 31, 1949.
"In August . . . the Yankees roster": Ed Sinclair, *NYHT*, August 7, 1949.
"It would be nice . . . twelve pitchers": Berkow, 97.
"The reserve strength of the Yankees": Dan Daniel, *TSN*, July 20, 1949.
"We must be the most-injured": *NWK*, September 12, 1949.
"According to my lists": Bob Cooke, *NYHT*, September 13, 1949.
"[I] declare, without reservation": Red Smith, *NYHT*, August 30, 1949.
"Lie down. . . . Don't get up": Halberstam, 238.
"Just imagine two crows like that": Dan Daniels, *TSN*, August 17, 1949.
"Rizzuto is the greatest shortstop": Dan Daniel, *TSN*, July 6, 1949.
"I now want all of DiMaggio": Dan Daniel, *TSN*, 6/15/49.
"It was trailing a banner": Halberstam, 157.
"Babe Ruth . . . match Joe's flair": Dan Daniel, *TSN*, July 6, 1949.
"Stengel came out of the dugout": Halberstam, 152.
"They told me he'd be back": *NYHT*, September 22, 1949.
"Joe McCarthy . . . with him": *NYHT*, September 27, 1949; *TSN*, October 5,
    1949.
"We're . . . gonna win two straight": Ed Sinclair, *NYHT*, October 1, 1949; *NYT*,
    October 1, 1949.
"I've never seen anything like it": *NYHT*, August 30, 1949.
"The old Yankees were a team": Red Smith, *NYHT*, September 10, 1949.
"You can ask Casey Stengel": Veeck, 94.
"He couldn't throw from here": Al, Jerry Coleman, August 4, 2003.
"In their best days, Hannibal": Ed Sinclair, *NYHT*, 7/29/49.

"When I thanked Page": Red Smith, *NYHT*, September 9, 1949.
"Joe Page is a relief pitcher": Anderson, 192.
"Baseball . . . anything else": Bob Cooke, *NYHT*, July 31, 1949.
"There are not many managers": Al
"If the Yankees are going down": Broeg, 130.
"How far can you go?": Anderson, 200.
"You did a fine job, Casey": Creamer, *Stengel*, 233.
"I want to thank all you players": Leonard Koppett, *NYHT*, October 2, 1949.
"Stengel put it, an anti-climax": Rud Rennie, *NYHT*, October 10, 1949.
"They're pretty nice": Ed Sinclair, *NYHT*, October 6, 1949.
"I was just thanking him": Al, Jerry Coleman.
"You're thanking me?": Meany, *Magnificent Yankees*, 194.
"I didn't catch a fly ball": Tom Meany, *TSN*, October 12, 1949.
"Gee! Most valuable?": Fred Down, *TSN*, October 12, 1949.
"That victory was sweet": Rice, 294.
"I believe . . . Casey will toss": *TSN*, September 7, 1949.
"I don't know of any manager": Collie Small, *Collier's*, March 28, 1953.
"He's nothing but a clown": Creamer, *Stengel*, 238.
"I won one! I won one!": Ward and Burns, 316.

BIBLIOGRAPHY

Non-Periodical Sources

Alexander, Charles. *Breaking the Slump*. New York: Columbia University, 2002.

———. *John McGraw*. New York: Penguin Books, 1988.

Allen, Lee. *The Cincinnati Reds*. New York: G. P. Putnam, 1948.

———. *The Giants and the Dodgers*. New York: G. P. Putnam, 1964.

———. *Hot Stove League*. New York: A. S. Barnes, 1955.

Allen, Mel and Ed Fitzgerald. *You Can't Beat the Hours*. New York: Harper & Row, 1964.

Allen, Maury. *The Incredible Mets*. New York: Paperback Library, 1969.

———. *Now Wait a Minute, Casey!* Garden City, New York: Doubleday, 1965.

———. *Where Have You Gone, Joe DiMaggio*. New York: E. P. Dutton, 1975.

———. *You Could Look It Up*. New York: Times Books, 1979.

Anderson, Dave. *Pennant Races*. New York: Doubleday, 1994.

Anderson, Dave et al. *The Yankees*. Revised ed. New York: Random House, 1980.

Anderson, Sparky and Don Ewald. *Sparky!* New York: Prentice Hall Press, 1990.

Angell, Roger. *Late Innings*. New York: Ballantine Books, 1982.

Asinof, Eliot. *Eight Men Out*. New York: Holt, 1963.

Bak, Richard. *Casey Stengel: A Splendid Baseball Life*. Dallas: Taylor, 1997.

Barrow, Edward Grant. *My Fifty Years in Baseball*. New York: Coward-McCann, 1951.

Bartell, Dick. *Rowdy Richard*. Berkeley, California: North Atlantic Books, 1987.

The Baseball Encyclopedia. 8th ed. New York: Macmillan, 1990.

Berkow, Ira and Jim Kaplan. *The Gospel According to Casey*. New York: St. Martin's Press, 1992.

Bjarkman, Peter, ed. *Encyclopedia of Major League Baseball: American League*. New York: Graf and Graf, 1993.

Bjarkman, Peter, ed. *Encyclopedia of Major League Baseball: National League*. New York: Graf and Graf, 1993.

Boudreau, Lou and Russell Schneider. *Lou Boudreau Covering All the Bases*. Champaign, Illinois: Sagamore, 1993.

Bouton, Jim and Neil Offen. *"I Managed Good, But Boy Did They Play Bad"*. New York: Dell, 1973.

Broeg, Bob. *Superstars of Baseball*. South Bend, Indiana: Diamond Communications, 1994.

Brown, Warren. *The Chicago Cubs*. New York: G. P. Putnam's, 1946.

Bryant, Howard. *Shut Out*. Boston: Beacon Press, 2002.

Cairns, Bob. *Pen Men*. New York: St. Martin's Press, 1992.

Cannon, Jack and Tom Cannon, eds. *Nobody Asked Me, But . . . The World of Jimmy Cannon*. New York: Holt, Reinhardt, and Winston, 1978.

Carmichael, John P. *My Greatest Day in Baseball*. New York: Grosset and Dunlap, 1963.

Carter, Craig, ed. *Daguerreotypes*. Eighth ed. St. Louis: The Sporting News, 1990.

————, ed. *Official Baseball Dope Book*. 1984 ed. St. Louis: The Sporting News, 1984.

Cataneo, David. *Casey Stengel*. Nashville: Cumberland House, 2003.

————. *I Remember Joe DiMaggio*. Nashville: Cumberland House, 2001.

Charlton, James, ed. *The Baseball Chronology*. New York: MacMillan, 1991.

Conlan, Jocko and Robert W. Creamer. *Jocko*. Lincoln, Nebraska: University of Nebraska Press, 1997.

Cramer, Richard Ben. *Joe DiMaggio: The Hero's Life*. New York: Simon and Schuster, 2000.

Creamer, Robert W. *Babe: The Legend Comes to Life*. New York: Simon and Schuster, 1974.

————. *Stengel: His Life and Times*. New York: Simon and Schuster, 1984.

Daniel, Daniel M. "Jester to Genius." In *Baseball Register*. 1959 ed. Ed J. G. Taylor Spink, 3–29. St. Louis: C. C. Spink and Son, 1959.

Davidson, Donald and Jesse Outlas. *Caught Short*. New York: Athenium, 1972.

Davis, Kenneth, S. *FDR: The War President*. New York: Random House, 2000.

DeGregorio, George. *Joe DiMaggio, An Informal Biography*. New York: Stein and Day, 1981.

Dewey, Donald and Nicholas Acocella. *The Biographical History of Baseball*. Chicago: Triumph Books, 2002.

Dickson, Paul. *Baseball's Greatest Quotations*. New York: Harper Collins, 1991.

Disneyland: The First Quarter Century. Walt Disney Productions, 1979.

Dobbins, Dick. *The Grand Minor League*. Emeryville, California, Woodford Press, 1999.

Durocher, Leo and Ed Linn. *Nice Guys Finish Last*. New York: Simon and Schuster, 1976.

Durso, Joseph. *Casey*. Englewood Cliffs, New Jersey: Prentice Hall, 1967.

———. *Casey and Mr. McGraw*. St. Louis: The Sporting News, 1989.

———. *DiMaggio: The Last American Knight*. New York: Little, Brown, 1995.

Einstein, Charles, ed. *The Baseball Reader*. New York: McGraw-Hill, 1980.

———, ed. *The Fireside Book of Baseball*. 2nd ed. New York: Simon and Schuster, 1987.

———, ed. *The Fireside Book of Baseball*. 4th ed. New York: Simon and Schuster, 1987.

Eskenazi, Gerald. *Bill Veeck*. New York: McGraw Hill, 1988.

Etkin, Jack. *Innings Ago*. Kansas City, Missouri: Normandy Square, 1987.

Felker, Clay. *Casey Stengel's Secret*. New York: Walker and Company, 1961.

Fjellman, Stephen M. *Vinyl Leaves*. Boulder, Colorado: Westview Press, 1992.

Fleming, G. H. *The Dizziest Season*. New York: William Morrow, 1984.

Forker, Dom. *The Men of Autumn*. Dallas: Taylor, 1989.

Furnas, J. C. *Stormy Weather*. New York: Putnam's, 1977.

Frick, Ford. *Games, Asterisks, and People: Memories of a Lucky Fan*. New York: Crown Publishers, 1973.

Frisch, Frankie and J. Roy Stockton. *The Fordham Flash*. New York: Doubleday, 1962.

Frommer, Harvey. *Baseball's Greatest Managers*. New York: Franklin Watts, 1985.

———. *New York City Baseball*. New York: Atheneum, 1985.

Fuchs, Robert S. and Wayne Soini. *Judge Fuchs and the Boston Braves*. Jefferson, North Carolina: MacFarland, 1998.

Furnas, J. C. *Great Times*. New York: G. P. Putnam, 1974.

Gallagher, Mark. *Day by Day in Yankees History*. New York: Leisure Press, 1983.

Gallen, David, ed. *The Baseball Chronicles*. New York: Carroll & Graf, 1991.

Geismar, Maxwell, ed. *The Ring Lardner Reader*. New York: Scribner's, 1963.

Gerlach, Larry R. *The Men in Blue*. New York: Viking Press, 1980.

Gilbert, Bill. *They Also Served: Baseball and the Home Front 1941–1945*. New York: Crown Publishers, 1992.

Goldstein, Richard. *Spartan Seasons: How Baseball Survived the Second World War*. New York: MacMillan, 1980.

———. *Superstars and Screwballs*. New York: Dutton, 1991.

Golenbock, Peter. *Amazin'*. New York: St. Martin's Press, 2002.

———. *Bums*. New York: Simon and Schuster, 1984.

———. *Dynasty: The New York Yankees 1949–1964*. New York: Berkley Books, 1975.

———. *Fenway*. New York: G. P. Putnam, 1992.

———. *Wild, High and Tight*. New York: St. Martin's Press, 1994.

Goodman, Jack, ed. *While You Were Gone*. New York: Simon and Schuster, 1946.

Gould, Stephen Jay. "SETI and the Wisdom of Casey Stengel." Chap. in *The Flamingo's Smile*. New York: W. W. Norton, 1985.

Graham, Frank. *The Brooklyn Dodgers: An Informal History*. New York: G. P. Putnam, 1945.

———. *McGraw of the Giants*. New York: G. P. Putnam, 1944.

———. *The New York Giants*. New York: G. P. Putnam, 1952.

———. *The New York Yankees*. New York: G. P. Putnam, 1947.

Graham, Frank Jr. *Casey Stengel* New York: John Day Co., 1958.

Gregory, Robert. *Diz*. New York: Viking, 1992.

Gross, Milton. *Yankee Doodles*. Boston: House of Kent, 1948.

Halberstam, David. *Summer of '49*. New York: Avon, 1989.

Henreich, Tommy and Bill Gilbert. *Five O'Clock Lightning*. New York: Carol Publishing Group, 1992.

Herzog, Whitey. *You're Missin' a Great Game*. New York: Simon and Schuster, 1999.

Hirshberg, Al. *The Braves, The Pick and The Shovel*. Boston: Waverly House, 1948.

Holtzman, Jerome. *No Cheering in the Press Box*. Revised ed. New York: Henry Holt, 1995.

Holway, John. *Voices from the Great Black Baseball Leagues*. 2nd ed. New York: Da Capo, 1992.

Honig, Donald. *A Donald Honig Reader*. New York: Simon and Schuster, 1988.

Hood, Robert E. *The Gas House Gang*. New York: William Morrow, 1976.

Ivor-Campbell, et al, eds. *Baseball's First Stars*. Cleveland: SABR, 1996.

James, Bill. *The Baseball Book 1991*. New York: Villard, 1991.

———. *The Bill James Guide to Baseball Managers*. New York: Scribners, 1997.

———. *The Bill James Historical Baseball Abstract*. New York: Villard Books, 1988.

———. *The New Bill James Historical Baseball Abstract*. New York: The Free Press, 2001.

James, Bill, John Dewan, Neil Munro, and Don Zminda, eds. *STATS All-Time Baseball Sourcebook*. Skokie, Illinois: Stats Publishing, 1998.

———. *STATS All-Time Major League Handbook*. Skokie, Illinois: Stats Publishing, 1998.

Johnson, Lloyd, ed. *The Minor League Register*. Durham: Baseball America, 1994.

Kaese, Harold. *The Boston Braves*. New York: G. P. Putnam, 1948.

Kahn, Roger. *The Era*. New York: Ticknor & Fields, 1993.

Kaiser, David. *Epic Season*. Amherst, Massachusetts: University of Massachusetts, 1998.

Kaplan, Justin, ed. *Bartlett's Familiar Quotations*. 16th ed. Boston: Little, Brown and Co., 1992.

Karst, Gene and Martin J. Jones, Jr. *Who's Who in Professional Baseball*. New Rochelle, New York: Arlington House, 1973.

Kavanaugh, Jack and Norman Macht. *Uncle Robbie*. Cleveland: SABR, 1999.
Kelley, Brent P. *The Early All-Stars*. Jefferson, North Carolina: McFarland, 1997.
———. *They Too Wore Pinstripes*. Jefferson, North Carolina: McFarland, 1998.
Kolbert, Jared Benjamin. *Major League Baseball During World War II*. The *National Pastime*, 1994, 102–105.
Koppett, Leonard. *All About Baseball*. New York: New York Times Book Co., 1974.
———. *The Man in the Dugout*. New York: Crown, 1993.
Kuenster, John, ed. *From Cobb to Catfish*. Chicago: Rand McNally, 1975.
LaBlanc, Michael L. *Football*. Detroit: Gale Research, 1994.
Lally, Richard. *Bombers*. New York: Three Rivers, 2002.
Lane, F. C. *Batting*. Reprint. Cleveland: SABR, 2001.
Langford, Walter. *Legends of Baseball*. South Bend, Indiana: Diamond Communications, 1987.
Lardner, Ring. *Ring Around the Bases*. New York: Scribner's, 1992.
Lieb, Fred. *Baseball as I Have Known It*. New York: Grosset and Dunlap, 1977.
———. *The Boston Red Sox*. New York: G. P. Putnam, 1947.
———. *The Pittsburgh Pirates*. New York: G. P. Putnam, 1948.
Light, Jonathan Fraser. *The Cultural Encyclopedia of Baseball*. Jefferson, North Carolina: McFarland, 1997.
Lindberg, Richard. *Who's on 3rd?* South Bend, Indiana: Icarus Press, 1983.
Lingeman, Richard R. *Don't You Know There's a War On?* New York: G. P. Putnam, 1970.
Linn, Ed. *The Great Rivalry*. New York: Ticknor and Fields, 1991.
Linthurst, Randolph. "Turner and Fette—Unlikely Rookie Phenoms." *Baseball Research Journal*. (1978): 6–9.
Littlefield, Bill and Richard A. Johnson. *Fall Classics*. New York: Crown Publishers, 2003.
Lowry, Phillip. *Green Cathedrals*. New York: Addison Wesley, 1992.
Mack, Connie. *My 66 Years in the Big Leagues*. Philadelphia: Universal House, 1950.
MacLean, Norman. *Casey Stengel, A Biography*. New York: Drake, 1976.
Madden, Bill. *Pride of October*. New York: Warner Books, 2003.
Mantle, Mickey. *The Quality of Courage*. New York: Doubleday, 1964.
———. *The Education of a Ballplayer*. New York: Simon and Schuster, 1967.
Mantle, Mickey and Herb Gluck. *The Mick*. New York: Jove, 1985.
Marazzi, Rich and Len Fiorito. *Aaron to Zuverink*. New York: Stein and Day, 1982.
Martin, Billy and Peter Golenbock. *Number 1*. New York: Dell, 1980.
Mayer, Ronald A. *The 1937 Newark Bears*. Reprint. New Brunswick, New Jersey: Rutgers University Press, 1994.
McGraw, Blanche S. and Arthur Mann, ed. *The Real McGraw*. New York: David McKay Company, 1953.

McGraw, John J. *My Thirty Years in Baseball*. New York: Boni and Liveright, 1923.

McMane, Fred. *Quotable Casey*. Nashville: TowleHouse, 2002.

McMillan, Ken. *Tales From the Yankees Dugout*. Champaign, Illinois: Sports Publishing, 2001.

Mead, William B. *Low and Outside*. Alexandria, Virginia: Redefinition, 1990.

Meany, Tom. *The Artful Dodgers*. New York: A. S. Barnes, 1954.

———. *The Magnificent Yankees*. New York: Grosset and Dunlap, 1952.

———. *The Miracle Braves*. New York: A. S. Barnes, 1954.

———. *Mostly Baseball*. New York: A. S. Barnes, 1958.

Metro, Charlie. *Safe By a Mile*. Lincoln, Nebraska: University of Nebraska, 2002.

Minor League Baseball Stars. Cooperstown, New York: SABR, 1978.

Murdock, Eugene. *Baseball Between the Wars*. Westport, Connecticut: Meckler, 1992.

———. *Baseball Players and Their Times*. Westport, Connecticut: Meckler, 1991.

Nathan, David H. *Baseball Quotations*. New York: Ballantine, 1991.

Neft, David S. and Richard M. Cohen. *The Sports Encyclopedia: Baseball*. 14th ed. New York: St. Martin's Press, 1994.

———. *The World Series*. New York: MacMillan, 1986.

O'Neal, Bill. *The Pacific Coast League*. Austin, Texas: Eakin Press, 1990.

O'Neil, Buck. *I Was Right On Time*. New York: Fireside, 1996.

Okkonen, Marc. *Baseball Memories, 1930–1939*. New York: Sterling, 1994.

Okrent, Daniel and Steve Wulf. *Baseball Anecdotes*. New York: Oxford University Press, 1989.

Okrent, Daniel and Harris Lewine, ed. *The Ultimate Baseball Book*. Boston: Houghton Mifflin, 1979.

Orodenker, Richard. *Dictionary of Literary Biography*. Vol. 171. Detroit: Gale Research, 1996.

Pappas, Doug. *Major League Baseball Profits and Player Salaries, 1920–1950*. February 23, 2003

Parker, Clifton Blue. *Fouled Away: The Baseball Tragedy of Hack Wilson*. Jefferson, North Carolina: McFarland, 2000.

Parrot, Harold. *The Lords of Baseball*. Reprint. Atlanta: Longstreet Press, 2001.

Peary, Danny, ed. *We Played the Game*. New York: Hyperion, 1994.

Pietrusza, David. *Judge and Jury*. South Bend, Indiana: Diamond Communications, 1998.

Pietrusza, David, Matthew Silverman, and Michael Gershman, eds. *Baseball: The Biographical Encyclopedia*. Kingston, New York: Total/Sports Illustrated, 2000.

Powers, Jimmy. *Baseball Personalities*. New York: Rudolph Field, 1949.

Price, Bill. "Braves Field." *Baseball Research Journal*. (1978): 1–6.

Reichler, Joseph L. *The Baseball Trade Register*. New York: Collier, 1984.

Reidenbaugh, Lowell. *The Sporting News: Take Me Out to the Ball Park*. St. Louis: The Sporting News, 1983.

Rice, Grantland. *The Tumult and the Shouting*. New York: A. S. Barnes, 1954.

Rickey, Branch. *Branch Rickey's Little Blue Book*. Edited by John J. Moaeleone. New York: MacMillan, 1995.

Ritter, Lawrence. *The Glory of Their Times*. New York: Vintage Books, 1966.

———. *Lost Ballparks*. New York: Viking, 1992.

Rizzuto, Phil and Tom Horton. *The October Twelve*. New York: Tom Doherty Associates, 1994.

Robinson, George and Charles Salzberg. *On a Clear Day they Could See Seventh Place (Baseball's Worst Teams)*. New York: Dell, 1991.

Robinson, Ray. *Baseball's Most Colorful Managers*. New York: G. P. Putnam, 1969.

———. *Matty: An American Hero*. New York: Oxford University Press, 1993.

Rosenthal, Harold. *Baseball's Best Managers*. New York: Thomas Nelson, 1961.

———. *The Ten Best Years of Baseball*. New York: Van Nostrand, 1979.

Ross, Alan. *The Yankees Century*. Nashville: Cumberland House, 2001.

Ruth, George Herman, and Bob Considine. *The Babe Ruth Story*. New York: E. P. Dutton, 1948.

Schacht, Al. *Clowning Through Baseball*. New York: A. S. Barnes, 1941.

Schoor, Gene. *Casey Stengel*. New York: Julian Messner, 1953.

———. *The Scooter*. New York: Scribner's, 1982.

Seidel, Michael. *Streak*. New York: McGraw-Hill, 1988.

Seymour, Harold. *Baseball: The Golden Age*. New York: Oxford University Press, 1971.

Shatzkin, Mike, ed. *The BallPlayers*. New York: William Morrow, 1990.

Sherwood, Robert E. *Roosevelt and Hopkins*. New York: Harper & Brothers, 1948.

Smith, Curt. *The Storytellers*. New York: MacMillan, 1995.

———. *Voices of the Game*. New York: Simon and Schuster, 1992.

Smith, Red. *The Red Smith Reader*. New York: Random House, 1982.

———. *Views of Sport*. New York: Alfred A. Knopf, 1954.

Smith, Richard Norton. *An Uncommon Man*. New York: Simon and Schuster, 1984.

Smith, Robert. *Baseball*. New York: Simon and Schuster, 1970.

Snelling, Dennis. *The Pacific Coast League: A Statistical History*. Jefferson, North Carolina: McFarland, 1995.

Spatz, Lyle. *Yankees Coming, Yankees Going*. Jefferson, North Carolina: McFarland, 2000.

Spink, J. G. Taylor, ed. *Baseball Register*. 1944 ed. St. Louis: Spink & Son, 1949.

———. *Baseball Register*. 1949 ed. St. Louis: Spink & Son, 1949.

Stadler, Ken. *The Pacific Coast League*. Los Angeles: Marbek Publications, 1984.

Stengel, Casey and Harry T. Paxton. *Casey at the Bat*. New York: Random House, 1961.

Stout, Glenn, ed. *Top of the Heap*. New York: Houghton Mifflin: 2003.

Sugar, Bert Randolph. *Rain Delays*. New York: St. Martin's Press, 1990.

Sullivan, Dean A. *Early Innings*. Lincoln, Nebraska: University of Nebraska, 1997.

———. *Middle Innings*. Lincoln, Nebraska: University of Nebraska, 1998.

———. *Late Innings*. Lincoln, Nebraska: University of Nebraska, 2002.

Sullivan, George and John Powers. *The Yankees: An Illustrated History*. Philadelphia: Temple University Press, 1997.

Sullivan, Neil J. *The Minors*. New York: St. Martin's Press, 1990.

Thompson, Fresco and Cy Rue. *Every Diamond Doesn't Sparkle*. New York: David McKay Company, 1964.

Thorn, John, ed. *The National Pastime*. New York: Warner Books, 1987.

Thorn, John and Pete Palmer, ed. *Total Baseball*. 7th ed. New York: Total Sports Publishing, 2001.

Tiemann, Robert L. and Mark Rucker, eds. *Nineteenth Century Stars*. Cleveland: SABR, 1989.

Tullis, John. *I'd Rather Be a Yankee*. New York: MacMillan, 1986.

U.S. Congress. Senate. Judiciary Committee. Subcommittee on Antitrust and Monopoly. *Organized Professional Team Sports*. 85th Cong., 2nd Sess.

Veeck, Bill and Ed Linn. *The Hustler's Handbook*. New York: Putnam, 1965.

———. *Veeck as in Wreck*. New York: Bantam Books, 1962.

Ward, Geoffrey C. and Ken Burns. *Baseball*. New York: Alfred A. Knopf, 1994.

Warfield, Don. *The Roaring Redhead*. South Bend, Indiana: Diamond Communications, 1987.

Werber, Bill and C. Paul Rogers III. *Memories of a Ballplayer*. Cleveland: SABR, 2001.

Westcott, Rich. *Diamond Greats*. Westport, Connecticut: Meckler, 1988.

———. *Masters of the Diamond*. Jefferson, North Carolina: MacFarland, 1994.

Whittingham, Richard. *The DiMaggio Albums*. Two vols. New York: G. P. Putnam, 1989.

Williams, Peter, ed. *The Joe Williams Baseball Reader*. Chapel Hill, North Carolina: Algonquin Books, 1989.

———. *When the Giants were Giants*. Chapel Hill, North Carolina: Algonquin Books, 1994.

Williams, Ted. *My Turn At Bat*. New York: Simon and Schuster, 1969.

Wright, Marhsall D. *The American Association*. Jefferson, North Carolina: McFarland, 1997.

Yardley, Jonathan. *Ring*. New York: Random House, 1977.

Zingg, Paul J. and Mark D. Medeiros. *Runs, Hits, and an Era*. Urbana, Illinois: University of Illinois: 1994.

AUTHOR INTERVIEWS

Yogi Berra
Hank Bauer
Jerry Coleman
Ryne Duren
Don Larsen
Bobby Richardson
Charlie Silvera
Bill Skowron
Enos Slaughter

INDEX

THE AUTHOR

Steven Goldman is the creator and author of the *Pinstriped Bible*, an irreverent look at the adventures of the New York Yankees. Published since 1998, it is now a featured part of www.yesnetwork.com, where it appears weekly. He is also one of the authors of the *Baseball Prospectus*, and writes two weekly columns for www.baseballprospectus.com. Presently completing a novel, Steven lives in New Jersey with his wife and daughter.